COMPETITION AMONG INSTITUTIONS

Competition among Institutions

Edited by

Lüder Gerken
Director of the Walter Eucken Institut
Freiburg, Germany

First published in Great Britain 1995 by
MACMILLAN PRESS LTD
Houndmills, Basingstoke, Hampshire RG21 6XS
and London
Companies and representatives
throughout the world

A catalogue record for this book is available
from the British Library.

ISBN 0-333-64204-X

 First published in the United States of America 1995 by
ST. MARTIN'S PRESS, INC.,
Scholarly and Reference Division,
175 Fifth Avenue,
New York, N.Y. 10010

ISBN 0-312-12581-X

Library of Congress Cataloging-in-Publication Data
Competition among institutions / edited by Lüder Gerken.
p. cm.
Includes bibliographical references and index.
ISBN 0-312-12581-X
1. Competition—Congresses. 2. Competition, International-
-Congresses. 3. Organizational change—Congresses. I. Gerken,
Lüder.
HB238.C64 1995
338.6'048—dc20   94-42269
                                                        CIP

---

10   9   8   7   6   5   4   3   2   1
04 03 02 01 00 99 98 97 96 95

Printed in Great Britain by
Ipswich Book Co Ltd
Ipswich, Suffolk

Contents

Acknowledgements

Early versions of the papers in this volume were presented at the international 1994 Friedrich August Hayek Symposium at Bleibach in the Black Forest, Germany. The conference was cosponsored by the Walter Eucken Institut at Freiburg, Germany, and the International Institute of George Mason University at Arlington, Virginia, USA. Funding by Daimler-Benz-Fonds, George Mason University Foundation, Rudolf Haufe Verlag and The Sarah Scaife Foundation is gratefully acknowledged.

In addition to the authors represented in this volume, the following delegates were also present at the Symposium: Peter Aranson, Louis DeAlessi, Douglas Ginsburg, Carola Lehmer, Henry Manne, Vitali Naishul, Steve Pejovich, Karl-Ernst Schenk, Dieter Schmidtchen, Kazimierz Stanczak, Manfred Streit, Gordon Tullock, Roland Vaubel, Stefan Voigt, Christian Watrin and Ulrich Witt.

The editor would like to thank, above all, John Moore of the International Institute for the co-operation in jointly organizing the conference. Advice and assistance by Wolfgang Kerber and Viktor Vanberg are also gratefully acknowledged. Daniela Gerbaldo of the Walter Eucken Institut coordinated the details of the conference. Wendula Gräfin von Klinckowstroem and Reinhard Cluse of the Walter Eucken Institut assisted in producing this volume.

Walter Eucken Institut   LÜDER GERKEN
Freiburg im Breisgau

Notes on the Contributors

Bruce L. Benson, Distinguished Research Professor at Florida State University, has written widely on spatial economics, public choice, and the economics of law, including books on *The Enterprise of Law* and *The Economic Anatomy of a Drug War* (with David W. Rasmussen).

Peter Bernholz is Professor of Economics and a director at the Basel Centre for Economics and Business, University of Basel.

Reiner Eichenberger is research associate at the University of Zürich. He is mainly interested in political economy, in the economics of information and in psychological economics.

Christoph Engel is Professor of Law at the University of Osnabrück, Germany. His main fields are economic law, media and communication law, European Union law, German public law.

Bruno S. Frey is Professor of Economics at the University of Zürich. He was Visiting Research Professor in the School of Business, Chicago University. His current main research areas are political economy, psychological economics and the economics of the arts.

Andreas Freytag is secretary and research associate at the Institute for Economic Policy, Cologne. His main fields of research are theoretical and empirical analysis of international economics and political economy.

Lüder Gerken is a Director of the Walter Eucken Institut at Freiburg, Germany. His main fields of research are the analysis of institutional competition, institutional economics and economic issues of the European Union.

Wolfgang Kerber is a Director of the Walter Eucken Institut at Freiburg, Germany. He has published on competition theory, antitrust policy, institutional economics and evolutionary economics.

John Kincaid is Robert B. and Helen S. Meyner Professor of Government and Public Service and director of the Meyner Center for the Study of State and Local Government at Lafayette College, Easton, Pennsylvania; former Executive Director of the US Advisory Commission on Intergovernmental Relations, Washington, DC; and Editor of *Publius: The Journal of Federalism*.

Günter Knieps is Professor of Economics and Director of the Institute of Transportation Economics and Regional Policy at the Albert-Ludwigs-Universität Freiburg i.Br.. His special fields are competition policy, industrial economics and the theory of regulation.

Matthias Lücke is a research associate in the Development Economics Department at the Kiel Institute of World Economics. His research has focussed on trade and industrialisation issues and more recently, on patterns of regional integration (and dis-integration) in the former Soviet Union.

Pavel Pelikan, a doctor in economics, is senior research fellow at the Industrial Institute for Economic and Social Research in Stockholm, Sweden, and regular visiting professor at the Université de Paris 1--Sorbonne. He has published on evolutionary comparative economics and post-socialist transformation.

Viktor Vanberg is Editorial Director at the Center for the Study of Public Choice and Professor of Economics, George Mason University, Fairfax, Virginia. He has published on the theory of social institutions and organizations and is editor of the *Journal of Constitutional Political Economy*.

Patrick Welter received a diploma degree in economics in 1990. Since that time he has been working as a research assistant at the Seminar for Economic Policy, University of Cologne. He is currently preparing a PhD thesis on the problems of establishing an international migration order.

Introduction

It is generally accepted by economists that competition is an essential pre-requisite for the increase of welfare in that it induces individuals to develop, for a specific problem, different solutions among which, in the course of time, inadequate solutions will be substituted by more efficient ones. Simultaneously, competition prevents the stabilization of accumu-lated power and thus enhances the preservation of individual freedom. However, these aspects of competition have been discussed mainly with reference to economic markets in which firms and households compete within a given set of institutions, that is within a legal order. The question arises as to whether competition may also evoke comparable effects on the institutional level, in the sense of competition among legal orders.

Economic science has only recently become more deeply involved in the analysis of institutional competition. One reason for this new interest may be the perception that the highly developed economies in Europe and North America are presently confronting considerable problems: The density of regulations, constraining particularly economic activity, has increased rapidly, despite the proclamations of politicians that they are aiming to promote deregulation. The public share of the gross national product has increased considerably, due to social benefits programmes, active employment policies and subsidization of industries. Regulatory competence has shifted from regional jurisdictions to the federal level, leading to a concentration of power. Government is perceived as acting inefficiently. The growing influence of competing interest groups prevents politicians and bureaucrats from adequately solving present-day problems. Institutional competition is increasingly suggested as a possible solution for such problems.

The term institutional competition is ambiguous in its meaning. On the one hand, in a more intuitive way, institution stands for organizations, par-ticularly jurisdictions like a state. Yet institutions can also be defined as rules that constrain actions of individuals. Accordingly, institutional compe-tition may be associated with both competition among jurisdictions, particu-larly states, and competition with or among rules. In many cases these meanings will coincide. However, this need not be the case. Jurisdictions may compete also on other grounds than with their legal systems, and com-petition among rules, in a wide sense, may also encompass the interactions between designed and spontaneously evolved rule systems.

The present book is an attempt to address some of the aspects associated with institutional competition and to identify some possible lines for further research. It is far from offering a coherent *theory* of institutional competition. The book is organized into two parts, which are preceded by a general orientation. The aim of the orientative paper, in Chapter 1, is to sketch the vast and complex spectrum of institutional competition with special reference to competition among states, and to construct a general framework that may help to identify the positions of the following papers within the overall context.

Part I examines basic issues of institutional competition. In Chapter 2, Wolfgang Kerber and Viktor Vanberg focus on two issues of competition among jurisdictions by using an evolutionary approach. First, they show that institutional competition can be profitably viewed as a knowledge-creating process that brings forth new and better rules. Second, they argue that, just as competition in ordinary markets has to be constrained by certain rules in order to ensure desirable outcomes, competition among jurisdictions also needs a framework of rules that constrains the strategies of the competitors (jurisdictions) and channels the competitive process into desirable directions.

Peter Bernholz, in Chapter 3, discusses from a long-term evolutionary perspective the factors that bring about changes in economic and political systems. He argues that democratic market economies regularly degenerate into excessive welfare states, thus leading to a crisis, that may give rise to ideological movements as well as the implementation of central planning and of a dictatorship. However, as Bernholz stresses, competition among states will eventually induce economic reforms towards a market economy, which sooner or later will also require a democratic regime and the implementation of the rule of law. Bernholz concludes that evolutionary cycles among political and economic systems have to be expected.

The paper by Christoph Engel, in Chapter 4, classifies and investigates the legal material with respect to institutional competition. Engel explores in what ways specific segments of the overall law system of a state may be exposed to competition. He concludes that institutional competition is much more frequent and manifold than economic analysis often perceives. He also explores the attitude of the legal orders toward institutional competition and finds that it is very pragmatic: While its positive effects are often applauded, the law in other instances is more reserved or even reluctant to competition. Engel finally analyzes the range of instruments that law has developed in order to reduce frequency or impact of unwelcome institutional competition.

Patrick Welter, in Chapter 5, provides a challenge to the argument that unregulated international migration is inherently inefficient (because migrants do not take into account fiscal externalities that they impose on the residents of the immigration country as well as of the emigration country) and that therefore an international agreement on migration policies is desirable in order to internalize these externalities. Welter argues that such an agreement may neglect the relevance of migration in promoting institutional competition. He models institutional competition on the basis of Hayek's evolutionary theory and analyzes from this perspective the set of migration policies: subsidies to migrants, migration taxes and transfers between states. Welter concludes that neither migration taxes nor transfers between states are adequate, while subsidies to migrants and, under certain conditions, immigration taxes are compatible with institutional competition.

Bruce Benson, in Chapter 6, explores the relationship between spontaneously evolved rules and designed rules. He argues that an individual can expand wealth through productive activities, particularly when these are complemented by voluntary interaction with others, and that spontaneously evolved legal institutions can facilitate both productivity and voluntary interaction. However, as Benson emphasizes, an individual can also expand wealth by taking from others, and the design of legal institutions can generate and enforce such a redistribution. He concludes that an analysis of the evolution of legal institutions must account for competition and interaction between those rules which evolve spontaneously to facilitate voluntary interaction, and those deliberately designed rules which alter spontaneous rules in order to take property.

The paper by Pavel Pelikan, in Chapter 7, draws a broad picture of social evolution by identifying and interrelating different types of institutions and competitive processes. Pelikan argues that institutional rules are the selection units of social evolution. He distinguishes between the analysis of given institutions (institutional statics), and the examination of how institutions themselves change and evolve (institutional dynamics). As for institutional statics, Pelikan assumes that in the competitive process some institutions win and others lose, and inquires into properties of potential winners. With regard to institutional dynamics, Pelikan provides a framework for understanding why, in the evolutionary process, democracy is superior to dictatorship and cultural reformism is superior to conservatism. He also argues that the deliberate design of rules is an important means for distinguishing and rectifying those institutions which eventually would be eliminated by social evolution, and that theoretical knowledge produced by the study of social evolution will play an increasingly important role in this respect.

Part II of this volume addresses specific aspects of institutional competition. In Chapter 8, Bruno Frey and Reiner Eichenberger derive a concept of functional, overlapping, competing jurisdictions (FOCJ) on the grounds of the economic theory of federalism. They argue that FOCJ have major advantages, in that governments of FOCJ face strong incentives to satisfy citizens' demands and that, as FOCJ are highly flexible, they adapt to the 'geography of problems'. Frey and Eichenberger stress that successful FOCJ have existed in European history, and that there are illustrative contemporary examples for FOCJ such as the US special districts and Swiss communes. They conclude that a future European constitution should actively support the evolution of FOCJ, thus complementing the policy of the European Union which so far excelled in strengthening economic competition, but neglected to promote competition among jurisdictions.

The paper by Andreas Freytag, in Chapter 9, provides in a public choice framework a model of competition among the European Commission and the national governments on the market for protectionism. According to Freytag, the European Commission as a new competitor is a serious threat to national suppliers of protectionism. He analyzes the competitive process, that he views as a Schumpeterian process of creative destruction with the European Commission being the innovator in that it supplies strategic trade and industrial policies as new products, while the national suppliers are imitators that try to survive on the market. Freytag discusses the set of possible strategies of the competitors and validates the theoretical findings by analyzing the Common Technology Policy and the subsidization of the European aircraft industry.

John Kincaid, in Chapter 10, argues that American federalism has entered a new era of coercion in which the federal government is engaged in unprecedented regulation of state and local governments and displacement of their sovereign powers. He inquires into the reasons for this development, which has given rise to what he calls 'coercive federalism'. Kincaid argues that institutional competition among subnational jurisdictions came to be seen as limiting the ability of governments to respond to social problems and especially to act against the powers of big business. He also finds that demands for more equality on a national scale, especially in protecting individual rights, generated political pressures against decentralized state regulations. According to Kincaid, federal policy-making has therefore shifted its attention from concerns about states' rights to concerns about individual citizens' rights. Kincaid concludes that, in order to provide economic benefits to persons and protect individual rights, the federal government is pre-empting state and local powers and has few incentives to co-operate with state and local governments.

Günter Knieps, in Chapter 11, focuses on institutional competition among standardization committees. He argues that hierarchical control of standard setting within large technical systems, like telecommunications and railway networks, no longer remains sustainable due to the recent trend towards vertical disintegration, deregulation and internationalization, and that therefore committees and regulatory commissions play an increasing role in the process of setting compatibility standards. Knieps undertakes two case studies, on telecommunications and railway systems, in order to point out the importance of variety and search for new solutions that is generated by competition among standards. Moreover, Knieps explores whether common rules with respect to standard-setting should be designed and enforced by regulatory authorities.

The final paper by Matthias Lücke, in Chapter 12, analyzes the potential contribution of competition among regional units to the economic transformation of the Russian Federation. Lücke finds that several presumed benefits of interregional competition are likely to apply also to the case of Russia. These include regional differentiation in the provision of public goods, enhanced public control over bureaucrats, and the discovery of knowledge that would not be disclosed in the case of centralized decision-making. However, as Lücke argues, interregional competition will only be effective if the national constitution guarantees basic rights, including the free movement of people, goods and money throughout the country. Furthermore, he makes an economic case for requiring all regions to share in the financial obligations that result from Russia's communist past, such as an oversized army and the dangers of ecological disaster.

1 Institutional Competition: An Orientative Framework*
Lüder Gerken

In economics, it is generally agreed that competition discloses knowledge, enhances efficiency and restrains power. It is also generally accepted that one main reason for the evolution of modern states has been that certain goods, due to their non-exclusive character, are not supplied by markets – for example, legislation and social services. It seems to follow logically that the state is forced to be in a monopoly position precisely because no one else is prepared to provide these goods. Unfortunately a monopolistic setting not only lacks a device that may serve as a discovery procedure for knowledge, but it also entails the dangers of inefficient provision of goods and a concentration of power that may eventually lead to a Hobbesian *Leviathan*. Therefore a predicament seems inevitable.

However, even though governments are monopoly-like organizations, which are not exposed to competition *within the state*, states do compete and always have competed *with each other*. In recent years, the argument has arisen that competition among states, just as competition within economic markets, may serve as a procedure of disclosing knowledge, inducing an efficient supply of public goods and limiting the power of government, thus compensating for the lack of competition within the state.

Public goods which are supplied by the state consist to a large extent of designed rules. In line with Institutional Economics, another term for rules is institutions. In so far as states compete with each other through designed rules, one may therefore speak of competition by legislation or of institutional competition. As in democratic constitutional states single actions, such as police operations and payments of social benefits or of subsidies, are generally based on a formal law, even in these cases legislation is essential. From this perspective, what is decisive for the competitive process is not the single action but the design of the underlying law. Therefore this paper will concentrate on competition by the design of law, that is institutional competition, viewing competition by single actions as a subordinate consequence of competition by legislative activities.

*Helpful comments by W. Kerber, G. Knieps and M.E. Streit on an earlier draft of this paper are gratefully acknowledged.

1

This paper will focus on competition among states. However, not only states but also other social entities may be exposed to some institutional competition. Therefore the concept of institutional competition in principle is not restrained to competition among states. In section 1, a concept of institutional competition for social groups in general is derived. Section 2 analyzes how institutional competition among states may come about and discusses economic policies that are commonly used in the competitive process. In section 3, vertical structures of states are incorporated into the model, and the impact of the formation of international trade associations on institutional competition is discussed. Section 4 relates competition among states to competition in economic markets and critically discusses the application of the neoclassical market model to institutional competition. Section 5 finally points to specific problems of a normative evaluation of economic policies when institutional competition is taken into consideration.

1   A GENERAL CONCEPT OF INSTITUTIONAL COMPETITION

In this chapter, section 1.1 discusses the fundamental question of how different types of rules come about and how they relate to different kinds of social orders. In section 1.2, concepts of competition are briefly discussed. Section 1.3 compares types of competitive actions, focusing on institutional competition. Finally, in section 1.4, institutional competition is related to the evolutionary process of rule selection.

1.1   Types of Rules and Their Formation

Institutions are rules that constrain actions of individuals and thus channel them into specific directions (North, 1990, pp. 3,4; see also Veblen, 1919, p. 225; North, 1989, pp. 238–40; Furubotn and Richter, 1991, pp. 2f). Rules form because individuals in social interaction aim at reducing complexity and uncertainty caused by their limited ability to gather information (Heiner, 1983) or at lowering transaction costs (Williamson, 1975, 1985). Social groups are characterized by systems of such rules. They coordinate in one way or another the actions of the individual members of the group and thus produce a certain social order as defined by Hayek (1973, p. 36), that is also called order of actions (for example 1967, p. 66, 1973, p. 67). Hayek distinguishes between two types of orders: organizations and spontaneous orders (1969, pp. 34–7, 1973,pp. 36–8).

Organizations are social entities constructed by deliberate human design (1973, p. 37) that serve a specific purpose of the organizer (1973, p. 38, North, 1990, p. 5). The main device within the organization for co-ordinating the actions of its members towards this objective is command (Hayek, 1973, p. 49). An organization thus involves some degree of hier-archial structure. Prominent examples of organizations are centrally planned economies and, in market economies, firms. *Spontaneous orders* form endogenously as a result of (decentralized) human action, but not of human design (Hayek, 1967, pp. 96–105) in an evolutionary process of selection (1973, pp. 37, 43). This is what Hayek calls the 'twin ideas of evolution and of the spontaneous formation of an order' (1978, p. 250). Examples from real life are street traffic and economic markets.

Orders are characterized by specific sets of rules. Corresponding to the two types of orders, Hayek distinguishes between two types of rules that govern the behaviour of individuals: rules of organization (1973, pp. 48–50) and rules of conduct (1973, pp. 43–6, 1976/1979, pp. 34–8). *Organizational rules* determine the internal structure of an organization, for instance the functions to be performed by each member (1973, p. 49). If the organizer possessed all relevant knowledge that was needed for the organization to work properly and to achieve its purpose, rules would be obsolete and the organization could be hierarchically directed only by command. To the extent to which this is not the case, organizational rules become necessary to make use of the knowledge of other members of the organization (1973, p. 49). Organizational rules are to serve the purpose of the organization and therefore have to be specific and positively formu-lated (1973, p. 49). *Rules of conduct*, on the contrary, are general – that is independent of purposes and individuals (1973, p. 50), and negative in that they only prohibit specific actions (1976/1979, p. 36). By channeling the interactions of the members of a social group, rules of conduct co-ordinate these interactions and thus bring about a spontaneous order of actions (1969, p. 173). As for those rules of conduct that are enforced by a ruler or an agency like government, Hayek terms these 'law' (1973, p. 72).

For the issue of institutional competition, it is important to stress that both kinds of rules – those of conduct as well as organizational ones – can principally form in two ways: by planned and conscious action, that is by human design (1973, p. 45), or spontaneously through an evolutionary process of social selection (1973, p. 45, 1979, pp. 155–63), this classi-fication being similar to the distinction by North between formal (1990, pp. 46–53) and informal (1990, pp. 36–45) constraints. To put it in other words, two different levels of formation have to be distinguished: at the

Table 1   Classification of orders and rule formation

Types of orders / Formation of rules	Organization	Spontaneous order
Design of rules	design of organizational rules (I)	design of rules of conduct (III)
Spontaneous formation of rules	spontaneous formation of organizational rules (II)	spontaneous formation of rules of conduct (IV)

lower level the formation of the order of actions, and at the upper level the formation of those rules that determine the order of actions.

Regularly, organizational rules are designed rules, invented by the organizer for the purpose of directing the organization towards its objective (I). However, theoretically, part of the organizational rules may also evolve spontaneously in an evolutionary selection process (II). A spontaneous order of actions may be the result of a set of rules of conduct that themselves have also evolved spontaneously as an unintended product of social interactions in the process of cultural selection (IV). This also holds for enforced rules of conduct, that is law (Hayek, 1973, pp. 72–4). Examples of spontaneous rules of conduct are the traditional, moral or religious behavioural norms of a society and unwritten customary business rules (1979, pp. 161–3). However, as Hayek admits (1973, p. 45), a spontaneous order of actions may also result from rules that are formed by conscious design (III). In reality, the system of rules of a social group will be partly of spontaneous and partly of designed origin.

1.2   Competition

Before relating the different types of rules and their formation as discussed in section 1.1 to institutional competition, some brief remarks on competition in general have to be made. Competition may be viewed as the striving of individuals, or groups of individuals, to improve by deliberate action their situation in relation to other individuals or groups. However, beyond this very general notion, a clearcut theory of competition on economic markets that is unequivocally agreed upon does not exist in economic science. The different approaches to competition stress very different aspects. Nevertheless, the array of models can with some simplification be divided into two categories.

An extensive set of models builds on the neoclassical general equilibrium paradigm with the notion of perfect competition (Walras, 1876/1954) as a reference system. As the real world contains market imperfections, rather than perfect competition, these original models have been supplemented in the past decades by much more sophisticated approaches. The *Theory of Workable Competition* (Clark, 1940, 1954) tried to derive normative second-best criteria for competition by assuming a causal link between market structure, conduct and performance. The empirical foundations were taken from the early *Industrial Organization Approach* (Bain, 1956, 1968), which stressed the relevance of concentration and structural entry barriers. The *Chicago School* (Stigler, 1968; Bork, 1978; Demsetz, 1973, 1976, 1982; Posner, 1977, 1979) to the contrary argues that competition permanently drives the economy to a constantly changing equilibrium, inducing the survival of the fittest. The relevance of entry barriers is denied, concentration is seen as the result of efficiency, and monopoly power is presumed to erode quickly due to the continuous development of markets. The *Theory of Contestable Markets* (Baumol, 1982; Baumol, Panzar and Willig, 1982; Baumol and Willig, 1986) generalizes the implications of the concept of perfect competition by using the notion of absolutely free entry into, and exit from a market as a reference system. If the criterion of contestability, that is the absence of sunk costs, is fulfilled, economies of scale and monopolistic market structures will have no relevance, due to the disciplining power of potential ('hit-and-run') competition, that was already stressed by Schumpeter (1942, p. 85). The *New Industrial Organization Approach*, as advanced by the *Harvard School* (surveys by Shepherd, 1985/1990, Scherer, 1986, Scherer and Ross, 1990, Tirole, 1988/1990), incorporates the theory of the firm as developed especially by Coase (1937) and Williamson (1975, 1985), and introduces concepts of strategic behaviour, including non-competitive strategies like the notion of raising rivals' costs (Salop and Scheffman, 1983).

The second category of models of competition stresses the importance of competition as a knowledge-creating process. This line of research is mainly associated with Schumpeter, Hayek and Kirzner. Schumpeter (1911/1993, pp. 110–39, 322, 334–48, English translation in 1934/1961, pp. 74–94, 216, 223–36, 1928/1929, pp. 312–5, 1942, pp. 81–6) views competition as a process of creative destruction, in which innovation is induced by creative entrepreneurs who invent new products or production techniques. This destroys a possibly existing economic equilibrium again and again, leading to a cyclical succession of innovation and imitation. Hayek (1948, pp. 77–91, 92–106, 1969, pp. 249–65, English translation in

1978, pp. 179–90, 1979, pp. 67–70) views competition as an evolutionary creative process of trial and error in which knowledge is acquired and communicated to other individuals. Competition thus serves as a discovery procedure. Kirzner (1973, 1979, 1992) stresses the role of arbitraging entrepreneurs who look for profitable co-ordination inefficiencies on markets and thus cause the economy to tend towards an equilibrium, that would in fact be achieved if the relevant environment remained constant.

Vihanto (1992) and Kerber and Vanberg (1995, in this volume) explicitly introduce the notion of competition as a knowledge-creating process into the analysis of institutional competition. Most of the current literature on institutional competition, however, applies the neoclassical paradigm (among others Tiebout, 1956, North, 1981, Oates and Schwab, 1988, 1991, H.-W. Sinn, 1990, Siebert and Koop, 1990, 1993, Musgrave, 1991, S. Sinn, 1992). In general, only the *basic* neoclassical model is applied, with the abovementioned more recent advances of this line of competition theory not being taken into consideration. It seems obvious that, if market imperfections prevail on economic markets, they are even more relevant in the field of institutional competition, where, for instance, the number of competitors is limited and more or less constant. Therefore, if one decides to argue within the general equilibrium paradigm, it certainly would be worthwhile exploring to what extent and in what particular way the more recent approaches may help to analyze and explain the phenomenon of institutional competition.

1.3 Institutional Competition

In line with Hayek (1948, pp. 1–32, 1955/1964, pp. 36–43, 53–63), Popper (1957/1960, p. 149) and Buchanan (1962/1965, pp. 315–17), the concept of methodological individualism will be presupposed for the present analysis. This means that the actions of individuals, as opposed to some social aggregate, are considered as the only source of social interaction. Social aggregates do not act, but rather are outcomes of actions of individual agents. Therefore, with respect to institutional competition, it is neither the institutions or rules nor the social groups as aggregates that compete by themselves, but rather individual human action which evokes competitive processes.

Competitive actions may take place in different settings. The most common one is that of individuals of the same social group competing with each other, that is *individual* competition *within* a social group. If the perspective is extended to a multitude of groups, two other possibilities of competition arise: Individuals of different groups may compete with each other, that is *individual* competition *among* social groups. Or the collectives of the individuals of different social groups as a whole may compete with each other, that is *collective* competition *among* social groups.

The standard example for individual competition within a group and among groups is that of suppliers or demanders competing on national respectively international economic markets. Collective competition among social groups is different. The members of a social group may, voluntarily or not, combine their resources and compete as a whole with other social groups. Collective competition thus contains the notion of at least some elements of an organization, possibly as a second layer in addition to an existing spontaneous order within the group. Regularly, a group disposes of an agency, like government, that co-ordinates the individual actions and acts on behalf of the group, this being one feature of organizations in general. In the process of collective competition, two kinds of instruments may be used: single actions and the design of rules. As mentioned above, in modern democratic states, single actions are generally based on a law, so that in the special case of competition among (democratic) states, collective competition among groups is mainly competition by the design of rules, that is institutional competition. An important example are the attempts of states to attract internationally mobile capital by creating a favourable legal framework.

In the process of collective competition among social groups, spontaneous rules as opposed to designed ones cannot be instrumentally used, because competition, as defined in section 1.2, requires deliberate action. They are exposed to an evolutionary selection process that is beyond human command and control. They may nevertheless be of considerable importance to the competitive process, as will be discussed in section 1.4.

Two kinds of designed rules have to be distinguished for the present context: constitutional and non-constitutional rules. Constitutional rules, as a specific variant of organizational rules, define and limit the powers of the rule-enforcing and rule-designing agency, like government, with respect to the members of the group (Hayek, 1973, pp. 124–6, 134–6, Buchanan, 1975, p. 72, 1991, p. 585). They are a constraint on and channel the design of non-constitutional rules because the agency may only design rules within its constitutional limits. Due to the character and the tasks of constitutions, competition with constitutional rules may not be very likely, although the possibility exists. Non-constitutional rules as the second form of designed rules channel social interaction among the members of the social group. They can be both general rules of conduct and organizational rules and are the main instruments of institutional competition.

It should not be neglected in this context, however, that to a considerable extent rules are designed for internal group reasons and not in order to gain a competitive edge over other social groups. Nevertheless even these rules may have an impact, albeit indirect, on the competitive position of the group. Engel (1995, in this volume) provides an extensive analysis of the legal material of states with respect to institutional competition.

1.4   Institutional Competition and Evolutionary Selection of Rules

As was argued in section 1.1, the rule systems of social groups consist of both spontaneous and designed rules. Spontaneous rules have evolved from and are constantly exposed to an evolutionary process of selection. For the present context, it is important that designed rules are also exposed to a process of selection in the sense that knowledge is created as to whether these rules combine to a consistent and adequate system for the social group. This knowledge may come about through competitive efforts among social groups with the systems of rules of other groups serving as a reference system. However, it can also be created within the group with its own set of spontaneous rules serving as a reference system.

In this context it matters if and to what extent spontaneous and designed rules are compatible with each other and how they interact. In this respect, deliberately designed rules can coincide with, specify, supplement, diverge from or contradict spontaneously-formed rules. Of particular interest are the cases of inconsistencies between a designed rule and spontaneously-formed norms. An important example of inconsistency is discussed by Benson (1995, in this volume) who argues that spontaneous rules evolve in order to facilitate productive and exchange activities, with the purpose of increasing individual wealth, while deliberately designed rules may be created in order to redistribute wealth, that is in order to overrule spontaneous rules.

Inconsistencies may result in three types of reactions. Firstly, the spontaneous rule system could adapt. This may happen if the contradicting spontaneous norm is not fundamental, only vague or a mere pattern of habit, such as not using seatbelts in automobiles. In these cases designed rules may channel the evolution of the system of spontaneous rules, as is stressed by Vanberg (1994). However, in other cases, the adaptation of spontaneous rules to designed ones seems rather unlikely, at least in a relatively short period of time, because of the low speed of cultural evolution compared to the velocity of rule design (North, 1990, p. 87). Thus in many cases only two possibilities remain: The designed rule is either changed or enforced by authoritarian means. However, in the case of fundamental inconsistencies within a rule system of a group, authoritarian enforcement will generally not be feasible in the long run, as the breakdown of the centrally-planned economies indicates. Less fundamental inconsistencies may prevail, but again, it is doubtful whether the designed rule can be effectively enforced, a problem that is indicated by the extent of black market economies even in the industralized countries with their developed law enforcement systems. Therefore in many cases the system of sponta- neous rules, at least its fundamental elements, must probably be consid- ered dominant (Hayek, 1969, pp. 103f). Similar problems may result when the system of spontaneous rules changes in the process of cultural evolution. The enforcing authority may try to keep up a formerly consis- tent designed rule, thus causing an inconsistency, as described by North (1990, pp. 87f). But again, in the long run, the spontaneous system will probably prevail in many cases.

However, very little is known about the formation, the contents, the degree of preciseness and the variability of spontaneous rules. The accept- ance of a designed rule, and thus its consistency with the overall set of spontaneous rules, could be due to the absence of a corresponding sponta- neous rule or the existence of some spontaneous meta-rule in accordance with the designed rule. But it could as well rest on an adaptation of the spontaneous norms to the designed rule.

Nevertheless, even though in certain cases designed rules may have an impact on the evolution of spontaneous rules, the system of spontaneous rules, especially its fundamental elements, will regularly constrain the set of feasible designed rules, which may also be considered as a case of path dependence in the sense of North (1990, pp. 93–100). This has important implications for institutional competition in that spontaneous rules thus also constrain the ability of a social group to compete with other groups.

Summarizing, only designed rules can be used instrumentally in the process of competition among social groups. However, designed rules will only be feasible in the long run if they do not contradict (fundamental) spontaneous rules. This dependence holds for both constitutional and non- constitutional rules. Non-constitutional rules are of greater relevance as instruments of institutional competition. However, they are constrained not only by spontaneous rules but also by designed constitutional ones. Finally, competitive single actions in democracies must generally be based on designed law, and therefore are determined by it. All three types of deliberate actions as well as their consistency with the system of sponta- neous rules contribute positively or negatively to the position of the group in the overall evolutionary process of social selection, as is analyzed more deeply by Pelikan (1995, in this volume).

The following sections of this paper will only deal with institutional competition among (nation-)states as a specific form of social groups. Competition among political units within a (nation-)state is discussed by Dye (1990) and, with special reference to the transition process in the Russian Federation, by Lücke (1995, in this volume). Knieps (1995, in this volume) explores the appropriateness of competition among standardization committees for the process of standard-setting, this being an important neighbouring field with comparable problems.

2   INSTITUTIONAL COMPETITION AMONG STATES

Competition among states affects, as is substantiated by Bernholz (1995, in this volume), the overall evolution of states and of political regimes. In this second section, an inquiry into the nature of such competition will be made. Section 2.1 stresses the role of specific individual actions as a prerequisite for institutional competition and discusses how they are transmitted to individuals in other states. Sections 2.2 and 2.3 deal with the two types of policies that aim at influencing institutional competition: policies of locational competition and of protectionism.

2.1   Transmission Mechanisms of Institutional Competition

For institutional competition among states to arise, the actions of political agents of different states must be linked to each other. In line with the individualistic approach in the sense of Hayek (1948, pp. 1–32, 1955/1964, pp. 36–43), the starting-point has to be an inquiry into the motives of political agents for acting in certain ways. Public choice theory (surveys by Mueller, 1991, Bernholz and Breyer, 1972/1994) argues in line with Schumpeter (1942, pp. 279, 282) that there is no reason to assume that political agents, politicians as well as bureaucrats, behave differently from agents on economic markets and that they also try to maximize their personal welfare (Downs, 1957, p. 27f, Buchanan and Tullock, 1962/1965, pp. 17–30, for bureaucrats Tullock, 1965, pp. 20–32, Niskanen, 1971, pp. 36–41), or, as North (1990, p. 25) puts it, their survival potential. Of course, the behaviour of political agents is also influenced by their basic beliefs and convictions and by their subjective perception of reality, that is by 'ideology' in the terminology of North (1990, p. 23). However, within these constraints, political agents, just like other individuals, strive for direct personal ends like power, reputation and wealth, and they especially strive for preservation of their position, that is, in democratic states, re-election (Downs 1957, pp. 28–31).

In the purely theoretical case that political agents have total control over the citizens and do not have to worry about preserving their power, they can use the state to serve only their ends – what corresponds to the *Leviathan* model as developed by Brennan and Buchanan (1980, pp. 26–30). Given the opposite extreme case that the citizens have complete knowledge and uniform preferences and can remove the government through elections at any time, political agents have to adapt their actions completely to the preferences of the citizens, if they want to be re-elected (Downs, 1957, pp. 54–63). Reality is somewhere between these extreme situations: Political agents have some scope for striving for their own ends, but they also have to serve the interests of the citizens.

The citizens are a heterogeneous group with diverging interests. Those with common interests may form interest groups (Olson, 1965) in order to seek rents (Krueger, 1974, Buchanan, Tollison and Tullock, 1980). Interest groups try to induce political agents to adopt a specific policy that is favourable to them, by claiming to represent voters and to be able to mould public opinion, and by offering to help political agents in their efforts to become re-elected (Downs, 1957, pp. 88, 90–4). Political agents adjust their actions if that increases the perceived probability of being re-elected.

The majority of citizens, however, are not organized in groups. Nevertheless, what may be called 'the' citizens, being the electorate as a whole, has an impact on the actions of political agents. In reflection of the heterogenity of preferences and of the existence of interest groups, the notion of political agents adjusting to the preferences of 'the' citizens, is, of course, theoretical. In the present context it is to be understood in the sense of how political agents would act if specific interest groups did not exist. This may result in adjusting to the preferences of the passionate majority of voters (Downs, 1957, pp. 64–6) or in any other adjustment. In any case, political agents do not rely completely on interest groups but also adapt, at least to some extent, to what they perceive as the preferences of 'the' citizens. These citizens, as opposed to interest groups, in many cases do not attempt actively to influence political agents. Rather the political agents will try to anticipate what the electorate favours.

Thus, there are three strings of interests that have an impact on and influence the actions of political agents: the interests of the electorate as a whole as perceived by the political agents, the interests of special interest groups and the ends of the political agents themselves. The preferences of the citizens and interest groups matter because of the sanctionary potential of elections, that is, in the terminology of Hirschman, 'voice' (1970, pp. 4, 15–29).

The relations discussed so far have been wholly domestic: Induced by the perceived interests of citizens, by interest groups or by their own ends, political agents act on behalf of the state in that they adopt a specific policy, thus binding all the citizens and the state as a whole. Competition among states may occur if these actions affect the citizens, interest groups or political agents in other states in their attempts to increase their welfare, so that political agents in these states are induced to react. Attempts to increase welfare can be affected from abroad either directly, for example through warfare or import and export restrictions of other states, or indirectly through what may be called transmission mechanisms.

One transmission mechanism is constituted by the terms of trade. If a specific action of a foreign state results in a deterioration of the terms of trade, which in turn leads to a decline of domestic welfare, the electorate or interest groups will at least in the long run induce the political agents, who are striving for re-election, to counteract. A devaluation policy that aims at raising employment via an increase of exports may at best in the short run be a rational policy to ensure re-election.

Another transmission mechanism (that may also have an impact on the terms of trade) is, in the terminology of Hirschman, 'exit' (1970, pp. 4, 15–20, 30–43, 1980, pp. 253–8, 277f) corresponding to the notion of 'voting with the feet' as forwarded by Tiebout (1956). Tiebout starts out from the argument, established particularly by Samuelson (1954, 1955), that no market-type solution exists to determine the optimal level of expenditures for public goods, because consumers will not reveal their true preferences for these goods (1954, pp. 388f). He shows that this statement is valid for federal expenditures, but not for local expenditures, if consumers are mobile and move to that community that best satisfies their preferences. Tiebout, however, only considers personal, physical exit, and ignores the possibility of a person not leaving physically, but rather exporting his capital.

Including the possibility of capital movements, the notion of exit as a transmission mechanism may be interpreted as follows: Owners of internationally mobile factors of production, mainly capital, will direct these to those locations where conditions are most favourable to them. If the exit of capital reduces the overall welfare it may result in reactions of voice in the next elections. Therefore, political agents have an incentive to prevent exit. Thus, voice and exit in the case of institutional competition are not necessarily either alternative or complementary options of the same logical level, as Hirschman (1970, p. 37, 1980, pp. 223–8, 257, 277) and Dye (1990, pp. 16f) state, but rather exit causes or may cause voice as that mechanism to which political agents react directly. Capital movements also indicate to less successful governments where more favourable conditions prevail and how these could be generated. These states have to adapt or they will drop back even further what again may be sanctioned by the electorate. Capital movements thus also contribute to the functioning of competition as a discovery procedure in the sense of Hayek (1969, pp. 249–65, English translation in 1978, pp. 179–90, 1979, pp. 67–70).

In principle, labour could also be an element of this second transmission mechanism, exit. However, to a large extent, labour is already immobile within a nation-state, and even more so in an international setting, where additional cultural and lingual barriers persist. Furthermore labour, as far as it is mobile, in most cases does not take the leading role in the decision of where to produce by moving to an attractive location first, but rather follows the movement of capital. Therefore, the movement of capital is the central variable for the second transmission mechanism, exit. Nevertheless labour movements may become highly relevant in the case of considerable differences in the living conditions, as migration from Europe to America in the nineteenth century and from Mexico to the USA during the past decades indicates.

Competition among states, as induced by terms of trade effects and voice, or exit and voice, comprises different economically relevant competition policies that with some simplification can be divided into two categories: policies of locational competition and of protectionism.

2.2 Policies of Locational Competition

Policies of locational competition aim at improving the legal framework in comparison to other states. To a large extent, both the attractiveness of a state to serve as location for foreign investments as well as the international competitiveness of the domestic industries are influenced by the quality of the legal framework (for instance of corporate law, of law on taxation or on environmental protection) and by the amount and the quality of the public infrastructure (for instance transportation networks, telecommunications networks and educational systems). As investments into the infrastructure, like other single actions, principally have to be based on some formal law, in the following they are subsumed under the legal framework.

A favourable legal framework enhances both capital import and the international competitiveness, which leads to the creation of jobs, that is income, and thus to additional welfare. This adds to the reputation of political agents and raises the probability of their re-election. Therefore political agents have a direct incentive to create a favourable legal framework.

Thus capital, in addition to being an element of the transmission mechanism may also be, together with international competitiveness, an intermediate target of institutional competition.

A policy that successfully improves the legal framework and thus induces capital import and/or an increased international competitiveness, may set off political reactions in other states: Capital import means capital export from another state. Increased international competitiveness means decreased competitiveness for another state. To the extent to which either development leads to a decline in welfare, political agents in that state, striving for re-election, will be induced to react.

Mobility of capital, that is a legal setting allowing for international capital movements, and free trade, that is a legal setting allowing for international exchange of goods and services, are of course important prerequisites for locational competition. As for capital mobility however, at least to some extent another setting can be imagined, in so far as the legal system need not necessarily be connected to the territory of the jurisdiction, but could be bound to persons, as was the case in certain variations in the ancient world (Honsell et al., 1987, pp. 51–7) and in the medieval world (Conrad, 1954, pp. 178–90). This would, for instance, enable a domestic firm to organize in a legal form provisioned by some foreign corporate law and be taxed by that state. Frey and Eichenberger (1995, in this volume) elaborate on this notion and suggest for the supply of certain public goods in the European Union a setting of competing jurisdictions that are not bound to a territory.

In the case of strong locational competition, the feasibility of redistribution policies is limited (H.-W. Sinn, 1990, pp. 500–2). For instance, an isolated increase of taxes on capital and capital income merely for redistribution purposes, and not in order to improve conditions for investors, has negative effects on the target variables, capital import and competitiveness, and will therefore only be feasible to a limited extent, if at all. The fact that locational competition reduces the scope for redistribution policies, may be one reason for interest groups, and even for citizens, to oppose locational competition and demand protectionist policies.

Siebert and Koop (1990, p. 442, 1993, p. 16), based on Giersch (1982, 1989), define competition among states as competition among immobile factors of production for mobile ones; government actions are seen as a composite commodity consisting of regulations, taxation and the provision of public goods; this commodity is assumed to be an immobile factor of production like land and the major portion of labour (Siebert and Koop, 1990, p. 440). As opposed to this view, however, it is not factors of production that compete, but individuals. And individuals are principally mobile, only facing barriers to exit of different degrees in that they may have to sell their immobile factors of production. Moreover, this conception only partially explains the phenomenon of competition among states: Competition for industrial primary products and machinery (a mobile factor of production until installation), as would have to follow from the definition, cannot regularly be observed; governments do not improve the legal framework in order to induce the import of primary products or machinery for the combination of these factors with domestic land and labour in the production process. Rather, the main factor of production that may serve as target of competitive actions of states is financial capital. In fact, the prevention of import of certain mobile factors like primary products and machinery, that is protectionist policies can regularly be observed and are a very common instrument of states in the international setting. They could not be modelled under the notion of competition among states being one of immobile factors for mobile ones.

2.3 Protectionist Policies

The argument put forward in section 2.2 dealt with a specific type of institutional competition, where capital import and the international competitiveness of domestic industries are intermediate targets of actions of political agents who aim at increasing their own welfare or that of interest groups or of the citizenry in general. However, throughout history states have, in order to increase welfare, also competed with each other on other grounds: Aggressive trade policies and the protection of domestic markets by tariffs and other trade barriers are no invention of modern days. The mercantilist notion of increasing national wealth through strengthening the domestic economy with respect to those of competing states by aspiring to a state of autarky and by reducing imports and increasing exports is probably as widely accepted today as it was three hundred years ago.

The array of protectionist instruments includes tariffs, quantity restrictions or import prohibitions, standards, voluntary export restraints, subsidies and migration restrictions. As these instruments channel actions of individuals into specific directions, are valid for an unlimited number of events and are a product of legislation, they are designed rules and therefore eligible instruments of institutional competition policy. However, compared to locational competition, there is one important difference in that, except for subsidization, protectionist instruments apply to foreign individuals and thus affect directly and not only indirectly the attempts of the latter to increase their welfare.

Commonly used arguments in favour of protectionism are the promotion of the competitiveness of domestic industries in relation to their foreign competitors, the protection or preservation of 'strategic' domestic industries (such as farming, mining, steel, electronics) in order to sustain some degree of autarky for the event of warfare or trade conflicts and defence against aggressive foreign actions that attempt at eliminating a domestic industry.

A positive theory of competition among states, renouncing normative criteria, must encompass and be able to explain all types of policy instruments that states employ to influence institutional competition. Therefore protectionism may not be simply excluded from the analysis by merely classifying it as non-competitive behaviour. In the terminology of Eucken (1952/1990, pp. 42, 247–50, 296), the analysis of economic markets has to incorporate both *Leistungswettbewerb* ('competition by performance and efficiency') and *Behinderungswettbewerb* ('competition by obstruction'): Attempts of firms to drive competitors out of the market in order to attain a monopoly position have to be modelled by economic theory as a strategy and an instrument in the competitive process, even though they are restraints of competition and might finally lead to its elimination. The same holds for protectionist policies in the field of competition among states. Therefore an inquiry into the rationale of such policies has to be made. The theories of public choice, of strategic trade policy and of clubs offer three explanations as to why political agents may favour protectionism.

A first reasoning for protectionist policies is provided by public choice theory (surveys by Frey, 1984, Nelson, 1988, Weck-Hannemann, 1992). Political agents, being mainly interested in re-election, are influenced in their actions by the citizens and by interest groups who aim at increasing their own welfare. If citizens or interest groups perceive that their welfare can be increased through some specific economic policy, they will demand it, be it an improvement of the legal framework or the implementation of protectionist regulations (Baldwin, 1982, 1989, p. 120, Frey, 1984, pp. 20–8, Nelson, 1988, pp. 800–17, Weck-Hannemann, 1992, pp. 50–62). Political agents concerned about their re-election have an incentive to come up to this demand (Frey, 1984, pp. 32–4, Nelson, 1988, p. 819, Weck-Hannemann, 1992, pp. 84–90). Of course an array of different preferences regularly prevails, resulting in simultaneously occurring inconsistent demands. Accordingly an interest group, for instance of an industry that is exposed to fierce foreign competition, may favour a specific protectionist measure while the majority of the citizens may oppose it. However, interest groups that favour a specific protectionist policy generally have the intrinsic advantage of being small in number so that they can become organized more easily than the inert mass of those opposing it (Olson, 1965, pp. 165–7, 1982, pp. 38–41). This asymmetry leads to an inclination of political agents towards protectionism. The asymmetry is even intensified if powerful organizations like labour unions also favour protectionism (Berthold, 1994).

Even though tariffs and subsidies have similar effects on the domestic market shares of the domestic and the foreign firms, there is a major difference with respect to institutional competition. Assuming normal demand and supply functions, tariffs relieve domestic taxpayers (up to the amount of the additional revenue) and burden domestic demanders of the good in question, while subsidies burden domestic taxpayers and relieve the demanders of the good. Thus, subsidies have to be financed by the taxpayer, so that voice is more reactive to them than to tariffs. Political agents, who are concerned about their re-election, will consider this difference when deciding upon what instrument, subsidization or tariffs, to employ in their efforts to support domestic industries with respect to foreign competitors.

A second rationale for protectionist policies is provided by the economic theory of international trade. From traditional trade theory (Haberler, 1933, English translation in 1936/1956, Dornbusch et al., 1977) it follows that a system of free trade is a first-best solution for the world economy, if certain conditions are fulfilled. However, as is shown in detail especially by the theory of strategic trade policy (surveys by Helpman and Krugman, 1985, 1989, Siebert, 1988, Grossman, 1992, Bletschacher and Klodt, 1992), under certain conditions, mainly imperfect competition and increasing returns of scale, national welfare can be improved even more by import restrictions (Krugman, 1984, Dixit, 1984, Venables, 1985, Dixit and Kyle, 1985) or by subsidization of domestic industries (Brander and Spencer, 1983, 1985, Dixit and Kyle, 1985, Venables, 1985, Dixit and Grossman, 1986). Only if other states follow in protecting their markets, a constellation of welfare losses for all states results (for instance Brander and Spencer, 1985, p. 95). For the same reason, international agreements to ensure free trade are permanently threatened by some state breaking or circumventing them, this being favourable as long as other states do not react. Protectionism as an instrument of institutional competition policy is therefore not only a real-life phenomenon, but can at least theoretically also be a rational policy that increases the welfare of a country as a whole and not only that of specific interest groups. Political agents striving for re-election therefore may have an additional incentive for protectionist policies, if they presume that these may increase the overall welfare of the electorate.

A third rationale for protectionist policies is supplied by the *theory of clubs* (Buchanan, 1965, Olson, 1965, survey by Sandler and Tschirhart, 1980) that analyzes the allocative efficiency of impure public goods which are characterized by either partial rivalry or some excludability of benefits, thus standing between purely public and purely private goods. A central question in club theory is that of determining the optimal size of the club, that is the number of members that maximizes welfare. From a supranational perspective the state can be interpreted as a club that supplies the impure public good of legislation to its members/citizens in exchange for a membership fee/tax, while non-members/foreigners are excluded. From the perspective of club theory, it is questionable why the state club should not limit the number of its members, that is restrict immigration, if additional members reduced the overall welfare, as is discussed in more detail by Welter (1995, in this volume). The same argument holds for a club decision to internally produce certain goods that are consumed by the members/citizens and to prohibit the sale of goods by non-members on the club territory, that is to restrict imports.

The three rationales as to why political agents may implement protectionist policies – public choice, strategic trade and club theories – by no means imply that protectionism will be more effective in increasing welfare than other policies. The analysis was strictly positive and merely tried to derive rationales as to why political agents may advance protectionism. As long as the state that follows a protectionist policy competes with other states that do not, it is institutional competition that may reveal information on whether protectionism can realistically be more effective than other policies. The terms of trade and, unless the movement of capital is restricted, exit in combination with voice will also serve as transmission mechanisms for spreading this knowledge about the effects of protectionist policies.

3   VERTICAL ASPECTS OF COMPETITION AMONG STATES

In both federally and centrally organized states, generally more than one level of political units exist, lower levels below the national one being those of communes, provinces or regions. Furthermore, in the case of international organizations like free trade zones, there is a level above that of nation-states. These vertical aspects have to be taken into consideration for the analysis of institutional competition. For the sake of brevity, in the following, the terms 'central unit' and 'regional units' are used so that the argument can be applied to all types of vertical political structures. Section 3.1 discusses general aspects of the vertical structures of states. In section 3.2, these are related to institutional competition. Section 3.3 finally sketches the impact of international economic associations on institutional competition.

3.1 General Issues of the Vertical Structures of States

Two aspects of vertical relations between different levels of political units have to be distinguished: One is the efficiency aspect of the optimal level of regulation as discussed by the fiscal federalism approach (Olson, 1969, Oates, 1972, surveys by Oates, 1991, Bird, 1993). The character of a public good, its production costs (economies of scale) and the preferences of the citizens (identical or regionally diverse), determine whether this good should be produced and financed on the central or on the regional level. A comparison of costs and benefits and the objective to prevent externalities are in the core of the argument.

The second vertical aspect is linked to the theory of public choice. Political agents of the central level strive for influence and power and therefore have incentives to take regulatory power from the regional level and to shift it to the central unit. Analogously, the political agents of the regional level have inverse incentives. In a strict hierarchical setting with the central unit precisely assigning tasks to and controlling the units of the regional level, only a few possibilities for such a struggle for power remain. The same holds if a constitution in great detail assigns the regulatory power to the different levels. However, in reality there is always a considerable degree of indefiniteness with respect to the division of power among the central and regional units, which makes a struggle for regulatory power possible. This struggle may take different forms: The fact that the division of power is generally institutionalized by a constitution implies that the political units on the different levels can use their granted jurisdictional competences as instruments in their struggle to acquire more power. Another strategy is the gradual reinterpretation of originally restrictive assignments of competence into general clauses, as was achieved by the European Commission under Article 235 of the EC Treaty. Further instruments include the engagement of the public opinion and the formation of alliances with non-state interest groups.

As for this second aspect of public choice, two more points have to be made. First, the central unit has an intrinsic advantage in that it can and will generally act uniformly whereas the different regional units may and probably will have diverging interests. Differences in opinion can weaken the regional level in its efforts to counterbalance the central unit. Under certain circumstances, the central unit may even succeed in forming an alliance with certain regional units against the rest, for instance by promising financial transfers or to buy from firms in the respective region. Second, a considerable readiness of regional political units to transfer regulatory power to the central unit can sometimes be observed, so that the interests of both levels seem to coincide. An example are the attempts of EU member states to harmonize parts of the national legal systems through the implementation of EU rules. This voluntary renunciation of regulatory power will be discussed in section 3.3.

Naturally, the struggle for power need not produce an outcome that is efficient. If the regional solution is efficient for a regulatory problem, the struggle for the regulatory competence may well result in the opposite outcome. Kincaid (1995, in this volume) explores in more detail for the USA the causes of power concentration on the federal level.

In recent years, a new line of research on the interactions among different political units within a nation-state has evolved (Oates and Schwab, 1988, Dye, 1990, Kenyon and Kincaid, 1991 with several contributions). It has become customary in this literature to distinguish between two types of interactions that are both defined as competitive: On the one hand competition among political units of the same level, as illustrated in section 2, for instance among communes or among states; this type has become known as interjurisdictional competition (Kincaid, 1991, pp. 89–91, Oates and Schwab, 1991, pp. 127f) or horizontal competition (Breton, 1991, p. 37, Kincaid, 1991, p. 89). On the other hand competition among political units of different levels, for instance between the federal and the state levels; this type has become known as intergovernmental competition (Kincaid, 1991, pp. 89–91) or vertical competition (Breton, 1991, p. 37, Kincaid, 1991, p. 89). However, 'interjurisdictional competition' and 'intergovernmental competition' could also be used interchangeably, and sometimes indeed are, as in Dye (1990) and Breton (1991). It is a matter of definition, whether the struggle for power between political units of different levels is considered competitive. Freytag (1995, in this volume) takes this view in arguing that the European Commission competes with the national governments on the market for protectionism, the firms being the demanders, and therefore tries to offer new products in the sense of new protectionist policies. In any case, vertical efficiency aspects and especially the vertical struggle for power may very well affect ('horizontal') institutional competition and therefore have to be incorporated into the analysis.

3.2   Impacts of the Vertical Structure of States on Institutional Competition

Institutional competition occurs simultaneously on all levels: States compete with each other in an international setting, while regional units compete within the state. At the same time, vertical struggles for power take place. These interactions have at least three implications for institutional competition.

First, the more extensive the regulatory power of the state, the less the regional units dispose of instruments that they can use for institutional competition on their level, so that regional competition will be less intensive.

Second, as the state is exposed to competition with other states, it is in its interest to co-ordinate or even restrain competition among its regional units, insofar as competitive actions on the regional level, in reality or only in perception, interfere with its efforts to compete on the international level. Therefore, competition among regional units in a hierarchical structure will always be constrained competition. The overall legal system at the central level as well as the prohibition of protectionist policies among regional units can be interpreted as such constraints on regional competition.

Third, institutional competition on the international level serves as a discovery procedure also with respect to the vertical division of power in a state in that it may reveal if the prevailing vertical division of jurisdictional competence is inferior to that of competing states. The state may thus be induced by international institutional competition to transfer power to the political units on the regional level or to take power from them.

3.3   Impacts of Supranational Economic Associations on Institutional Competition

A worldwide tendency towards the construction of free trade zones, customs unions and common markets – in short of international economic associations – can be observed. In most cases this development was not caused by citizens with corresponding preferences who induced political agents to act. Nor was it caused by interest groups that are at best able to adapt gradually to the international scale (Olson, 1982, pp. 125f). Therefore, this development seems, at first sight, to be inconsistent with the theory of public choice: Why should political agents voluntarily give up regulatory power? One reason may of course be that political leaders seeking reputation and historical immortality may be tempted to construct an epochal peace order. Another reason could be the attempt of political agents to eliminate, at least in part, troublesome institutional competition by forming cartel-like associations. A third reason could be the attempt, induced by institutional competition, to adapt to the progressively increasing entanglement of the world economy, that is to reach an efficient size, in order to preserve at least some regulatory power over supranational firms. After all, concentration processes can also be observed on economic markets, where firms merge and co-operate on an international level at an ever-increasing rate.

A thorough inquiry into these and other reasons why supranational economic associations have been forming, cannot be made here. This section will rather elaborate on the question of how they affect institutional competition. For the analysis, internal effects within the association, that is between member states, have to be distinguished from external aspects between members and non-members.

As for the internal perspective, the creation of a multinational economic association has three essential consequences. First the set of instruments that is employable in the process of institutional competition changes: On the one hand, free trade zones, customs unions and common markets explicitly aim at eliminating protectionist policies within the community. In addition, policies of locational competition are eliminated to the extent to which the legal systems of the member states are harmonized. On the other hand, multinational economic associations often not only guarantee, but actively promote the free movement of capital and labour. Therefore it can be expected that in those fields of the legal framework that have not been harmonized locational competition increases, as the member states have to be more responsive to the preferences of investors and of highly qualified labour. It should be noted that harmonization of law may reduce transaction costs, but it will also prevent competitive processes that could serve as a discovery procedure for finding better legal rules, so that the association might remain stuck in a harmonized, but inferior legal system. Moreover, without institutional competition, there are less incentives for political agents to adjust the legal system to changing conditions.

The second internal consequence is linked to the creation of a supranational agency. Such an agency is assigned certain competences that were formerly exercised by the member states, in order to co-ordinate common activities of the association. As there is no reason why the political agents of this agency should behave differently from those in national governments, a struggle for regulatory power between the supranational and the national levels will arise, entailing the possibility of increasing centralization not only for efficiency reasons.

The third internal effect of the creation of a supranational economic association is a combination of horizontal and vertical aspects. Through the formation of a supranational association a new policy instrument is created that directly affects the process of institutional competition. How will member states react that, on the one hand, are on the verge of dropping behind in locational competition, because they are incapable of sufficiently adapting their legal systems to the economic development and on the other hand are not allowed to react with protectionist policies, because these are explicitly ruled out in supranational economic associations? Locational competition and the competitiveness of a more successful member state can be eliminated, if the rules in question are no longer a matter of the individual member states but are harmonized on the level of the association. Therefore, less successful member states have an incentive to form an alliance with the supranational agency in order to jointly induce harmonization. The supranational agency will readily assist, as harmonization means an increase of its power. Opposing member states may then be bribed with grants-in-aid or other benefits. These considerations are not restricted to economically less developed states. A highly industrialized member state which, due to the influence of interest groups, is not capable of deregulating its expensive and inefficient social security system, may also call for supranational harmonization.

As for external aspects, member states might alter their foreign trade policies towards non-member states, after forming a supranational economic association, for example by jointly shifting towards protectionism with respect to non-member states once they are exposed to increased locational competition from inside (Berthold, 1995). This situation can be seen in Europe with the development of what has been termed 'Fortress Europe'.

4 INSTITUTIONAL COMPETITION VERSUS MARKET COMPETITION: COMPETITION AMONG STATES OR COMPETITION AMONG GOVERNMENTS?

Commonly, the standard (neoclassical) economic market model is also applied to politics, the central field in this context being competition among political agents for votes within a state (for example Downs, 1957), which gave rise to the terminological distinction between economic and political markets.

However, besides this internal perspective, also most of the literature on institutional competition applies the (neoclassical) market model to the presumedly similar phenomenon of institutional competition (for instance Tiebout, 1956, North, 1981, Oates and Schwab, 1988, 1991, H.-W. Sinn, 1990, Siebert and Koop, 1990, 1993, Musgrave, 1991, S. Sinn, 1992). The general concept is that governments compete by offering a commodity, called legislation, to individuals who pay for it through taxes. This notion of institutional competition is one of competition among governments rather than states, in that it distinguishes between government as the supplier and individuals or citizens as demanders, whereas the notion of competition among states as developed in this paper views them as an entity. It follows from the application of the market model either that government is an autonomous organization, independent from the citizens, or that the citizens are both the sovereigns that appoint and control government and the demanders that buy legislation from it. In the analogy of economic markets, this would correspond to the owners of a firm being the main, if not the only, clients of that firm.

In addition to this rather peculiar construction of a twin role of the citizens, the market model, if applied to institutional competition, has more caveats: First, while 'demanders' with mobile taxable resources, especially financial capital, may choose between either 'contracting' the commodity or exporting their resources, 'demanders' with immobile taxable resources, land and immobile capital, do not have this choice. To them government is a monopolist who can compel them to 'contract' the supplied commodity at a 'price' set by the monopolist, unless they sell their resources, the feasibility of this option depending on individual circumstances.

Second, while most transactions on economic markets are based on short-term contracts involving just one transaction, the decision of a 'demander' with mobile resources to 'buy' the commodity of a specific government implicitly establishes, if at all, a long-term 'contract'. However, even such a 'contract' differs from economic long-term contracts in two important aspects: Not only can the 'supplier' unilaterally change the 'conditions of contract' at any time, for instance by raising taxes, but also in most cases a 'notice of termination' of the long-term 'contract' is no more possible because, as soon as financial capital is transformed into real capital, it becomes immobile.

Third, mismanagement of government is not exposed to sanctions corresponding to those on economic markets. Governments cannot go bankrupt, as long as there are immobile resources that can be taxed in order to make up for financial losses caused by the government. In the worst case, governments can even prevent 'demanders' from exporting mobile resources by means of legislation. This equates to the notion that the 'clients' will be liable for a mismanagement of the supplier. The only sanctions governments face are generally those of democratic elections, corresponding to a dismissal of the managers.

Finally, as was already stated in section 2.2, the application of the market model to institutional competition neglects the relevance of protectionist policy instruments to influence institutional competition.

Admittedly, for the analysis of the internal structure within the state a distinction between government and the citizens is useful. However, that is another perspective and a different setting. For institutional competition, the notion of a club seems more adequate, implying that competition takes place not among governments but among states, as entities composed of citizens and government. As such, states do not offer anything on some market, but merely act in order to do better than others, as an athlete strives to do better than his competitors.

5   INSTITUTIONAL COMPETITION AND THE RELATIVITY OF NORMATIVE CRITERIA

A positive theory has to comprise and be able to explain both types of policies that are used in the process of institutional competition among states, that is locational competition and protectionism. However, it is another question as to how these policies are evaluated in a normative sense. The normative aspect of institutional competition is discussed by Kerber and Vanberg (1995, in this volume). Therefore only a brief remark shall be made here, pointing to a general aspect that arises from the fact that institutional competition is inter-group competition.

A normative criterion that is consistent with the concept of methodological individualism may not be constructed 'externally' (Buchanan 1977, p. 142), but must be erected directly on the individuals. Accordingly, Buchanan and Tullock (1962/1965, pp. 88–90) and Buchanan (1975, pp. 38–41, 70–3, 82–4, 1977, pp. 102–4, 221–3), building on Wicksell (1896, pp. 110–24, English translation in 1958, pp. 87–97), suggest for constitutional rules the normative criterion of unanimity, that is a rule must be unanimously agreed to by all members of the group in order to be 'efficient'.

The essential point is that this criterion is generally related to the individuals *within* a specific group, whereas institutional competition amounts to interactions *between* different groups. A normative criterion for the evaluation of policies of institutional competition will therefore have to be formulated for the aggregate level, consisting of the totality of individuals of the competing groups taken together. To put it in other words, under the normative criterion of unanimity a system of internationally-designed meta-rules that constrain competition among states has to be agreed to by all citizens of all states in order to be 'efficient'.

Nevertheless, normative criteria on the national scale are not superfluous. They supply a reference system for those cases in which the meta-rules on institutional competition, that comply with the aggregate, supranational normative criterion, accord scope for different competitive actions. It follows of course, that the criterion of the national level is only a relative one in that it is constrained by those meta-rules. Even if the citizens of a state unanimously vote in favour of a specific policy of institutional competition, for instance the introduction of a tariff, this policy is only 'efficient' if it does not contradict the supranational criterion, that is if the world population has unanimously consented to tariff policies.

In a more pragmatic sense, the national criterion is also 'constrained' in another way, as unanimously adopted policies are also exposed to the process of institutional competition in which they have to prove their efficiency and in which they may turn out to be inferior to differing policies of competing states. However, institutional competition, serving as a discovery procedure, does reveal to the citizens that certain policies may be unfavourable to the objective of increasing welfare. Only if the citizens do not incorporate this information into their preferences, they may sooner or later face problems in the overall process of social evolution. This, by the way, may be one explanation for the decreasing competitiveness of the European economies on world markets.

References

Bain, J.S. (1956) *Barriers to New Competition. Their Character and Consequences in Manufacturing Industries* (Cambridge, Mass.: Harvard University Press).
_____ (1968) *Industrial Organization* (New York: Wiley).
Baldwin, R.E. (1982) 'The Political Economy of Protectionism', in J.N. Bhagwati (ed.), *Import Competition and Response* (Chicago: University of Chicago Press), pp. 263–92.
_____ (1989) 'The Political Economy of Trade Policy', *Journal of Economic Perspectives*, 3, pp. 119–35.
Baumol, W.J. (1982) 'Contestable Markets: An Uprising in the Theory of Industry Structure', *American Economic Review*, 72, pp. 1–15.
Baumol, W.J., J.C. Panzar and R.D. Willig (1982) *Contestable Markets and the Theory of Industry Structure* (New York: Harcourt Brace Jovanovich).
Baumol, W.J. and R.D. Willig (1986) 'Contestability: Developments Since the Book', *Oxford Economic Papers* (Supplement), 38, pp. 9–36.
Benson, B.L. (1995) 'Competition Among Legal Institutions: Implications for the Evolution of Law'. In this volume.
Bernholz, P. (1995) 'Causes of Changes in Political–Economic Regimes'. In this volume.
Bernholz, P. and F. Breyer (1972/1994) *Grundlagen der Politischen Ökonomie* (Tübingen: J.C.B. Mohr (Paul Siebeck)).
Berthold, N. (1995) 'Regionale wirtschaftliche Integration – Ordnungspolitischer Sündenfall oder Schritt in die richtige Richtung?', in W. Zohlnhöfer (ed.), *Weltwirtschaft im Wandel* (Berlin: Duncker & Humblot). Forthcoming.

Bird, R.M. (1993) 'Threading the Fiscal Labyrinth: Some Issues in Fiscal Decentralization', *National Tax Journal*, 46, pp. 207–21.

Bletschacher, G. and H. Klodt (1992) 'Strategische Handels- und Industriepolitik: Theoretische Grundlagen, Branchenanalysen und wettbewerbspolitische Implikationen', *Kieler Studien*, 244 (Tübingen: J.C.B. Mohr (Paul Siebeck)).

Bork, R.H. (1978) *The Antitrust Paradox: A Policy at War with Itself*, (New York: Basic Books).

Brander, J. and B. Spencer (1983) 'Strategic Commitment with R&D: The Symmetric Case', *The Bell Journal of Economics*, 14, pp. 225–35.

___ and ___ (1985) 'Export Subsidies and International Market Share Rivalry', *Journal of International Economics*, 18, pp. 83–100.

Brennan, G. and J.M. Buchanan (1980) *The Power to Tax: Analytical Foundations of a Fiscal Constitution* (Cambridge: Cambridge University Press).

Breton, A. (1991) 'The Existence and Stability of Interjurisdictional Competition', in D. Kenyon and J. Kincaid (eds), *Competition Among States and Local Governments* (Washington: Urban Institute Press), pp. 37–56.

Buchanan, J.M. (1962/1965) 'Marginal Notes on Reading Political Philosophy', in J.M. Buchanan and G. Tullock, *The Calculus of Consent* (Ann Arbor: The University of Michigan Press), pp. 307–22.

___ (1965) 'An Economic Theory of Clubs', *Economica*, 32, pp. 1–14.

___ (1975) *The Limits of Liberty: Between Anarchy and Leviathan* (Chicago: University of Chicago Press).

___ (1977) *Freedom in Constitutional Contract: Perspectives of a Political Economist* (College Station and London: Texas A&M University Press).

___ (1991) 'Constitutional Economics', in J. Eatwell, M. Milgate and P. Newman (eds), *The New Palgrave*, Vol. 1 (London: Macmillan), pp. 585–8.

Buchanan, J.M., R.D. Tollison and G. Tullock (eds) (1980) *Toward a Theory of the Rent-Seeking Society* (College Station: Texas A&M Press).

Buchanan, J.M. and G. Tullock (1962/1965) *The Calculus of Consent* (Ann Arbor: The University of Michigan Press).

Clark, J.M. (1940) 'Toward a Concept of Workable Competition', *American Economic Review*, 30, pp. 241–56.

___ (1954) 'Competition and the Objective of Government Policy', in E.H. Chamberlain (ed.), *Monopoly and Competition and their Regulation* (London: Macmillan), pp. 317–37.

Coase, R.H. (1937) 'The Nature of the Firm', *Economica*, 4, pp. 386–405.

Conrad, H. (1954) *Deutsche Rechtsgeschichte, Band I, Frühzeit und Mittelalter* (Karlsruhe: C.F. Müller).

Demsetz, H. (1973) 'Industry Structure, Market Rivalry and Public Policy', *Journal of Law and Economics*, 16, pp. 1–10.

___ (1976) 'Economics as a Guide to Antitrust Regulation, *Journal of Law and Economics*, 19, pp. 371–88.

___ (1982) 'Barriers to Entry', *American Economic Review*, 72, pp. 47–57.

Dixit, A.K. (1984) 'International Trade Policy for Oligopolistic Industries', *The Economic Journal Conference Papers*, 94, pp. 1–16.

Dixit, A.K. and G.M. Grossman (1986) 'Targeted Export Promotion with Several Oligopolistic Industries', *Journal of International Economics*, 21, pp. 233–49.

Dixit, A.K. and A.S. Kyle (1985) 'The Use of Protection and Subsidies for Entry Promotion and Deterrence', *American Economic Review*, 75, pp. 139–52.

28   *Institutional Competition: An Orientative Framework*

Dornbusch, R., S. Fischer and P.A. Samuelson (1977) 'Comparative Advantage, Trade, and Payments in a Ricardian Model with a Continuum of Goods', *American Economic Review*, 67, pp. 823–39.

Downs, A. (1957) *An Economic Theory of Democracy* (New York: Harper & Row).

Dye, T. (1990) *American Federalism, Competition Among Governments* (Lexington, Mass. and Toronto: D.C. Heath and Company).

Engel, C. (1995) 'Legal Experiences of Competition Among Institutions'. In this volume.

Eucken, W. (1952/1990) *Grundsätze der Wirtschaftspolitik* (Tübingen: J.C.B. Mohr (Paul Siebeck)).

Frey, B.S. (1984) *International Political Economics* (Oxford: Basil Blackwell).

Frey, B.S. and R. Eichenberger (1995) 'Competition Among Jurisdictions: The Idea of FOCJ'. In this volume.

Freytag, A. (1995) 'The European Market for Protectionism: New Competitors and New Products'. In this volume.

Furubotn, E.G. and R. Richter (1991) 'The New Institutional Economics: An Assessment', in E.G. Furubotn and R. Richter (eds), *The New Institutional Economics* (Tübingen: J.C.B. Mohr (Paul Siebeck)), pp. 1–32.

Giersch, H. (1982) 'Schumpeter and the Current and Future Development of the World Economy, in H. Frisch (ed.), *Schumpeterian Economics* (New York: Praeger), pp. 49–59.

____ (1989) 'Anmerkungen zum weltwirtschaftlichen Denkansatz', *Weltwirtschaftliches Archiv*, 125, pp. 1–16.

Grossman, G.M. (1992) 'Introduction', in G.M. Grossman (ed.), *Imperfect Competition and International Trade* (Cambridge, Mass. and London: The MIT Press), pp. 1–19.

Haberler, G. (1933) *Der internationale Handel. Theorie der weltwirtschaftlichen Zusammenhänge sowie Darstellung und Analyse der Außenhandelspolitik*, (Berlin: Springer-Verlag).

____ (1936/1956) *The Theory of International Trade with its Applications to Commercial Policy* (London, Edinburgh and Glasgow: William Hodge & Company Ltd.) (English Translation of 1933).

Hayek, F.A. (1948) *Individualism and Economic Order* (Chicago: The University of Chicago Press).

____ (1955/1964) *The Counter-Revolution of Science* (London: The Free Press of Glencoe Collier-Macmillan Limited).

____ (1967) *Studies in Philosophy, Politics and Economics* (Chicago: The University of Chicago Press).

____ (1969) *Freibuger Studien* (Tübingen: J.C.B. Mohr (Paul Siebeck)).

____ (1973) *Law, Legislation and Liberty, Vol. 1, Rules and Order* (Chicago: The University of Chicago Press).

____ (1976/1979) *Law, Legislation and Liberty, Vol. 2. The Mirage of Social Justice* (London and Henley: Routledge & Kegan Paul).

____ (1978) *New Studies in Philosophy, Politics, Economics and the History of Ideas* (London and Henley: Routledge & Kegan Paul).

____ (1979) *Law, Legislation and Liberty, Vol. 3, The Political Order of a Free People* (London and Henley: Routledge & Kegan Paul).

Heiner, R.A. (1983) 'The Origin of Predictable Behavior', *American Economic Review*, 73, pp. 560–95.

Helpman, E. and P. Krugman (1985) *Market Structure and Foreign Trade: Increasing Returns, Imperfect Competition and the International Economy* (Brighton: Wheatsheaf).

___ and ___ (1989) *Trade Policy and Market Structure* (Cambridge, Mass.: The MIT Press).

Hirschman, A. (1970) *Exit, Voice and Loyality. Responses to Decline in Firms, Organizations and States* (Cambridge, Mass.: Harvard University Press).

___ (1980) *Essays in Trespassing. Economics to Politics and Beyond* (Cambridge: Cambridge University Press).

Honsell, H., T. Mayer-Maly and W. Selb (1987) *Römisches Recht* (Berlin and Heidelberg: Springer-Verlag).

Kenyon, D. and J. Kincaid (eds) (1991) *Competition Among States and Local Governments* (Washington: Urban Institute Press).

Kerber, W. and V. Vanberg (1995) 'Competition Among Institutions: Evolution Within Constraints'. In this volume.

Kincaid, J. (1991) 'The Competitive Challenge to Cooperative Federalism: A Theory of Federal Democracy', in D. Kenyon and J. Kincaid (eds), *Competition Among States and Local Governments* (Washington: Urban Institute Press), pp. 87–114.

___(1995) 'Liberty, Competition, and the Rise of Coercion in American Federalism'. In this volume.

Kirzner, I.M. (1973) *Competition and Entrepreneurship* (Chicago and London: University of Chicago Press).

___ (1979) *Perception, Opportunity and Profit* (Chicago and London: University of Chicago Press).

___ (1992) *The Meaning of Market Process: Essays in the Development of Modern Austrian Economics* (London and New York: Routledge).

Knieps, G. (1995) 'Standardization: The Evolution of Institutions versus Government Intervention'. In this volume.

Krueger, A.O. (1974) 'The Political Economy of the Rent-Seeking Society', *American Economic Review*, 64, pp. 291–303.

Krugman, P. (1984) 'Import Protection as Export Promotion: International Competition in the Presence of Oligopoly and Economies of Scale', in H. Kierzkowski (ed.), *Monopolistic Competition and International Trade* (Oxford: Clarendon Press), pp. 180–93.

Lücke, M. (1995) 'Transformation of the Economic System in the Russian Federation: What Role for Competition Among Regional Governments?'. In this volume.

Mueller, D.C. (1991) *Public Choice II* (Cambridge: Cambridge University Press).

Musgrave, P.B. (1991) 'Merits and Demerits of Fiscal Competition', in R. Prud'homme (ed.), *Public Finance with Several Levels of Government* (Den Haag and Königstein: Foundation Journal Public Finance), pp. 281–97.

Niskanen, W.A. (1971) *Bureaucracy and Representative Government* (Chicago and New York: Aldine & Atherton).

Nelson, D. (1988) 'Endogenous Tariff Theory: A Critical Survey', *American Journal of Political Science*, 32, pp. 796–837.

North, D.C. (1981) *Structure and Change in Economic History* (New York and London: W.W. Norton & Company).

___ (1989) 'Institutional Change and Economic History', *Journal of Institutional and Theoretical Economics*, 145, pp. 238–45.

_____ (1990) *Institutions, Institutional Change and Economic Performance* (Cambridge: Cambridge University Press).

Oates, W. (1972) *Fiscal Federalism* (New York: Harcourt Brace Jovanovich).

_____ (1991) 'Fiscal Federalism: An Overview', in R. Prud'homme (ed.), *Public Finance with Several Levels of Government* (Den Haag and Königstein: Foundation Journal Public Finance), pp. 1–18.

Oates, W. and R. Schwab (1988) 'Economic Competition Among Jurisdictions: Efficiency Enhancing or Distortion Inducing?', *Journal of Public Economics*, 35, pp. 333–54.

_____ and _____(1991) 'The Allocative and Distributive Implications of Local Fiscal Competition', in D. Kenyon and J. Kincaid (eds), *Competition Among States and Local Governments* (Washington: Urban Institute Press), pp. 127–45.

Olson, M. (1965) *The Logic of Collective Action, Public Goods and the Theory of Groups* (Cambridge, Mass.: Harvard University Press).

_____ (1969) 'Strategic Theory and Its Applications. The Principle of Fiscal Equivalence: The Division of Responsibilities Among Different Levels of Government', *American Economic Review*, 59, pp. 479–87.

_____ (1982) *The Rise and Decline of Nations (New Haven: Yale University Press).*

Pelikan, P. (1995) 'Competitions of Socio-Economic Institutions: In Search of the Winners'. In this volume.

Popper, K.R. (1957/1960) *The Poverty of Historicism* (London: Routledge & Kegan Paul).

Posner, R.A. (1977) Economic Analysis of Law (Boston and Toronto: Little, Brown and Co.).

_____ (1979) 'The Chicago School of Antitrust Analysis', *University of Pennsylvania Law Review*, 127, pp. 925–48.

Salop, S. and D. Scheffman (1983) 'Raising Rivals' Costs', *American Economic Review*, 73, pp. 267–71.

Samuelson, P.A. (1954) 'The Pure Theory of Public Expenditures', *Review of Economics and Statistics*, 36, pp. 387–9.

_____ (1955) 'Diagrammatic Exposition of a Pure Theory of Public Expenditures', *Review of Economics and Statistics*, 37, pp. 350–6.

Sandler, T. and J. Tschirhart (1980) 'The Economic Theory of Clubs: An Evaluative Survey', *Journal of Economic Literature*, 18, pp. 1481–1521.

Scherer, F.M. (1986) 'On the Current State of Knowledge in Industrial Organization', in H.W. de Jong and W. Shepherd (eds), *Mainstreams in Industrial Organization* (Dordrecht, Boston and Lancaster: Kluwer Academic Publishers), pp. 5–22.

Scherer, F.M. and D. Ross (1990) *Industrial Market Structure and Economic Performance* (Boston: Houghton Mifflin Company).

Schumpeter, J.A. (1911/1993) *Theorie der wirtschaftlichen Entwicklung. Eine Untersuchung über Unternehmergewinn, Kapital, Kredit, Zins und den Konjunkturzyklus* (Berlin: Duncker & Humblot).

_____ (1928/1929) 'Der Unternehmer in der Volkswirtschaft von heute', in B. Harms (ed.), *Strukturwandlungen der Deutschen Volkswirtschaft, Band 1* (Berlin: Reimar Hobbing), pp. 303–26.

_____ (1934/1961) *The Theory of Economic Development: An Inquiry into Profits, Capital, Credit, Interest and the Business Cycle* (New York: Oxford University Press) (English Translation of 1911/1993).

Lüder Gerken   31

_____ (1942) *Capitalism, Socialism and Democracy* (New York: Harper and
  Brothers).
Shepherd, W.G. (1985/1990) *The Economics of Industrial Organization*
  (Englewood Cliffs, NJ: Prentice Hall).
Siebert, H. (1988) 'Strategische Handelspolitik. Theoretische Ansätze und
  wirtschaftspolitische Empfehlungen', *Außenwirtschaft*, 43, pp. 549–84.
Siebert, H. and M. Koop (1990) 'Institutional Competition. "A Concept for
  Europe?"', *Außenwirtschaft*, 45, pp. 439–62.
_____ and _____ (1993) 'Institutional Competition versus Centralization: "Quo Vadis
  Europe?"', *Oxford Review of Economic Policy*, 9, pp. 15–30.
Sinn, H.-W. (1990) 'Tax Harmonization and Tax Competition in Europe',
  European Economic Review, 34, pp. 489–504.
Sinn, S. (1992) 'The Taming of *Leviathan*: Competition Among Governments',
  Constitutional Political Economy, 3, pp. 177–96.
Stigler, G.J. (1968) *The Organization of Industry* (Homewood, Ill.: Irwin).
Tiebout, C. (1956) 'A Pure Theory of Local Expenditures', *Journal of Political
  Economy*, 64, pp. 416–24.
Tirole, J. (1988/1990) *The Theory of Industrial Organization* (Cambridge, Mass.
  and London: The MIT Press).
Tullock, G. (1965) *The Politics of Bureaucracy* (Washington DC: Public Affairs
  Press).
Vanberg, V. (1994) 'Cultural Evolution, Collective Learning and Constitutional
  Design', in D. Reisman (ed.), *Economic Thought and Political Theory*. (Boston,
  Dordrecht, London: Kluwer Academic Publishers), pp. 171–204.
Veblen, T. (1919) *The Place of Science in Civilization and Other Essays* (New
  York: Huebsch).
Venables, A.J. (1985) 'Trade and Trade Policy with Imperfect Competition: The
  Case of Identical Products and Free Entry', *Journal of International Economics*,
  19, pp. 1–19.
Vihanto, M. (1992) 'Competition Between Local Governments as a Discovery
  Procedure', *Journal of Institutional and Theoretical Economics*, 148,
  pp. 411–36.
Walras, L. (1876/1954) *Elements of Pure Economics* (Homewood, Ill.: Irwin).
Weck-Hannemann, H. (1992) *Politische Ökonomie des Protektionismus: Eine
  institutionelle und empirische Analyse* (Frankfurt and New York: Campus).
Welter, P. (1995) 'International Migration and Institutional Competition: An
  Application of Hayek's Evolutionary Theory'. In this volume.
Wicksell, K. (1896) *Finanztheoretische Untersuchungen nebst Darstellung und
  Kritik des Steuerwesens Schwedens* (Jena: Gustav Fischer).
_____ (1958) 'A New Principle of Just Taxation', in R.A. Musgrave and A.T.
  Peacock (eds), *Classics in the Theory of Public Finance* (London: Macmillan),
  pp. 72–118.
Williamson, O.E. (1975) *Markets and Hierarchies: Analysis and Antitrust
  Implications* (New York: The Free Press).
_____ (1985) *The Economic Institutions of Capitalism: Firms, Markets, Relational
  Contracting* (New York: The Free Press).

Part I

Basic Issues of Institutional Competition

2 Competition among Institutions: Evolution within Constraints

Wolfgang Kerber and Viktor Vanberg

Competition among institutions is a wide topic with many different aspects and problems to discuss. The purpose of this paper is to outline an evolutionary approach to the process of competition among institutions. For a more thorough analysis we will draw a parallel between ordinary market competition and the subject of our interest, competition in the realm of institutions. We shall focus, in particular, on two issues. First, the role of the competitive process as a knowledge-creating process. In this respect, we will show that institutional competition leads to the creation and spreading of new institutions. Secondly, we ask what inferences, if any, can be drawn from the nature of this process of competition among institutions to the desirability of its outcomes. Here we will argue that in the same way that competition on ordinary markets has to take place under certain rules, which ensure the desirability of these competitive processes, competition among institutions also requires a framework of rules channelling the competitive processes into desirable directions. Before we begin our discussion on these issues, however, some clarifying comments are in order to narrow down what we mean by 'evolutionary approach' and 'competition among institutions'.

1 CLARIFYING CONCEPTS: EVOLUTION AND COMPETITION AMONG INSTITUTIONS

1.1 Population Thinking in Biological Evolution

Evolution and competition are closely-connected concepts. The notion of competition is as central to evolutionary biology as it is to economics, and in both fields it is directly linked to the notion of scarcity.[1] Yet, the theoretical perspectives that the two disciplines bring to bear on their common subject differ significantly.

In economics the principal interest has been in determining the equilibria that are supposed to result from the competitive process. Furthermore,

35

it is assumed that these equilibria can be derived from the relevant data of any given situation, and that therefore a detailed study of the workings of the competitive process itself is not a necessary part of such equilibrium analysis. By contrast, the principal interest of evolutionary biology is exactly in the process of competition itself. More precisely, its interest is in examining how this process affects the distribution of characteristics in a 'population' over time, a perspective that is called 'population thinking'. There is no presumption that process can be best understood in terms of predeterminable equilibria. Instead, the emphasis is on the continuous endogenous generation of novelty within populations.

Population thinking establishes a connection between competition and adaptation. It argues 'that if there is a population of entities with multiplication, variation and heredity, and if some of the variations alter the probability of multiplying, then the population ... will evolve so that the entities come to have adaptations' (Maynard Smith 1987, p. 120). The 'entities' of which populations consist are unique individuals, and it is the very emphasis on their uniqueness and diversity that characterizes population thinking. The focus of population thinking is on intra-population competition, i.e. on competition among the individual entities making up a population. And its interest is in examining how differences between individuals' capacities to secure resources affect their prospects of being represented by their likes in future generations.

When we speak of an 'evolutionary approach' to competition we mean an approach that employs population thinking.[2] And our main purpose in this paper is to explore the insights that can be gained by applying population thinking to the study of competition among institutions. The essential ideas that we shall borrow from the biological model are the following:

- There is a population of individual entities who compete with each other for scarce resources/rewards;
- The individual entities differ in their traits and in the strategies that they employ, and these differences influence their relative success in securing resources/rewards;
- Their differential success translates into different probabilities for the respective traits or strategies to be represented, or practiced, in future populations;
- New variation is continuously generated within the population and induces change in the distribution of traits/strategies within the population.

It is the competition-induced change in the composition of a population over time that is meant by the term 'evolution'.[3]

1.2 The Meaning of 'Competition Among Institutions'

In order to apply the population perspective to the study of 'competition among institutions', we need to make clear what we regard as the relevant population and the individual entities of which it consists. This task is not only made difficult by ambiguities that surround the concept of institutions. It becomes apparent, upon closer inspection, that the notion of 'competition among institutions' may, indeed, be a somewhat misleading description of what we want to study.

In the social sciences the term 'institution' is so generously employed that one can hardly find a definition that would cover all its various uses, even though they all pertain, in one way or another, to social rules. Something like 'configuration of interconnected rules' comes perhaps closest to an encompassing definition. Yet, this leaves still considerable room for ambiguity, a major instance of which is pointed out, for instance, by the sociologist Talcott Parsons (1975, p. 97), when he observes that we speak of the institutions of property and contract, but also speak of organizations or collectivities (university, state, etc.) as institutions, despite the apparent difference between the two kinds of phenomena.[4] As Parsons illustrates the difference, we can, for instance, meaningfully speak of 'membership of an institution' when we think of organizations or collectivities as institutions, but not when we use the term in the other sense.[5]

The term 'institution' will be used here in its wide definition, that is as a 'configuration of interconnected rules'. Yet, in order to avoid the above-noted ambiguity, we add an explicit distinction between two kinds of rule-configurations, namely configuration of general rules of conduct and configurations of organizational rules. This is a distinction which parallels Hayek's well-known contrast between two kinds of social order, spontaneous order and organized or corporate order, and between the two different kinds of rules that underlie these orders, general rules of conduct and organizational rules. By configurations of general rules of conduct we mean institutions of spontaneous order like, for instance, property and contract. By configurations of organizational rules we mean the kind of institutions that constitute organized or corporate orders, for instance, state and government or business corporations. We suggest that an institution of spontaneous order like, for instance, property can be said to exist where individuals in their dealings with each other respect the various rules of conduct that regulate the uses of, and transactions associated with, property. By contrast, an institution, like a business corporation, can be said to exist, where, among a group of individuals, the rules are followed that constitute the organization in question. In both settings, though, we deal with social arrangements that involve a plurality of actors who follow rules and whose rule-following reinforces the rule-following of others, and vice versa.

If by institutions we mean, as suggested here, configurations of interconnected rules, in what sense can we then speak of 'competition among institutions'? What are the individual entities that are supposed to compete, and how do we define the populations that consist of these entities? As one seeks to answer these questions it becomes apparent that 'competition among institutions' may not be the most appropriate name for what we want to investigate. Certainly, one can think of a 'population of rules', e.g. the different rules by which a business firm could be organized. And the process in which, over time, the relative frequencies change with which the different rule-configurations are adopted in an economy could be interpreted as 'competition among rules'. 'Competition among rules' could, in this interpretation, be viewed as competition among rules *for* firms who, by selecting from the population of rule-configurations, decide which rules will multiply and which will shrink in numbers. Yet it seems to us that it is not the most natural and most useful way of approaching the issue at hand. Instead, we suggest considering the entities that can adopt or discard rules, namely individual persons and groups of persons, as the units that compete, and regarding rules as one of the properties or strategies by which they compete. To use an analogy, instead of speaking, as we commonly do, of competition among firms, and of production technologies as one of the variables in terms of which they compete, we could, of course, speak of 'competition among technologies' and think of a population of technologies that compete for firms that adopt them. Yet, the latter approach would seem to us less appropriate and fruitful than its more common counterpart.

By analogy to production technologies, institutions can be thought of as social technologies, as technologies for co-ordinating interaction and co-operation among groups of persons, an analogy that Hayek has emphasized by likening rules to 'tools'.[6] As different production technologies can be more or less effective in generating valued output, different institutions can be more or less effective in allowing the groups that adopt them to generate social surplus, i.e. valued output in excess of what the individual participants could realize in separation. From such a perspective, the individuals or groups of individuals are viewed as the 'users' or 'carriers' of rules. They are viewed as the entities that compete for resources/rewards, and the rules or rule-configurations that they adopt are seen as one of the instruments by which they compete. The populations that we are interested in are, then, populations of individuals or groups, who are more or less different from each other in terms of the rules that govern their behaviour or operation. And what we actually mean when we speak of 'competition among rules' is the competition between individuals and groups that is carried out by means of rules and institutions. We seek to understand how the distribution of a population, of individuals or groups, along the rule-dimension is affected by the relative success to which different rules help their respective users.

Accordingly, the main ingredients of the population approach that we want to apply here to the study of institutional dynamics can be summarized as follows:

- We view institutions or rule-configurations as traits or attributes of social groups;
- The groups are viewed as the entities that compete for resources/ rewards;
- The relevant 'populations' are composed of such groups;
- The groups of which a population consists differ in terms of their rule-configurations;
- There is constantly new variation introduced by deliberate and non-deliberate experimenting with alternative rules and practices;
- Differences in rule-configurations have an impact on the groups' relative success in securing resources;
- Differences in relative success affect the probabilities for groups to have 'their likes' represented in future populations;
- This induces a change, over time, in the composition of the relevant population along the rule-dimension.

This perspective can be applied to a wide variety of processes that we may be inclined to describe as 'competition among institutions'. It can be applied to various kinds of populations and to various kinds of rule-configurations. Our analysis here will primarily focus on a particular kind of 'group', namely polities or jurisdictions. A principal characteristic of these entities is their 'territorial' nature, i.e. the fact that residence in a particular territory is the essential criterion that decides whether one is subject to a polity's rules or not.[7] We want to examine the process of competition among polities/jurisdictions insofar as it pertains to the institutions that they use in their efforts to gain resources. More specifically, we want to argue that this competitive process works as a knowledge-creating process, in the same sense in which ordinary market competition works, in Hayek's terms, as a 'discovery procedure'. We begin with a discussion of the latter.

2   COMPETITION AS A KNOWLEDGE-CREATING EVOLUTIONARY PROCESS

2.1   Competition Among Firms in Ordinary Markets

The notion that competition in 'ordinary' markets, i.e. markets for goods and services, can be understood as an evolutionary process in which new knowledge is created and spread, has its main roots both in Schumpeter's notion of cyclical processes of innovation and imitation as the driving-force of economic development (Schumpeter, 1934) and in Hayekian ideas of 'competition as a discovery procedure' (Hayek, 1948, 1978). Based upon their contributions several strands of thought have been developed[8] that focus on the idea that the significance of competition lies not so much in the fact, emphasized by traditional price theory, that it pushes prices down to marginal costs but, instead, in the role it plays in creating and spreading knowledge about what consumers want, and how their preferences can be satisfied in a better or less costly way.[9]

The focus of this approach is on the knowledge problem that economic agents face. They are not assumed to command 'perfect knowledge'. The assumption rather is that producers of goods and services, for instance, cannot really know in advance what current consumer preferences are, nor can they know in advance which products, which product qualities or which design will satisfy consumers best, or which technologies, which inputs and what organizational structure are best in producing these products. All these things (preferences, products, technologies), which in neoclassical microeconomics are treated as 'given' data, known by the agents, are in fact not known by them. Economic agents or, in our example, producers can base their actions only on conjectures about these things, conjectures that may be correct or mistaken. Their subjective knowledge of the relevant 'data' is always fallible and therefore capable of improvement. This knowledge problem, which has been addressed, in particular, by Hayek,[10] is aggravated by the rapid change of today's economic world which constantly 'turns former knowledge into present ignorance' (Lachmann, 1977, p. 140).

From the above perspective, competition can be seen as a trial-and-error process, in which firms compete in trying out new products and new marketing techniques, new technologies and new inputs, new forms of organization and new ways of financing. All these innovations can be understood as manifestations of conjectures or hypotheses of firms or, rather, entrepreneurs about what current consumer preferences are and how they can be best satisfied. By expressing with their buying decisions which goods and services they prefer, consumers confirm or refute these hypotheses. They are the ultimate judges in this contest, and hence can be understood as the 'reality', against which these hypotheses are tested. Since the agents in this process are seen as creative, entirely new hypotheses can be generated which, by definition, cannot be anticipated. Consequently, evolutionary market processes have to be seen as open processes without predefined ends.[11]

In many respects, such an evolutionary concept of competition as a process of trial-and-error, of conjecture and refutation, has important parallels with the process of scientific discovery.[12] Trying out new hypotheses referring to new products, marketing instruments or technologies and testing them in the market is similar to the testing of new hypotheses by scientists. As Lachmann (1977, p. 90) puts it: 'The business man who forms an expectation is doing precisely what a scientist does when he formulates a working hypothesis. Both business expectation and scientific hypothesis serve the same purpose; both reflect an attempt at cognition and orientation in an imperfectly-known world, both embody imperfect knowledge to be tested and improved by later experience.'[13]

Crucial for the dynamics of these evolutionary competitive processes in ordinary markets are the built-in incentives for experimentation and exploration. Those agents who offer the relatively best hypotheses gain a competitive advantage and hence advance in comparison with their competitors. This lead implies a temporary monopolistic position and the opportunity to realize supernormal profits. While these profits from successful innovations can be seen as the necessary incentives for taking the efforts and risk of trying out new hypotheses, the less successful competitors – by losing market shares – are automatically put under pressure to improve their achievements, either by imitating the successful firms, and hence taking advantage of the knowledge of the leaders and spreading it, or by innovating themselves. Their following up or even outstripping the initially advanced firms eliminates the temporary market power of the latter and puts them again under competitive pressure.[14] Hence their competitive process can be described as a perennial, dynamic process of advancing and pursuing, of gaining and eliminating market power and profits.[15]

An important determinant of the extent of knowledge which is being created in these competitive processes is the heterogeneity of the competitors. The more heterogeneous the firms and hence their products/ hypotheses are, the more knowledge is likely to be generated. Since consumers can select from a broader set of hypotheses, the probability of them finding superior solutions to their problems than they knew before increases. Consequently, heterogeneity of firms and diversity of their 'conjectures' are not shortcomings of the market process, as the concept of market imperfections suggests, but an essential positive resource. Evolutionary competitive processes generate more knowledge if a larger variety of hypotheses are advanced and tried out. Or as J. Röpke (1977, 1990) put it, innovations – increasing the variety of behaviour – are crucial for the problem-solving capacity of market systems, and hence also for their stability and survivability in an uncertain and changing environment where unanticipated shocks are a constant possibility.[16]

Looked at from the perspective of population thinking, the evolutionary approach to competition can be said to be about the process in which the composition of a population of firms changes over time as a result of the interaction of competitive and innovative forces. Different from the process of natural selection, in the evolution of a population of firms human choice plays a critical role in the generation of new variation as well as in the selection among, and 'retention' of, variants. Yet the general scheme of 'variation, selection, and retention' (Campbell, 1965, pp. 26ff) applies here as well. Firms are not identical: they vary in terms of the characteristics of the goods and services they offer; they also vary in their advertising, in their technology, organizational structure and many other things. The constant emergence of new variation (innovations) in their performance characteristics is a crucial ingredient in the evolutionary process. The selection environment, which encompasses all determinants which influence the survival of firms in the market, defines what 'better performance', 'fitness' or 'adaptedness' mean in this evolutionary process. Profits and losses are the mechanism that leads to the spreading/elimination of the superior/inferior 'hypotheses', to the elimination of poorly performing variants and the 'preservation, duplication, or propagation of the positively selected variants' (Campbell, 1965, p. 27). Hence by these variation–selection–retention processes knowledge is being produced and spread,[17] and these processes must be regarded as an unintended product of the efforts of many agents, i.e. as the outcome of a spontaneous process in the Hayekian sense.

2.2 Institutional Competition Among Jurisdictions as a Knowledge-Creating Process

We noted above that 'competition among institutions' may actually be a misleading label for the phenomenon that we want to examine, since it is not the institutions themselves, as rule-configurations, that we regard as the competing units, but rather the 'carriers' or 'users' of institutions, i.e.

the individuals or groups that employ rules and institutions as 'social technology'. It may be better to use the term 'institutional competition' in
analogy to such terms as 'price-' or 'quality-competition', by which we
obviously do not mean that prices or qualities compete but, rather, that
sellers compete through their prices and the qualities of their products. In
the same sense 'institutional competition' means the competition among
'carrier-' or 'user-units' in terms of institutions. It is via the effect that
rules/institutions have on the success of their users – 'success' in terms of
the users' capability to solve the problems they face in their environment –
that rules/institutions survive and multiply, i.e. are being used more
widely. What we are interested in here is the issue of how institutional
competition affects the population of 'user-units'. Or, more specifically,
we want to examine how differences in institutional structure among
'user-units' translate into differential success in competition, and how the
latter affects the representation of institutional types in future populations
of 'user-units'.

Institutional competition is going on in multiple ways and within
various kinds of populations of 'carriers' or 'users', such as religious communities, business firms, sports clubs or political entities like local governments or states. Which entities constitute the relevant population is an
analytical issue; it depends on the explanatory problem that is to be
addressed. The competition among firms in ordinary markets, for instance,
includes an institutional dimension in the sense that the firms' organizational structure, that is, their internal rule-configuration, is one of the variables in terms of which they compete. And to the extent that differences in
their rule-structure affect firms' market success, one should expect this to
be reflected in the distribution of future populations of firms along the
institutional dimension.[18]

As noted above, we want to focus here on competition among polities
or jurisdictions, i.e. social entities that can be characterized, in analytical
terms, as 'territorial clubs'. Approaching such competition among jurisdictions from a population perspective, we need to ask what the relevant
populations of jurisdictions are and through what kinds of feedback mechanisms differences in institutional attributes can be expected to translate
into changes in the composition of populations over time. There exist
various levels of jurisdictions and, accordingly, various levels of competition, from local communes to nation states and beyond. Which set of jurisdictions constitutes the relevant population will, as noted before, depend
on the nature of the explanatory issue at hand.

As for the 'feedback mechanisms' there seem to be essentially two
kinds, which we propose to label as 'political selection' and 'market-type

selection' (Vanberg and Buchanan, 1991). By 'political selection' we mean the choice among potential alternative institutional regimes through collective political decision procedures such as, in particular, legislation. By 'market-type selection' we mean the choice of individuals – or of 'non-territorial clubs' like, for instance, firms – to locate in a particular jurisdiction or to move from one jurisdiction to another. These two selection processes are not mutually exclusive alternatives but typically operate simultaneously. Indeed, the way in which 'market-type selection' impacts on 'political selection' is important for the population effects of institutional competition.

Furthermore, both processes are about 'human selection' as opposed to 'natural selection', i.e. they do not operate directly through 'objective' success, but through human perception of success, even though we can assume that learning will impose a limit on the extent to which the two can diverge.[19] The potential difference between human perception and the factual performance of institutions means that there is not only an interaction between the two feedback mechanisms distinguished above, i.e. political selection and market-like selection, but also an interaction between the feedback via 'objective' consequences of rules/institutions for the problem-solving capacity of their carriers/users, and the feedback that works through perceived success, where 'perception' implies the possibility of error. The interaction of these various feedback mechanisms is bound to generate considerable complexity and should lead us to expect that we will hardly find simple regularities in the 'evolution of institutions' that hold widely across time and across social environments.

The issue that we are interested in is how competition among governments/jurisdictions affects the distribution of institutional properties within a relevant population of jurisdictions over time. That competition among jurisdictions can serve functions similar to those that we associate with ordinary market competition is a theme that, at least since Tiebout's (1956) classic article, has found considerable attention, in particular, in the theory of fiscal federalism. Yet, much of this discussion remained within a standard equilibrium framework, concerned with such issues as the matching of policies with 'given' citizens' preference, and left unexplored the issue that is our principal concern here, namely the role of competition as a knowledge-creating discovery procedure.[20]

The knowledge problem that we discussed earlier with regard to entrepreneurs in ordinary markets applies with full force to political entrepreneurs as well, where under the label of 'political entrepreneur' we subsume all agents who are in a position to shape the institutional attributes of jurisdictions, i.e., in particular, governments and legislators. What we said about the former can, by analogy, be extended to the latter. They also do not know, and cannot know, in advance most of the things that an equilibrium framework treats as 'given data'. They cannot know in advance what kinds of institutional provisions are best suited to solve diagnosed problems, nor can they know in advance what citizens will consider relevant problems in the future. Like entrepreneurs in ordinary markets, they have to act on conjectures, conjectures that may turn out to be right or wrong. And the process of competition among governments/jurisdictions can be seen, in analogy to market competition, as a process of experimenting, exploration and discovery, a process in which alternative institutional arrangements or social technologies are tried out, in an arena in which new arrangements and institutional inventions can constantly appear on stage, challenging established solutions.

In analogy to market competition, jurisdictions which introduce new superior institutions or abolish old ones, which outlived their usefulness, can – by winning a competitive advantage – advance in their respective competition among cities, regions or nations. This improvement in the interregional/international competitiveness of jurisdictions will attract the influx of factors of production (labour and capital). The advantages of this influx for the jurisdiction correspond to the profits of leading firms in market competition. Other jurisdictions, which now have a relatively inferior institutional structure, will fall back, losing labour and capital (investments) to the leading jurisdictions. These effects will put the jurisdictions under competitive pressure to improve their attractiveness, such as by imitating the institutional innovations of the leading countries. Hence there are incentives that successful institutional innovations of jurisdictions are being tried out and spread by imitation.[21] Before elaborating the knowledge-creating effect of this competition in more detail, we want to point to some particular problems for the workability of these competition processes.

One significant difference between ordinary market competition and competition between governments/jurisdictions that does not allow for the latter the degree of flexibility that we find in market competition has to do with the previously mentioned fact that jurisdictions are territorial clubs. When a dissatisfied customer of a seller in the market decides to take his business elsewhere, the costs or inconvenience of doing so are normally relatively modest. When residents are dissatisfied with 'their' government, they can escape that government only by moving into a different jurisdiction, a transaction that is in general significantly more costly than changing sellers in market exchange. There are potentially considerable exit costs involved, in particular in the form of 'sunk capital' that has to be given up or is devalued significantly by the change in residential location.

This includes as a major component accumulated knowledge, skills and expertise that are adapted to the particular environment, but have comparatively little value in alternative environments.

The problem of exit-costs certainly means that interjurisdictional migration will, in general, be less effective in making political entrepreneurs responsive to citizens' wants than mobility in ordinary markets is in making producers responsive to consumer preferences. However, this does not mean that it is not an important instrument in inducing responsiveness. Several facts have to be considered here. One important fact is that in competition among jurisdictions marginal residents, i.e. residents to whom the opportunity costs of moving to a different jurisdiction are low, can play a role similar to that which we ascribe to marginal consumers in ordinary market competition. Another fact is that persons may be able to move their resources, in particular capital, much more easily, i.e. at lesser costs, between jurisdictions, than they themselves could migrate, thus penalizing/rewarding governments by the withdrawal/investment of taxable funds.[22]

A further problem for the proper working of the process of competition among jurisdictions are the positive and negative incentives for those who decide on the institutional structure of the jurisdictions. Since jurisdictions have no single owner, who can claim the residual, but have to be seen as clubs consisting of many members with a collective decision procedure ('one citizen, one vote'), the incentive mechanism, which provides for the feedback by assigning profits and losses according to the relative position in the competition among jurisdictions seems to be much more difficult and hence may work considerably less efficiently than in ordinary markets, in which the capital owners simultaneously have both the ultimate authority to make decisions and can claim the profits or have to bear the losses, respectively. By contrast, the advantages and disadvantages of advancing or falling back in competition among jurisdictions may be both widely dissipated and presumably unevenly distributed among the citizens of jurisdictions.[23] Compared to the clearcut role of entrepreneurs in ordinary markets, the incentives for political entrepreneurs to search for institutional innovations in order to improve the competitiveness of his or her jurisdiction may be rather weak.

In regard to institutional competition among jurisdictions the imitation of successful institutions by other jurisdictions which have fallen back in competition can be a major problem, since it may be difficult to find out, to which part of the complex institutional structure the success of leading jurisdictions has to be attributed. If a jurisdiction imitates some of the institutions of the successful jurisdictions, it cannot be excluded that its competitiveness even deteriorates. There are primarily two reasons for that. One possibility is that the jurisdiction has imitated the wrong rules, i.e. rules which also affect negatively the competitiveness of the leading jurisdiction but which are counterbalanced by the positive effects of other rules. The second possibility, causing many more problems, is that rules fostering the competitiveness of the leading jurisdictions lead to negative effects on the imitating jurisdiction, because the effect of rules may differ depending on the existence of other rules and the habits of the individuals dealing with them. A considerable part of the problems the former centrally-planned economies are facing by implementing market institutions may be explained by that. Consequently, also the imitation of successful institutions by other jurisdictions may be a difficult and risky task.

Yet, even if the competition processes among institutions may not be as effective as those in ordinary markets, the essential fact remains that competition among jurisdictions provides for the possibility of alternative institutional arrangements to be tried out, and that it provides incentives for political entrepreneurs to seek to provide attractive institutional environments for citizens/taxpayers and mobile resources. And we can observe that such institutional competition among jurisdictions takes place. New institutional arrangements have been created and tried out by some jurisdictions, and after positive experiences have been later imitated by others. For example, in the 1980s, deregulation, liberalization and privatization have been strategies of jurisdictions to improve their competitiveness in the international competition for investments and new jobs. Through the experimentation with new institutional arrangements in these competition processes among jurisdictions, experiences are made and knowledge is being created and spread. As in competition on ordinary markets, the heterogeneity of the institutions of different jurisdictions has to be seen as positive for the process of finding better institutions.[24]

The knowledge-creating effect of institutional competition among jurisdictions elaborated above, also leads to important conclusions in regard to the internal multi-layered, hierarchical structure of jurisdictions, because from this perspective, an additional argument for a further decentralization in federally-organized jurisdictions can be derived. Shifting the solving of a certain problem from the level of the nation-state to a lower level as, for example, regions or local communes, leads to an additional competitive process among these territorial subunits concerning the finding of better ways to fulfill this task. Since many of these subunits try their own way of solving a certain problem, as, for example, what rules should be implemented to deal with the problem of waste disposal, hundreds of different hypotheses about the best way to handle such a problem will be tried out within one nation-state, and according to that much knowledge about better institutions for solving certain problems will be won and spread. Because of this knowledge-creating effect of institutional competition, it can be argued that decentralization should be pushed further ahead than purely static efficiency criteria would recommend.[25] Finally, it should be noted that the institutional competition among nation states can force the central level to shift the solving of certain problems to lower levels to take advantage of this knowledge-creating effect.

3   EVOLUTION WITHIN CONSTRAINTS

3.1   Market Competition as Constitutionally-Constrained Competition

Market competition can be carried out in many different ways and with a broad variety of strategies. Burning down the factories of one's competitors, bribing their employees for disclosing business secrets, or spreading false rumours about poisonous ingredients in their products might be just as effective strategies in seeking business success as creating a new product, improving one's service or the launching of a more impressive advertising campaign. There are many potential strategies that competitors could consider, and it is the function of the 'rules of the game' to draw a dividing line between strategies that may be employed, and those that may not be. To the extent that they are effectively enforced, rules determine which strategies a firm cannot use in order to gain a competitive advantage. In other words, in the 'market competition game' not all conceivable strategies are admissible. Market competition is competition within rules, it is (constitutionally) constrained competition (Vanberg, 1993).

What is the effect of rules on the evolutionary competitive process? Since the rules determine which strategies are allowed and which prohibited, they, in effect, direct the search efforts of the competitors for innovations into certain directions, and discourage search in other directions. If, for instance, rules prohibiting industrial espionage or trademark piracy are effectively enforced, agents will not expect a positive pay-off from efforts to improve their knowledge and capabilities in these kinds of activities. As a further consequence, firms need not search for ways how to defend themselves from these activities. That is, rules – by assigning positive and negative incentives to different strategies – influence the direction of innovative efforts, and hence the direction of the knowledge-creating and -spreading process (Kerber, 1992a, 1993, 1994b).[26] So the rules of the 'market competition game' also influence the direction of the process of economic development, or, as Witt (1987b) has observed, rules 'channel innovativeness'.

In terms of the variation–selection–retention framework we can interpret the hypotheses of the firms as the variants and the rules that define the terms of market competition as a relevant part of the selection environment. Different rules constitute different selection constraints, and it depends on the particular rules of the game which performance characteristics of firms make for success or failure in market competition. If, for instance, property rights are not sufficiently protected – either by lack of appropriate rules or by failure of enforcing them – incentives exist to violate the property of competitors, and, consequently, the necessity arises of defending one's own property against intrusion. In such an environment, it is not enough to produce better products to succeed; it is also necessary to develop knowledge about how to defend one's business against predatory action. A firm without such appropriate skills would not be sufficiently adapted to this problem environment. Since the rules are part of the selection criteria of market competition games, different sets of rules will lead to the survival of different kinds of firms with different knowledge and capabilities. They lead to the survival of different products, services and technologies in the market. And they determine which kind of knowledge will be selected or suppressed in market competition.

The recognition that it depends on the 'rules of the game' which kinds of firms, i.e. firms with what kinds of performance characteristics, will tend to be successful in market competition should alert us to the fact that there are clearly assumptions about 'appropriate rules' implied when we ascribe efficiency attributes to markets. The population of firms operating in an economy will always 'adapt' to the existing problem-environment (and the 'rules of the game' define relevant characteristics of that environment), i.e. there will be a shift in the distribution of the population in favour of superior problem-solving capacity. In this sense, it is always true that the 'successful' – successful relative to the respective problem-environment – will survive. Whether what survives is 'desirable' in terms of some separately defined normative criterion is, of course, a totally different matter. The terminology of 'survival' and 'success', of 'fitness' and 'adaptedness' may seem to imply that evolutionary processes necessarily lead to 'beneficial' or 'efficient' outcomes. Yet, it should be clear that such characterization is always relative to a particular problem-environment. In the case of market competition to say that the firms that survive are the most successful, the fittest, or the most adapted can only mean that they are the most successful, the fittest, and the most adapted *relative* to the specific market competition game, defined by a particular set of rules. Under a different set of rules, i.e. under a different selection environment, other firms with other attributes would be the most adapted and the fittest.[27]

The claim that in an evolutionary competitive process the successful survive has, *per se*, no normative content. It tells us that what survives is better adapted to the relevant selection conditions of the respective environment. It does not tell us whether what survives is 'desirable' in terms of some independent normative criterion, like, for instance, in terms of what the persons involved consider desirable. Whether that is the case is clearly a factual matter. Where such an independent criterion is applied, it will depend on the nature of the selection environment whether that which *de facto* survives is 'desirable' in terms of that criterion. If we regard the preferences and values of the persons involved as the relevant normative standard, the desirability of evolutionary competitive processes will depend on whether the selection environment makes for responsiveness to these interests and values. When we consider market competition as 'efficient', we, in effect, mean that it is a competitive process constrained by rules that encourage responsiveness to consumer interests. This is what the concept of 'consumer sovereignty' is meant to imply. Stated in terms of the variation–selection–retention framework, a normative standard like 'consumer-sovereignty' defines what the relevant selection criteria in the evolutionary competitive process *should* be, and, consequently, in what direction firms should search for new and better knowledge.

Another way of approaching the problem under discussion is in terms of the distinction between conditional and unconditional conjectures about the workings of evolutionary processes (Vanberg, 1994). Unconditional evolutionary conjectures are hypotheses about evolution that do not specify the selective forces under which the process occurs. Without any such specification we can still say that what survives must be 'successful' in coping with the problem-environment. But, not knowing what selective forces will operate, we cannot make any predictions about what it is that will be successful, and what attributes that which survives is likely to exhibit. Without knowing anything about the attributes of that which will be successful and survive, we surely cannot say whether what survives will be 'desirable' in terms of any specified normative criterion. By contrast, conditional evolutionary conjectures are statements about the workings of evolutionary processes under specified environmental constraints. Where relevant selective conditions in evolutionary processes can be identified, conjectures can be made about what is likely to be successful, and hence to survive, given those specified constraints. Since such conditional evolutionary hypotheses provide information about the likely attributes of what survives, they also allow for a meaningful discussion on whether these evolutionary processes lead to 'beneficial' results.

The above considerations reinforce our earlier argument on market competition as constitutionally-constrained competition. The claim that markets serve consumer interests is a conditional claim about the working of competition within 'appropriate rules'. It is the assumption that certain rules are in place that allows us to draw conclusions regarding, for instance, the general direction into which the search efforts of the agents are guided, or regarding the feedback mechanisms that, via the assignment of profits and losses, determine the dynamics of the process.[28] In every environment we can expect humans to experiment around what exists, and to explore new and potentially better solutions to the problems they face.[29] What is critical for the general direction into which man's explorative efforts are directed is the nature of the problem-environment. If markets are to serve consumer interests, they need to be framed by rules that make better service to consumers the principal avenue to success rather than, for instance, lobbying efforts for protective legislation.

Liberal advocates like Hayek have always emphasized that, in order to work beneficially, competition is to be 'restrained by appropriate rules of law'.[30] Also the German Ordo-liberals (Freiburg School) have emphasized that a system of rules is necessary to check both private and political power. This institutional framework, called 'competitive order' (*Wettbewerbsordnung*) and conceived as a 'rule of law', has the task to maintain the proper functioning of the competitive process, i.e. to safeguard competition against restraints of competition and the use of 'unfair means'. The basic idea of the Ordo-liberal concept of competition is that competition should be *Leistungswettbewerb*, i.e. that competition should take place within rules that assure 'that the only road to business success is through the narrow gate of better performance in service of the consumer'.[31] The Ordo-liberal *Leistungswettbewerb* hence can serve as a heuristic term, which may help in the search for the appropriate rules ('competitive order') to channel the innovative efforts of entrepreneurs in ordinary market competition into the direction of a better fulfillment of consumer preferences.

3.2 The Necessity of Constitutional Constraints for Institutional Competition

To institutional competition among governments/jurisdictions the same arguments that have been made above about market competition as constitutionally-constrained competition can also apply. Competition among jurisdictions can, in principle, be carried out in many ways with a wide variety of strategies or instruments. They can compete with each other by making their institutions more attractive to citizens and investors, by providing a more hospitable environment in terms of such things as regulatory provisions, their educational system, environmental and cultural attractiveness. But they can also compete by protectionist policies and export subsidies, the use of military force, by terrorist acts, by restricting their citizens' mobility, by confiscating property, and an array of other measures. Which kinds of institutions allow a jurisdiction to compete successfully, will surely depend on the nature of the relevant competitive constraints.

Looking at institutional competition as an evolutionary process, we can, again, predict that there will be a 'survival of the successful'. But, as in the previously discussed context, this does not tell us very much as long as we have no knowledge about the terms of competition, and about the nature of the selective forces that operate in the relevant environment. It tells us that whatever will make jurisdictions more successful in coping with their problem-environment will further their 'survival' and enhance the prospects that 'their likes' will be better represented in future populations of jurisdictions. But it does not tell us what properties 'successful' jurisdictions will tend to have, nor can it tell us whether what 'survives' will be 'desirable' in terms of whatever normative criterion we want to apply. As an unconditional evolutionary conjecture, i.e. a conjecture that does not specify the selective constraints and hence the particular nature of the competitive process, such a 'prediction' is without empirical and normative content.

A meaningful discussion on whether the outcomes of a process of institutional competition are 'desirable', is possible only to the extent that two questions can be answered. Namely, first, what kinds of properties are likely to promote 'success' and will, therefore, tend to be attributes of what 'survives'? And, second, what is considered 'desirable'? In order to answer the first question we need to know what the selective constraints and the terms of competition are. Only then can we specify what the likely characteristics of 'survivors' will be, and only then can we meaningfully begin to ask whether jurisdictions with such characteristics are 'desirable'. In order to answer the second question, we obviously need to specify a normative criterion that allows us to decide what, in terms of this criterion, is or is not desirable.

For market competition we adopted the individualist-liberal criterion of 'consumer sovereignty' that sees the desirability of the competitive order (*Wettbewerbsordnung*) of markets in its effectiveness in making producers/suppliers responsive to consumer interests. For institutional competition among governments/jurisdictions we suggest an analogous criterion that may be called 'citizens'sovereignty', a criterion that takes the preferences of the constituents of, or residents in, a jurisdiction as the relevant measuring rod against which the desirability of its institutional features has to be measured.

According to the criterion of 'consumer sovereignty' markets can be said to work the better, the better they are in serving consumer interests. The institutions that define the competitive order of markets can, accordingly, be said to be desirable to the extent that they enhance producers' responsiveness to consumer interests. By analogy, we can now also introduce the idea of a set of rules or a competitive order for competition among jurisdictions. And it can be said that these rules work the better, the better they induce the governments of the jurisdictions to direct their innovative competitive efforts to the serving of the interests of the citizens. Hence the set of rules that define the competitive order of institutional competition can be said to be desirable to the extent that they induce responsiveness to citizens' preferences. And to 'improve' such a competitive order means to improve the rules for institutional competition so as to channel the innovative efforts of the political entrepreneurs in the direction of a greater fulfillment of citizens' sovereignty.

Since the 'rules of the game' are a significant part of the framing conditions that constitute the problem-environment in which institutional competition takes place, different rules will guide the explorative efforts of jurisdictions into different channels, and, surely, not all of these efforts will be laudable in terms of our stated criterion. That is, as with market competition, we have to think of institutional competition as constitutionally constrained competition – as competition that occurs within the constraints of appropriate rules of the game. In markets, these constraints restrict the strategies that market participants may use in their competitive efforts. In the political realm, they restrict the strategies that governments are allowed to use in their competition for taxpayers and taxable resources.

4 A COMPETITIVE ORDER FOR INSTITUTIONAL COMPETITION AMONG INSTITUTIONS

From our above considerations, the following conclusion can be drawn: If the working properties of competitive evolutionary processes in the social realm are to a significant extent a function of the rules under which they operate, and if we can determine which kinds of rules are more likely than others to make these processes work in a way desirable to the persons involved, then, it would seem, efforts to install and maintain a suitable rule-framework should be one of the principal means by which we can hope to improve our social condition.

For markets this case has been forcefully argued by German Ordo-liberals with their plea for *Ordnungspolitik*, by which they meant an economic policy that sees its principal role in the continuous monitoring, enforcing and improving of the framework of rules. The perspective on institutional competition that we have outlined here suggests that for competition among governments/jurisdictions there should be an equivalent to the *Ordnungspolitik*-approach, i.e. a suitable framework of rules (competitive order) should be established. The general task of *Ordnungspolitik* in all its potential varieties, therefore, is to steer the competitive process in a desirable direction in the sense of consumer sovereignty or citizens' sovereignty. Or, stated in terms of the population paradigm, its task is to assure that selective forces operate on the relevant population (of e.g. firms or jurisdictions) in such a way as to shift the distribution of properties of the competing entities (firms, jurisdictions) in the direction of increased 'fit' with consumer/citizens preferences. Or, stated in still another way, the task of *Ordnungspolitik* is to encourage *Leistungswettbewerb* in ordinary markets as well as in politics, i.e. a kind of competition that approaches the ideals of consumer sovereignty and citizens' sovereignty.

But the statement that the task of *Ordnungspolitik* is to encourage *Leistungswettbewerb* does not mean that we should have a ready-made answer to the question of what constitutes an appropriate or desirable competitive order, either for market competition or for institutional competition. The concept of *Leistungswettbewerb* is an analytical concept, whose basic idea is that firms should advance in competition by better performance, and not by impeding their competitors, but it is not always easy to distinguish between these two kinds of competitive behaviour.[32] For market-oriented *Ordnungspolitik* there have been considerable efforts to specify what *Leistungswettbewerb* may mean in particular contexts. How *Ordnungspolitik* may advance *Leistungswettbewerb* in the realm of competition among governments/jurisdictions is a much less explored issue, though Public Choice and Constitutional Economics, as well as other branches of the 'new institutional economics', have provided useful insights.

Although we can specify the general theoretical meaning of the concept of *Leistungswettbewerb* with some clarity, its actual implementation is, however, a continuous task that must be solved in view of factual contingencies that we cannot all know in advance, nor determine once and for all. Like its correlatory terms, consumer sovereignty and citizens' sovereignty, the concept of *Leistungswettbewerb* is a general guideline rather than a specific blue-print for economic policy. To work out what this guideline suggests with regard to specific problem-situations is a permanent task of *Ordnungspolitik* in a changing world. And it will largely be a matter of learning from experience, by trial and error. After having expressed our doubt that appropriate solutions can easily be found, we want to mention, at least briefly, some aspects that seem to us of particular significance for the establishment of a suitable competitive order for institutional competition among jurisdictions.

If we have a multi-layered structure of jurisdictions (from local communes to nation-states), institutional competition can take place at all of these different levels. Therefore a multi-layered structure of institutional competition exists. In this case, the competitive order we are looking for has two intertwined dimensions. First, the institutional competition among jurisdictions of a certain level is in need of rules directing the competitive efforts of their respective governments to the fulfillment of their citizens' preferences. Usually, a higher-level jurisdiction is considered to be the appropriate unit for establishing such rules. But there is also a second dimension: by defining which strategies jurisdictions of lower levels may use in their competition, the higher-level jurisdiction simultaneously decides also about the vertical structure of competences within such a multi-layered system.

A different way of expressing this is that in such a federal system 'institutional *Ordnungspolitik*' would not only imply the establishment of rules for horizontal institutional competition among jurisdictions, but would also demand an integrated system of rules for the whole multi-layered structure, since the defining of the permissible competitive strategies on all levels of jurisdictions and the vertical distribution of competences are closely interdependent. Consequently, such an integrated framework of rules should also take into account our conclusion (derived above on p. 47f) that a further decentralized federal structure allowing for more institutional competition will create and spread a larger amount of knowledge about better ways to solve the problems of their citizens.

Returning to the problem of the appropriate rules for horizontal institutional competition, the principal selective force in the process of institutional competition among jurisdictions that we envision here, is the locational choices of entities – citizens/taxpayers, firms and investors – that can move taxable resources in and out of jurisdictions. Their choices constitute the essential feedback link between the institutional characteristics of jurisdictions and their success in attracting valued resources. The more responsive these locational choices are to changes in, and differences among, the institutional properties of jurisdictions, the closer the feedback link will be. Consequently, rules securing the mobility of persons/resources between jurisdictions are, therefore, a principal component of a *Wettbewerbsordnung* for institutional competition. Similar considerations may apply to the issue of 'collective' exit and entry, i.e. the possibility for subunits to secede from a polity of which they are part, and to operate as an independent unit or to associate with other polities. Appropriate rules for such 'jurisdictional mobility' may also help to promote responsive government.

But neither the right to compete with other jurisdictions through a certain set of strategies nor a perfect mobility between jurisdictions may be sufficient to ensure the working of these competition processes. It seems that a competitive order for institutional competition among jurisdictions may also have to address issues which on ordinary markets are the concern of antitrust policy. If there is to be genuine competition among governments/jurisdictions, the competitive order (*Wettbewerbsordnung*) has to effectively limit the scope for cartel-like *ex-ante* co-ordination among governments. No less than firms in ordinary markets, governments have incentives to seek to escape competitive constraints by concerted action. And there is a significant repertoire of arguments that allow governments to mask as legitimate concerns what, in effect, are only means to reduce competition. This would include the many varieties in which 'externality' arguments can be used to justify arrangements that limit the possibility of, and the incentives for, independent competitive efforts.[33]

Looking at competition among governments from an antitrust perspective, one is tempted to think about the idea of limiting the 'concentration' of jurisdictions, e.g. by a 'merger control' or by 'breaking up' large jurisdictions into smaller ones, in order to stimulate institutional competition. Taking into account the multi-layered structure of jurisdictions, each form of further centralization can be interpreted as a kind of 'concentration', since referring to the specific task that has been transferred to a higher level now only one unit instead of several offers its solution to the citizens. Consequently, a process of decentralization in a federal system does imply simultaneously a process of deconcentration with respect to the offering of institutional arrangements by jurisdictions to the citizens.

We cannot deal here with the questions, whether jurisdictions can have 'market power' in a sense analogous to the market power of firms, and to what extent it would be controlled by competition from other jurisdictions, because this would require a much longer discussion. But we want to point out that in one respect an important (and perhaps crucial) difference exists between competition among firms and competition among jurisdictions regarding the control of 'market power'. In ordinary market competition, an important limit to the market power of firms is the freedom of new firms to enter the market. But in competition among jurisdictions market entry is in some sense very difficult or impossible, because jurisdictions are territorial clubs, and there is no more free territory on the earth. Hence new jurisdictions can only emerge by seceding from old ones. Therefore the above-mentioned right to secede might also be a crucial one for maintaining institutional competition among jurisdictions.

As already suggested above, we do not have ready-made and definite answers as to how these problems, and many others, can be best accounted for in a competitive order for institutional competition among jurisdictions. Rather it has to be seen as an issue that requires continuous attention and further research. But it is important to recognize that the definition of a framework of rules for competition among jurisdictions is an essential part of the role that the constitutions of polities and federations have to play.

5 CONCLUSION

In regard to the wide topic 'competition among institutions', our purpose with this paper was twofold. We wanted to show that, similarly to market competition, institutional competition ought to be viewed as a knowledge-creating discovery process. And we wanted to argue that, again like market competition, institutional competition can be expected to work to the benefit of the persons involved only if it is constrained by appropriate rules. Institutions as rule-configuration can be viewed as 'social tools' or 'social technologies' that help to solve problems that persons face in their dealings with each other. As with problem-solving devices in other areas, we can never know in advance what the best technology is to solve the problems in human interaction and co-operation. Here, as there, we have to rely on experimenting, experience and learning, and our interest should be in utilizing the explorative potential of a competitive, evolutionary process. Since the selective constraints under which such a process operates are critical for the direction into which explorative efforts are guided, we need to subject institutional competition to appropriate rules if we want to assure responsiveness to the interest of the persons involved.

The combination of competitive evolutionary forces, and of institutional design, is what the concept of a competitive order (*Wettbewerbsordnung*) is all about. To generalize this notion from market competition to the realm of institutional competition, i.e. of competition among governments/jurisdictions, is no more than a logical extension of the research program of the Freiburg School.

Notes

1. Exemplifying references for economics are hardly needed here. For references from evolutionary biology see McIntosh (1992). As Mayr (1982; p. 484) notes, the Darwinian 'struggle for existence ... rarely takes the form of actual combat. Ordinarily it is simply competition for resources in limited supply'.

2. Note that not all of the unorthodox approaches in economics that are labelled 'evolutionary' are either based on, or compatible with, population thinking (on this issue see Witt, 1991, 1992). For an evolutionary approach in economics that explicitly adopts population thinking, see Metcalfe (1989).

3. As Allen and McGlade (1987, p. 729) phrase the 'question of evolution': 'How does the "character" of a population change over time in response to the "rewards and dangers" of particular strategies?'

4. The significance of this particular ambiguity in the use of the term 'institution' is discussed in some detail in Vanberg (1983).

5. '[O]ne simply cannot speak of being a member of the institution of property. Institutions in the latter sense ... are complexes of normative rules and principles which ... serve to regulate social action and relationships' (Parsons 1975, p. 97).

6. Hayek (1976, p. 21) speaks of rules as 'general purpose tools' that are 'adapted to the solution of recurring problem situations' and he argues: 'Like a knife or a hammer they have been shaped not with a particular purpose in view but because ... they have proved serviceable in a great variety of situations ... The knowledge which has given them their shape ... knowledge of the recurrence of certain problem situations or tasks'. – For a discussion on Hayek's use of the 'rule as tools' analogy, see Vanberg (1992, pp. 109ff; 1994, pp. 186ff).

7. In order to keep things simple we disregard here the issue of potential differences between citizens and resident non-citizens, as well as issues that concern the status of non-resident citizens.

8. One of these approaches consists of the German concepts of 'dynamic competition' and evolutionary market process (Arndt, 1952, Heuss, 1965, Hoppmann, 1988, J. Röpke, 1977, 1990, Fehl, 1986; for an overview see Kerber, 1994a), which originally have been based primarily upon Schumpeterian thinking and which later have also been influenced by Hayek. Austrian economists, particularly Kirzner (1992), have explicitly adopted the Hayekian notion of competition in their studies of market processes. Schumpeterian approaches to innovation and economic development have also influenced the evolutionary approach of Nelson and Winter (1982) and much of the vast theoretical and empirical literature about innovation and technical change (e.g. Dosi et al., 1988). For an overview including the new discipline of evolutionary economics, see Witt (1987a, 1992).

9. A more detailed exposition of the following argument can be found in Kerber (1992b).

10. See Hayek (1948, p. 101 in particular) and Hayek (1979, pp. 66ff).
11. For the creative character and the resulting open-endedness of the process see e.g. Shackle (1972) and Buchanan and Vanberg (1991). P. Allen (1990, p. 16) notes about the generalized evolutionary perspective: 'The fluctuations, mutations and apparently random movements which are naturally present in real complex systems, constitute a sort of "imaginative" and creative force which explores around whatever exists at present. Selection, or rather the mechanisms which constitute its dynamics, operate on these initiatives which will either regress, or on the contrary will sweep the system off to some new state of organization.'
12. Hayek (1979, p. 68): 'Competition is thus like experimenting in science, first and foremost a discovery procedure.'
13. According to Hayek (1978, p. 181): '[T]he difference between economic competition and the successful procedures of science consists in the fact that the former is a method of discovering particular facts relevant to the achievement of specific, temporary purposes, while science aims at the discovery of what are sometimes called "general facts", which are regularities of events'.
14. To this notion of dynamic competitive processes, the power-limiting effect of competition lies in the temporariness and not in the non-existence of market power.
15. This dynamic analysis of the competitive process has especially been elaborated in the German approach of 'dynamic competition' (see above n. 8). For the potential negative effects on the wealth of competitors, which follow from the introducing of new innovations by others, see Witt (1987b, pp. 182ff), Streit and Wegner (1992, pp. 142ff), and Kerber (1993, pp. 443ff).
16. The importance of the heterogeneity of firms has been especially emphasized by Heuss (1965, pp. 145ff) and Fehl (1986).
17. As Hayek (1978, p. 236) has noted, the competitive market process 'provides incentives for constant discovery of new facts which improve adaptation to the everchanging circumstances of the world in which we live'. See also Popper's claim of a universal Darwinian concept of the growth of knowledge, based upon the principle of trial-and-error elimination (Popper 1972, p. 255). In the evolutionary approach of Nelson and Winter (1982) such a variation–selection reasoning has been combined with Schumpeterian dynamics to provide for a more adequate explanation of economic development than the traditional neoclassical growth theory which always had difficulties in explaining technical progress. For a combination of this literature with evolutionary epistemology see Metcalfe and Boden (1992).
18. The evolutionary approach of Nelson and Winter (1982), in which firms are conceived as consisting of 'routines' in the sense of repetitive patterns of activity, comes close to this notion.
19. As Allen (1990, p. 20) notes on this issue: 'In human systems, at the microscopic level, decisions reflect the different expectations of individuals, based on their past experience. The interaction of these decisions actually creates the future, and in so doing fails to fullfill the expectations of many of the actors. ... Evolution in human systems is therefore a continual, imperfect learning process, spurred by the difference between expectation and experience, but rarely providing enough information for a complete understanding.'

20. Discussing 'competition between local governments' explicitly as a 'discovery procedure' Vihanto (1992, p. 434) notes as a defect of the traditional analysis that it regards competition as 'a procedure by which the competitors can be induced to act so as to produce foreseeable outcomes that are known to be efficient or inefficient on the basis of current information', and that it ignores that 'many of the outcomes of competition cannot be known' in advance. For other approaches regarding the competition among jurisdictions for better institutions, which are based upon these Hayekian ideas, see Wohlgemuth (1994, pp. 24ff) and especially Fehl (1990, pp. 13–24), who analyses the transmission processes of successful institutions among nation states via 'political selection' and 'market-type selection' (including various interactions between them) in more detail.

21. For a Schumpeterian analysis of international competition, in which the competition among countries is seen as a rivalry process, consisting of 'moving ahead and falling back', of 'leaders' and 'followers' and their mutual interaction, see Abramovitz (1988). For an argument along somewhat similar lines, see Porter (1990) who applies his concept of 'competitive advantage' to the competition among nations. But in contrast to our approach Porter does not stress the institutional dimension of international competition.

22. For an explicit analysis of the effects of competition among governments for capital, see Sinn (1992).

23. Since e.g. the prices for real estates react especially sensitively on any inflow or outflow of labour and capital, the owners of real estates may be much more affected by changes in the competitiveness of their jurisdiction than other members.

24. Campbell (1965, p. 28): 'The more numerous and the greater the heterogeneity among variations, the richer the opportunities for an advantageous innovation'.

25. For an interesting argumentation in favour of decentralization which is derived from the Hayekian notion of competition, see Vihanto (1992, p. 415), who emphasizes that it is 'the nature of competition as an open-ended process of discovery' that provides an essential 'argument for a decentralized government'.

26. See also Demsetz (1991, p. 230): 'The importance of the private property system is not in furthering or reducing rivalry generally but in the direction it gives to rivalry. The harm to one individual in allowing competition may be as great as that resulting from theft, but we approve of the incentive effects of the former and disapprove of those of the latter.' And: 'The question is not whether to compete, it is what *kind* of competition to sanction' (ibid, p. 229).

27. The idea that the prevailing set of rules influences the selection criteria of the market, and hence that the 'superiority' of products and firms is always relative to these rules, was put forward by J. Röpke (1977, p. 275).

28. Without specification of the selective conditions any variation–selection argumentation remains empty, an insight that can already be drawn from Alchian (1950) and Penrose (1952, pp. 809ff).

29. As the eighteenth century Scottish moral philosopher A. Ferguson (1767/1980, p. 6) put it: Man 'is destined, from the first age of his being, to invent and contrive. ... He would be always improving on his subject, and he carries this intention where-ever he moves, through the streets of the populous city, or the wild of the forest.'

30. Hayek (1978, p. 125; 1988, p. 19); or as Edwards (1949, pp. 2ff) has characterized the issue: 'Competition necessarily takes place within the limits of certain rules of the game established by law and custom. These rules provide a setting within which commercial intercourse is carried on. ... In general, ..., rules of the game are designed to direct competitive behaviour into desirable channels without reducing the intensity of competition ... When the rules are too lax, the competitive game is played by undesirable means and produces undesirable results. When they are too tight, desirable activities are forbidden and experiment becomes difficult'.
31. W. Röpke (1960, p. 31); for a short presentation of the Ordo-liberal concept of *Wettbewerbsordnung*, see Möschel (1989) and Vanberg (1991).
32. For example, in Germany the concept of *Leistungswettbewerb* partly also has been abused in the application of the 'Law Against Restraints of Competition' (GWB) and the 'Law Against Unfair Competition' (UWG) for reducing competition (see e.g. Mestmäcker, 1984).
33. For example, 'revenue sharing' or 'intergovernmental transfers' (Vihanto, 1992, pp. 430ff; Dye, 1990, pp. 114ff). From that perspective, the efforts to a greater harmonization of laws and regulations within the European Union can also be seen as a step to a further cartelization of the member states. But to make sure, we do not want to deny that there may be also 'economies of scale' effects and legitimate arguments in regard to externalities, which should be taken into account.

References

Abramovitz, Moses (1988) 'Following and Leading', in Horst Hanusch (ed.), *Evolutionary Economics: Applications of Schumpeter's Ideas* (Cambridge: Cambridge University Press) pp. 323–41.
Alchian, Armen A. (1950) 'Uncertainty, Evolution, and Economic Theory', *Journal of Political Economy*, 58, pp. 211–21.
Allen, Peter M. (1990) 'Why the Future is not what it was: New Models of Evolution' *Futures*, 22, pp. 555–70. (Here quoted from typescript, International Ecotechnology Research Centre, Cranfield Institute of Technology, Bedford, England.)
____ and J. M. McGlade (1987) 'Evolutionary Drive: The Effect of Microscopic Diversity, Error Making, and Noise', *Foundations of Physics*, 17, pp. 728–38.
Arndt, Helmut (1952) *Schöpferischer Wettbewerb und klassenlose Gesellschaft* (Berlin: Duncker & Humblot).
Buchanan, James M. and Vanberg, Viktor (1991). 'The Market as a Creative Process', *Economics and Philosophy*, 7, pp. 167–86.
Campbell, Donald T. (1965) 'Variation and Selective Retention in Socio-Cultural Evolution', In H.R. Barringer, G.I. Blanksten, and R.W. Mack (eds.), *Social Change in Developing Areas* (Cambridge, Mass.: Schenkman) pp. 19–49.
Demsetz, Harold (1991). 'Perfect Competition, Regulation, and the Stock Market', in Harold Demsetz, *Efficiency, Competition, and Policy. The Organization of Economic Policy, Vol. II* (Cambridge and Oxford: Basil Blackwell) pp. 225–41.
Dosi, Giovanni, Freeman, Christopher, Nelson, Richard, Silverberg, Gerald, and Luc Soete (eds) (1988) *Technical Change and Economic Theory* (London and New York: Pinter Publishers).

62   *Competition among Institutions: Evolution within Constraints*

Dye, Thomas R. (1990) *American Federalism – Competition Among Governments* (Lexington, Mass.: Lexington Books).

Edwards, Corwin D. (1949) *Maintaining Competition. Requisites of a Government Policy* (New York, Toronto and London: McGraw-Hill).

Fehl, Ulrich (1986) 'Spontaneous Order and the Subjectivity of Expectations: A Contribution to the Lachmann–O'Driscoll Problem', in Israel M. Kirzner (ed.), *Subjectivism, Intelligibility and the Economic Understanding: Essays in Honor of Ludwig M. Lachmann* (New York: New York University Press) pp. 72–86.

_____ (1990) 'Wachsende internationale Interdependenz und Transmission von Effekten binnenwirtschaftlicher Politik auf das Ausland', in Erhard Kantzenbach (ed.), *Probleme der internationalen Koordination der Wirtschaftspolitik* (Berlin: Duncker & Humblot) pp. 9–43

Ferguson, Adam (1767/1980). *An Essay on the History of Civil Society* (New Brunswick and London: Transaction Books).

Hayek, Friedrich A. von (1948) 'The Meaning of Competition', in Friedrich A. von Hayek, *Individualism and Economic Order* (Chicago: University of Chicago Press) pp. 92–106.

_____ (1976) *Law, Legislation, and Liberty. Vol. 2: The Mirage of Social Justice* (London: Routledge & Kegan Paul).

_____ (1978) *New Studies in Philosophy, Politics, Economics and the History of Ideas* (Chicago: University of Chicago Press).

_____ (1979) *Law, Legislation, and Liberty. Vol. 3: The Political Order of a Free People* (London: Routledge & Kegan Paul).

_____ (1988) *The Fatal Conceit: The Errors of Socialism* (London: Routledge & Kegan Paul).

Hesse, Günter (1990) 'Evolutorische Ökonomik oder Kreativität in der Theorie', in Ulrich Witt (ed.), *Studien zur Evolutorischen Ökonomik I* (Berlin: Duncker & Humblot) pp. 49–73.

Heuss, Ernst (1965) *Allgemeine Markttheorie* (Tübingen and Zürich: J.C.B. Mohr (Paul Siebeck) and Polygraphischer Verlag).

Hoppmann, Erich (1988) *Wirtschaftsordnung und Wettbewerb* (Baden-Baden: Nomos).

Keller, Evelyn Fox and Loyd, Elisabeth A. (1992). *Keywords in Evolutionary Biology* (Cambridge, Mass. and London: Harvard University Press).

Kerber, Wolfgang (1992a). 'Innovation, Handlungsrechte und evolutionärer Marktprozess', in Ulrich Witt (ed.), *Studien zur Evolutorischen Ökonomik II* (Berlin: Duncker & Humblot) pp. 171–95.

_____ (1992b) *Competition as a Knowledge-Creating Process. Towards a Comprehensive Theory of Evolutionary Market Processes*. Mimeo.

_____ (1993) 'Rights, Innovations, and Evolution. The Distributional Effects of Different Rights to Innovate', *Review of Political Economy*, 5, pp. 427–52.

_____ (1994a). 'German Market Process Theory', in Peter J. Boettke, (ed.), *The Edward Elgar Companion to Austrian Economics* (Aldershot: Edward Elgar) pp. 500–7.

_____ (1994b) 'Some Notes on the Distributional Effects of Different Rights to Innovate', *Review of Political Economy*, 6, pp. 240–5.

Kirzner, Israel M. (1992). *The Meaning of Market Process. Essays in the Development of Modern Austrian Economics* (London and New York: Routledge).

Lachmann, Ludwig M. (1977). *Capital, Expectations, and the Market Process. Essays on the Theory of the Market Economy* (edited by W. Grinder) (Kansas City: Sheed Andrews and McMeel Inc.).

Maynard Smith, John (1987) 'How to Model Evolution', in J. Dupre (ed.), *The Latest on the Best – Essays on Evolution and Optimality* (Cambridge, Mass.: The MIT Press), pp. 117–31.

Mayr, Ernst (1982) *The Growth of Biological Thought* (Cambridge, Mass. and London: The Belknap Press of Harvard University Press).

McIntosh, Robert (1992) 'Competition: Historical Perspectives', in Evelyn Fox Keller and Elisabeth A. Loyd (eds.), *Keywords in Evolutionary Biology*, (Cambridge, Mass. and London: Harvard University Press) pp. 61–7.

Metcalfe, J.S. (1989) 'Evolution and Economic Change', in A. Silberston (ed.), *Technology and Economic Progress* (London: Macmillan) pp. 544–85.

——— and Boden, M. (1992) 'Evolutionary Epistemology and the Nature of Technology Strategy', in R. Coombs, Paolo Saviotti and Vivien Walsh (eds), *Technological Change and Company Strategies.* (Academic Press) pp. 49–71.

Mestmäcker, Ernst-Joachim (1984) *Der verwaltete Wettbewerb: eine vergleichende Untersuchung über den Schutz von Freiheit und Lauterkeit im Wettbewerbsrecht* (Walter Eucken Institut: Wirtschaftswissenschaftliche und wirtschaftsrechtliche Untersuchungen 19), (Tübingen: J.C.B. Mohr (Paul Siebeck)).

Möschel, Wernhard (1989) 'Competition Policy from an Ordo Point of View', in Alan Peacock and Hans Willgerodt, (eds), *German Neo-liberals and the Social Market Economy* (London: Macmillan) pp. 142–59.

Nelson, Richard. R., and Signey G. Winter. (1982) *Evolutionary Theory of Economic Change* (Cambridge, Mass: Harvard University Press).

Parsons, Talcott (1975) 'Social Structure and Symbolic Media of Exchange', in P.M. Blau (ed.), *Approaches to the Study of Social Structure* (New York and London: The Free Press) pp. 94–120.

Penrose, Edith T. (1952) 'Biological Analogies in the Theory of the Firm', *American Economic Review*, 72, pp. 114–32.

Popper, Karl R. (1972) *Objective Knowledge. An Evolutionary Approach* (Oxford: The Clarendon Press).

Porter, Michael E. (1990) *The Competitive Advantage of Nations* (New York: The Free Press).

Röpke, Jochen (1977) *Die Strategie der Innovation* (Tübingen: J.C.B. Mohr (Paul Siebeck)).

——— (1990) 'Evolution and Innovation', in K. Dopfer and K.-F. Raible (eds), *The Evolution of Economic Systems. Essays in Honour of Ota Sik* (Houndmills and London: Macmillan) pp. 111–20.

Röpke, Wilhelm (1960) *A Humane Economy. The Social Framework of the Free Market* (South Bend, Ind.: Gateway Editions).

Schumpeter, Joseph A. (1934) *The Theory of Economic Development. An Inquiry into Profits, Capital, Credit, Interest, and the Business Cycle* (Cambridge, Mass.: Harvard University Press).

Shackle, G.L.S. (1972) *Epistemics & Economics. A Critique of Economic Doctrines* (Cambridge : Cambridge University Press).

Sinn, Stefan (1992) 'The Taming of *Leviathan*: Competition Among Governments', *Constitutional Political Economy*, 2, pp. 177–96.

Streit, Manfred E. and Gerhard Wegner (1992) 'Information, Transactions, and Catallaxy: Reflections on some Key Concepts of Evolutionary Market Theory', in Ulrich Witt (ed.), *Explaining Process and Change. Approaches to Evolutionary Economics* (Ann Arbor: Michigan Press) pp. 125–49.

Tiebout, Charles M. (1956) 'A Pure Theory of Local Expenditure', *Journal of Political Economy*, 84, pp. 416–24.

Vanberg, Viktor (1983) 'Der individualistische Ansatz zu einer Theorie der Entstehung und Entwicklung von Institutionen', *Jahrbuch für Neue Politische Ökonomie*, 2, pp. 50–69.

____ (1991) 'Review of Ordo, Vls. 40 and 41', *Constitutional Political Economy*, 2, pp. 397–402.

____ (1992). 'Innovation, Cultural Evolution, and Economic Growth', in Ulrich Witt (ed.), *Explaining Process and Change. Approaches to Evolutionary Economics* (Ann Arbor: The University of Michigan Press) pp. 105–21.

____ (1993) 'Constitutionally Constrained and Safeguarded Competition in Markets and Politics. With Reference to a European Constitution', *Journal des Economistes et des Etudes Humaines*, 4, pp. 3–27.

____ (1994) 'Cultural Evolution, Collective Learning and Constitutional Choice', in David Reisman (ed.), *Economic Thought and Political Theory* (Boston, Dordrecht and London: Kluwer Academic Publishers) pp. 171–204. (English version of Viktor Vanberg, *Kulturelle Evolution und die Gestaltung von Regeln*, Walter Eucken Institut, Vorträge und Aufsätze 144 (Tübingen: J.C.B. Mohr (Paul Siebeck)).

____ and James M. Buchanan (1991) 'Constitutional Choice, Rational Ignorance and the Limits of Reasons', *Jahrbuch für Neue Politische Ökonomie*, 10, pp. 65–78.

Vihanto, Martti (1992) 'Competition Between Local Governments as a Discovery Procedure', *Journal of Institutional and Theoretical Economics*, 148, pp. 411–36.

Witt, Ulrich (1987a) *Individualistische Grundlagen der evolutorischen Ökonomik* (Tübingen: J.C.B. Mohr (Paul Siebeck)).

____ (1987b). 'How Transaction Rights are Shaped to Channel Innovativeness?' *Journal of Institutional and Theoretical Economics*, 143, pp. 180–195.

____ (1991). 'Reflections on the Present State of Evolutionary Economic Theory', in G. Hodgson and E. Screpanti (eds.) *Rethinking Economics: Markets, Technology, and Economic Evolution* (Aldershot: Edward Elgar) pp. 83–102.

____ (1992). *Evolutionary Economics: An Interpretative Survey.* Paper presented at the Eastern Economic Association Meeting, New York. Mimeo.

Wohlgemuth, Michael (1994) *Economic and Political Competition in Neoclassical and Evolutionary Perspective.* Diskussionsbeiträge des Max-Planck-Instituts zur Erforschung von Wirtschaftssystemen, No. 02–94, Jena.

3 Causes of Changes in Political-Economic Regimes*

Peter Bernholz

1 INTRODUCTION

If we want to speak about the causes of changes of political-economic regimes or systems we should first try to formulate what we understand by the latter concepts. In this paper, a political-economic regime is defined by the set of relatively stable and long-lasting rules (including the legal system), rights and government organizations within and through which it operates.

In the past, ideal systems described by concepts like market or planned economy, private or public property, monarchy, aristocracy, democracy, dictatorship, totalitarianism, rule of law, division of power, have been applied by economic and political theory to come to grips with the manifoldness of systems which have developed in reality. We will follow this precedence, but keep in mind two reservations. First, the different systems have themselves evolved in history. The stone age hunters did not have the knowledge of a market economy, and it is dubious whether we can speak of democracies before the Greek innovations. Second, we certainly can sometimes observe rather abrupt changes from one political–economic regime to another one. Russia after 1917 and West Germany from 1948 are telling examples. But we should not forget that in most historical cases, the change of political–economic regimes was a nearly continuous evolutionary process, in which subsequent changes, and the abolishment or introduction of rules and organizations followed each other and accumulated to a transformation of political–economic systems.

---

*Parts of this paper are reprinted with kind permission from 'Efficiency, Polictical–Economic Organization, and International Competition Among States', *International Journal of the Unity of the Sciences*, 1992, 5, pp. 443–83.

2   FORCES RESPONSIBLE FOR CHANGES OF POLITICAL–ECONOMIC REGIMES

Let me state at the very beginning the forces which I believe to be responsible for the change of political–economic regimes:

1.   The divergent performances concerning economic efficiency and innovative capabilities of different economic systems.
2.   Political competition inside states for domestic power.
3.   Competition of states in the international system for dominance and survival.
4.   The influence of ideological or religious belief systems succeeding during crises.

In the following sections we will sketch how these forces work together to change political–economic regimes. We will also point to historical evidence supporting our hypotheses.

3   REASONS FOR THE VASTLY DIVERGING ECONOMIC PERFORMANCES OF DIFFERENT ECONOMIC REGIMES

Let us first turn to the reasons for the divergent economic performance of different economic systems.

By now we know quite well that this performance, that is efficiency, innovativeness and growth of gross national product per capita depend mainly on the economic and political, as well as on the legal, institutions of a country. The main relationships have been summed up in Figure 1. A so-called planned socialist economy with state property is unable to motivate people to work efficiently and to be innovative. Since people cannot earn higher incomes or profits as a consequence of greater efforts, they are not motivated to work industriously and efficiently. Because of the same reasons, they have no cause to innovate, since they cannot earn the fruits of their ingenuity. On the contrary, they have even to fight a stubborn bureaucracy to get the necessary inputs to innovate, that is, to invent and to introduce new and better production processes and goods. Since there is no competition which is threatening to throw them out of business, they are also not driven to be efficient and innovative because they are afraid to lose their present position. The whole problem is made worse by the fact that there are no market prices which give reliable information on the relative scarcities of factors of production and of other goods. As a

Figure 1   Consequences of Different Economic Systems

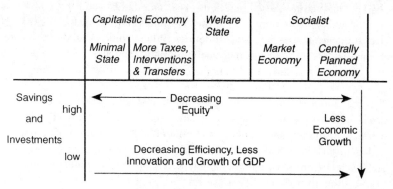

consequence, no manager or worker in state-owned plants knows how to combine best the factors of production to reach the highest productivity and to produce the goods most wanted by the population or even by oligarchic leadership (v. Mises,1920/1935, Hayek, 1935, Bernholz, 1975 chapter 6, Pejovich, 1987). The central planning agency suffers from a similar defect. It can, through lack of information, never know how to combine best, and where and when to use the scarce factors of production. All this leads to an inefficient economy and to a lack of innovation. Resources are squandered and productivity is rather low. Because of central planning, freedom cannot be granted and the wishes of the population for goods cannot be taken into account. On the other hand, the oligarchy is always able to reserve for themselves enough goods like dachas, cars and resorts at the Black Sea.

Moreover, 'socialism with a human face', some kind of socialist market economy, does not seem to provide a much better solution (Ward, 1967, Bernholz, 1979 chapters 1–2, Pejovich, 1987). Though informational problems can be solved better with the help of markets, inefficiency, a strong tendency towards unemployment and inflation, and distorted investment policies of labour-managed firms with weak and unsaleable property rights of workers remain. The empirical evidence from former Yugoslavia with very high unemployment, inefficiency and rampaging inflation is also not encouraging.

On the other hand, it should not be overlooked that free market economies only work adequately if certain conditions are met. A legal framework assuring the safety of property rights and a stable monetary system (Dorn and Schwartz, 1987) allowing extensive credit and capital markets are among these conditions. The same holds true for the absence of too many government regulations and interventions, of too high taxes and of unsustainable high budget deficits. Where some or all of these conditions are not met, no adequate economic efficiency and development can be expected, as is shown by example of several Latin American and other underdeveloped countries.

It has also to be stressed that a regime of at least relatively free international trade in goods and services and of free international capital movements is of the greatest importance for an efficient allocation of resources and a high level of innovative activity. Not only efficiency and thus welfare is increased by the international division of labour and the international allocation of capital according to its greatest productivity. But foreign competition is also necessary to limit the power of domestic cartels and monopolies and to motivate firms to innovate to keep abreast with competitors from abroad.

The recent literature on economic development has demonstrated (Donges, 1976, Krueger, 1978, Little, Scitovsky and Scott, 1970) that a foreign trade regime trying to further development through import substitution by creating import barriers or by using foreign exchange controls, has been a dismal failure. Cartels and monopolies sheltered from foreign competition produce inefficiently and need not innovate. Productive activity and resources are misdirected because of distorted relative prices. Firms are competing for import or foreign exchange quotas and thus dissipate resources to obtain rents. Corruption of politicians and bureaucracy are furthered.

It is thus not surprising that several of the so-called newly developing countries (Taiwan, South Korea, Singapore, Hong Kong, Thailand, Malaysia) have all pursued an export-oriented policy and in time reduce import and foreign exchange restrictions. Unfortunately, especially in democracies, political forces are usually pressing for restrictions on foreign trade and foreign exchange.

The better performance of 'pure' market economies with private property does not imply that they can solve all problems adequately. Among these are the so-called negative externalities, e.g., environmental pollution, the scarcity of non-reproducible and of 'positional' goods (Hirsch, 1978) and the just distribution of income and wealth. Though environmental pollution seems to fare even worse in planned economies, measures by the government to internalize these negative externalities are clearly needed to reduce pollution to permanently sustainable levels. Economists have shown that these measures should, whenever possible, consist not in regulations but in taxes or fees on the firms, households and communities according to the amounts of pollution caused by them. Only then are they strongly motivated not only to reduce the level of pollution but also to find and to introduce more adequate new technologies (Faber and Manstetten, 1989). Thus quasi-market mechanisms should be used, whenever feasible.

4 THE INFLUENCE OF THE DOMESTIC POLITICAL REGIME

Let us turn now to the fourth factor influencing the change of political–economic regimes, namely political competition inside states.

A developed system of free markets and of private property requires the existence of a strong but limited state to protect the safety of property rights and, if necessary, to adjudicate and enforce privately agreed contracts. Government has to be limited to prevent excessive tax burdens, frequent and incalculable changes in law, discretionary interventions in the economy and excessive taxes. Only under such conditions can private initiative unfold its benevolent consequences.

Government has, moreover, to provide public goods like internal order and safety and defence against foreign aggression. We have already seen that it has also to play a role in removing and preventing environmental pollution and in bringing about some limited income or wealth redistribution.

It has to be stressed that not democracy but limited government and some rule of law is necessary for the success of a free market economy with private property. The rapid economic development of Hong Kong, Taiwan and South Korea provides empirical evidence for this proposition. By contrast, a decentralized market economy seems to be a precondition for long-lasting democratic regimes.

Let us point out in this context what we understand by a democracy. A democracy is a political regime in which most issues within the jurisdiction of government are decided upon by simple majority voting in legislative bodies (parliaments) or in referenda, and in which the members of parliament are elected by the population at regular intervals. A democracy, in this sense, is not congruent with a regime dominated by the rule of law. First, the rule of law can also be present in monarchies, aristocracies and in pluralistic regimes not dominated by one specific group. Secondly, in a democracy with a total domain, i.e., in which all problems can be taken up and be decided by government and/or parliament, the rule of law may be threatened. This usually happens if a democratic regime is not restricted in its domain by constitutional or other safeguards, so that shifting simple majorities in parliament, i.e., small minorities of the population only inadequately controlled by rationally uniformed voters, can impose their will on the rest of the population. For if shifting majorities can legislate on everything they select, individuals have no secure rights. Their rights can be abrogated any time by the legislature. Majorities in the latter are not bound by the rule of law, and thus individuals have only rights conditional on the intentions of different potential majorities. Ethnic and other minorities may be suppressed or disadvantaged by the majority. This, in its turn, may engender international tensions, especially if the respective minority group forms a majority in other states. We will see in this section that unrestricted or even only moderately limited democracies show tendencies not only to weaken the rights and thus the freedom of individuals, but also to erode the efficiency and innovative capabilities of market economies with dominating private property (Figure 2).

Democracy is not only no precondition for a capitalist market economy but may even endanger it in the long-run and, from the above remark, thus even threaten its own existence. With several parties competing in capitalist market economies for votes and the necessity of financial assistance to cover the costs of their organizations and election campaigns, this results in growing public expenditures, excessive regulations by government, tax loopholes and subsidies to special minority interests and pressure groups *whenever the majority of voters is rationally uninformed about the issues* (Figure 3). This will be the case *if decisions impinge only marginally on the situations of citizens*, since then they have little reason to inform themselves, given the fact that the influence of individual votes on election outcomes is negligible. As a consequence, we observe, for example, protection of certain industries against foreign competition, the fixing of agricultural prices above market-clearing levels or subsidies to the energy industry, although it is clear that a majority of voters is hurt by higher taxes and/or prices. Only if economic developments like rent increases are perceived by a majority of people, since the respective expenditures amount to a substantial part of their budgets, will government action favour the majority e.g., by imposing rent controls (Downs, 1957, Bernholz, 1966).

Note that the influence of minorities just discussed depends on the rational ignorance of the majority of the population. It implies thus no contradiction to the decisiveness of shifting majorities mentioned above, which is always working whenever the respective majority is well-informed about the issues at stake.

It follows from the above analysis that unlimited democracies show a tendency to introduce subsidies, transfers and regulations in favour of dif-

Figure 2 Consequences of Growing Government Activity in Democratic Market Economies

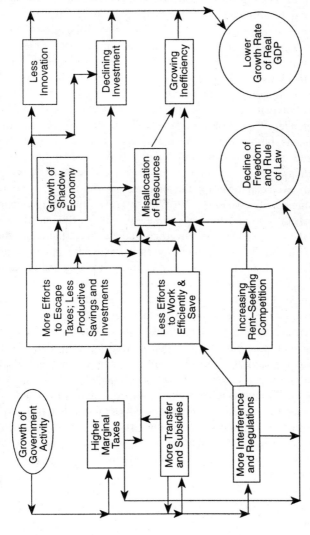

Figure 3   Growth of Government in Market Economies

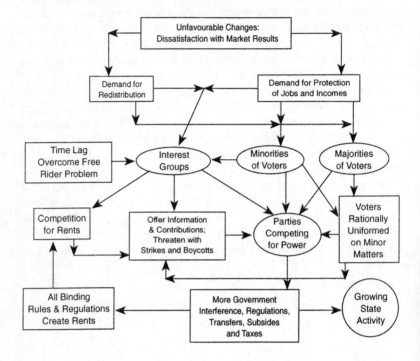

ferent minorities of voters, of interest groups and, in some cases, of shifting majorities. Since it is often difficult to form interest groups because they provide a public good to their members, it takes time to organize them. The more diverse the interests and the greater the number of potential members, the more difficult the task to form an interest group and the more time this will take (Olson, 1965, Bernholz, 1969). Moreover, time is needed to introduce new legislation, taxes and subsidies. Finally, political interests and party competition will respond to shifting economic conditions, which are at least partially brought about by the process of economic growth itself.

From all these factors it has to be expected that state activity will be growing in time. A democratic regime with competing parties responds to the demands of different groups of voters and of special interest groups arising over time. Thus the older and the less disturbed by wars or revolution a democracy the higher the level of regulations, of taxes, subsidies and transfers one would expect with comparable levels of per capita incomes (Olson, 1982, 1983). But since excessive state activity also makes for less efficiency and innovation – as stated in the last section – one would also expect negative consequences for real economic growth, a result which seems to be corroborated by empirical evidence (Figures 4 and 5) (Bernholz, 1986, 1990, Marlow, 1986, Peden and Bradley, 1989, Weede, 1984, 1990).

If democracy is unrestricted, government activity tends to grow to unsupportable levels and to erode the efficiency, productivity and innovative capabilities of the capitalistic market system. In doing so, it not only destroys the economic basis of the welfare state it has developed, but by necessity, restricts more and more the freedom of its citizens by regulations and discretionary interventions, high taxes and obligatory social security premia. Since the underlying process feeds on the rational ignorance of voters and depends on the high initial productivity of the capitalist market economy, the erosion of the basis of a free society, the burdens and disadvantages are not felt by citizens for a long time. Thus a crisis has to develop to cause a political turnaround through political entrepreneurs, which may, but need not, come too late and may lead in the wrong direction of a dictatorship or an oligarchic regime. Argentina and Uruguay, which were

Figure 4   Growth of Real GDP for Seventeen OECD Countries (1960–93)

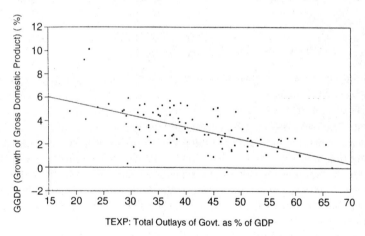

Notes:
Averages of 4 Seven-Year and   FINV: Fixed Investment/GDP
1 Six-Year Periods   ADEM: Undisturbed Age of Democracy
Regression Equation Estimated:
GGDP = 8.31 – 0.107TEXP + 0.041FINV – 0.030ADEM
        (7.21)   (–8.61)   (1.222)   (–6.082)
        n = 85   t-Statistics in Brackets
        $R^2 = 0.60$

Figure 5   Growth of Real GDP for Seventeen OECD Countries (1950–93)

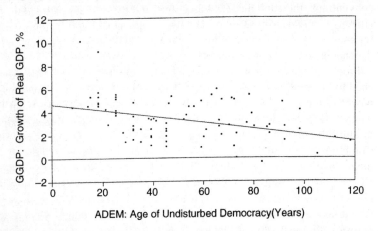

Notes:
Averages of 4 Seven-Year and   FINV: Fixed Investment/GDP
1 Six-Year Periods   TEXP: Total Govt. Expenditures/GDP
Regression Equation Estimated:
GGDP = 8.31 – 0.107TEXP + 0.041FINV – 0.030ADEM
    (7.21)   (–8.61)   (1.222)   (–6.082)
          n = 85   t-Statistics in Brackets
                            $R^2 = 0.60$
Sources for figure 4 and 5: For Age of Democracy Hewitt (1977) with appropriate
modifications by Weede (1986). All other data are from OECD.

among the wealthiest democracies around 1930, are telling examples of
such developments.

To preserve freedom, productivity and innovative capabilities in the
long-run, a democracy with a capitalistic market regime has thus to limit
constitutionally or by other means the domain of majority decision-making
by parliament. How such restrictions can be reached and maintained permanently is still an open question (Buchanan, 1987, Gwartney and Wagner,
1988). We know that a division of government power, an independent judiciary, federalism, an independent central bank, a guarantee of property
rights and constitutional restrictions on the domain of government all help.
But historical examples like that of the USA show that even such provisions hold, at best, only for several decades, and will slowly be eroded.

We have already mentioned that not a democratic but only a restricted
government and the rule of law are necessary to maintain a productive
free market economy. But in an authoritarian system safeguards against a
removal of the limitations of government are obviously weak. For the
rulers can themselves determine the domain of their power, if they are not
bound by religious, quasi-religious or social conventions or by a delicate

balance among several oligarchs. With the modern weakening of such conventions, the capitalist market regime and the domain of freedom for citizens from state intervention are always threatened under authoritarian regimes, since they depend mainly on the goodwill of rulers or even on the delicate balance of power among oligarchs.

Freedom, the rule of law and the capitalistic regime can also be threatened by the emergence of totalitarian movements striving for government power (Arendt, 1968, Bernholz, 1991a, 1991b). According to them the whole fabric, organizations and institutions of society have to be reshaped in subordination to their supreme values, like those of the Nazis, the Communists and of recent Islamic Fundamentalism. Thus, if such movements gain power, individual freedom will be limited to the domain allowed by the corresponding supreme value system. The former organization of government, the constitution, the legal system and even the capitalist market regime will be reshaped, abolished and substituted by radically new institutions as far as they do not correspond to the goals of the supreme value system. Democracy is abolished or degenerates and conflicting value systems are no longer tolerated.

5 COMPETITION OF STATES AS A REASON FOR THE EVOLUTION OF A FREE AND PROSPEROUS SOCIETY

Let us now discuss the role played by the international competition of states in the changes of political–economic regimes.

As discussed above, it seems to be rather clear today under which conditions prosperity will develop in a society. But given an oligarchic, totalitarian and/or despotic regime, why should the ruling elite agree to strong and safe property rights for everybody, to minimal state intervention and regulation, to a strong limitation of taxes and thus of its own powers to command and to take away goods and resources at their discretion? This question is the more important, since despotic regimes have ruled for the greatest part of history in most countries, and in fact, even today. Dictatorships, oligarchy and despotism as regimes have been rather stable systems in the course of history. Freedom, rule of law, safety of property rights and democracy have been the exception and not the normal state of affairs in history.

Fortunately, well-known historical explanatory sketches of 'the Rise of the West' by new economic historians (North and Thomas, 1973, North, 1981, Jones, 1981) are now available to answer our question.

As Erich Weede (1987) puts it, 'European *disunity* has been our good luck' (p. 2). After the breakdown of the Roman Empire, feudalism with its many power centres developed and a split opened up between religious and temporal power (Pope and Emperor and Kings). A strong rivalry arose between these emerging states and their rulers to gain, to preserve and to extend their powers. This forced European rulers to become interested in the well-being and loyalty of their subjects and above all in economic development to secure a greater tax base and thus stronger armies. But economic development itself depended on the development of adequate property rights and on free markets. As a consequence, a competition among states forced on reluctant rulers a limitation of their domestic powers. The development of competing legal systems and the rule of law, of property rights and of due process of law was helped, not only by inter-state competition but also by the separation of church and state, the pre-venting of a theocracy (Berman, 1983). Limited government and pluralistic society were thus a predemocratic achievement. They were not planned by anybody, but emerged and proved to be successful. First Capitalism and later Democracy were their progeny.

But why did first capitalism and only then democracy develop? Now, it is obvious that economic decentralization and development within free markets require safe property rights and the rule of law. This makes many individuals and groups rather independent from political interference, at least in the economic sphere. They learn to form their own judgements, to make independent decisions and to shoulder the risks and benefits of the consequences. But independence and self-reliance further the demand for rational decision-making and participation in the political domain. As Andreski (1965) states: 'Up till now representative government has flour-ished only where there was in existence a large class of economically inde-pendent persons, not necessarily independent in the sense of enjoying unearned incomes but in the sense of having no boss' (p. 357). Thus apart from primitive systems with self-supporting peasants, only market economies with private property and a minimal concentration of production seem to be a fertile ground for the development of democracies.

From these arguments it seems to be clear that a multipolar international system like Feudalism in Europe is especially favourable to engender the chain of developments just sketched. And, indeed, outbursts of innovative activities in many fields of life as well as strong economic performance characterized not only the Renaissance with its many Italian city-states, but also early Greece with Ionia and especially Milet as its centre, and classical Greece with Athens as a leader. And in both these cases a tough military and political competition between many city-states was present. The flowering of Phoenicia and even the remarkable successes of Sumeria may also have been caused by the competition of several city-states. Note also that Greece in its early and classic periods faced the crisis of threats from Lydia and Persia, and that Phoenicia, too, had to cope with the powers dominating its hinterland, like Assyria and later Persia.

To substantiate these claims it is appropriate to discuss at least one of the cases, namely early Greece, in greater detail.

In early Greece (700–500 BC) there existed many states involved in severe military and foreign policy competition. This situation was furthered by geography which split the country into many small regions. Military competition led to the introduction of hoplite armies, of the phalanx and of mercenaries. Mass commodities like grain, bronze and pottery vessels and slaves were traded (Murray, 1980), which implied an international division of labour and discouraged piracy or confiscatory taxes. For only those states could, under such conditions, strengthen the economic base of their military power which attracted trade by low duties and safe property rights and thus furthered the development of their own economy.

The international competition of early Greek city states led to the following consequences (Murray, 1980):

1. The introduction of the hoplite army based on all capable male citizens (and not only the nobility) who could afford the weapons entailed a broadening of the number of people sharing political powers.
2. A legal order began to develop. The fixation of law in writing especially in trading cities was enforced by the lower strata of citizens. The law was published (Seventh century).
3. A strong international trade developed and many new colonies were founded. Both presupposed economic development and furthered it again. Trading posts like Al Mina in Syria, Pithekussai (now Ischia), Naukratis in Egypt, Graviscae and Spina in Etruria were founded by Greek cities. They all were neighbouring important raw material sources or highly civilized regions. Strong trade competition between states developed, e.g., already rather early between Korinth and Aigina.
4. Coins were invented and this helped to further trade and economic development.
5. General economic prosperity and relative individual freedom allowed and made partly profitable inventions and innovations in science and the arts. In as far as they were related to geography – cartography, the description of countries and peoples, the development of prose and the debate about political reforms – they were themselves instrumental in promoting trade and economic growth.
6. Economic growth led to a restructuring of the economy and of society. Conflicts between nobility and the new wealthy class arose,

which were described by Alkaios and Theognis. Very rich traders like Sostratos from Aegina entered the scene, a trader who regularly traded with Graviscae in Etruria.

7. The restructuring of the economy caused a redistribution of income and wealth which implied political tensions. Thus reforms, like those introduced by Solon in Athens, became necessary. The reforms, however, entailed also a change of the political system.

Our hypotheses seem to be corroborated by these observations. They are also supported by the cases of stagnation observed under different conditions. First, not all states are forced to undertake or succeed with reforms as a consequence of international political competition. They rather stick to inefficient rules and regulations hindering the developments sketched above. Or secondly, they are subjugated by great powers stifling them again. Thus the historical evidence shows that:

1. The relative economic importance of Sparta decreased. This deterioration was obviously caused by a great number of state regulations for its citizens. Already Plutarch mentioned in his *Lykourgos* that merchants, poets and artists would have to be paid. Sparta, however, outlawed the new Greek currency.

2. The great original empires with their system of discretionary government interventions stagnated. Even the successful development of Ionia and Phoenicia ended in the Persian empire, whereas it continued on the Greek mainland (especially Athens) and in Phoenicia's daughter, Carthage.

The motivation of rulers to limit their domestic powers, to strengthen economies as a base of their power in the international system, is also present today. It is highly probable that the efforts to decentralize and to move towards market economies in China since 1979 and recently in the Soviet Union and Eastern Europe have more to do with the aim of China and the Soviet Union to build up or to maintain a Great Power status than with the wish to supply the population with more and better goods or even to grant them greater freedom.

We can now understand why Gorbachev tried to move the Soviet Union to undertake far-reaching institutional and economic reforms. Before he became Secretary-General of the Politbureau, he already stressed the necessity for reform in the Soviet Union. According to the *Neue Zürcher Zeitung* of December 13 1984, which referred to reports in the Soviet press: 'The youngest member of the Politbureau was the main speaker at a

(Communist Party) conference on Ideology'. The article reports that Gorbachev stated that 'it was essential to transform the Soviet economy and to raise its technical and organizational performance to a qualitatively higher level. ... Only such a modernized economy could meet the necessities of the population, allow a strengthening of the position of the USSR on the international stage and make it possible for her to enter the new millenium as a powerful and flourishing state.' The report went on to state that 'One could not learn from the presentation, in which way the Soviet economic production should be modernized and which reform ideas Gorbachev would like to apply'.

From this statement the reasons for reforms from above seem to be obvious. Note also that only reforms by the rulers seem to be possible in dictatorships and/or totalitarian regimes. For, as Gordon Tullock has argued convincingly (1974), a free economic and democratic regime are public goods and the risks for life and family implied in a revolution or *coup d'état* far outweigh the possible gains for the ordinary person not in control of at least part of military or police power.

Also the wish of rulers to grant more economic freedom to realize a more successful economic regime does not mean that the reforms are adequate and will be successful.

An example of a successful reform of the constitutional, legal and economic regime is provided by Japan during the second part of the nineteenth century, a reform which, in a sense, was fully completed only with the new Japanese constitution introduced by General MacArthur in the wake of World War II. The Meiji Restauration of the 1860s was also a revolution from above, led by parts of the nobility against the weakened power of the *shogun* and skillfully using the device of restoring factual power to the *Tenno*. The restoration was decisively shaped, or even caused by, the realization of the superiority of the powers of Western states after the forced opening of Japanese harbours to Western trade, beginning with Commodore Perry in 1854. Thus the new slogan of the day became '*fukokukyohei*', 'rich country, strong arms', (*Encyclopedia Britannica*, vol. 12, p. 924). The reforms took the form of a wholesale adoption of Western constitutional, legal, educational, economic, technical, administrative and military systems, which proved so successful in the long-run.

If we turn to the cases of South Korea and Taiwan it seems also that the foreign policy situation *vis-à-vis* North Korea and Red China may have been the most important consideration for the leaders to give Capitalism a chance. The international position would thus have been the reason causing the rulers of South Korea and Taiwan to allow and even to further a capitalist development, to limit their own powers and thus indirectly to motivate their populations to ask also for more political rights and even for democratic regimes. Similarly, Communist China, which has been rather successful with its stepwise economic reforms in the direction of a market economy since 1979, probably wanted to reach a stronger position as a big power in international competition.

What other reasons exist for motivating the rulers in oligarchies or even in democracies to limit their own powers and to allow safe property rights, free markets and low taxes? I am under the impression that only some kind of crisis can bring about such a response. First, the United Kingdom had fallen back behind France and West Germany for decades in its economic performance. This may have been more important for the Thatcher turnaround than the fact 'that by 1979, the British had experienced the practical consequences of all ideas propounded by the politicians in all the parties' (Seldon, 1988, p. 19). Similarly Hong Kong and Singapore faced the challenge of supporting a big inflow of refugees and of the separation from their hinterlands in China and Malaysia.

6   THE ROLE OF CRISES AND OF IDEOLOGY IN THE CHANGE OF ECONOMIC AND POLITICAL REGIMES

Until now we have mentioned only in passing the roles played by ideology and crises in influencing or bringing about the eruptions which may lead to changes of political and economic regimes. But ideology and crises, until now rather neglected by Public Choice, play a major part as a cause and as a beneficiary of such eruptions.

We have already discussed the tendency of democratic market regimes towards an ever-increasing intervention and/or welfare state. This development, however, leads in time to less and less efficiency, freedom, innovation, productive investment and to a misallocation of resources and decreasing growth rates of GNP. As a consequence, in the end the political–economic regime enters a crisis because of widespread voter dissatisfaction.

Crises can also develop because of other reasons, namely, wars, religious and ethnic strife, hyperinflations, depressions, etc. Obvious examples are: the consequences of World War I, especially for the defeated countries with the harsh peace treaties of Versailles, St. Germain, Trianon and Neuilly; the Great Depression, beginning in 1929; and the hyperinflations in Germany, Austria, Hungary and Poland in the 1920s, in China in the 1940s, in the countries of the former Soviet Union and in some Latin American countries.

Crises are obviously a fertile ground for reform plans designed to introduce new political–economic regimes. Crises are thus also fertile ground for the application of ideas or the success of ideologies purporting to have the right recipe for solving the perceived problems. For instance, German neo-liberals like Eucken, Böhm, Röpke and Müller-Armack, had already prepared their ideas or theoretical vision about a new free market regime during the Nazi regime and the war (Peacock and Willgerodt, 1989). These ideas were available at the time of the currency reform of 1948 and were implemented by Ludwig Erhard, Müller-Armack and others in West Germany. A regime change from the degenerating system of a planned economy to a free market system was successfully engineered. Here again, it is interesting to note that well-known economists like Walter Heller (1950) and Thomas Balogh (1950) criticized the reforms and predicted dire consequences for the West Germany economy.

During other crises, different theories and ideologies competed with similar proposals for problem solutions. By an ideology I understand a worldview, a *Weltanschauung*, trying to interpret major aspects of the world and their interrelationships. Usually such an ideology contains also supreme values which have to be pursued according to the creed to solve the problems of individuals and/or society. An ideology thus fulfills a latent human demand for spiritual goods, since the *Weltanschauung* provides safety and meaning in an otherwise incomprehensible world. A sharing of this world view with others, offers a feeling of warmth and belonging, of safety in the womb of collectivity. Examples for ideologies of this kind are major religions, but also Communism and National Socialism.

It is obvious that ideologies become most attractive to disoriented and suffering people in time of crises, especially if they seem to propose through their world view solutions to problems perceived by the masses. Thus, during the crisis of the Great Depression in the wake of the Wall Street Crash, both Nazis and Communists gained strong voter support in Germany (Frey and Weck, 1981), after they had widely lost it with the end of the German hyperinflation in 1923. It was also not coincidental that Lenin and his supporters gained power in Russia in the débâcle of defeats and suffering brought about by World War I. And we may also ask whether Mao and his communists would have defeated the Kuomintang so easily in 1949 without the dismal economic plight, the corruption and the ravaging hyperinflation in China.

We conclude that ideological movements enjoy a good chance to grasp power during crises, if they have an attractive belief system promising to solve the problems perceived by the masses of the population. Once having succeeded, such an ideological movement may then even turn the nation into a totalitarian state, if the supreme values of their creed seem to demand it (Bernholz, 1991a).

At the moment we are, however, interested in another trait of ideological movements. Their supreme values usually contain certain rules referring to the economic regime wanted. Islam does not allow interest, Christianity forbade usury. Communism and Nazism imply a more or less centrally-planned economy, the former additionally including socialist or state property. We note that ideologies contain fixed, i.e. constitutional, rules which are binding for everybody, even the leadership. For even Stalin or Lenin could not preach capitalism or introduce free markets except for a short intermediate period with the purpose of moving on towards Socialism and Communism. There thus exists what I have called a 'Constitution of Totalitarianism' (Bernholz, 1991b). And as far as such a written or unwritten constitution contains comprehensive rules referring to the organization of the economy, the political success of an ideological movement necessarily leads to a change not only of the political but also of the economic regime. And this is exactly what happened in the Soviet Union, in Nazi Germany, in Eastern Europe, Communist China, Cuba, Vietnam and Cambodia.

We all know that in countries in which the communists came into power, the economic regime was changed to collectivized or state-owned property and to more or less central planning instead of markets. But it has already been mentioned that such a regime must, in time, lead to growing economic inferiority compared to free market economies with strong private property rights, because it cannot solve the informational and motivational problems implied by it (Pejovich, 1987). The resulting weakening of the relative economic base of military and political power leads to increasing tensions which finally result in another major eruption as witnessed by recent events in Eastern Europe.

7 CYCLES OF POLITICAL–ECONOMIC REGIMES OR BACK TO ARISTOTLE?

Our analysis suggests the existence of a long-term cyclical movement from one economic, and perhaps also political, regime to another: democratic free market economies in time degenerate into excessive welfare and/or intervention states. The ensuing crisis allows ideological movements to grasp power and to transform the economic regime by introducing central planning and perhaps collective property. Central planning requires a central political authority, preferably a dictatorship. But the economic

Figure 6 Bases for Long-Term Predictions of Changes in Relative International Power

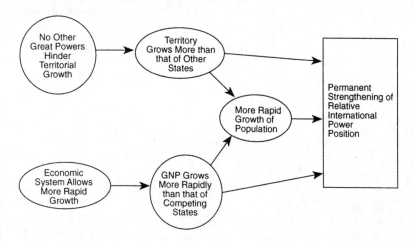

regime thus established leads, in time, to a deterioration of the relative power position in the international system of competing states (Figure 6). Finally reforms from above are taken and a free market economy with dominating private property is introduced or emerges from the chaos of reform. But economic liberalization requires political decentralization and promotes again the latter. Thus the rule of law and democracy emerge. Here the cycle can begin again. Given these stylized relationships, it may be asked whether we are back to some kind of political cycle as already proposed by Plato (1965, Book 8) and critically discussed by Aristotle (1965, Book 5)?

Though there are certainly forces working towards such a definite long-term cyclical movement among political–economic regimes, there are other factors which may push the process into other directions or cycles (Figure 7). An excessive welfare or intervention state may be reformed by cutting back government regulations, taxes and redistribution, if only an opposition party with a corresponding reform programme presents itself to the voters at the time of crisis. Or neither such reformers nor an ideological movement are present during the crisis to recommend themselves as alternatives. In this case, the political–economic system may slowly degenerate and in time turn into an underdeveloping country like Argentina after the 1930s, with increasing budget deficits, corruption, exchange controls and rising rates of inflation. The same may happen if inadequate or unsuccessful reforms are taken in formerly planned socialist economies. Or, if a strong economic deterioration results from the reform

84

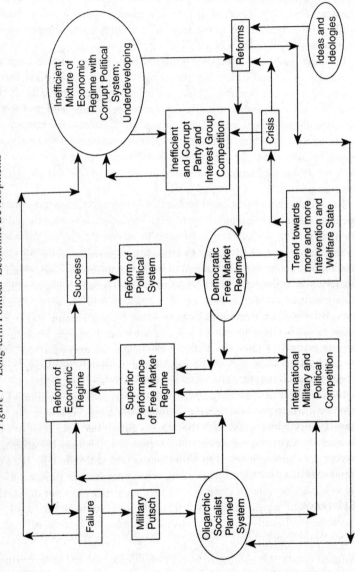

Figure 7 Long-term Political–Economic Developments

process, a military coup may move back the country to dictatorship and central planning. Recent events in the (former) Soviet Union from 1989 to 1992 show that especially the former alternative may happen with a quite substantial probability. And in fact, it is always much more difficult and politically dangerous to move from a less complex to a more complex economic system than vice versa.

In short, political–economic systems may not substitute each other cyclically in a fixed order, but short cuts or moves back to the formerly ruling regime are possible. Also, the economy may move away in an unstable process from any stable economic regime and end up for a long period with inadequate and weak political and economic institutions which imply an underdeveloped or underdeveloping economy. Obviously, economics broadly speaking and public choice theory specifically have still to do a lot of work to understand better the preconditions and the dynamics of these processes.

But let me end with another problem. Given the broad evolutionary perspective taken, is there anything left for fundamental economic policy, or for that matter, for economists trying to advise politicians on adequate strategies for how to introduce and maintain, let's say, the institutions of a free market economy? I think what I have said allows at least one answer: namely, that if the right ideas are available at the right time in crises, they may prove successful if they win the battle with other ideas and ideologies. But how can we ensure that our ideas win this battle? True, we can point to the better empirical record of free market economies with strong private property rights. But is this sufficient to convince a power-hungry oligarchy or a rationally badly-informed population and their feelings? Feelings which may be influenced by ideological fanatics and by the intellectuals of the mass media who are mostly hostile to a free market economy and to private property (Schumpeter, 1943, chapter XIII). Do we perhaps need a religion or ideology incorporating the tenets of a free market economy among its supreme values to solve these problems? Max Weber's *Capitalism and the Protestant Ethic* (Weber, 1965) seems to point into that direction.

References

Andreski, Stanislav (1965) *The Uses of Comparative Sociology* (Berkeley and Los Angeles: University of California Press).

Aristotle (1965) *Politics*. (Edited by N. Tsongopoulos and E. Grassi, translated by Franz Susemihl).

Arendt, Hannah (1968) *Origins of Totalitarianism*, 4th edition (New York: Harcourt, Brace and World).

Balogh, Thomas (1950) 'Germany: An Experiment in "Planning" by the "Free" Price Mechanism', *Banca Nazionale di Lavoro*, 3, pp. 71–102.

Berman, Harold J. (1983) *Law and Revolution* (Cambridge, Mass. and London: Harvard University Press).

Bernholz, Peter (1966) 'Economic Policies in a Democracy', *Kyklos*, 19, pp. 48–80.

_____ (1969) 'Einige Bermerkungen zur Theorie des Einflusses der Verbände auf die politische Willensbildung in der Demokratie', *Kylos*, 22 pp. 276–87.

_____ (1975) *Grundlagen der Politischen Ökonomie* (Tübingen: J.C.B. Mohr), vol. 2

_____ (1979) *Grundlagen der Politischen Ökonomie*, vol. 3 (Tübingen: J.C.B. Mohr).

(1986) 'Growth of Government, Economic Growth and Individual Freedom', *Journal of Institutional and Theoretical Economics* (Zeitschrift für die gesamte Staatswissenschaft), 142: pp. 661–83.

_____ (1990) 'The Completion of the Internal Market: Opportunities and Dangers Seen from an Institutional Perspective', in CEPS (ed.), *The Macroeconomics of 1992*. Brussels; Centre for European Policy Studies, pp. 59–105.

_____ (1990a) *The Importance of Reorganizing Money, Credit and Banking When Decentralizing Economic Decision-Making*. Paper presented at the Shanghai Conference of Cato Institute and Fudan University, Sept. 12–15, 1988.

_____ (1991a) 'Notwendige Bedingungen für Totalitarismus: Höchste Werte, Macht und persönliche Interessen', in Gerard Radnitzky and Hardy Bouillon (eds), *Ordnungstheorie und Ordnungspolitik* (Berlin, Heidelberg and New York: Springer) pp. 241–84.

_____ (1991b) 'The Constitution of Totalitarianism', *Journal of Institutional and Theoretical Economics*, 147(3), pp. 425–40.

Buchanan, James M. (1987) 'The Constitutional Strategy and the Monetary Regime'. Comments in James A. Dorn and Anna J. Schwartz (eds) pp. 119–27.

Donges, Juergen B. (1976) 'Comparative Survey of Industrialization Policies in Fifteen Semi-Industrial Countries', *Weltwirtschaftliches Archiv*, 112, pp. 626–57.

Dorn, James A. and Anna J. Schwartz (eds) (1987) *The Search for Stable Money* (Chicago: The University of Chicago Press).

Downs, Anthony (1957) *An Economic Theory of Democracy* (New York: Harper & Row).

Encyclopaedia Britannica (1962) Article on Japan, vol. 12. (London, Chicago, Geneva, Sydney and Toronto: William Benton).

Faber, Malte and Rainer Manstetten (1989) 'Rechtsstaat und Umweltschutz aus ökonomischer Sicht' *Zeitschrift für angewandte Umweltforschung*, 2(4), pp. 361–71.

Frey, Bruno and Hannelore Weck, (1981) 'Hat Arbeitslosigkeit den Aufstieg des Nationalsozialismus bewirkt?', *Jahrbuch für Nationalökonomie und Statistik*, 196(1), pp. 1–31.

Gwartney, James D. and Richard E. Wagner (eds) (1988) *Public Choice and Constitutional Economics* (Greenwich, Conn. and London: JAI Press).

Hayek, Friedrich A. (ed.) (1935) *Collectivist Economic Planning* (London: Routledge & Sons).

Heller, Walter W. (1950) 'The Role of Fiscal-Monetary Policy in German Economic Recovery', *American Economic Review*, Papers and Proceedings, 40, pp. 531–47.

Hewitt, Charles (1977) The Effect of Political Democracy and Social Democracy on Equality in Industrial Societies, *American Sociological Review*, 42, pp. 450–64.

Hirsch, Fred. (1978) *Social Limits to Growth* (London: Routledge).

Jones, Eric L. (1981) *The European Miracle* (Cambridge: Cambridge University Press).

Krueger, Anne O. (1978) *Foreign Trade Regimes and Economic Development: Liberalization Attempts and Consequences* (New York: National Bureau of Economic Research).

Little, Ian, Tibor Scitovsky and M. Scott (1970) *Industry and Trade in Some Developing Countries. A Comparative Study* (London, New York and Toronto: OECD Paris and Oxford University Press).

Marlow, Michael L. (1986) 'Private Sector Shrinkage and the Growth of Industrialized Economies', *Public Choice*, 49(2), pp. 143–54.

Mises, Ludwig von (1920/1935) 'Economic Calculation in the Socialist Commonwealth', in Friedrich A. Hayek (ed.), *Collectivist Economic Planning*. First published as 'Die Wirtschaftsrechnung im sozialistischen Gemeinwesen', *Archiv für Sozialwissenschaften*, 47.

Murray, Oswyn (1980) *Early Greece* (London: William Collins Sons & Co. Ltd).

Neue Zürcher Zeitung, December 13, 1984.

North, Douglass C. (1981) *Structure and Change in Economic History* (New York: W.W. Norton & Co.).

_____ and Roberth Thomas (1973) *The Rise of the Western World: A New Economic History* (Cambridge: Cambridge University Press).

Olson, Mancur (1965) *The Logic of Collective Action* (Cambridge, Mass.: Harvard University Press).

_____ (1982) *The Rise and Decline of Nations: Economic Growth, Stagflation, and Social Rigidities* (New Haven: Yale University Press).

_____ (1983) 'The Political Economy of Comparative Growth Rates', in Dennis C. Mueller (ed.), *The Political Economy of Growth* (New Haven: Yale University Press).

Peacock, Alan and Hans Willgerodt (1989) *German Neo-Liberals and the Social Market Economy* (London: Macmillan).

Peden, Edgar A. and Michael D. Bradley (1989) 'Government Size, Productivity, and Economic Growth: The Post-War Experience', *Public Choice*, 61, pp. 229–45.

Pejovich, Svetozar (ed.) (1987) *Socialism: Institutional, Philosophical and Economic Issues* (Dordrecht, Boston and Lancaster: Kluwer Academic Publishers).

Plato (1965) 'Politics', in *Sämtliche Werke*, edited by W.F. Otto, E. Grassi and G. Plamboek. Translated by F. Schleiermacher. Vol. 3, Rowohlt.

Schumpeter, Joseph A. (1943) *Capitalism, Socialism and Democracy*, (London: Unwin University Books) Fifth Edition, 1952.

Seldon, Arthur (1988) Paper Presented at the Meeting of the Mont Pelerin Society in Kyoto, Japan.

Tullock, Gordon (1974) *The Social Dilemma: Economics of War and Revolution* (Blacksburg: Center for Study of Public Choice).

Ward, Benjamin (1967) *The Socialist Economy* (New York: Random House).

Weber, Max (1965) *Die protestantische Ethik* (München: Siebenstern Taschenbuch Verlag).

Weede, Erich (1984) 'Democracy and War Involvement'. *Journal of Conflict Resolution*, 28(4), pp. 649–64.

___ (1986) Catch-up, Distributional Coalitions and Government Growth or Decline in Industrialized Democracies, in: *The British Journal of Sociology*, 37, pp. 194–220.

___ (1987) From 'The Rise of the West to Eurosclerosis: Are There Lessons for the Asian-Pacific Region?', in: *Asian Culture Quarterly*, 15(1): pp. 1–14, (Taipei, Taiwan).

___ (1990) *Wirtschaft, Staat und Gesellschaft* (Tübingen: J.C.B. Mohr).

4 Legal Experiences of Competition among Institutions*

Christoph Engel

1 INTRODUCTION

Thomas Hobbes would not have liked our topic. The very purpose of his *Leviathan* was to end chaos and bloodshed, which had been lasting in his country for decades, by the voluntary submission of everybody under a unified and strong state. The law as the primary emanation of the state must therefore be obeyed without exception. This implies a negative attitude towards institutional competition (Hobbes, 1668, ch. 26).[1]

Meanwhile the law has become more indulgent, or more realistic, if you prefer. Nearly every lawyer would admit that setting a rule is not tantamount to changing life in the intended direction. The lower classes do it by simple disobedience. The upper classes and in particular firms can pay for a cunning lawyer and do it legally. The lawyer will often advise them to play the game of institutional competition; lawyers would rather call it circumvention. The economic concept of institutional competition helps to a better understanding of what is going on and it is an extraordinarily useful tool for assembling and organizing legal phenomena that are usually dealt with in isolation.

While thus the positive value of the concept is strongly supported by legal empiricism, the normative prejudice of at least many of the economic analysts receives less empirical support. The law so far seems to have a more pragmatic attitude: Institutional competition is sometimes uniformly assented to, sometimes it is a means to serve very specific ends, sometimes it is reacted to as an exogenous factor and often it is combated fervently. Behind all this is obviously the traditional public interest model of regulation, to which many economists have important objections (see Posner, 1974). But even for those who share that critique, the following might prove useful since it shows how the law handles institutional competition in day-to-day business.

*Helpful comments by Lüder Gerken and a survey of current thinking on institutional competition by Stefan Tontrup are gratefully acknowledged.

To be specific, this paper is purely empirical. It is written from the perspective of real-world regulators and outlines their attitude and action *vis-à-vis* institutional competition. It furthermore uses on purpose a very broad concept of (institutional) competition. It may well be that economists, at the end of the day, might prefer to reserve the term for a narrower set of phenomena. But since it has not been safely established so far that the normative value judgements inherent in the concept of competition on the product markets may be extended to any form of institutional competition, it appears legitimate to use the term here in a way broad enough to encompass all instances in which individuals, organizations and officials may effectively choose among different institutions.

Other, related phenomena have to be left out. Economists have stressed that informal constraints are often more powerful institutions than formal ones (North, 1989, p. 239). Being a legal endeavour, this paper, however, will only briefly allude to the interface of formal and informal institutions (Section 2.3), while informal institutions proper are left aside.

Also omitted is the purely persuasive authority of legal institutions, although this phenomenon has high practical importance. For setting up a coherent legal system is an extremely costly and time-consuming process. Less developed and especially newly-independent states have therefore often chosen to copy a foreign legal order in full or at least to duplicate whole codes. This is true for most former colonies. Even more interesting are cases like Israel, which combines areas of Roman origin with others of common law origin. The phenomenon is obviously important for international trade. The saying: 'He who has the standard, has the market' applies to whole legal orders as well. The United States is particularly aware of such opportunities and sent a whole army of legal counsels to the newly independent East European countries. Many of these countries, however, seemingly prefer to return to the pre-World War II German roots of their private law. I nonetheless leave the question aside, since the national legislator in this type of competition is the client, while the focus of this symposium is on the rule-maker as the supplier of rules among which is competition.

Even further away from this focal point is competition of whole political systems. Obviously there is such competition. Many assert that the collapse of the Eastern Bloc was not solely the result of a credible nuclear threat, but that western information policy has a considerable share in it. Under the heading of humanitarian improvements the Conference of Security and Co-operation in Europe (CSCE) succeeded in opening the eastern markets for some western media products. The eastern population thereby began to realize how extraordinarily inefficient their economic system was. But the client, so to speak, in this competition is not even the legislator acting within the constitutional framework, but the constitution giving power itself.[2]

At first sight one might expect that the considerable literature on 'regulation on demand' or on a 'market for regulation' could illuminate our topic. But this literature is concerned with addressing a different question. It stresses that firms are not always interested in less or no regulation. They may wish to overcome a 'Prisoners' Dilemma' situation or to guarantee the public the demanded quality of a product (Holcombe and Holcombe, 1986, Haddock and Macey, 1987). They further elaborate on the conditions under which the legislator should meet such demand for regulation (Bongaerts and van Schaik, 1984). This literature touches upon institutional competition only in so far as competing fora for meeting the demand are contemplated (Holcombe and Holcombe, 1986).

Another phenomenon shall be neglected in order not to overburden the model: regulatory dumping. It consists of varying regulatory standards according to whether the product remains in the market of origin or whether it is destined for exportation. In this context, the low standard is an instrument of industrial policy. Well studied is the lenient attitude of most states towards export cartels (Maloney, McCormick and Tollison, 1984).

My paper is organized as follows. Section 2 shows how wide institutional competition as understood here is spread and details the instances as well as the driving forces behind such competition. Section 3 elaborates on the differentiated, sometimes even ambivalent, attitude of the legal order towards such competition. Section 4 switches from purpose to action and presents the major instruments by which the law tries to influence the degree of competition. Section 5 briefly looks at meta-meta-rules: is the rule-maker free in its attitude and action towards institutional competition or has it to abide by some sort of constitutional standards?

2   CLASSIFICATIONS

There are frequent and multifold opportunities to choose among different institutions. Such competition may be classified according to its subject matter (1) and to the connecting factors employed (2). Horizontal instances may be distinguished from vertical ones (3). Competition beyond the reach of the rule-maker may be distinguished from instances within its sphere of influence (4).

2.1 Subject-Matter

The subject-matter of competition may be a single institution as shaped by law. Different sets of rules may compete. Finally competition may affect the institutions for applying, not for setting up rules.

Institutions at choice

Sometimes the regulator decides to offer the public a set of institutions from which they may choose at will. The most common example is corporation and partnership. German law offers no less than eight primary types and allows for a lot of additional hybrid forms, ranging from the partnership of two or more fully responsible entrepreneurs[3] up to the large public corporation the shares of which are traded at the stock exchange.[4] Similarly, firms and unions as their counterparts may, under German law, choose whether the amount of wages and the conditions of work are specified in conventions for the whole industry or for each firm separately. The regulator may even offer institutions that it has not set up itself. The most important example are transnational contracts. Almost without exception the parties have power to submit them to whatever legal order in the world they deem fit.

Competing sets of rules

The bulk of this paper will be concerned with competition among regulation. At this moment two examples will suffice: air pollution under German law is combated by public law,[5] by torts law and by penal law. Can a neighbour to a polluting factory, who did not succeed in influencing the licensing authority, switch to the private law courts under the heading of private neighbour law, or can he call the attorney-general for help (Schröder, 1991, Jarass, 1991)? The second example stems from the European Union. As a rule, Member states are no longer allowed to close their markets against goods and services originating in other Member states. Consequently, the different regimes of Member states for the production of the same or similar goods and services compete over the quality of the products.

Competing institutions for the application of rules

The third type of competition is more visible under Continental than under Anglo-American law. For Continental Law draws a strict line between setting and applying rules. The first is the domain of the legislator, the second the domain of administration and of the courts. Competition for application matters, since application is not a mechanical action, but a hermeneutical one. The authority has to enter the hermeneutical circle, playing 'ping-pong' between the rules framed *in abstracto* and the case before it. Since the law never fully determines the outcome of this endeavour, applying the law inevitably is progressively developing it.

Competition comes up since the legal order normally creates more than one institution for the application of rules, and since their powers are not always clearly delineated. In torts cases the victim may choose between suing the tort-feasor at his home or at the place where the tort has been committed. When he feels that a public undertaking has gone beyond its public law limits, a private competitor may ask the German public law courts for help, but he may also go to the private law courts pretending that the public corporation by one and the same action has engaged in unfair competition.

2.2 Connecting Factors

The major opportunity for institutional competition is created by connecting factors. Each rule has to specify its territorial, historical, personal and material field of application. Additional competition stems from the limited jurisdiction of rule-makers.

Choice among institutions and connecting factors

Sometimes the choice among institutions is totally unrestricted. This is in particular the case for some forms of institutions at choice (Section 2.1). A case in point is the already mentioned choice of the appropriate organizational structure for a firm. But even in private law, such a choice is normally not unfettered. Take the law of obligations: the parties are largely free to give a contract whatever contents they prefer; but they are not free to call a contract agency that, from an objective point of view, is one of master and servant. Freedom of contract does not, in other words, encompass freedom of classification (Gernhuber, 1989, p. 153). The question becomes important whenever the parties to the contract have left unregulated a detail. It is, in our example, supplemented by the statutory rules on agency, not on master and servant.

While in these cases at least a certain influence by those to which the rule is addressed on its application is intended, the actual competition is often very much against the will of the rule-maker. It is the work of clever lawyers who have played on the connecting factors of the pertinent rules, thereby switching from cumbersome regulation to a more lenient regime. Experience shows that such a strategy is all the more promising the more complex a regulatory network is. Less regulation is therefore usually more powerful regulation.

Let us examine these connecting factors. In theory, every rule has a territorial, a historical, a personal and a material dimension.

Territorial field of application

The territorial validity of the rule normally is identical with the territory for which the rule-maker is responsible. To take the German example: Rules by the municipalities are valid within the municipality, rules by the *Länder* within the Land, rules by the federation within the whole country. But the law distinguishes between validity and application. The rule applies when the case has taken place within the constituency. But is it enough that the person or interest protected by the rule be located here? Or must the prohibited action have taken place here? Must the defendant live in the constituency? Must there at least be some property that avoids useless administrative or court proceedings? These questions have attracted particular scientific interest in transnational cases and are the domain of international economic law (see in great detail Schnyder, 1990). But sometimes they also arise within a federal state. A case in point are German nationwide private television programmes. The programme providers claim that they should only be regulated by the *Land* which has granted them a licence, while some regulation authorities argue that the attribution of a terrestrial frequency gives them independent regulatory powers (see in detail Engel, 1993).

Historical field of application

Similar considerations concern time. Again the law distinguishes between validity and application. Of particular importance is retroactive application. When the law replaces one regime by another, it normally specifies which cases shall be dealt with by the new rules and which by the old ones. To do so, it states connecting factors. Practising lawyers try to play on those factors in the interest of their client.

To give an example. Under German public construction law, a construction permit is issued, if and when the planned building is in conformity with the city construction plan. If the city has announced its intention to set up such a plan, the applicant may try to get the permit on pre-plan rules. It then is necessary and sufficient that the building be in line with existing neighbouring buildings. Or he may prefer to place it under the (more favourable) future plan. The law expressly provides for the case and gives the construction authority discretion to follow such a proposal by the applicant (section 33 of the *Baugesetzbuch*).

Personal field of application

To this, the personal dimension is added. A rule is valid for every person under the jurisdiction of the rule-maker. In the case of the nation-state, this would mean all the inhabitants whatever nationality they have, and all the nationals wherever they live. But the rule-maker often sees reason to delineate the personal field of application more narrowly by connecting factors. A typical example is German social security legislation. It does not apply to persons with a regular income above certain limits. They are free to take private insurance. Since private insurance for these persons is much cheaper, they have an incentive to make their income look higher in order to evade social security.

Material field of application

While in territorial, historical and personal respect, there is a difference between validity and application, a similar distinction makes no sense with respect to the subject-matter of the rule. Any rule must define the questions to which it shall be applied. But the delineation of the material field of application is an important source for institutional competition: By influencing the connecting factor, persons try to opt for a more favourable regime. My example is again taken from German media law. While broadcasting in Germany is under extremely dense regulation, there are only a few scattered provisions on communication services. Media enterprises therefore consider services such as pay-per-view and video-on-demand, hoping to free themselves from broadcasting legislation.

Rule-makers with limited jurisdiction

The preceding analysis starts from the standard rule-maker, the jurisdiction of which is, in principle, universal. Institutional competition is then above all the result of meta-rules on the field of application. There are, however, many rule-makers with only limited jurisdiction. An opportunity for institutional competition exists where these jurisdictions overlap. This is particularly frequent in the international arena. States sometimes employ these overlaps strategically. Thus the US were dissatisfied with the work of the World Intellectual Property Organisation and started the trade-related intellectual property negotiations within the Uruguay Round of

GATT (Beier and Schricker, 1989). This type of competition is customarily called the 'battle of the forum'.

2.3 Horizontal and Vertical Competition

So far, we have dealt with horizontal competition, in that the institutions concerned originated in rules by one and the same or by parallel rule-makers. If one of the rule-makers concerned is subordinated to the other, one may talk about vertical institutional competition (Trachtman, 1993, pp. 53 and 80). It may further be distinguished according to whether a hierarchical element is present or not, a question that is not always easy to assess.

Vertical competition without hierarchy

Vertical competition without hierarchy is not fundamentally different from horizontal competition. Such is, for instance, the case where the jurisdiction to legislate within a federal state is distributed among the federation and the members by subject matter. That is the system followed by the German *Grundgesetz*. The *Länder* have had a hard time resisting attempts by the federation to encroach ever further on their jurisdiction. Particularly dangerous in this respect was article 74 no. 11 of the Fundamental code, under which the federation is competent to legislate on 'economic matters'.[6] As nearly any activity may be defined as 'economic', this might prove far-reaching (Ipsen 1986/1993, marginal notes pp. 524–9). In this instance, the federation tries to make profit from a broad interpretation of the (material) connecting factor. Another example is merger control. While Germany has relatively strict rules, the European regulation is so weak, that within five years of existence no more than one single merger has effectively been forbidden.[7] Whether a merger falls under German or European rules depends on the turnover of the participating firms. In practice, German corporations have therefore tried to find particularly big partners in order to overstep the German limit.

Competition with hierarchy

Competition implying a hierarchical element might be called 'limping' competition. The term indicates that the two institutions are not on an equal footing. The institution with superior rules could take over if and when it feels that the inferior institution leads to unsatisfactory results. Such competition is relatively frequent. A prominent example is so-called 'economic self-regulation' (Holcombe and Holcombe, 1986, Schmidt,

1993). In Germany the case of package refuse is notorious. The Minister of the Environment has its power to oblige retailers to take back old packaging materials within their premises. Retailers have therefore pressed producers to set up a private system that collects package material directly from households. Of course, without such a threat, they would not have created such a costly system. Another example is what German lawyers call co-operative federalism.[8] Under the German constitution, the federation has the unwritten, subsidiary power to regulate inter-land matters, if the *Länder* themselves prove unable to settle things. Under that threat, the *Länder* have for instance set up the *Zentralstelle für die Vergabe von Studienplätzen*, which distributes students nationwide, thus giving as many as possible the opportunity to take up university education.

Borderline cases

Sometimes the hierarchical element exists, but is weak. This gives the subordinate institution a certain amount of freedom. The most important case involves competition among the rule-maker and the rule-applier. In theory, the rule-maker might revoke any new development of the rules by the rule-applier (supra 2.1). But the legislative process is much more cumbersome than administrative or court procedure. Most alterations of the original rule will therefore persist. This weakness of the hierarchical element may even be introduced on purpose. For instance the appeal against arbitration awards to the courts is possible, but it is confined to cases where either the arbitration procedure was illicit or where the award was manifestly wrong.

2.4 Competition Within and Beyond the Sphere of Influence of the Pertinent Authority

If the law provides for different institutions, it is likely that the ensuing competition is intended by the legislator. From a superior, constitutional law point of view, competition within a federal state, competition between the municipalities and the state, and competition between the rule-maker and the rule-applier is assented to. That the federation, the state as opposed to the municipalities and the rule-makers are somewhat impeded in their action, is the price the constitution willingly pays in order to introduce checks and balances and to further political ends. The pertinent rule-makers and rule-appliers, however, will consider these influences as exogenous and they will try to combat them, lest the constitution forbids such defence or reduces it to a small array of instruments. On the contrary, competition with national institutions from abroad may be regarded

as entirely exogenous. Not surprisingly, it is here that we will find the
richest arsenal of defence instruments. The reason is the relative weakness
of public international law. To date, it has not really overcome the
Hobbesian 'war of everybody against everybody'.

An overall view of the classifications developed in section 2 results in
the taxonomy presented in Figure 1.[9]

Figure 1   Classification of Competition Among Institutions

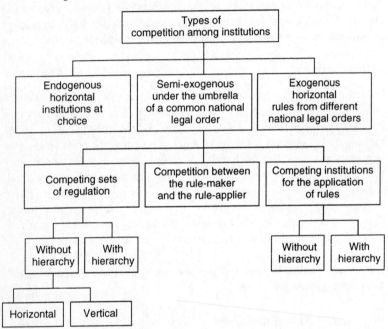

3   THE ATTITUDE OF THE LAW TOWARDS INSTITUTIONAL COMPETITION

In forming an attitude towards institutional competition, the regulator first
needs knowledge about possible driving forces (1). It is evident that the
attitude will not solely rely on considerations of public interest (2).
Decisive, however, is the purpose sought by the institution (3). Basically,
it is this purpose that determines whether institutional competition is
regarded as healthy (4) or noxious (5), a question that is sometimes not
easy to settle (6).

3.1 Driving Forces

Four classes of actors may influence the actual degree of institutional competition: the entities affected by rules, the rule-appliers, the rule-makers and the constitution-maker.

The parties may choose directly, if the institutions are at offer. If not, they have to influence one of the connecting factors. In practice, the credible threat of doing so is often enough to bring about substantial changes. For example, in 1981 the German Constitutional Court laid down such strict conditions for private broadcasting that it seemed practically forbidden.[10] Five years later the court became much more indulgent.[11] Commentators argued that German publishing houses had credibly enough announced the intention of using a Luxembourg satellite in order to broadcast to Germany. They would then have been beyond any German control. In order to preserve at least some regulatory influence, the Court overruled its elder judgement.

It is important to keep in mind, that not only the addressees, but also the rule-makers and rule-appliers behave competitively. They may do so for economic reasons, considering the already mentioned saying: 'He who has the standards, has the markets'. But they evidently also strive for individual political power. Finally, seemingly aggressive competition by the courts is often motivated by the intention to help the parties before them. Unfortunately, lawyers have long known that bad cases make bad laws; courts often willingly neglect that insight.

3.2 Considerations Beyond Public Interest

From the traditional public-interest perspective, which I have confessed in the introduction, state practice on institutional competition reveals a number of purposes one would hardly be able to welcome. Others appear somehow neutral. Yet in order not to become myopic, a general theory of institutional competition should keep both in mind.

The rule-maker is frequently motivated by protectionism. It may shift substantial power beyond its (visible) sphere of influence. In Germany, the degree to which fundamental political decisions are taken by the Constitutional Court rather than by Government or by Parliament has long been deplored. The political parties seem to be quite content with this development, since it has considerably weakened their dependence on the electorate. The actual intention of the regulator may remain disguised for a long time. The best example seems to be the European Union. Its policy, over the last twenty years, has commonly been perceived as a huge machinery for deregulation. The major tool for liberalization seemed competition among the regulation of Member states. But the more this process reaches its conclusion, the more it becomes apparent that the European Union is neither liberal nor federalist. The overall purpose seemingly was to create a sort of *tabula rasa*, on which a Europe-wide mercantilistic policy could be built.

3.3   The Primary Importance of the Purpose Sought by the Institution

Sometimes, institutional competition is openly employed by the law. The most important instances are institutions at choice (supra 2.1) and competition with hierarchy (supra 2.3). For the remaining instances, competition among institutions is not considered a value as such, but rather as a means to help or to hinder the law to meet the goal for which the respective institution has been set up. It is therefore important to note from where a general theory of institutional competition takes its empirical evidence. The focus of the American debate on the Delaware phenomenon (Cary, 1974, Charny, 1991, Bebchuk, 1992) should therefore not distort economic theory.

Roughly we may distinguish institutions as a prerequisite for market economy, regulation as a means to overcome market failure, regulation serving other ends chosen by the political system, and redistribution. Let us briefly consider each.

Redistribution is an obvious case where each legal order will fervently combat competition (Maloney, McCormick and Tollison, 1984, p. 330). For new beneficiaries from abroad would either diminish the capital available for the original beneficiaries or increase the burden on those who have to pay for the subsidy. This is one of the main reasons why social states usually have a strict immigration policy.

Regulation intended to correct market forces or to change market results normally asks for a differentiated attitude towards institutional competition (see in greater detail Engel, 1990). Two regulators may seek different or even contradictory purposes. A good example is the study of antitrust policies. While German legislation, under the influence of the Freiburg School, has adopted relatively strict rules and set up the powerful *Bundeskartellamt* to apply them, the attitude of our French neighbours is much more influenced by the fear of American economic dominance. They accordingly welcome huge French and even European corporate groups as a counterpart to would-be American power on the world market. Germany seems to have lost the battle, if we look at the already mentioned European merger control. Were there not this regulation, Germany should be expected to prevent firms from changing the connecting factor in a way that makes French antitrust legislation applicable or French authorities competent. But even if the purpose sought is identical or the foreign purpose appears at least tolerable, regulators often engage in defensive activities. In fact, an opportunity for arbitrage may also be created by the mere difference of instruments. This, of course, provides a promising case for harmonization.

Finally most legal orders are relatively open-minded with respect to foreign institutions as a prerequisite for a market economy. It comes therefore as no surprise that most states are, by virtue of their (autonomous) private international law, willing to apply foreign legislation and to enforce foreign court decisions.

3.4 Effects of Institutional Competition Welcomed by the Regulator

It goes without saying that the law expects positive effects where it openly offers a choice of institutions (supra 2.1, 2.3). This subsection is concerned with less evident favourable effects. Economists frequently recommend competition among institutions as a stimulus for innovation. The law seems to be relatively sceptical. More important is the power of such competition to break up political deadlocks and to balance the negative effects of public choice.

Institutional competition generating, testing and adjusting regulatory concepts

In a Hayek Symposium it is appropriate that the innovative effects of institutional competition receive a great deal of interest. One should indeed expect, from a theoretical point of view, that institutional competition spurs creativity, as it does in the marketplace (Charny, 1991. p. 441, Vihanto, 1992). The legal order should be even more interested in getting reliable information where the aim is not less, but smarter regulation. Take the example of pollution: Political proposals range from the abolition of property rights (for rubbish), traditional police law, private torts law, fiscal instruments and even pollution certificates. Is one concept better than all others? Should the choice be governed by the type of pollution? How great is the impact of the political and legal culture of the country concerned? Moreover, institutional competition should help institutions adjust in time to technical, economic, cultural and political changes of its subject matter (Hutter, 1989, Schmidtchen and Leder, 1990, Priest, 1993).

There is astonishingly little practical evidence, however. Some twenty years ago, most German *Länder* supplemented traditional law faculties by institutions that integrated theoretical and practical training of law students and that amalgamated traditional legal techniques with social sciences. A few years ago a federal statute converted all these reform faculties into traditional ones without making much profit of their (scientifically well-studied) experiences. The main argument of traditionalists ran as follows: Reform faculties had an optimum student–professor ratio, while one professor was responsible for up to ten times as many students in normal faculties. This, of course, one knew in advance.[12]

Another problem is highlighted by the gradual introduction of private broadcasting in Germany. The *Länder* agreed to gain experience by a couple of pilot projects. Some *Länder* claimed greater legislative freedom during the testing phase. The Constitutional Court, however, was reluctant for fear that the test would generate results which would be hard to reverse at a later stage.[13]

Breaking a political deadlock

We still have to consider the adjustment value of institutional competition. In this respect the law, indeed, seems to be very sensitive. One may, in theory, distinguish two models: gradual adjustment and eruptive breaking of political deadlocks. The first is the task of the administration and the courts when applying the law. The inevitable competition between them and the legislator finds here its justification (section 2.3).

While the administration and the ordinary courts should be confined to careful and gradual elaboration on the original intention of the legislator, there is sometimes a need for more radical reform. It should, in principle, be for the legislator itself. But the legislator may be paralysed. Thus the Council of the European Union was often unable to act, because it had to take its decisions unanimously. The European Court of Justice stepped in and reached the same result by a broad construction of the EC Treaty. Similarly, fundamental freedoms as administered by the Strasbourg Commission on Human Rights or by the German Constitutional Court have helped to overcome political deadlocks, as did the US Supreme Court in *Wabash*, when it curtailed the ability of the states to regulate railroads engaged in interstate commerce (Poole and Rosenthal, 1993).

Institutional competition may also help to overcome a related problem: burdensome regulation may, over time, become so deeply embedded in the minds of lawyers that nobody even tries to think of smarter solutions (Kübler 1994, p. 88).

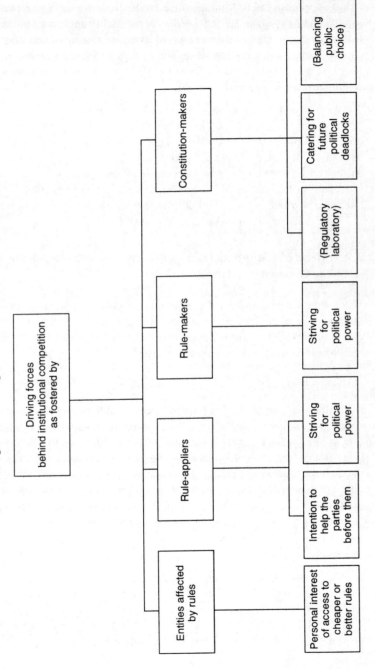

Figure 2   Driving forces behind institutional competition

Yet in order to break deadlocks effectively, these competing institutions must be very powerful. All legal orders concerned struggle hard to confine their activities to cases where there is indeed a deadlock. Solutions are not easy to frame, since such situations are difficult to define in advance.

Balancing public choice

The most important argument in favour of institutional competition seems to be rarely raised: such competition may help to counterbalance the negative effects of public choice (cf. Butler, 1985, p. 166). This is particularly clear in the case of locational competition. While legislators in principle would have an interest in winning the next election by giving preference to consumer interests over the interests of the much smaller number of shareholders, they must also be afraid of the danger of firms moving away from their location.

Figure 2 summarizes the insights gained so far.

3.5 Effects of Institutional Competition to which the Regulator would be Opposed

When they limit institutional competition, regulators primarily do so in order to prevent circumvention or arbitrage, to protect different markets, to maintain democracy, participation and the sense of responsibility or the individual interests of third parties affected.

Circumvention

If institutional competition is brought about by influencing the respective connecting factor (supra 2.2), regulators normally regard it as circumvention. In the case of competition among different authorities for the application of rules, they call it forum shopping. Since it becomes more difficult to reach the regulatory goal, the regulator will usually combat such activities. Yet the decisive factor is always the purpose sought by the institution (section 3.3). Take pollution tax: its very purpose is to induce the polluters to avoid the tax by generating less or even no pollution.

Arbitrage

A specific form of circumvention is arbitrage, to which 'free-riding' and 'cream-skimming' are related. The opportunity for such behaviour is created whenever regulation sets up or protects institutions that could not survive under market conditions. Much attention is given to remailing, these days. It makes profit of cross-subsidization within the German postal service. The German postal office charges customers transportation rates for letters that are above costs and uses the profits reaped thereby in order to offer highly subsidized services for the delivery of personal packages or of newspapers. Since the postal service of the Netherlands has adopted a different policy and since the European Union has obliged the postal services of all Member states to forward letters into other Member states at inland rates, remailing agencies have arisen that collect letters at large German corporations, drive them by car to the Netherlands and post them there. The *Bundespost* tries hard, but so far without success, to stop this business.

Unfavourable effects on other markets

Lively institutional competition may hamper competition on the product markets (Bebchuk, 1992, p. 1467). For instance the broadcaster of the German nationwide TV channel RTL complains about allegedly stricter application by the Niedersachsen broadcasting authority of the Interland Treaty on Broadcasting, as compared to the Rheinland-Pfalz authority responsible for its main competitor SAT 1. RTL pretends that it has to compete under different, stricter rules.

Similarly, institutional competition may have an unfavourable effect on the market for corporate control. This question has received much attention in the US. Competition among incorporation regimes has been blamed for giving managers an opportunity to insulate themselves against shareholders' influence (cf. Butler 1985, pp. 164–6).

Democracy, participation and sense of responsibility

Competition among jurisdictions makes it more difficult for the legislator to bring about those changes it has been elected for. Competition between the rule-maker and the rule-appliers takes power away from the rule-maker. Usually the rule-appliers are not directly responsible to the electorate. The opportunity to play on institutional competition is mostly not equally distributed in the population, but the wealthy stratum and in particular firms have – through the retention of well-trained lawyers – much easier access to it. Institutional competition can therefore serve as the tool for taking away benefits from the general public that it ought to have according to the will of the legislator. Finally, as has already been mentioned (see section 3.2), institutional competition may serve as a pretext for inefficient government and it may deteriorate the sense of responsibility of those in power. None of these arguments will suffice to support a fundamentalist struggle against institutional competition (North

1989, p. 242). But these arguments should be kept in mind when assessing the adequate degree and form of institutional competition.

Individual interests of third parties affected

Finally, no legal order will be content with having superior rules at the end of the day; it will also be concerned with the costs of the rule-making process for individuals. Such costs may take the form of simple external effects on the products or control market; we have already alluded to the alleged 'race to the bottom' in US corporation law, that would in particular have been to the detriment of small shareholders and of creditors (Bebchuk, 1992, p. 1485). More interesting are the costs of institutional competition itself. A case in point is that of reverse discrimination. This arises whenever European Union law obliges Member states to let products into their markets that have been produced at standards below those usually applied in the country of destination. Since less regulation is normally tantamount to less costs, the home industry perceives a competitive disadvantage. Businesses affected over a long period have tried to rely on an appeal to fundamental standards in order to alleviate their situation (König, 1993).

3.6 Ambivalent Features

Last but not least we should point to a few features of institutional competition that may, according to circumstances and interests, either support an argument for or against such competition.

Institutional competition helps to unify the law in that onerous legislation can be evaded and will, ultimately, be abandoned; we have seen the example of the European Union. But unification may be endangered if all but a few small jurisdictions have developed a uniform standard, because firms will avoid the quasi-general standard and make profit from the more comfortable solution of the few. This is the case with regulatory havens.

Institutional competition will, as with any form of competition, bring about new information that could otherwise not be obtained. It thereby enhances transparency on a general level. But since the process of regulation on the inferior level becomes tilted, institutional competition simultaneously decreases transparency.

Finally, institutional competition has distribution effects. It may shift business and income to a powerful jurisdiction, since the latter has succeeded in forcing less powerful countries to adopt its home solutions – the markets will normally follow. On the contrary, a small jurisdiction can

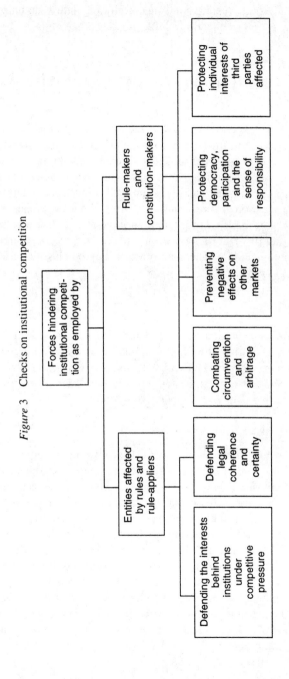

Figure 3   Checks on institutional competition

effectively attract business and income by regulatory dumping. That is sometimes its sole competitive edge.

Figure 3 summarizes the section.

4 INSTRUMENTS FOR COMBATING UNWANTED COMPETITION

If a legal order expects favourable effects from institutional competition, it is relatively easy to foster it, even if the conditions are beyond its sphere of influence: the legal order may give foreign products and producers easy access to its market, and it may allow its own nationals to act under foreign rules or to go abroad. If institutional competition within the framework of a legal order turns out not to bring about the effects it has been introduced for, the legal order may, in principle, reverse it at any time.[14] Much more difficult is attempting to defend an institution against unwanted competition. The state practice may be classified according to form (1) and substance (2).

4.1 Form

Defending an institution against competition is easiest, if and when the competing institution is under the influence of a legal order superior to both institutions. We might call that situation semi-exogenous competition. In exogenous competition proper, the legal order may choose between autonomous and co-operative solutions.

Semi-exogenous competition

Semi-exogenous competition is typical for institutions set up by different members of a federal state. The defending member may then have access to federal law and institutions instead of employing the techniques available in the international context. Federal law may even prevent members from making use of these traditional instruments. The point is well illustrated by the law of the European Union, which in this respect behaves like a federation. The EC Treaty expressly forbids that Member states close their markets against products or investments from other Member states, and it further rules out any treatment discriminating against such products or investments. The Member state affected by unjust, or even allegedly illegal, competition is therefore confined to suing the originating state before the European Court of Justice, a few protection clauses notwithstanding.

It should be noted, however, that the superior legal order will not necessarily behave like a disinterested arbiter. It may, on the contrary, curtail competition among inferior units in order to increase its own sphere of action. What looks like supervision of horizontal competition may thus turn out to be competitive vertical action.

Autonomous defence against exogenous competition

Unilateral defence against unwanted institutional competition is traditional power policy. It may reach the diplomatic level. The US, for instance, have made use of their economic (and, tacitly, military) strength in order to force their main trading partners into laws against insider trading and money laundering that largely follow the American blueprint, thus excluding what they regard as international circumvention of their domestic rules. But small countries may engage in unilateral defence as well. For they may have power *vis-à-vis* the individual who would otherwise play on institutional competition. Such is in particular the case when the individual has property in the defending state, or when it does business in its markets. Property and business relationships may then be taken as hostages.

Co-operative defence against exogenous competition

Where they lack power, states will strive for co-operative solutions. More importantly, co-operation is usually more effective and less costly than unilateral defence. The classical co-operative tool is a treaty. There are plenty of these on international trade matters, be they bilateral or multilateral. Treaties are difficult to adjust to new developments, however. Where subtle management is required, states will set up an international organization and give it power to recommend or even to decide. The gradual development of GATT into the Multilateral Trade Organization (MTO) is a good example.

Finally, an instrument one might label 'limpingly co-operative' has considerable practical impact: reciprocity. States have access to it when nationals or products of each state are present on the territory of the other. They then legislate to the detriment of foreign nationals and products, but the provision expressly provides for its removal, if the legislating state is satisfied that its own nationals or products receive favourable treatment in the other country. This is again a hostages' solution. But the hostage is neither personally responsible for the attacked competitive behaviour of its national state, nor could it even influence it. The question has therefore been raised whether reciprocity is in line with fundamental freedoms of the individuals and firms affected.[15]

4.2 Substance

If we now turn from form to substance, we find four major defence techniques: blocking , marginalizing, bundling and corridoring.

Blocking

Having framed the problem as one of unwanted exogenous competition, the evident reaction should expectedly be as powerful a defence as is available. There has indeed been some experience of blocking, but it has not been widely used.

Most interest has been drawn to UK blocking statutes directed against what was considered as an unwarranted intrusion by the US into its economic sovereignty. These statutes went so far as to expressly forbid and sanction behaviour that was mandatory under US law (for the details see Lowe, 1988). Similarly severe are Australian, UK and Canadian 'claw-back clauses. They are a reaction to US court decisions in antitrust cases. Under US antitrust law the plaintiff is entitled to treble damages. The claw-back' clauses allow Australian, British and Canadian defendants to sue the original plaintiff for recovery of the extra two-thirds (Schnyder, 1990, marginal note 133).

An elegant blocking technique has been invented by Canada. The country was concerned by the impact of US TV programmes from across the border on its national culture, and, of course, on its media industry. Since it is costly and politically touchy to prevent the reception of terrestrial broadcasting by a disturbing signal, Canada instead influences the economic foundations of trans-border broadcasting: Canadian firms may not deduct advertising costs from their income tax when they advertise in US programmes which are directed to the Canadian public (Matte and Jakhu, 1987; 81 s.).

Instead of outright blocking, defending legal orders may also make institutional competition dependent upon authorization. Such is, in principle, the attitude towards foreign judgements. Most procedural codes ask for an express recognition of every single foreign judgement before it may be relied on or even enforced.[16]

Marginalizing

Fully insulating a legal order from institutional competition is tantamount to realizing autarky. Even Albania had to give up that policy, because its costs were so extreme. Moreover, institutions often do not need absolute protection in order to fulfill the purpose for which they have been created.

Legal orders are therefore often content to make sure that the choice of foreign institutions remains a marginal phenomenon.

Thus, German insurance law, long before the overall EC liberalization, allowed for foreign insurance by correspondence, provided the foreign insurer neither advertised nor deployed personnel in Germany. Similarly, the European Convention on Broadcasting, signed under the auspices of the Council of Europe, entitles broadcasters to Europe-wide distribution of their programmes, but obliges them to abide by the advertising legislation of the country of destination when their programme is specifically directed to this public.[17] The spillover of programmes directed to the public of the originating country and pan-European programmes thus are under a more liberal regime, since they will normally have no more than a marginal impact on the domestic broadcasting order.

Marginalizing is also behind private international law. The apparently extremely liberal attitude towards foreign private law and foreign decisions is acceptable, since the connecting factors are determined in a way that excludes a massive influx of foreign institutions. Thus freedom to bring a contract under whatever legal order the parties deem fit is confined to transnational contracts; contracts with no international aspect, and that is the absolute majority of contracts, fall under domestic contract law. Of course, a legal order may go beyond, as the US and the UK do when they allow corporations to incorporate wherever they prefer. German private international law is less liberal and accepts only incorporation in the country from which the corporation is effectively managed.[18] Evading German corporation law thereby becomes marginal: the company must change the place of effective management. Couched in terms of competition theory, this is a rule-making demand for other institutions less elastic.

Bundling

The elasticity of the demand for competing institutions is also reduced by a related technique, which one might call bundling.

It has been observed that institutions are mostly bundled products (Trachtman, 1993, p. 79): A limited corporation as opposed to a partnership are both complex legal institutions which the parties, *grosso modo*, must elect as such. If the company, under US legislation, incorporates in Delaware and not in New York, in principle it has to accept the totality of Delaware corporation law and not just a single rule it might be specifically interested in. If the plaintiff in a torts case goes to the courts of the place where the defendant has its residence, and not to the place where the tort has been committed, he has to accept the court procedure as such and may not supplement a judge or a procedural rule by one from the other place.

Often the defending legal order is content with the (low) natural elasticity of institutional demand. This is particularly true where the only way of changing institutions is to permanently change the residence of a natural person. If people move at all, they usually do so because they have found a new and better job.[19] Strategic changes occasionally happen when, for example, the school system in the place of residence dramatically deteriorates. Even then people hesitate, since other places cannot easily make a credible commitment in the durability of a better school system: after the next elections it might be changed. The reluctance to move may be well explained in terms of transaction costs economics: the choice of residence is an investment with very high (pecuniary and non-pecuniary) sunk costs.

The users of institutions sometimes engage in unbundling. Such activities are frequently combated by the legal order. Thus transnational contracts may normally not be legally placed under the so-called *lex mercatoria*, the law of international commerce as developed by the business community itself (Spickhoff, 1992). For state contract law, however liberal it may be, always contains a couple of mandatory provisions in order to protect the weaker party or third persons. If the parties to the contract choose another state contract law, however, the dominating party cannot entirely avoid legal control.

In business practice, the most important technique for unbundling is setting up a corporate group. The separate legal entity of the subsidiary allows the insulation of the remaining firm from legal influence. This is particularly effective in the case of multinational enterprises. Strict legislation on corporate groups is therefore an important technique for reducing the elasticity of demand for institutions.

A last example are rules of origin that are typical for external trade in goods. Since, for instance, the importation of consumer electronics from Japan to the European Union is burdensome because of high tariffs and of quantitative restrictions, the Japanese manufacturers have tried to circumvent these restrictions by assembling their products within the European Union. The Union has defended itself by rules of origin asking for a relatively high degree of value added within the Community. Otherwise the products are treated as if they came from abroad.

Sometimes the legal order even packs bundles thicker than they naturally were, in order to shelter its institutions from competition. A case in point for a long time was insurance. The German statute on insurance only not forced foreign insurers to take residence in Germany. Once they did, they were prohibited to serve German customers on a correspondence basis from their headquarters.[20] A similar result is reached by the appropriate choice of the connecting factor: it is for instance easier to change the place of residence than to change nationality.

Corridoring

Marginalizing and bundling reduce the number of cases in which institutional competition takes place. Corridoring, to which we turn now, reduces the impact of competition on domestic institutions, once it takes place. If one again uses economic language, one might talk about measures that reduce the elasticity of the offer.

The most sophisticated examples are to be found in the law of the European Union. Let us have a closer look at the Directive concerning construction products.[21] The free circulation of such products within the whole European Union is impeded by two types of obstacles: by national rules restricting their marketing and by prescriptions for construction. Difficult to remove is the second type of obstacles, since Member states have a legitimate interest to prevent buildings from collapse and to protect the health of inhabitants or workmen. The Directive makes market access dependent on the following conditions: the Directive itself states basic security requirements; these requirements may be detailed in a Community document at the request of any Member state; the originating state is obliged to allow the marketing of a construction product only if the product abides by the common European standard or has been approved *in concreto* by a European authority set up for the purpose; the conformity of every single entity of the product with these standards is tested and certified in a manner that is regulated by the Directive; and if the Member state of destination has legitimate reasons to believe that the producer or the Member state of origin violate the Directive, it may exceptionally forbid the use of the product.

Corridoring is not confined to the European Union, however. Another example may be found in the German Constitution. Although the *Länder* have the character of proper states with their own constitution, they are not entirely free to adopt whatever constitution they please. Article 28 II Basic Law obliges them to keep in line with fundamental federal principles like democracy, the rule of law and the social state. Moreover, their constitution may not hamper the workability of federal organs within which the *Länder* are represented, and they may not deny minimum solidarity with their fellow-states.

Even where the law gives considerable leeway for institutional competition, one corridoring technique is still prevalent: protection clauses cater

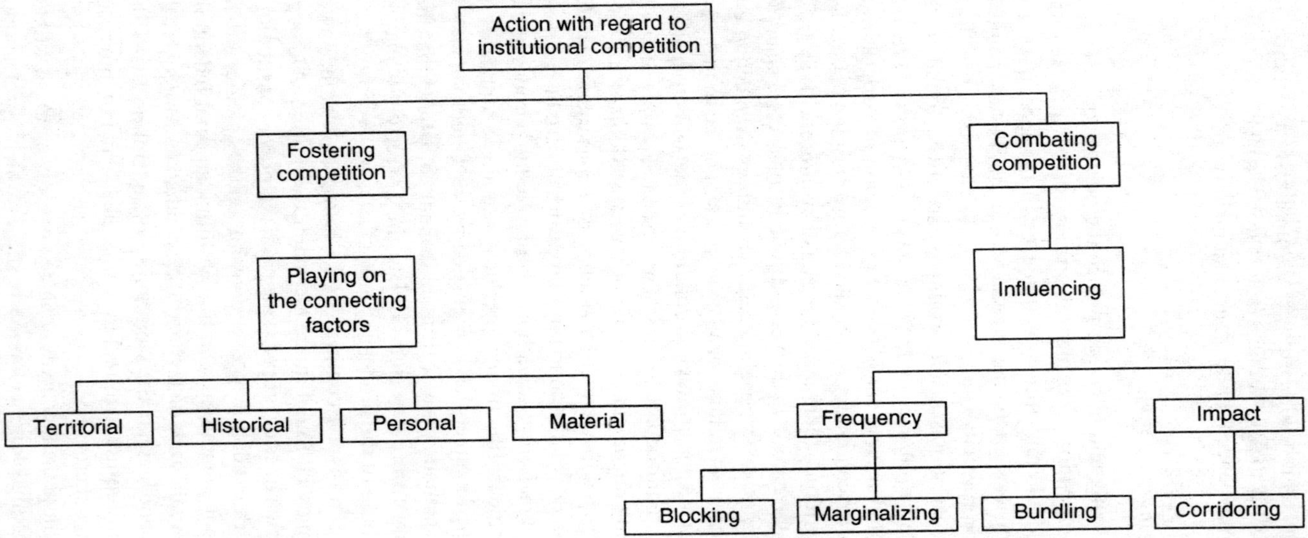

Figure 4   Institutional Competition : Fostering and Combating

for unforeseeable detrimental effects. In private international law one talks about *ordre public*. Similar clauses are contained in Article 36, 56 and 115 of the EC Treaty or in Article XIX to Article XXI of the GATT.

Figure 4 gives an overall picture of section 4, including pertinent aspects of previous sections.

5 META-META-RULES

So far, the law has been treated as empirical evidence: for the diversity of institutional competition, for the attitude of states towards it and for the instruments employed when they wish to combat unwanted exogenous competition. Of course, such analysis is not only of use to economists, but also to lawyers when they are framing new rules on institutional competition; we have already mentioned that rule-appliers potentially always are in the position of subtly reforming the law (supra 2.1).

But institutional competition might also directly be addressed as a legal problem, since there are rules on the admissibility and on the form of such competition. One might call them meta-meta-rules. In order to operate, they either are part of a superior legal order or they take the character of general principles that amalgamate specific rules.

It would stretch beyond the limits of a conference paper (and beyond the interest of the audience present) to go into the details. A few sketches must suffice. Meta-meta-rules may foster or discourage institutional competition. Fostering effects have constitutional guarantees of autonomy for federal states, municipalities or autonomous units like universities. Discouraging effects have rules that guarantee a minimum of homogeneity like the just mentioned Article 28 II German Basic Law. Meta-meta-rules may look at the economic effects of institutional competition. It has been argued that lax regulation is a hidden subsidy (Trachtman, 1993) and that making profit from a regulatory slope is a case of unfair competition (Oesterhaus, 1991). Finally, fundamental freedoms may work in both directions. The access to the opportunities of institutional competition may be within the field of application of a fundamental freedom. For instance, freedom of association might oblige the state to develop a sufficient range of corporate forms and to guarantee easy access to them. On the other hand, freedom of property might protect persons from becoming a hostage under the guise of reciprocity.

Thus a coherent legal theory of the admissibility and framing of institutional competition has still to be written – but certainly not without making profit of this symposium.

Notes

1. He accordingly accepts customary law only in so far as it is approved by the Sovereign. Judges and, of course, law professors are only allowed to find out the true intention of the sovereign rule-maker, while they are forbidden to modify rules under the pretext of interpreting them. Some caveats are in place, however. Hobbes did expressly allow for rules that apply only to (newly acquired) parts of the territory or only to some persons at the exclusion of others (Hobbes, 1668, ch. 26), thereby creating the opportunity for institutional arbitrage. And above all Hobbes never intended to overcome the national state, but rather was one of its major advocates.

2. The French would talk about the *pouvoir constituant* as opposed to the mere *pouvoir constitué*.

3. *Offene Handelsgesellschaft.*

4. *Aktiengesellschaft,* for the details s. Schmidt (1986/1991).

5. *Bundesimmissionsschutzgesetz.*

6. *'Das Recht der Wirtschaft'.*

7. EC Commission 2 October 1991, OJ 1991 L 334/42 – de Havilland.

8. American readers should be warned that US political science uses the same term with a different meaning. In the US it characterizes situations in which federal and state authorities co-operate. German lawyers would in the equivalent situation talk of *Mischverwaltung.*

9. In order not to present connecting factors twice, they are omitted here and integrated into Figure 4 below.

10. BVerfG 16 June 1981, BVerfGE 57, 295 – FRAG.

11. BVerfG 4 November 1986, BVerfGE 73, 118 – Niedersächsisches Landesrundfunkgesetz.

12. Economists might step in and elaborate on the workability of competition among non-homogenous, but related products.

13. BVerfG 24 March 1987, BVerfGE 74, 297 (pp. 338 ff) – Baden-Württemberg.

14. In practice, things are somewhat more complicated in the interest of individuals affected. They may ask for the protection of legitimate expectations. Often they have even acquired a property right under old rules, that cannot be revoked without giving them just compensation.

15. BVerfG 3 November 1982, BVerfGE 62, 169 – *Konten von DDR-Bürgern in der Bundesrepublik.*

16. But courts are normally content if minimum procedural and material standards have been met.

17. Art. 16 of the Convention, European Treaty Series 132.

18. German lawyers talk about *Sitztheorie* as opposed to *Gründungstheorie.*

19. Or, of course, if they want to profit from foreign redistribution, as in section 3.3 above.

20. So-called *Kumulverbot,* see Roth 1990: 257 s.; the rules are now modified under the influence of EC law.

21. Directive of 21 December 1988, OJ 1988 L 40/12.

References

Bebchuk, Lusian Arye (1992) 'Federalism and the Corporation: The Desirable Limits on State Competition in Corporate Law', *Harvard Law Review*, 105, pp. 1437–510.

Beier, Friedrich Karl and Gerhard Schricker (eds) (1989) *GATT or WIPO? New Ways in the International Protection of Intellectual Property* (Weinheim: V.C.H. Verlagsgesellschaft).

Bongaerts, J.C. and A.S. van Schaik (1984) 'The Demand for Regulation: The Case of Dutch Inland Shipping', *International Review of Law and Economics*, 4, pp. 199–212.

Butler, Henry N. (1985) 'Nineteenth-Century Jurisdictional Competition in the Granting of Corporate Privileges', *Journal of Legal Studies*, 14, pp. 129–66.

Cary, William L. (1974) 'Federalism and Corporate Law: Reflections upon Delaware', *Yale Law Journal*, 83, pp. 663–705.

Charny, David (1991) 'Competition among Jurisdictions in Formulating Corporate Law Rules: An American Perspective on the "Race to the Bottom" in the European Communities'. *Harvard International Law Journal*, 32, pp. 423–56.

Engel, Christoph (1990) 'Trade in Services between the European Community and Third Countries – Its Regulation by Community Law', in Daniel Friedmann and Ernst-Joachim Mestmäcker (eds), *Rules for Free International Trade in Services* (Wirtschaftsrecht und Wirtschaftspolitik (107) (Baden-Baden: Nomos) pp. 107–75.

—. (1993) 'Vorsorge gegen die Konzentration im privaten Rundfunk mit Mitteln des Rundfunkrechts – eine Analyse von § 21 Rundfunkstaatsvertrag 1991', *Zeitschrift für Urheber- und Medienrecht*, 37, pp. 557–85.

Gernhuber, Joachim (1989) *Das Schuldverhältnis: Begründung und Abänderung. Pflichten und Strukturen. Drittwirkungen* (Handbuch des Schuldrechts 8) (Tübingen: Mohr).

Haddock, David D. and Jonathan R. Macey (1987) 'Regulation on Demand: a Private Interest Model, with an Application to Insider Trading Regulation', *Journal of Law and Economics*, 30, pp. 311–52.

Hobbes, Thomas (1668) *Leviathan*.

Holcombe, Randall and Lora P. Holcombe (1986) 'The Market for Regulation', *Journal of Institutional and Theoretical Economics*, 142, pp. 684–96.

Hutter, Michael (1989) *Die Produktion von Recht: Eine selbstreferentielle Theorie der Wirtschaft, angewandt auf den Fall des Arzneimittelrechts* (Die Einheit der Gesellschaftswissenschaften 60) (Tübingen: Mohr).

Ipsen, Jörn (1986/1993) *Staatsorganisationsrecht* (Frankfurt: Metzner).

Jarass, Hans Dieter (1991) 'Verwaltungsrecht als Vorgabe für Zivil- und Strafrecht', *Veröffentlichungen der Vereinigung der Deutschen Staatsrechtslehrer*, 50, pp. 239–74.

König, Doris (1993) 'Das Problem der Inländerdiskriminierung', *Archiv des öffentlichen Rechts*, 118, pp. 591–616.

Kübler, Friedrich (1994) 'Rechtsbildung durch Gesetzgebungswettbewerb? Überlegungen zur Angleichung und Entwicklung des Gesellschaftsrechts in der Europäischen Gemeinschaft', *Kritische Vierteljahresschrift*, 77, pp. 79–89.

Lowe, A. Vaughari (1988) 'Extraterritorial Jurisdiction – The British Practice', *Rabels Zeitschrift*, 52, pp. 157–204.

118   *Legal Experiences of Competition*

Maloney, Michael T., Robert E. McCormick and Robert D. Tollison (1984) 'Economic Regulation, Competitive Governments, and Specialized Resources', *Journal of Law and Economics*, 27, pp. 329–38.

Matte, Nicolas Mateesco and Ram S. Jakhu (1987) *Law of International Telecommunications in Canada* (Law and Economics of International Telecommunications 3) (Baden-Baden: Nomos).

North, Douglas C. (1989) 'Institutional Change and Economic History', *Journal of Institutional and Theoretical Economics*, 145, pp. 238–45.

Oesterhaus, Henning (1991) *Die Ausnutzung des internationalen Rechtsgefälles und § 1 UWG* (Frankfurt: Lang).

Poole, Keith T. and Howard Rosenthal (1993) 'The Enduring Nineteenth-Century Battle for Economic Regulation: The Interstate Commerce Act Revisited', *Journal of Law and Economics*, 36, pp. 837–60.

Posner, Richard (1974) 'Theories of Economic Regulation', *Bell Journal of Economics and Management Science*, 5, pp. 335–58.

Priest, George L. (1993) 'The Origins of Utility Regulation and the "Theories of Regulation" Debate', *Journal of Law and Economics*, 36, pp. 289–323.

Roth, Wulf-Henning (1990) 'International Free Trade in Insurance Services', in Daniel Friedmann and Ernst-Joachim Mestmäcker (eds), *Rules for Free International Trade in Services* (Wirtschaftsrecht und Wirtschaftspolitik 107) (Baden-Baden: Nomos) pp. 243–74.

Schmidt, Karsten (1986/1991) *Gesellschaftsrecht* (Köln: Heymanns).

Schmidt, Marek (1993) *Standesrecht und Standesmoral: Ein Beitrag zu den rechtlichen Grenzen der Wettbewerbsregulierung durch Standesorganisationen* (Wirtschaftsrecht und Wirtschaftspolitik 127) (Baden-Baden: Nomos).

Schmidtchen, Dieter and Matthias Leder (1990) 'Die Produktion von Recht', *Journal of Institutional and Theoretical Economics*, 146, pp. 749–57.

Schnyder, Anton K. (1990) *Wirtschaftskollisionsrecht: Sonderanknüpfung und extraterritoriale Anwendung wirtschaftsrechtlicher Normen unter besonderer Berücksichtigung von Marktrecht* (Zürich: Schulthess).

Schröder, Meinhard (1991) 'Verwaltungsrecht als Vorgabe für Zivil- und Strafrecht', *Veröffentlichungen der Vereinigung der Deutschen Staatsrechtslehrer*, 50, pp. 198–237.

Spickhoff, Andreas (1992) 'Internationales Handelsrecht vor Schiedsgerichten und staatlichen Gerichten', *Rabels Zeitschrift*, 56, pp. 116–41.

Trachtman, Joel P. (1993) 'International Regulatory Competition, Externalization and Jurisdiction', *Harvard International Law Journal*, 34, pp. 48–104.

Vihanto, Martti (1992) 'Competition between Local Governments as a Discovery Procedure', *Journal of Institutional and Theoretical Economics*, 148, pp. 411–36.

5 International Migration and Institutional Competition: An Application of Hayek's Evolutionary Theory[*]

Patrick Welter

> However, in assessing the economic effects of the migration of a factor of production, the relevant criterion is not marginal *private* productivity, but marginal *social* productivity.
>
> Brinley Thomas (1968, p. 298)

> Competition between local authorities or between larger units within an area where there is freedom of movement provides in a large measure that opportunity for experimentation with alternative methods which will secure most of the advantages of free growth.
>
> Friedrich A. von Hayek (1960, p. 263)

1 INTRODUCTION

In the last decade, the number of migrants on the international level, especially migrants to western welfare states, has increased to unforeseen heights. The United States has experienced a level of legal immigration unseen since the beginning of the century, and the number of illegal immigrants to the US is supposed to have increased as well. Due to liberal asylum laws, asylum-seekers have flooded Western Europe, which has been exacerbated by an influx of immigrants from post-communist countries. As legal immigration is restricted, unregulated immigration takes place, to a large part, under the guise of asylum-seeking, especially in the

[*]The author would like to thank Barbara Dluhosch and Clemens Fuest for helpful comments, as well as the participants of the symposium, especially Louis De Alessi and Stefan Voigt. Major parts of the research were done while the author was Hume fellow at the Institute for Humane Studies, George Mason University, Fairfax, VA. Financial support of the IHS as well as useful suggestions by staff members there are gratefully acknowledged. Errors and omissions remain the responsibility of the author.

European states. There are worries that these huge migration flows will be detrimental to western wealth, and that they will prove inefficient world-wide. Therefore, governments are trying to tighten immigration laws, especially in the field of asylum policy. They find support from economists, who propose an international migration order to control migration and to co-ordinate migration policies. Analogous to the GATT, this proposal is named GAMP, the General Agreement on Migration Policies.

> It should provide rules of entry permission, rules of exit permission, rules of taxing migration, treatment of foreign labour, and other migration aspects which have to be fixed within this multilateral agreement (remittances, transfers, social rights, pension transfers etc.).[1]

The assumption behind the proposal is that unregulated migration is inherently inefficient. Pareto-efficiency, it is argued, would dictate a co-ordinated regulation of migration.[2] However, policy co-ordination always includes the danger of governmental policy cartelization in order to escape from institutional competition. This must be considered when analyzing the GAMP proposal.

The assumed inefficiency of migration between states is based on an idea of external effects that migrants impose on 'those left behind' (Bhagwati, 1979, p. 18) as well as 'those already there'. Migrants, it is argued, impose negative or positive effects on the (broadly defined) wealth of non-migrants.[3] Since migrants do not take into account these externalities, it is usually argued in the Pigou tradition that the migration decision is individually efficient, but socially inefficient. Thus, a control of migration flows would be necessary in order to correct externalities. It is important to note the implicit underlying assumptions: a certain definition of a state, and a certain idea of property rights as far as migration is concerned.[4]

If proponents of regulation suggest that the migrant has to take into account the externalities he imposes on the immigration country, they acknowledge, to a certain degree, a right of 'those already there' to be economically undisturbed through immigration. In an extreme interpretation, the immigrant is not allowed to influence their level of wealth. In the same way, a property right of 'those left behind' to the migrant's social contribution – for example tax payments – is recognized.[5] This expresses nothing else than a right to co-operate and to exclude others if one's own interests are harmed. Therefore, a common interest of citizens is acknowledged; the theoretical discussion of international migration is based on the idea that a state is a club.

The basic purpose of a club, in common language as well as in economic theory, involves the pursuit of a common objective, for example the production of a common good (a survey of economic club-theory is given by Cornes and Sandler, 1986). If states are seen in that way as clubs, the common good can be found in the realm of the productive or of the protective state (Buchanan, 1975). The discussion in this paper will be restricted to the productive state, as the economic theory of (regional) clubs only deals with the common provision of club goods. Under the notion 'club goods' I subsume the following: (i) goods that allow for exclusion (at the border); (ii) goods with certain economies of scale in consumption and (iii) the possible existence of congestion costs.

In the following discussion, I will focus on one argument of the migration externality kind, namely the argument of fiscal externalities that is most prominent in the literature. I will discuss the neoclassical rationale for migration inefficiency in section 2 and present the usual policy implications that follow. Hayek's evolutionary theory will be introduced in section 3, as it forms the basis for the following discussion of institutional competition. Section 4 analyzes migration policies from the Hayekian perspective and compares the results with migration policies derived from the neoclassical argument. The paper aims at showing that the usual policy proposals concerning fiscal externalities are incompatible with an evolutionary interpretation of rule-competition. It is not only that the Pigou tradition ignores several important aspects – more significantly, to implement a GAMP on that basis would destroy institutional competition.

2   THE RATIONALE FOR MIGRATION INEFFICIENCY

The argument that, due to fiscal externalities, unrestricted migration between jurisdictions does not lead, from a global point of view, to an efficient allocation of individuals is based on the locationally-fixed character of club goods or services.

Most of the tasks modern states fulfill are locationally fixed, since states normally provide their services on a regional, not on a personal basis. Transaction costs, or simply the physical impossibility of providing goods like highways on a personal basis without regard to location, explain from an economic point of view, why states or jurisdictions are regionally-bounded entities. This locational fixity does not necessarily apply with respect to state interventions in the field of pure redistribution, for example transfers in cash.[6] However, it applies to a productive state and to a certain degree to a protective one as well. The law-enforcement task of the latter suggests at least some degree of locational fixity: territorial law-enforcement seems to imply subadditive cost functions, which are not present when law is enforced for a group of geographically-scattered individuals (Schmidt-Trenz and Schmidtchen, 1993). Furthermore, locational fixity follows from the assumption that the geographical size of state-clubs is fixed. Neither secession nor splitting-off of states is taken into consideration. It is claimed that, out of this double locational fixity, migration inefficiencies arise – inefficiencies that call for correction.

Tiebout (1956) has claimed that migration between jurisdictions can serve as a 'voting-with-the-feet' mechanism and, therefore, guide governmental decisions on club goods. The resulting Tiebout hypothesis states that interjurisdictional competition through 'voting-with-the-feet' leads to an efficient provision of club goods. The proponents of inefficient migration due to locational fixity argue that this hypothesis can no longer be justified.[7] A regulation of international migration would be necessary in order to secure the welfare-enhancing properties of migration.

Assume that there is a given set of jurisdictions each offering public consumption goods of a given type.[8] The government of each jurisdiction collects taxes in exchange for a certain amount of club goods. Also, assume that the supply of club goods satisfies the Samuelson criterion for efficiency in every jurisdiction.[9] The private sector is characterized by a competitive Ricardian economy: land is combined with homogeneous labour in a linear-homogeneous production function. Labour migrates from one jurisdiction to another in order to maximize utility. The arguments in the utility function of a representative individual are: real income earned from the private sector, a lump-sum tax paid by the individual,[10] and benefits from the club good provided by the respective government. The private sector is assumed to be competitive.[11] There are – for the moment – no migration costs.

Consider now the migration behaviour of individuals, as well as an efficiency condition, in order to analyze the case for regulation. Following Buchanan and Wagner (1970) and Buchanan and Goetz (1972), Pareto-optimality demands that the marginal value an individual contributes to social welfare in any jurisdiction is the same. This marginal value is the sum of the marginal value in the private sector as well as in the public (governmental) sector. Assume that there are two jurisdictions, 1 and 2. Then the condition of Pareto-optimality can be written as:

$$MVP_1^i + MVG_1^i = MVP_2^i + MVG_2^i \tag{1}$$

where *MVP* stands for marginal private-goods value and *MVG* for marginal club-goods value. The exponents i and j stand for individuals i, $j = 1...N$, $i \neq j$. The marginal private-goods value in a particular jurisdiction equals (in equilibrium) the marginal social value. The marginal value an individual contributes to the public sector in a given jurisdiction, *MVG*, is given by the effects on fiscal surplus – the difference between total benefits and total tax payments. *MVG* can therefore be broken up into a benefit term (B) and a tax term (T). Seeing that immigration (emigration) influences the benefits received,[12] as well as the tax payments of 'those already there' ('those left behind'),[13] equation (1) changes to:

$$MVP^i_1 + (B^i_1 - T^i_1) + \left[\frac{\partial(\Sigma B^j)}{\partial N_1} - \frac{\partial(\Sigma T^j)}{\partial N_1} \right] = \qquad (2)$$

$$MVP^{\,i}_2 + (B^i_2 - T^i_2) + \left[\frac{\partial(\Sigma B^j)}{\partial N_2} - \frac{\partial(\Sigma T^j)}{\partial N_2} \right]$$

Now, equation (2) states the migration equilibrium condition for a Pareto-optimum. The terms in square brackets show the values of fiscal externalities, which the migrant exercises on the non-migrating individuals. As long as migration is unregulated, the migrant does not take into account these externalities, neither with respect to the immigration jurisdiction nor to the emigration jurisdiction. Instead of fulfilling the efficiency-conditions of equation (2), the individual migration equilibrium satisfies equation (3):

$$MVP^i_1 + (B^i_1 - T^i_1) = MVP^i_2 + (B^i_2 - T^i_2) \qquad (3)$$

Imagine now that country 1 is larger with respect to land size than country 2. If the migration equilibrium were determined only by the private sector, there would be more people in jurisdiction 1 than in jurisdiction 2. As a result, the relative price per head for the club good would be lower in 1 than in 2.[14] Jurisdiction 1 would be more attractive for potential migrants, since either the migrant would have to pay less for the same amount of club goods, or he could profit from more club goods for the same amount of taxes.

Out of this regional difference, an incentive arises for individuals in 2 to migrate to 1 until equation (3) is satisfied. However, the migrant does not take into account all effects he exerts. It is highly probable that the social costs he imposes on 'those left behind' diverge from the externalities he imposes on 'those already there', as the land sizes differ.[15] Therefore, the migration that takes place is suboptimal: either there are too many migrants, or too few.

Note that this inefficiency does not appear in the classic Tiebout model, as the assumptions differ in important aspects. Tiebout (1956) assumes an unlimited number of jurisdictions, as well as the irrelevance of an individual's location with respect to income.[16] In his model, individuals guide their locational residence decision solely by comparing bundles of tax payments and club goods. Then, the assumption of an unlimited number of jurisdictions allow for sorting of individuals into clubs with an optimal size. Tiebout establishes migration efficiency by dividing the private income rationale for migration (in fact, he assumes it away) from the club good rationale for migration. In this way, locational fixity loses importance and cannot imply migration inefficiency. However, compared to the prerequisites of the Tiebout model, the ones of the model used here come closer to reality. In particular, the assumption of a limited number of jurisdictions is more appropriate in dealing with migration on an international level than the one set by Tiebout.[17]

The situation with inefficient migration is a special case of the well-known problem of the commons (Gordon, 1954). Instead of being guided by the total marginal value of his presence in a specific jurisdiction, the individual migrant is guided by private marginal value and social average value. The resulting inefficiency appears since the per capita tax system does not allow for an internalization of the fiscal externalities: no discrimination between migrants and 'those already there' is allowed.

An internalization may arise out of the property of locational values to be capitalized in the price of immobile factors, for example land. In order to change residential location, the migrant must bid for immobile resources either as buyer or as tenant. If the complete value of fiscal externalities were to be capitalized in the piece of land the migrant buys or rents, internalization could occur. However, this does not take place: the fiscal externalities are dispersed over all non-migrants, and are capitalized in the summed value of the immobile resource, not in the value of individual parcels of land. A correction of the individual migration calculus would take place only under the condition that the migrant were to bid for the whole of the immobile resource. The argument can be stated in another way: the owner of a certain piece of land does not have complete control over the fiscal externalities the migrant imposes on all of 'those already there' (see for a similar argument Buchanan, 1969b, p. 268). Therefore, he will not internalize the complete value of the fiscal externalities in his reservation price. Capitalization only leads to a partial internalization and will be disregarded from this point on.

Usually two policy-options to the internalization problem are discussed in the respective literature, either a property-rights solution or a transfer solution. The former specifies state-club property rights to the fiscal surpluses they generate, the latter relies on international transfers in order to prevent inefficient migration.

The specification of property-rights would guide the allocation toward an efficient equilibrium. (The classic paper in this respect is Knight, 1924.) If jurisdictions were to possess property rights to fiscal surpluses, they would pursue a migration policy that internalizes fiscal externalities. This first-best solution is dismissed in the literature, since the authors normally deal with migration within federal states. (For an exception see Myers, 1990.) It is assumed from the beginning that individuals should be allowed to migrate freely in the sense of being treated equally in federal sub-jurisdictions. On an international level, there seems to be greater consent to assigning property rights to states,[18] thus, the analogy of a state-club is generally accepted.

Granting property rights to state-clubs leads to a system of migration taxes and subsidies, geared toward internalization of fiscal externalities as in the classic Pigou argument. Figure 1 shows the subsidy and tax options for a state-club.[19] Note that for a complete internalization of the externalities, both sides, the external effect in the emigration as well as in the immigration state, have to be corrected. The necessity of immigration taxes arises only in the case of congestion-prone club goods.

Migration policies that follow these lines have been proposed by several authors. The competition for citizens via subsidies was discussed by Buchanan and Wagner (1970) and Buchanan and Goetz (1972). A historical example is the policy of the Prussian monarchy with regard to the Huguenots, who received subsidies in the form of free land and temporary tax relief.[20] Immigration taxes are proposed out of a club-theoretical reasoning, for example, by Becker (1992).[21] The most famous proposal for an emigration tax comes from Bhagwati (Bhagwati and Partington, 1976). He proposed to tax high-qualified emigrants in order to internalize the negative externality (brain drain) they impose on the growth prospects of their home country. Historical examples can also be found in the history of the former communist bloc.

Figure 1   Options for migration policy in a state-club

| | | *policy concerning* | |
		immigrants	*emigrants*
population	*too small*	subsidy	tax
	too large	tax	subsidy

As illustrated above, an assignment of property rights in fiscal surpluses could solve the inefficiency arising out of the divergence between private and social cost or utilities. However, it is not at all clear whether this solution is feasible, since an implicit prerequisite is that states have control over their borders. Seeing the difficulties the United States encounters, while attempting to control immigration at the Mexican border, as well as the degree of permeability of Western Europe's eastern border, other methods of correcting migration inefficiency may gain in importance.[22]

The proposal to implement transfers between states does not rely on border controls. The fundamental idea behind this policy option is easily understood. The prevention of inefficient migration requires an internalization of the externalities in the individual migration calculus. This internalization could occur via direct measures, for example raising migration taxes, or indirectly, by transferring wealth to the emigration country in order to raise the standard of living there.[23] An adequate transfer from the potential immigration to the potential emigration country could stop inefficient migration, and thus help both countries. The transfer payments West Germany supplied to East Germany with the unification treaty have been proposed as an example for such a policy (Hercowitz and Pines, 1991, p. 180).

Summarizing the rationale behind the proposed policy options will give the basis for a comparison with an evolutionary approach. Inefficient migration occurs, since state-clubs do not completely control the number of their inhabitants. State-clubs generate rents (fiscal surpluses) through cost-sharing agreements or economics of scale in the consumption of club goods. Migrants contribute to and participate in these fiscal surpluses and, thus, impose fiscal externalities. Since the property rights to these rents are not completely specified, in other words controlled by the respective state-club, a problem of common property results, leading to inefficient migration. Fundamental for this inefficiency is the difference in state-club sizes. Assigning property rights to fiscal surpluses would be the first-best remedy in this setting. In the event this solution is not feasible, transfer payments between states could correct the inefficient migration decisions as well.

Oddly enough, all the proponents of these arguments assume that governments pursue their citizens' interests and have the knowledge necessary for providing club goods according to the Samuelson condition. (Exceptions are Buchanan and Wagner (1970) and Buchanan and Goetz (1972).) Such a modelling is quite astonishing, as it fails to grasp the basic motivation of the idea behind 'voting-with-the-feet'. This mechanism was proposed by Tiebout especially to solve the fundamental knowledge problem governments normally encounter when trying to supply club goods in an efficient way. In the Tiebout setting, a spontaneous sorting process would lead to an efficient outcome, guided solely by individual calculus. But as soon as policy proposals require the evaluation of different outcomes – as the proposed migration policies do – an outside observer is assumed to analyze values, including costs. Thus, governments are supposed to have full knowledge of individual values for the club good,[24] as well as the knowledge of the costs a new citizen imposes. This assumption neglects the subjectivist insights into cost-theory (Alchian, 1968, Buchanan, 1969a). The government cannot possess this ability, nor can the value difference in fiscal externalities be measured by any other outside observer. The political process does not bring about a revelation of subjectivist values either. All these insights into the practicability are missed by the Pigouvian approach, and there is no way to solve them other than to rely on individual decision-making, that is to say individual migration.

Additionally, 'voting-with-the-feet' is often seen as an exit-option (Hirschman, 1970) that restricts the governmental power to tax (Brennan and Buchanan, 1980, Jones, 1987). Governments pursue self-interests, and do not act directly in the interest of their citizens. Seeing that the political-democratic process does not constitute an obstacle to the *Leviathan's* appetite, one possibility to diminish over-taxation might be an unrestricted exit-option. This aspect of intergovernmental competition is missed as well by the conventional club-theoretical analysis.

The knowledge problem points to the fundamental incapability of governments to provide an efficient amount of club-goods by satisfying the Samuelson condition. The power-problem points to the fundamental unwillingness of governments to respect citizen's preferences. Out of this criticism emerges a different approach to the analysis of international migration. To analyze such a self-interested government in a world without social welfare functions, it seems more adequate to look at the rules that restrict governmental action, as it is the rule-system that determines the degree of inefficiency in the supply of club-goods. These rules might be constitutional rules, which define governmental tasks and permit a certain power to tax, or organizational rules that govern the provision of club-goods. Migration between state-clubs is then to be seen as migration between institutional systems that constitute states.[25]

Assuming away the knowledge as well as the power problem – as does the analysis of international migration in the Pigou tradition – invalidates the value of free migration for the choice of rules and institutional competition. In order to analyze the institutional competition through international migration, I refer to Hayek's theory of cultural evolution. Clarifying in that way the importance of free migration for institutional competition allows elaboration on the shortcomings of the conventional approach and the derived migration policies.

3   THE HAYEKIAN EVOLUTIONARY APPROACH TO INSTITUTIONAL COMPETITION[26]

In his theory of cultural evolution, Hayek delivers an explanation for the evolution of rules. More precisely, Hayek concentrates predominantly on a theory of rule-selection rather than one of rule-emergence.[27] According to him, rules are tested for their success (functional utility) and rejected if unsuccessful. This selection takes place in a polycentric order, and is not guided by a central authority. Implicitly, Hayek transfers the idea of a competitive market process to the realm of rule-selection, and describes in this way a process of institutional competition. One of the main elements of his theory is the interplay between two market processes: the market for goods and the 'market for rules'. To show this interdependence, I propose a two-level scheme for spontaneous order (Figure 2).

On the first level of spontaneous order, individuals compete for goods. In the competition for private goods, a 'first-best solution' is given by the market order (catallaxy). However, the catallaxy does not include the

Figure 2   A two-level scheme of spontaneous order

	determines	*innovation*	*selection*
First level of spontaneous order: **'market order':** competition for goods	result of co-operation (wealth)	innovation • economic (products, processes) • political (club goods, services)	selection in the realm of economic and political competition (under given rules) via individual, entrepreneurial actions
Second level of spontaneous order: **evolution:** competition for rules	form of co-operation (taxis, cosmos)	innovation of rules • accidental • deliberate	group-selection via individual actions

opportunities that arise from the existence of club goods, that is to say the possibilities of gaining from joint production and consumption (Hayek, 1979/82, pp. 44 ff). Therefore, a certain kind of political competition is needed in order to exploit these economic opportunities. Both kinds of competition are inferred by 'competition for goods'. Individuals are interested in utility-maximizing and will be served to that end by economic or political entrepreneurs (Downs, 1957), who innovate in the field of products (private and public) or processes. In the club-theoretical reasoning, individuals choose among state-clubs in an effort to maximize utility, taking into account income prospects as well as net utility from public action.

To avoid any misunderstanding: the outcome on the first level of spontaneous order cannot be evaluated with the help of equilibrium theory, as was assumed in the neoclassical argument. Hayek proposes – as criterion for an evaluation of governmental intervention in the catallaxy – a kind of Wicksellian unanimity criterion over the whole bundle of collective goods (Hayek, 1979/82, p. 45). He stresses the ambivalent character of governmental action: on the one side, coercion (at least with respect to taxes) is necessary in order to provide collective goods; on the other, governmental intervention always represents a danger to the economic wealth the catallaxy guarantees. Due to this ambiguity, he emphasizes the necessity of submitting the government as collective-good producer to the same set of general rules as private providers of goods.[28] This fits the interpretation of governmental submission to (general) rules as a criterion for evaluation, rather than a Samuelsonian equilibrium solution. Migration policies derived in a Hayekian framework cannot be based on an equilibrium that will never be reached in a dynamic competitive process, but must take into account the institutional differences of state-clubs. The issue here is not an equilibrium that guarantees Pareto-optimality, but rules that control the division between the private catallaxy and the public sector, as well as the organizational rules governing the latter.[29]

These different institutional structures are selected on the second level of spontaneous order, where the competition between rule-systems take place. It is the *form* of economic co-operation that is selected on this level, not the outcome. Rule-innovation happens accidentally or deliberately. Rules are sorted out by a mechanism of group selection: co-operation rents are generated in the economic game, for example through common action in providing club goods. The amount of these rents depends on the quality of the rules governing the economic game. Differences in co-operation rents form the competitive advantage of rule-systems. Co-operation rents in this terminology arise out of the common submission to certain rules. To a certain degree, they coincide with the idea of fiscal surpluses that was used in the neoclassical argument. But in that argument institutions do not play a role; fiscal surpluses are the result of scale effects in the production of club goods. Co-operation rents include these fiscal surpluses, but – additionally and more importantly – may also include rents emerging out of different qualities of rule-systems.

One of the main elements of Hayek's evolutionary theory is the interdependence between both levels. The rules that govern the ordering process on the first level are the outcomes of the competitive process on the second one. However, on the second level, rules are selected for the economic success they initiate on the first level. In that way, both levels of spontaneous order are combined in a feedback mechanism and developed in a mutually self-enforcing manner.[30]

The implications of Hayek's evolutionary theory for migration between state-clubs are two-fold. On the one hand, the second level of competition enters the analysis. Competition between rule-systems is necessary in order to promote and secure rules that generate wealth. One way this competition takes place is through individual migration between state-clubs, that is to say institutionalized forms of alternative rule-systems. On the other hand, Hayek's evolutionary approach emphasizes the importance of economic rents for rule selection. Individuals generate co-operation rents in submitting to abstract rules of behaviour. Utility-maximizing individuals join groups with higher per capita co-operation rents. In leaving, an individual withdraws his contribution to the co-operation rents that are generated through the rules of the emigration state, and contributes to the rents in the immigration country. Thereby, the migrant exercises pressure on unsuccessful rules to be changed or to be abolished.

These implications apply to the problem of state-clubs in a special form, since governmental services are locationally fixed. An individual change to more successful rules requires physical migration from one club to another, or rule innovation inside the respective state-club. On the international level, both individual options – *exit* and *voice* in the sense of Hirschman (1970) – are characterized by high costs: either migration costs, or costs of political action, which are especially high, since the possibility of changing an established rule-system is small. The latter follows out of the low probabilities of an individual voter to influence the political decisions in a majority democracy.[31] Due to the high migration costs, a massive flow of migrants is likely to be witnessed only in situations of drastic differences in co-operation rents.[32] The competitive pressure on the second level is, therefore, not really strong and certainly does not generate an outcome analogous to the law of one price.

Evolutionary rule competition among locationally-fixed state-clubs has to deal with another peculiarity: it is to be expected that co-operation rents will be capitalized as locational rents in the price of land. In that way, immigrants might not profit from co-operation rents, as these would be appropriated by land owners. Besides the argument against capitalization mentioned above, another aspect that is closely related to the idea of institutions can be emphasized in this context. Co-operation rents depend on governmental power, as governments are responsible for and guarantee the rules that permit the generation of these rents. A full capitalization does not take place since there is, due to the governmental power, no complete, secure individual property right to co-operation rents that can be tied to the land (Buchanan, 1969b).[33]

4   MIGRATION POLICIES FOR INSTITUTIONAL COMPETITION

Migration policy based on the standard theory of local public goods leads either to a system of property rights to co-operation rents, or to transfers between the state-clubs in order to correct fiscal externalities. Both proposals have been elaborated on the basis of the first level of competition, and do not consider the implications for competition on the second, the institutional level. An analysis of their effects on the latter will show that there are incompatibilities.

For this analysis it is helpful to assume *Leviathan*-governments, since the implications of the policy proposals on the exit-option are to be analyzed.[34] Under this assumption, the only way for a state-club member to influence a government is by withdrawing or granting his personal tax base. (A possible escape to leisure is not regarded here.) Choosing among state-clubs means selecting among different wealth prospects that arise out of particular rule-systems including, for example, tax-rules and rules for the provision of club goods. In migrating between states and, at the same time, by granting the right to be taxed to a government that acts under a certain rule-system, the individual expresses his approval of these rules. In *Leviathan*-states (as well as in modern democracies), constitutional rules and organizational rules for the provision for club goods are more or less managed by the government, and it is therefore the government that limits its actions in keeping certain rules. Governmental provision of club goods can, thus, be understood as a voluntary submission to certain rules. In this way, governments attract citizens and secure tax payments; the more efficient the supply of club goods, the more rents that could be appropriated by governments. With these additional assumptions, the ground is set for analyzing migration policies for institutional competition.

Assume first that governments are interested in increasing the number of citizens of their respective state-clubs.[35] Allowing them to compete for citizens, therefore utilizing subsidies, would not distort incentives in institutional competition. On the other hand, the proposal to tax emigration is not compatible with competition on the rule-level.

This result arises out of the different allocation of the right to migrate in an institutional competition via subsidies and via emigration taxes: subsidies leave the right to migrate with the individual, emigration taxes effectively do not. The success of institutional competition depends absolutely on the allocation of the right to migrate. Having the right to emigrate is the same as having the right to withdraw the personal tax base. Subsidies in this respect do not disturb the competition on the rule-level, but if the potential migrant had to pay for negative fiscal externalities he imposes on 'those left behind', there would be no way to 'vote-with-the-feet' and the exit-sanction would be barred to him.[36] In this way, allowing governments to tax emigrants means in essence granting monopoly rights to exploit the citizens.

Note that subsidies geared at attracting additional citizens (or preventing them from leaving) must be financed by tax payments of the residents. 'Those already there' will agree to these additional taxes if there are still economies of scale in the club good-provision that could be exploited. However, these subsidies would be used in favour of the residents only in the case that *Leviathan*-governments were to act under high competitive pressure. A certain number of competing state-clubs as well as a high mobility of residents are, therefore, required. Otherwise, *Leviathan*-governments could exploit immobile residents without taking directly into consideration their interest in possible economies of scale in club good-provision. Fiscal surplus out of these scale effects would be appropriated by the *Leviathans*. However, there remains a difference to emigration taxes. Governmental exploitation of citizens through 'regular' tax payments relies on insufficient competition. In contrast to this, emigration taxes permit citizens' exploitation at any rate.

Taking institutional competition into account, the case against emigration taxes is clearcut. Whether immigration taxes are compatible with competition on the second level of spontaneous order is questionable. From a club-theoretical point of view, immigration taxes are easily justified. Imagine there were no political principal–agent problem in a regional club, in other words, the interests of the government and the constituency coincide. If there were a neoclassical club-theoretical argument for an optimal population, the club would have to possess the possibility of excluding outsiders from common property. As soon as there are congestion-proned club goods, it must be possible for a club to experiment with immigration taxes in order to internalize the negative externalities the immigrant imposes, that is to say the raising of congestion costs. This argument is valid in the context of institutional competition as well, assuming again *Leviathan*-governments: these compete for taxpayers through organizational rules that secure an efficient provision of club goods, as well as through immigration rules in an effort to approach an optimal club size. The former can be seen as competition through reduction of inefficiency, the latter as competition in the realm of scale effects.

It might be argued that immigration taxes should be abolished as they permit a discrimination between residents and immigrants, assuming that it is not possible to discriminate in taxation inside a state-club. However, it is this very discrimination at the border that is necessary for institutional competition to work. If *Leviathan*-governments are not allowed to compete through immigration rules, that is to say immigration taxes, they could not compete through the number of residents, which is important if we are concerned with club goods.[37] In such a situation, there would be no incentive for citizens to submit to tax rules which secure an efficient provision of club goods, as the population size could not be controlled. Note that this rationale for immigration taxes relies on a competitive process of rule-selection. It is not assumed that governments can calculate fiscal externalities out of an equilibrium approach; but it is argued that competition through immigration taxes will generate the necessary knowledge of the efficient number of residents and of the club goods demanded by potential citizens. In this respect, immigration taxes do not serve to internalize – through co-ordinated governmental action – fiscal externalities that arise out of locational fixity, but rather act to give state-clubs the right to experiment with different population sizes.

However, the argument for immigration taxes in institutional competition must be qualified. The right to tax immigrants equals the right to appropriate locational rents immigrants would gain in the respective state-clubs. A lower limit to these locational rents would be established by the fiscal externalities the migrant would impose, but the locational rents might be even higher. Immigration taxes permit governments to appropriate this part of the locational rents as well, thereby strengthening their power to tax. Certainly, in a neoclassical setting this rent-shifting must be judged as pure redistribution, implying no inefficiency in governmental competition. If governments were interested in the total of locational rents, their self-interest would induce an efficient immigration policy with respect to the optimal population size of a state-club.[38]

But, emphasizing institutional competition's task to limit the power to tax, this rent-shifting means a reallocation of property rights to locational rents from the constituency to the government. Immigration taxes strengthen the power to tax and are, in this respect, inconsistent with the objective of institutional competition. Nonetheless, this reasoning is questionable. *Leviathan*-governments might already tax residents more than necessary for club good-provision, thereby taking away maximal locational rents. In such a situation, there would be no need for governments to tax immigration as they could appropriate locational rents from immigrants as soon as they are residents in the jurisdiction. If there were no advantage for *Leviathan*-governments in using immigration taxes compared to income taxation, a ban on immigration taxes could not be justified with the needs of a proper working of institutional competition.

There are some arguments seeming to imply, however, governmental preferences for immigration taxes (additional to income taxation) since they allow discrimination between immigrants and residents with regard to locational rents. Residents are submitted to income taxation, but as citizens they can use their voice-option in order to influence tax payments. Until now, 'voice', that is to say the vote-mechanism, was assumed away, but it might have a certain influence on the power to tax: compared to immigrants, residents can vote, and might, therefore, secure a lesser degree of governmental exploitation. Immigration taxes, in this respect, permit additional governmental rent appropriation. Banning immigration taxes would strengthen the position of the potential immigrant, as he would be equal to 'those already there'; immigrants could not be exploited to a higher degree than former residents, neither through *Leviathan*-governments, nor through 'those already there'. (For the effects of income tax discrimination on the power to tax see Brennan and Buchanan, 1980, pp. 44–54.) Additionally, it seems to be more difficult for a government to acquire knowledge about locational rents inside a country rather than at the border. This is true, if it is easier for a government not to let someone in than to expel him from the country.

If these arguments are valid, it should be easier for governments to appropriate locational rents from immigrants than from residents. (These arguments require individual differences in income or tastes.) In an individual constitutional decision, income taxation would be, therefore, preferred to immigration taxes. A ban on the latter fits the Hayekian concept of general rules, as immigration taxes discriminate between immigrants and 'those already there' with regard to rent exploitation.[39]

Immigration taxes (as well as income taxation) would not pose such problems if they were placed under competition. Contrary to emigration taxes, which imply a governmental right to exploitation, immigration taxes set under high competitive pressure would provide no opportunity for appropriating locational rents higher than fiscal externalities. It is for this reason that the number of state-clubs becomes relevant, as in the case of subsidies. The less possibilities to immigrate, the more likely that a ban on immigration taxes is justified. This argument is amplified by the importance of an effective right to emigrate. Immigration taxes – though set by benevolent governments – make it more difficult for people to leave their home states, thereby expressing disapproval for a certain rule-system. This aspect is not incorporated in the traditional, neoclassical club-theoretical reasoning, and it might be a reason strong enough for banning immigration taxes in a GAMP.[40]

It can be concluded, therefore, that the assignment of property rights to state-clubs is only partially compatible with competition on the institutional level. An emigration tax can be helpful in internalizing the fiscal externalities on the first level but, in the same way, diminishes the incentive for *Leviathan*-governments to improve policies – the incentive that is necessary for the competition on the rule-level to work. Immigration taxes show a certain ambiguity: on the one hand, they are compatible with the club-theoretical reasoning, as they allow for a maximization of per capita locational (co-operation) rents in case of congestion costs; on the other hand, they shift the property rights to these co-operation rents from the constituency to the government. It is the latter aspect that forms the main argument for a ban on immigration taxes in a situation with a small number of state-clubs and resulting low competitive pressure between governments. Additionally, in such a setting the state-club right to tax immigrants goes hand in hand with a diminution of the effective right to emigrate from other states.[41] Subsidies do not seem to distort institutional competition. However, an incompatibility results between a migration policy, which corrects fiscal externalities, and a migration policy, which sets the right incentives for institutional competition.

A similar trade-off characterizes the proposed transfer solution on the one hand and institutional competition on the other. In order to show why, it is helpful to look once more at fiscal externalities from another point of view. As people segregate into state-clubs and submit to certain rules, they generate co-operation rents, for example, through sharing agreements in the financing of club goods. Viewed from this perspective, members of a state-club exert fiscal externalities through their impact on the net rent per head.[42] The transfer solution, in this respect, suggests an equalization of individual co-operation rents between state-clubs, so that individual migration decisions are exclusively guided by income out of the private sector. Co-operation rents would be socialized, and the influence of the public sector on migration decisions would be eliminated.

To evaluate this proposal it is necessary to recall once again the source of the rents. In the neoclassical literature on the subject, it is most often assumed that state-clubs are different in size, resulting in different amounts of fiscal externalities exerted by the marginal migrant. (For example Buchanan et al., 1970, 1972; Flatters et al., 1974; Stiglitz, 1977.) Other authors further the analysis, at least verbally, by including rents out of various amounts of public capital.[43] Migration externalities in this respect arise out of scale effects, either positive ones in jointly producing and using a club good, or negative ones in sharing a common resource. At any rate, these rents depend on governmental action: if there were no club good or public capital, there would be no co-operation rent.[44] A second factor influences, therefore, the per capita level of co-operation rents: the efficiency of the governments in fulfilling the tasks club members assign to them. Using the Hayekian notion, the more efficient the rule-system in a certain state-club is, *ceteris paribus*, the higher the per capita co-operation rent. Population concentration in state-clubs is, therefore, determined by scale effects as well as by differences in governmental efficiency. The latter factor determines the differential degree of efficiency that drives institutional competition, that is the competition on the second level of spontaneous order.

The argument for internalization of fiscal externalities does not take into account the problems which arise out of this double character of co-operation rents. Truly, different land sizes can disturb the competition on the second level, as they result in different co-operation rents between state-clubs, although their governments are equally efficient and submit to equivalent rules. (This seems to be emphasized by Boadway and Flatters, 1982, p. 615.) However, it does not seem to be possible to isolate these 'unwelcomed' rents that arise only out of scale effects. Only under the strong assumption that governments are (equally) successful in fulfilling the Samuelson condition is it plausible to assign differences in the attractiveness of state-clubs solely to scale effects; competition on the second level would no longer be necessary and would cease to exist. In any other case, a clearcut separation of the different rent components is not feasible. Therefore, transfers from the more attractive state-club to the less attractive one, in order to internalize fiscal externalities, are most likely to disturb institutional competition. The incentives for less attractive state-clubs to improve their provision of club goods would be diminished as the transfers from the more efficient state-club provide a substitute for these efforts.

Furthermore, it is necessary to evaluate the importance of the various components of co-operation rents. As long as international differences in co-operation rents are as high as they are today, it can be plausibly argued that the influence of land (and thereby scale effects) on these rents is negligible, while the main part of the difference seemed to be better explained by various rule-systems. (This argument is even more convincing if one introduces in the analysis differences in the realm of the protective state.) Moreover, if capital is highly mobile and forms a good substitute to land, differences in rule-systems gain additional importance; under these conditions differences in co-operation rents are not founded on land sizes.[45]

The transfer solution does not realize the importance of institutions in generating co-operation rents. The argument for transfers restricts the analysis to fiscal surpluses, instead of taking into account the institutional competition. From the latter perspective, the proposed transfer solutions cannot be justified.

5 CONCLUDING REMARKS

The argument for regulation of international migration in order to internalize fiscal externalities does not persist if one introduces an evolutionary, rule-oriented explanation of governmental action. The criticism of the club-theoretical reasoning along neoclassical lines is directed at two apparent misconceptions: (i) it is not sensible to assume implicitly that governments act in the interest of their citizens; (ii) the importance of rents due to differences in land sizes (fiscal surpluses through scale effects) seems to be overemphasized in the usual analysis. Therefore, the proposed policy options are not totally compatible with competition on the rule-level, as they do not recognize the influence of co-operation rents.

Emigration taxes and transfers directly violate conditions necessary for the success of institutional competition. Immigration taxes are not necessarily detrimental to institutional competition, but as the number of competing state-clubs is relatively small, a ban on immigration taxes might be justified. At the same time, subsidies to individuals pose no problem for the competition among rule-systems. Therefore, a GAMP should not co-ordinate governmental action in setting migration taxes, but rather should ban emigration taxes. Transfers between states in order to prevent inefficient migration should not be introduced on an international level.

These results are valid for institutional competition as far as it concerns club goods. The derived proposals need not reflect the outcome of an analysis that broadens the assumptions. Two aspects are especially likely to change the results: the introduction of regionally-based redistributional policies, as well as the phenomenon of mass migration due to differences in the economic constitutions of states.

6 APPENDIX

This appendix discusses several objections that might be raised against the proposed understanding of Hayek's evolutionary theory. Three aspects are approached: (i) Does Hayek's evolutionary theory include designed rules? (ii) Are rules that overcome prisoner's dilemmas incorporated in the evolutionary explanation? (iii) Is the notion of group selection compatible with the understanding given in section 3?

It might be objected that Hayek is concerned with the spontaneous evolution of cultural rules in the sense that they are not the result of human design, but rather of human action. Certainly the evolution of such cultural rules is an important element in Hayek's work, but the presentation of his evolutionary theory seems to be much too sketchy to restrict it only to this aspect.

Concerning the emergence of rules, Hayek himself is not without ambiguities. There are quotations where he emphasizes an unplanned, accidental emergence, but he underlines equally the importance of individual action in innovating and testing new rules.[46] Individual action necessarily means deliberate and planned action.[47] Therefore, elements of planning and conscious action do not seem to be excluded from Hayek's evolutionary theory. Does this fact contradict the characterization of rule-evolution as spontaneous order, which Hayek emphasized with the notion 'twin idea of evolution and spontaneous order' (Hayek, 1978, p. 250)? Not necessarily, as the concept of spontaneous order emphasizes the notion of unplanned emergence as well as the idea of competitive selection. (See Ullmann-Margalit, 1978 for a sharp differentiation of both aspects.)

Seen from the latter perspective, the spontaneous order is given by the outcome of a decentralized competitive process, but not necessarily by the unplanned emergence of the rules to which individuals adhere (Hayek, 1960, p. 37, Bouillon, 1991, pp. 60ff; for a contrary opinion, see Barry, 1982, p. 45). In this understanding of the Hayekian evolutionary theory, the aspect of competitive selection among rules is more important than the fact of how rules come into being. Evolution as spontaneous order, therefore, in no way restricts innovation procedures to accidental, unplanned events. On the contrary, man's ability to invent and his inclination to try out new solutions in order to improve his situation drive cultural evolution of rules as well as accidental events (see for example Witt, 1989, p. 146). To exclude deliberate human action from an evolutionary theory would invalidate the explanation, as long as it is based on methodological individualism.

Constitutions of state-clubs in the above sense are rule-systems that allow for certain economic activities and guide the economic game within the club. These constitutional rules can be seen as the outcome of a collective decision-making process. Despite the presented understanding of Hayek's evolutionary theory, its appropriateness for explaining such constitutional rules might be questioned.

Along this line, it is sometimes argued that an individualistic invisible-hand notion of evolution could not explain the 'constitutional' result of collective or political processes. Constitutional rules are necessary to overcome Prisoner's Dilemmas (PD). For this aim, they rely on coercion, external to the individuals involved in a PD-game. A solution of Prisoner's Dilemmas without external coercion is proposed by evolutionary game theoretical approaches, but only under very restrictive assumptions (see for example Axelrod, 1984, Sugden, 1986). Thus, it is argued that an evolutionary invisible-hand explanation of constitutional rules is inappropriate.[48] From an institutional club-theoretical perspective, this argument does not really seem convincing. The evolutionary process selects different rule-systems specifically on the grounds of their efficiency in overcoming Prisoner's Dilemmas. It is just for different qualities of state-clubs in solving PD-situations that individuals choose their location. (Critical to this position is Bouillon, 1991, pp. 47–9; compare this analysis with Gray, 1984, pp. 70–1.) This argument applies to the protective state-club as well as to the productive state-club. The former solves the basic free-rider problem of securing property rights, the latter offers solutions to free-rider problems in the financing and provision of club goods.

Migration between state-clubs can thus be understood as a mechanism of an evolutionary selection of rules, no matter how these came into being. Constitutional rules are not excluded from this individualistic choice process, if one relies more on the notion of evolutionary selection than on the idea of spontaneous emergence.

Hayek himself introduces the idea of group selection between rules. The idea of group selection is often interpreted in a social Darwinistic manner as a non-personal, non-individualistic selection via physical extinction. As several authors have pointed out, this explanation is not very convincing in contemporary situations or for explaining short-run phenomena (Witt, 1989, p. 145, Radnitzky, 1984, p. 22, Vanberg, 1986, p. 89, fn. 14).

Surviving in an absolute sense depends on medical care and a minimum level of food. Both require a certain absolute level of wealth that can be attained today without too much difficulty (Witt, 1989, pp. 145 ff). Note that this is rather a theoretical statement than a description of the real world. The conclusion from this argument is that an evolutionary theory, which is based on the idea of group selection, cannot explain selection processes between jurisdictions that have already reached the required minimum level of wealth.[49]

However, arguing in a marginalistic way with an economic concept of individual utility-maximizing, there is no difference between 'surviving' and 'improving one's position'. As long as one adheres to an economic calculus which forms the basis of human action, the selection process need not proceed via physical extinction. It can equally work via individual intergroup migration or imitation of successful rules.[50] Growth of a group would then simply mean that the quantitative relation of rule-adhering individuals to 'outsiders' rises. To state it most clearly: group selection in this understanding does not mean that individuals have to survive, but requires that certain rules survive (Hayek, 1960, p. 59).

Such an interpretation understands group selection as an individualistic concept of choice, so that it may be objected that the term itself becomes meaningless. The club-theoretical approach offers an alternative. The basic reason for the existence of clubs is given by mutual gains in producing or consuming goods jointly. These gains can result out of a common agreement to respect private property rights and to submit to a law-enforcing agency. Furthermore, gains arise as well in using club-goods jointly and in sharing the financing via taxation. In this way, rules that guide economic interaction as well as political competition allow for the generation of co-operation rents. Since these rents are the outcome of human interaction, they form a basis for group selection, as individuals alone cannot generate them. Individuals choose between groups (or clubs) in an attempt to maximize their share of co-operation rents. Seen from this perspective, the notion of group selection still has validity upon removal of the social Darwinistic foundation.

The idea of co-operation rents supports the interpretation of Hayek's evolutionary theory given above, as it concerns the selection between constitutional rules. To profit from co-operation rents in a larger society requires that human action is guided by certain rules – for example the rule of law, which has to be secured by a player external to the underlying Prisoner's Dilemma. Given this understanding, in which Hayek's group selection operates through co-operation rents, it seems appropriate to agree that Hayek's evolutionary theory fits constitutional rules.

Notes

1. Straubhaar and Zimmermann (1992, p. 26). The authors proposed a GAMP only for Europe, but their arguments should be valid on the worldwide level as well.
2. The argument for a GAMP is, furthermore, often based on a public-good problem, since a migration order is assumed to be an international public good. See for example Straubhaar (1990, p. 543). See also Stiglitz (1977) and Myers (1990). This aspect is excluded in this paper.
3. By migration externalities, a variety of economic effects are implied. The following compilation gives, without any claim to completeness, an overview of the most common migration externalities specified in the respective literature. That compilation is mostly based on Grubel (1992) and Layard et al. (1992). For the brain drain see especially Bhagwati and Partington (1976) and Webb (1985). Migration externalities appear in the form of:

- Income redistribution through private markets, especially from labour to capital. For Grubel, these effects form a social externality.
- Population stock externalities and effects on the size of markets: for example, economies of scale in production, the common use of social overhead capital and economies of agglomeration; or – on the other hand – diseconomies of congestion and the problem of pollution.
- Adjustment externalities – as immigration spurs economic growth and therefore promotes structural adjustment; or adjustment diseconomies – because of rapid construction of social overhead facilities and private investment.
- Fiscal externalities through government taxation and spending.
- Effects on the dependency rates in combination with governmental programs on pensions, education and health care.
- 'Social (or cultural) externalities' through social, intellectual and cultural enrichment; or negative externalities, since culture, value systems and social structures have to change. The idea of social externalities closely approaches the communitarian justification of a state (see Walzer, 1983, ch. 2).
- 'Political externalities', since migration prevents governments from reaching certain objectives like educational goals ('brain-drain'), distributional goals, the provision of certain amounts of public goods.

Siebert and Koop (1990) discuss, in the context of institutional competition, the notion of externalities with the help of the differentiation in pecuniary and technological externalities. However, they only refer to the well-known problem of spillover effects of governmental policies. Migration externalities are not discussed in their elaboration on institutional competition.

4. In stating that unregulated migration requires a GAMP, the proponents of migration policies compare institutional settings on the basis of the standard Pareto criterion. However, it is not at all clear whether this criterion would be accepted by the individuals in question as the standard for evaluating migration policies. De Alessi (1992) discusses the problems that arise when institutional solutions are evaluated by an outside standard. Without going into

detail, this paper assumes the underlying standard to be Pareto-efficiency. The reader may either accept this assumption as a value-loaded one, or regard the analysis as an 'as-if' analysis. The question that will be discussed is then: Given Pareto-efficiency as the relevant criterion, how are the arguments for migration policies to be evaluated?

5. This is an example for a more general principle: the recognition of an externality as economically relevant (or irrelevant) always means the acknowledgement of a certain set of property rights (see Demsetz (1982)).

6. In the following discussion I will exclude any redistributive government intervention, since on account of its specific character it poses different problems for migration policies.

7. There are many arguments against an efficient working of the 'voting-with-the-feet' mechanism. As stated, the paper will only discuss the inefficiency arising out of fiscal externalities. This argument was introduced by Buchanan and Wagner (1970) and Buchanan and Goetz (1972). For other 'market failures' in Tiebout-like markets, compare Stiglitz (1977) or Bewley (1981).

8. A public consumption good enters directly into the utility function of individuals, while a public capital good changes the marginal productivity of other factors within the jurisdiction in question. The formal presentation of the migration inefficiency will only include public goods. Congestion costs are not explicitly discussed, as they do not change the fundamental argument. The presentation borrows heavily from Buchanan and Goetz (1972).

9. This assumption is implicitly made in the cited articles and helps to make clear the (claimed) basic inefficiency. The assumption is highly problematic and will be relaxed later.

10. The assumption of a lump-sum tax does not change the results of the analysis, as long as individuals are homogeneous in income and tastes. The effects of alternative tax systems are not analyzed here. Introducing heterogeneous individuals does not change the nature of the assumed inefficiency that will be discussed.

11. The modelling neglects differences between landowners and workers. This assumption is innocent insofar as it does not influence the fundamental argument that is made for migration inefficiency. Land rents are explicitly incorporated for example in Flatters et al. (1974), Stiglitz (1977), Boadway and Flatters (1982).

12. As long as we are concerned with pure public goods, the benefits received by 'those already there' out of a given supply of public goods do not change, if more individuals live in the jurisdiction.

13. Every fiscal externality with respect to the immigration country takes place in a reversed manner with respect to the emigration country. From now on, I will present the argument with the example of immigration and will no longer mention explicitly the emigration country.

14. If the government provided a club good with congestion externalities, the individual benefit out of a given supply of the good would depend on the number of users. Therefore, an optimal size for a jurisdiction would result, as in Tiebout (1956).

15. Flatters et al. (1974) show that, in the case of a pure public good, a compensated elasticity of demand for the public good of unity guarantees the equality of the fiscal externalities.

Another argument for a divergence of the fiscal externalities could be different levels of public capital (see Boadway and Flatters, 1982, Usher, 1977). Furthermore, instead of changing the amount of the immobile factor, land, one could assume different production functions in the jurisdictions in order to generate the claimed inefficiency. Insofar as differences in the production function could mirror different qualities of the law-enforcing state, the presented analysis has relevance for competition between law-enforcing states as well.

16. In the Tiebout model, individual incomes are dividend incomes, and thus do not influence the decision where to locate. Tiebout's analysis approaches, therefore, more nearly a pure club-theoretical analysis than a theory of local public goods.

17. The literature on the subject makes no explicit assumption about the number of jurisdictions, but the prerequisite of locational fixity implies a certain restricted set of regional clubs.

18. The declaration of human rights does not include the right to enter every state one chooses. This leads to the conclusion that state-clubs are seen to have the right to exclude individuals (see Bhagwati (1984)).

19. Sometimes another policy option is discussed. Wildasin (1980) proposed restricting taxation to immobile factors, and allowing taxation of mobile factors only in order to internalize congestion externalities.

The integer problem is assumed away. This problem emerges, when the total number of individuals is not a multiple of the optimal club-size, given that efficient clubs are of the same size. In such a situation, inside efficiency of the clubs does not guarantee overall efficiency of the economy. Compare Ng (1973).

20. It is reported that representatives of several states competed for the Huguenots at Frankfurt, where the latter arrived after being chased by the French government.

21. Note that in reality the price system is already used for immigration policies, e.g. in Canada. In the former GDR, after the wall fell down, citizenships had been sold to Chinese from Hong Kong.

22. Another reason for a certain reluctance towards the practicability of the first-best solution is the political process in modern welfare states. It seems to be quite difficult to implement a long-lasting purely economically-motivated immigration policy, as the history of the European states, as well as that of the United States, shows. In the 1970s the European states – after stopping guest-worker recruiting – allowed the families of foreign workers to follow. This was a change from a purely economic rationale of immigration policy to a policy guided by purely social motivation. An analogy might be the US Immigration Act of 1965, if one adheres to the notion of 'social externalities'. The 'racist' immigration policy – letting in white immigrants from the western hemisphere much more easily than people from the eastern hemisphere – was changed to a quota system with much less discrimination with respect to cultural backgrounds.

23. Pareto-optimal transfers in this respect have been discussed verbally by Buchanan and Wagner (1970) and Buchanan and Goetz (1972). A theoretical modelling can be found in Flatters et al. (1974). See also Boadway and Flatters (1982), Myers (1990), Hercowitz and Pines (1991). See Myers (1990)

for a discussion of problems posed by the implementation of the transfers solution.

24. This knowledge could be generated in a fully competitive Tiebout process, that requires especially an (nearly) unlimited number of state-clubs as well as flexible land markets among jurisdictions. As these conditions are not given, politics inside the state-clubs are necessary as well. Thus, the usual revelation problem for preferences for public goods re-emerges. See for example Epple and Zelenitz (1981). The same aspect is emphasized by Buchanan and Goetz (1972), who argue that, if states were to raise taxes on the basis of pure locational rents, any rational relationship between tax payments and the public (consumption) services paid out of them would be lost.

25. States are not only characterized by formal rules, but also by informal ones. On the one hand, informal rules, as they adapt to formal rules, are indirectly influenced through governmental action. On the other hand, governmental action – in order to be successful – has to take into account the influence of rather stable, cultural informal rules. North (1990) discusses this interdependency at length. The subject of this paper is rule-competition among formal rules set by the government. Informal rules are not discussed explicitly.

26. It is not intended to give an ultimate interpretation of Hayek's evolutionary theory (see especially Hayek, 1960, 1973/83, 1979/82, 1988). Instead I hope to give an understanding that allows conclusions to be drawn for institutional competition between state-clubs. In the appendix, several problems arising out of the proposed reading of Hayek are discussed. In the main text, I will concentrate on its implications for international migration policy.

27. This is not to say that Hayek has nothing to say about the emergence of rules, but he presents only sketchy remarks concerning the emergence of rules. See the appendix (section 6)

28. Hayek (1979/82, pp. 44 ff) Hayek stresses that no governmental monopoly should be guaranteed in the production of collective goods. This implies even an individual right to a reimbursement of tax-money, when the individual gets the service in some other way (Hayek, 1979/82, p. 147).

29. The following quotation underlines this point: '... but in some of these cases [governmental services, P.W.] the question whether the government ought to possess an exclusive right to them is of decisive importance, not merely a question of efficiency but of crucial significance of the preservation of a free society. In these cases the objection against any monopoly powers of government must preponderate, even if such a monopoly should promise services of a higher quality.' Hayek (1979/82, p. 148).

30. In sketching a conjectural history of human development from the hunter society to the Open (Great) Society, Hayek builds explicitly on this feedback mechanism. The economic success of a spontaneous market order, he claims, has allowed for the growth of mankind and forced the involved individuals and groups to rely on abstract rules in order to be competitive. For an interpretation of Hayek's evolutionary theory as fictitious history along these lines, see Pies (1993, ch. 2).

31. See also the analysis of path-dependency in institutional change, for example North (1990, ch. 11). Due to this phenomenon, it might be less costly for an individual to switch to another rule-system by moving to another geographical state-club, than by raising its voice inside its home state-club.

32. The reader might be reminded that, by assumption, there is no redistributive policy involved.
33. Please remember that the analysis does not allow for taxation of land.
34. For that objective, an explicit modelling of the democratic process inside the states is not necessary. Therefore, monopolistic governments that are not submitted to political competition inside the states, that is to say *Leviathan*-governments (see Brennan and Buchanan, 1980), are appropriate. *Leviathan*-governments exclusively provide constitutional rules and club goods in their respective jurisdictions. This kind of modelling does not violate the analogy of a state as a club, since club-members will most likely delegate some tasks to a centralized bureaucracy; then, the emerging principal-agent problem in the political realm can be interpreted, in an extreme case, as a *Leviathan*-government.
35. Governments could profit from a higher number of citizens: (a) as there would be more taxable factors (for example citizens), and (b) as more citizens may be necessary to exploit economies of scale in consumption of the club good, thus leading to higher per capita consumer-rents that could be taxed away.
36. Therefore, the Bhagwati proposal of a never-ending tax obligation to the native state cannot be justified at all on efficiency grounds.
37. A similar point is made by Schwarz (1993), who questions (out of a club-theoretical reasoning) the liberal idea of an unrestricted right to live wherever one wants.
38. The government would aim to maximize per capita fiscal surplus. See for this conclusion Buchanan and Goetz (1972), as well as the literature on the Henry George theorem, for example Stiglitz (1977).
39. Hayek himself makes a similar point in his discussion of federalism and governmental supply of collective goods. He never differentiates between emigration and immigration (see for example 1939/48) and explicitly forbids discrimination in taxation for governments:

> Assuming their powers to be so limited by law as not to restrict free migration, and that they could not discriminate in taxation, their interest would be wholly to attract those who in their particular conditions could make the greatest contribution to the common product. (Hayek, 1979/82, p. 146)

Nonetheless, in the footnote to that paragraph Hayek acknowledges a right to exclude others, at least under a structure of property rights that secure a homogenity of interests in communities and is not built on collective property (1979/82, p. 195, fn. 14). However, this discussion of Hayek is related to local and 'even regional governments' (1979/82, p. 146), and it is highly improbable that the required homogeneity of interests is given on an international level. For federalism on an European scale, Hayek obviously sees a necessity for totally free migration in order to secure a competitive pressure between the states (1939/48). He would sacrifice the efficiency of governmental provision of collective goods, if the foundations of a free society were endangered (1979/82, p. 46, 148). It seems, therefore, that Hayek tends, in order to further institutional competition, more toward a ban on immigration taxes than to their club-theoretical justification.

Concerning the effects of redistribution on migration policy, namely the guarantee of a certain minimal income standard, Hayek is realistic about the possibilities to reintroduce a regime of free migration between states. On the one hand, Hayek denies a personal right to profit from redistribution. He points to the incompatibility of redistributive policy with the idea of a free society, as such a policy would be based on a kind of collective ownership that is not a necessary consequence of governmental service functions (1979/82, pp. 55 ff):

> The fact that all citizens have an interest in the common provision of some services is no justification for anyone's claiming as a right a share in all the benefits... The conception that citizenship or even residence in a country confers a claim to a particular standard of living is becoming a serious source of international friction. (Hayek, 1960, pp. 101 ff)

On the other hand, he acknowledges that, under the given circumstances, the minimum incomes that are secured by different states will differ to such a degree that restrictions on migration are unavoidable.

> We must face the fact that we here encounter a limit to the universal application of those liberal principles of policy which the existing facts of the present world make unavoidable. (Hayek, 1979/82, p. 56)

40. In an extreme situation, there would be no way for citizens of an exploitative state to vote-with-their-feet, as all other states would have reached the optimal club-size and closed their border. See for this 'partition-problem' Ng (1973). Certainly, this is an extreme situation, but it is a further example showing that the competitive pressure exerted via the exit-option is not necessarily strong enough in a neoclassical setting to assure governmental efficiency. See endnote 24.

41. Broadening the assumptions of the discussion here, a further argument against immigration taxes could be brought forward: immigration will affect residents of the immigration country to different degrees. There is a strong presumption that especially workers will oppose immigration. Therefore, in a majority-democracy, it is much more likely to see an immigration policy guided by special interest-groups than by the club-theoretical interest of the whole population. Compare Mises (1985, pp. 136 ff).

42. Seen in this way, the differentiation introduced by Boadway and Flatters (1982, p. 621) in fiscal externalities and rent-sharing externalities becomes irrelevant.

43. See Boadway and Flatters (1982), Myers and Papageorgiou (1993). Boadway and Flatters allow for any sort of resource, while Myers and Papageorgiou assume the amount of the resource to be fixed. If the law-protective state is interpreted as producing public capital (Buchanan, 1975), the analysis fits in this respect the protective state as well.

44. To put it more precisely, there would be no co-operation rent in the public sector of an economy. Co-operation rents through division of labour might arise through network effects in the division of labour. The efficiency of migration might be questioned as the migrant would not take into account the

'division of labour externalities' he imposes on others. Ferrie and Mokyr (1994, p. 119) discuss in this way the efficiency of entrepreneurial immigration to USA in the last century. However, these effects seems to be pecuniary externalities and are normally assumed to be internalized as far as necessary through factor prices in the competitive private economy. This is true at least, as long as one deals with open economies and tradeable goods.

45. Viewed from a dynamic point of view, individuals orientate their migration decisions on growth prospects. From that perspective, land loses importance, as economic growth seems to be much more the result of efficient rules than of differences in land sizes (or other fixed factors). See for example North (1990), Jones (1987), Olson (1993).

46. 'Auch die Regeln, die das Entstehen dieser komplexen Ordnung möglich machten, waren nicht im Vorausblick auf dieses Ergebnis entworfen worden, sondern es haben jene Menschen, die zufällig geeignete Regeln annahmen, infolgedessen eine komplexe Zivilisation entwickelt, die sich als anderen überlegen erwies.' Hayek (1969, p. 42). '... practices adopted for some unknown and perhaps purely accidental reasons.' Hayek (1979/82, p. 155). 'Most of these steps in the evolution of culture were made possible by some individuals breaking some traditional rules and practicing new forms of conduct – not because they understood them to be better, but because the groups which acted on them prospered more than others and grew.' (Ibid., p. 161). 'Even the success of an innovation by a rule-breaker, and the trust of those who follow him,...' (Ibid., p. 167).
For further quotations see Radnitzky (1987, fn. 25).

47. This is true at least for the last stage in Hayek's fictitious history of the evolution of mankind. See Pies (1993).

48. See for example Vanberg (1986, p. 97): 'But the range of its [the individualistic, invisible-hand notion of cultural evolution, P.W.] explanatory applicability and the normative inferences it allows for are clearly limited, not only because ... many rules upon which spontaneous market orders are based are implemented and enforced by some organized apparatus, but also because, for systematic reasons, certain kinds of rules cannot be expected to emerge from and to be enforced by a spontaneous process, except under certain restrictive conditions.'

49. The idea of group selection is often dismissed (Steele, 1987, Vanberg, 1986) as violating the methodological individualism that forms the basis of the idea of spontaneous order (Barry, 1982, p. 2). This criticism is not really convincing as Hayek's theory is much too sketchy in order to argue that he excludes individualistic explanations (like migration between different rule-systems) from his theory. Therefore, Steele's 'Alternative View of Natural Selection of Culture' (1987, p. 186) is not necessarily different from Hayek's point of view.
Note that Pies (1993, p. 51, fn. 38) refuses the criticism of the idea of group selection for another reason. He develops Hayek's evolutionary theory in a three-part historical sketch of the development of mankind. Then, he interprets Hayek as reserving the idea of group selection (in a social Darwinian sense) to the second step in this historical sketch. In this second stage, deliberate conscious action does not yet exist. Man follows rules without knowing why. Therefore, criticisms like Vanberg's (1986), which argues that deliberate conscious action of rule-creating is not explained by Hayek's theory, fade.

50. Hayek might have thought of a social Darwinistic concept. But enlarging, along the lines described, the evolutionary theory he developed will not change the fundamental insights of his work. He himself notes that the spreading of rules takes place by rule-imitation of individuals. '... rules ... which have spread because some practices enhanced the prosperity of certain groups and led to their expansion, perhaps less by more rapid procreation than by the attraction of outsiders.' Hayek (1979/82, p. 159).

References

Alchian, Armen A. (1968) 'Cost', in David L. Sills (ed.), *International Encyclopedia of the Social Sciences* (New York: Crowell Collier and Macmillan) 3, pp. 404–15.

Axelrod, Robert (1984). *The Evolution of Co-operation* (New York: Basic Books).

Barry, Norman (1982) 'The Tradition of Spontaneous Order', *Literature of Liberty*, 5, pp. 7–58.

Becker, Gary S. (1992) 'Comments on Julian Simon on Immigration'. Mont Pèlerin Society General Meeting 1992, Vancouver, Canada, Aug. 30 to Sept. 4.

Bewley, Truman F. (1981) 'A Critique of Tiebout's Theory of Local Public Expenditures', *Econometrica*, 49, pp. 713–40.

Bhagwati, Jagdish (1979) 'International Migration of the Highly Skilled: Economics, Ethics and Taxes', *Third World Quarterly*, 1; pp. 17–30.

____ (1984) 'Incentives and Disincentives: International Migration', *Weltwirtschaftliches Archiv*, 120, pp. 678–701.

____ and Martin Partington (eds.) (1976) *Taxing the Brain Drain: A Proposal, vol. 1* (Amsterdam: North-Holland).

Boadway, Robin and Frank Flatters (1982) 'Efficiency and Equalization Payments in a Federal System of Government: A Synthesis and Extension of Recent Results', *Canadian Journal of Economics*, 15, pp. 613–33.

Bouillon, Hardy (1991) *Ordnung, Evolution und Erkenntnis* (Tübingen: J.C.B. Mohr (Paul Siebeck)).

Brennan, Geoffrey and James M. Buchanan (1980) *The Power to Tax* (Cambridge: Cambridge University Press).

Buchanan, James M. (1969a) *Cost and Choice: An Inquiry in Economic Theory* (Chicago: The University of Chicago Press).

____ (1969b) 'Überfüllung der öffentlichen Einrichtungen: Ein Argument für Staatseingriffe', *Ordo*, 20, pp. 261–76.

____ (1975) *The Limits of Liberty: Between Anarchy and Leviathan* (Chicago: The University of Chicago Press).

____ and C. J. Goetz (1972) 'Efficiency Limits of Fiscal Mobility: An Assessment of the Tiebout Model, *Journal of Public Economics*, 1, pp. 25–43.

____ and Richard R. Wagner (1970) 'An Efficiency Basis for Federal Fiscal Equalization', in J. Margolis (ed.), *The Analysis of Public Output* (New York: NBER, pp. 139–58.

Cornes, Richard and Todd Sandler (1986) *The Theory of Externalities, Public Goods, and Club Goods* (Cambridge: Cambridge University Press).

De Alessi, Louis (1992) 'Efficiency Criteria for Optimal Laws: Objective Standards or Value Judgements', *Constitutional Political Economy*, 3, pp. 321–42.

Demsetz, Harold (1982) 'Barriers to Entry', *American Economic Review,* 72, pp. 47–57.

Downs, Anthony (1957) *An Economic Theory of Democracy* (New York: Harper & Row).

Epple, Dennis and Allan Zelenitz (1981) 'The Implications of Competition among Jurisdictions: Does Tiebout Need Politics?', *Journal of Political Economy,* 89, pp. 1197–1217.

Ferrie, Joseph P. and Joel Mokyr (1994) 'Immigration and Entrepreneurship in the Nineteenth-Century US', in Herbert Giersch (ed.), *Economic Aspects of International Migration* (Berlin: Springer), pp. 115–38.

Flatters, F., B. Henderson and P. Mieszkowski (1974) 'Public Goods, Efficiency, and Regional Fiscal Equalization', *Journal of Public Economics,* 3, pp. 99–112.

Gordon, H. Scott (1954) 'The Economic Theory of a Common-Property Resource: The Fishery', *Journal of Political Economy,* 62, pp. 124–42.

Gray, John (1984) *Hayek on Liberty* (Oxford: Basil Blackwell).

Grubel, Herbert G. (1992) 'The Economic and Social Effects of Immigration', in Steven Globerman (ed.), *The Immigration Dilemma* (Vancouver, BC: The Fraser Institute), pp. 99–127.

Hayek, Friedrich A. von (1939/48) 'The Economic Conditions of Interstate Federalism', in Friedrich August von Hayek, *Individualism and Economic Order* (Chicago: The University of Chicago Press), pp. 255–72.

____ (1960) *The Constitution of Libery* (London: Routledge).

____ (1969) 'Arten der Ordnung', in Friedrich August von Hayek, *Freiburger Studien* (Tübingen: J.C.B. Mohr (Paul Siebeck)), pp. 32–46.

____ (1973/82) *Law, Legislation and Liberty, Vol. 1: Rules and Order* (London: Routledge), 1st ed. 1973, pbk. ed. 1982.

____ (1978) 'Dr. Bernard Mandeville', in Friedrich August von Hayek, *New Studies in Philosophy, Politics, Economics, and the History of Ideas* (London: Routledge & Kegan Paul), pp. 249–66.

____ (1979/82) *Law, Legislation and Liberty, Vol. 3: The Political Order of a Free People* (London: Routledge), 1st ed. 1979, pbk. ed. 1982.

____ (1988) *The Fatal Conceit: The Errors of Socialism* (Edited by W.W. Bartley III (ed.)) (London: Routledge).

Hercowitz, Zvi and David Pines (1991) 'Migration with Fiscal Externalities', *Journal of Public Economics,* 46, pp. 163–80.

Hirschman, Albert O. (1970) *Exit, Voice and Loyalty: Responses to Decline in Firms, Organizations and States* (Cambridge, Mass. and London: Harvard University Press).

Jones, Eric L. (1987) *The European Miracle,* 2nd ed. (Cambridge: Cambridge University Press).

Knight, Frank H. (1924) 'Some Fallacies in the Interpretation of Social Cost', *Quarterly Journal of Economics,* 38, pp. 582–606.

Layard, Richard, Olivier Blanchard, Rudiger Dornbusch and Paul Krugman (1992) *East–West Migration: The Alternatives* (Cambridge, Mass. and London: MIT Press).

Mises, Ludwig von (1985) *Liberalism,* 3rd ed (Irvington-on-Hudson/NY: FEE and San Francisco/CA: Cobden Press).

Myers, Gordon M. (1990) 'Optimality, Free Mobility, and the Regional Authority in a Federation', *Journal of Public Economics,* 43, pp. 107–21.

____ and Yorgos Y. Papageorgiou (1993) 'On the Economic Impact of Political Boundaries Over a Resource-Diversified Territory', in Hiroshi Ohta and Jacques-Francois Thisse (eds), *Does Economic Space Matter? Essays in Honour of Melvin L. Greenhut* (New York: St. Martins Press), pp. 81–94.

Ng, Yew-Kwang (1973) 'The Economic Theory of Clubs: Pareto Optimality Conditions', *Economica*, 40, pp. 291–8.

North, Douglass C. (1990) *Institutions, Institutional Change and Economic Performance* (Cambridge: Cambridge University Press).

Olson, Mancur (1993) 'Why Are Differences in Per Capita Income So Large and Persistent?, in Horst Siebert (ed.), *Economic Growth in the World Economy* (Tübingen: J.C.B. Mohr (Paul Siebeck)), pp. 193–214.

Pies, Ingo (1993) *Normative Institutionenökonomik, Zur Rationalisierung des politischen Liberalismus* (Tübingen: J.C.B. Mohr (Paul Siebeck).

Radnitzky, Gerard (1984) 'Die ungeplante Gesellschaft: Friedrich von Hayek's Theorie der Evolution spontaner Ordnungen und selbstorganisierender Systeme', *Hamburger Jahrbuch für Wirtschafts- und Gesellschaftspolitik*, 29, pp. 9–33.

____ (1987) 'An Economic Theory of the Rise of Civilization and Its Policy Implications: Hayek's Account Generalized', *ORDO*, 38, pp. 47–90.

Schmidt-Trenz, Hans-Jörg and Dieter Schmidtchen (1993) 'Theorie optimaler Rechtsräume, Die Regulierung sozialer Beziehungen durch die Kontrolle von Territorium'. Mimeo, Universität des Saarlandes.

Schwarz, Gerhard (1993) 'Der Bodenmarkt zwischen Freizügigkeit und lokaler Identitätsbewahrung: Einige möglicherweise gar nicht so ketzerische Überlegungen', in Helmut Gröner and Alfred Schüller (eds), *Die europäische Integration als ordnungspolitische Aufgabe* (Stuttgart: Fischer), pp. 261–77.

Siebert, Horst and Michael J. Koop (1990) 'Institutional Competition. A Concept for Europe?, *Aussenwirtschaft*, 45, pp. 439–62.

Steele, David Ramsay (1987) 'Hayek's Theory of Cultural Group Selection', *The Journal of Libertarian Studies*, 8, pp. 171–95.

Stiglitz, Joseph E. (1977) 'The Theory of Local Public Goods', in M.S. Feldstein and R.P. Inman (eds), *The Economics of Public Services* (London: Macmillan), pp. 274–333.

Straubhaar, Thomas (1990) 'Eckpfeiler einer europafähigen schweizerischen Migrationspolitik', *Aussenwirtschaft*, 45, pp. 517–51.

____ and Klaus F. Zimmermann (1992) *Towards a European Migration Policy* Münchener Wirtschaftswissenschaftliche Beiträge, 92–02.

Sugden, Robert (1986) *The Economics of Rights, Co-operation, and Welfare* (Oxford: Blackwell).

Thomas, Brinley (1968) 'Migration, Economic Aspects', in David L. Sills (ed.), *International Encyclopedia of the Social Sciences* (New York: Crowell Collier and Macmillan) vol. 10, pp. 292–300.

Tiebout, Charles M. (1956) 'A Pure Theory of Local Expenditure', *Journal of Political Economy*, 84, pp. 416–24.

Ullmann-Margalit, Edna (1978) 'Invisible-Hand Explanations', *Synthese*, 39, pp. 263–91.

Usher, Dan (1977) 'Public Property and the Effects of Migration Upon Other Residents of the Migrants' Countries of Origin and Destination', *Journal of Political Economy*, 85, pp. 1001–20.

Vanberg, Viktor (1986) 'Spontaneous Market Order and Social Rules: A Critical Examination of F.A. Hayek's Theory of Cultural Evolution', *Economics and Philosophy,* 2, pp. 75–100.

Walzer, Michael (1983) *Spheres of Justice: A Defense of Pluralism and Equality* (New York: Basic Books).

Webb, M.A. (1985) 'Migration and Education Subsidies by Governments: A Game-Theoretic Analysis', *Journal of Public Economics,* 26, pp. 249–62.

Wildasin, David E. (1980) 'Locational Efficiency in a Federal System', *Regional Science and Urban Economics,* 10, pp. 453–71.

Witt, Ulrich, (1989) 'Bemerkungen zu Hayeks Theorie Sozioökonomischer Evolution', *Wirtschaftspolitische Blätter,* 36, pp. 140–8.

6 Competition among Legal Institutions: Implications for the Evolution of Law[*]

Bruce L. Benson

1 INTRODUCTION

Fuller (1964, p. 106) explains that law is 'the enterprise of subjecting human conduct to the governance of rules'; that is, law includes both rules of obligation and institutions to induce recognition of, clarify, and change those rules. The actual characteristics of rules and legal institutions depend on their purpose, however. An individual can expand wealth through productive activities, particularly when they are complemented by voluntary interactions with others, including economic interaction such as co-operative production (e.g., due to specialization and the division of labour) and trade, *and* legal institutions to define and support private property rights facilitate both productivity and voluntary interaction. Hayek distinguishes between the 'order of actions' and the 'order of rules' (1973, p. 98), arguing that the order of rules can emerge spontaneously, just as an order of action does. Rules and their supporting institutions evolve spontaneously because individuals discover that in their voluntary interactions the rules are co-ordinated more effectively under one system or process than under another (Benson, 1989). The relative effectiveness of rules and institutions are discovered as individuals innovate and as they observe, learn from, imitate and migrate to competitive alternatives. Some of the innovations in rules may be deliberately created by co-operating individuals facing a new situation (e.g., new contract clauses) and voluntarily adopted by others, while others evolve even more spontaneously through changes in behaviour that are observed and copied.

[*]This paper draws from a larger project on 'The Evolution of Law' which has been supported by the Earhart Foundation. Discussions with and comments by Randy Holcombe and Kevin Reffett led to significant improvements in the development and presentation of the arguments, as did discussant comments made by Douglas Ginsburg and participants in the Friedrich August von Hayek Symposium on 'Competition Among Institutions' in Freiburg, Germany, June 1–4, 1994, sponsored by the International Institute and the Walter Eucken Institut.

153

An individual can also expand personal wealth by taking wealth from others, however. And significantly, rules and institutions can be developed to generate and/or enforce such a redistribution. Individuals with relatively substantial capacities to use force may design rules for their own benefit and induce those who are harmed to acquiesce out of fear of the coercive institutions of violence. Indeed, only part of the rules in virtually every society evolve through a consensual and largely spontaneous process to facilitate voluntary interaction. Some rules are also deliberately imposed by relatively powerful individuals in order to influence the distribution of wealth.

The fact that some rules are deliberately designed does not mean that the concept of spontaneous evolution does not apply, however. Deliberately-made rules tend to set off spontaneous reactions, whether the rules are intended to facilitate voluntary interaction or to facilitate trans-fers. For instance, deliberate actions which take property rights away from some individuals or make property rights less secure will, in effect, place part of those rights in the 'public domain', thus creating incentives to recapture them (Cheung, 1974). Efforts to deliberately control the evolu-tion of law simply influence the path of that evolution, often in unantici-pated and unintended ways. The analysis of legal evolution must account for the competition and interaction between those rules and institutions of law which evolve to facilitate voluntary interaction, and deliberate com-mands which alter either rules or institutions in order to take property.[1]

2   LAW BY VOLUNTARY CONSENT OR BY COERCIVE COMMAND?

Let us begin with the Hobbesian 'state of nature', assuming that there is no co-operative interaction between individuals. Further assume that while there is considerable uncertainty, and therefore high transactions costs, decisions are *not* made behind a Rawlsian 'veil of ignorance'. Thus, this analysis focuses on the rules and institutions that would emerge assuming that rational decision makers recognize their alternatives and anticipate potential outcomes.

In the absence of scarcity, there would be no reason for conflict and, therefore, no reason for rules, but because of scarcity, conflict over the use of property is inevitable. Securing property claims requires recognition of the owner's 'rights' by others (Umbeck, 1981, p. 39). Therefore, success in turning a property claim into actual ownership requires that an individ-ual acting unilaterally must back a claim with a sufficiently strong threat of violence to induce others to abandon their conflicting claims. Umbeck (1981, pp. 40–1) explains that 'The concept of violence ... could include the actual use of guns, knives or fists, or merely the threat of their use. It could also include building a fort or other protective structures'. Violence is defined here as the use of resources (e.g., capital to build a fort, labour time) allocated to excluding other individuals from using claimed property. Since several individuals are likely to have similar incentives with regard to any particular scarce resource, the competitive process could consume vast amounts of resources as each invests to build a capacity for violence in order to exclude others. Property rights are never completely secure, of course, but if violence can increase the security of an individual's claims it can increase the individual's wealth, as long as the cost of violence is less than the benefits. If this is not the case, violence may not actually materialize.

2.1 Violence Versus Co-operation: Static Considerations

Skaperdas (1992) and Rider (1993) develop two-person, one-period models of co-operation, conflict, and power and deduce three possible outcomes: (i) full co-operation; (ii) partial co-operation; and (iii) conflict.[2] 'Full co-operation', which implies that neither person invests in the tools or violence, occurs *if* it is very difficult for either person to increasing the probability of winning a violent conflict and *if* both parties recognize this (other reasons for co-operation arise in a multi-period game, as suggested below). That is, if the marginal product of investing in conflict is very low so that a large differential in the tools of violence produces only a small change in the probability of winning, then incentives to tacitly co-operate arise. The result is a private property arrangement as each party does not attempt to claim the resources or outputs of the other (Rider, 1993, p. 152), and in contrast to the Hobbesian assumptions and to 'Prisoners' Dilemma' models. 'Conflict' arises when the marginal product of violence is expected to be high for both parties: each believes that increasing investments in the capacity for violence substantially enhances their probabilities of winning. The result may be open conflict, or a stalemate enforced by mutual deterrence, depending on the relative capabilities of the two parties and their perceptions of those capabilities.

'Partial co-operation' occurs when one party's opportunity cost of investing in conflict differs substantially from the other party's. Thus, one individual invests in violence but the other does not. This 'command' arrangement means that the person with a relatively low opportunity cost for violence subjugates and extracts tribute from the relatively productive individual (the individual with a high opportunity cost for violence because of a comparative advantage in the production of consumption goods; that is, new wealth). Such tribute is 'extortion' because the payment is for 'protection' from the individual receiving the payment rather than from other threats. Nonetheless, the subjugated individual chooses a co-operation strategy because yielding to subjugation and command produces greater wealth than he expects to be able to claim through violent conflict, given his comparative disadvantage in violence.[3]

2.2 Dynamic Considerations and Incentives to Contract

If information was costless, so that every individual knew every other individuals' capacity for violence, each individual would only claim the amount of property that he could defend (Umbeck, 1981, p. 41). Indeed, given such knowledge, a stable property rights arrangement could arise. No enforcement mechanism other than the implicit threat of violence would be needed, and no actual investment in violence would occur. Thus, conflict and partial conflict would 'look like' full co-operation. However, this hypothetical outcome is impossible. The requisite knowledge is far from costless to obtain, after all, and in more realistic dynamic situations, individuals' relative capacities for violence change over time.[4] Indeed, this hypothetical is raised because it points to a second complementary reason for Hobbesian conflict; scarcity means competition but transactions costs and uncertainty turn that competition in the direction of violence. The cost of establishing property rights in such a setting can be considerable since it includes the costs that both winners and losers incur. Furthermore, in a dynamic setting, winning is temporary unless the capacity for violence is maintained, and it may be temporary even then. After all, incentives for entry of new competitors exist if the entrants believe that they are stronger than a current successful claimant, and both potential entrants and previous losers have incentives to search for superior technology for violence. Thus, the winner also has incentives to both maintain his existing capacity for and to search for new technologies in violence, to deter existing and potential rivals' investments in violence. Property rights enforced by violence can only be made more secure by investing in a greater capacity for violence.

The Hobbesian conflict results from at least three conditions: (i) scarcity and (ii) uncertainty, as noted above, and (iii) absence of recognized rules. However, any subset of individuals can reduce the costs of conflict by agreeing to establish rules recognizing some subset of each others' claims (Vanberg and Buchanan, 1990, p. 18), *given* that the promise each makes is credible. A sufficiently strong threat of violent retaliation can produce credible promises, but in a dynamic setting other sources of credibility, discussed below, can create an environment of trust rather than fear. Given the option of employing violence as a means of securing property claims, however, a voluntary 'agreement ... must ration to each individual as much wealth as he could [expect to] have through the use of his own force' (Umbeck, 1981, p. 40). Thus, as Umbeck (1981) concludes, force determines the distribution of wealth rather than fairness, even when that distribution is voluntarily agreed upon. Nonetheless, if wealth can be increased for everyone involved relative to what it was expected to be in the absence of such an exchange, then individuals have incentives to enter the exchange, thereby making property rights to some resources more secure without increasing investments in violence. As Umbeck (1981, p. 45) concludes, in an agreement to end conflicts each 'individual gives up any claim he might have made (through force) on the other [persons' resources] ... in exchange for the agreement that other individuals will not exercise (through force) any claims on his assigned [property]'. The substitute 'investment' is acceptance of a rule of obligation to respect others' property rights.

The degree to which individuals reduce their investments in the tools of violence after the agreement depends on how credible the promises are, *and* on the source of the credibility. If the agreement stems from an initial situation involving either partial co-operation or asymmetric conflict the dominant power will demand a relatively large share of the wealth arising from clarified property rights, but he is likely to have to maintain his position of dominance in order to assure credibility on the part of the weaker party. The institutions that evolve to support credible commitments to respect the property rights arrangements will be those of coercion and command. After all, the incentives for a weak party to accept this contract are relatively 'negative' – subjugation is expected to be better than the alternative high probability of losing everything through violent confrontation.

On the other hand, if the agreement arises out of symmetric conflict, the parties may be able to reduce their investments in violence, perhaps even to zero, thereby producing a full co-operation outcome through contracting. The incentives to co-operate in this case are positive: individuals enter the contract because they expect to increase wealth by shifting resources into productive activities as a result of securing property rights claims through contract rather than through mutually-deterring investments in violence. The resulting property rights arrangement still requires the support of legal institutions, as noted below, but they will not rely exclusively on coercion. Under these circumstances, sources of credibility other than violence also will evolve.

2.3   Evolving Sources of Credibility

When an individual's choices regarding interaction with others are part of
a continuous process, with each unique decision representing only one link
in a long-time chain of social interaction, a non-violent source of credibility arises. Promises to accept a commonly recognized set of rules of
behaviour are relatively credible in such a repeated game because each
individual recognizes the long-term benefits of remaining on good terms
with the other party, which may be greater than the immediate benefits of
not co-operating (e.g., violating the rules, investing in and using violence).

Repeated games do not guarantee credibility, of course, but even the
repeated game situation involves weaker incentives for co-operation in
this fashion than those which develop for many individuals who interact
with one another (Tullock, 1985; Benson, 1994a). In particular, if each
individual enters into several different games (whether repeated or one-
shot) with different players, then violence, refusal to recognize widely-
held rules of conduct within one game, etc., can affect the person's
reputation and limit his ability to enter into other games, given that reputation travels from one game to another. When there are players who value
relationships with other reliable players more than the potential benefits
associated with using violence or refusing to follow accepted conduct in
any one single game, the incentives to keep promises that arise from
repeated games are effectively reinforced, because anyone who chooses a
non-co-operative strategy in one game will have difficulty finding a
partner for any further game (Tullock, 1985, pp. 1075–6). Therefore, in
order to maintain a reputation for dealing under recognized rules of behaviour (i.e., for fair and ethical dealings or 'high moral standards'), each
player's dominant strategy may be to behave as expected throughout each
game, whether it is a repeated or a one-shot game. Repeated-game reciprocities and reputation effects should evolve as individuals begin to contract and co-operate, thereby providing alternative sources of credibility
that can, over time, allow reductions in investments in violence.

3   LEGAL INSTITUTIONS: SUPPORTING CONSENT OR COMMAND?

The potential outcomes alluded to above provide the basis for different
kinds of evolving legal systems. At one extreme of a continuum of possible legal institutions, rules and institutions develop exclusively from the
'bottom-up' through voluntary co-operation so the institutions of gover-

nance allow a reduction in investments in violence, and the resulting legal system might be described as one of purely voluntary or consensual law. At the other extreme, if the rules develop from the top down as a powerful individual with an absolute advantage in violence makes slaves of other individuals, the result is a legal system of pure 'authoritarian command'. In between, many other possibilities exist. Some involve predominantly private rights with modest payments of tribute or taxes to someone who has a comparative advantage of violence, and some involve a large degree of extortion and attenuation of property rights through a continued and possibly increasing investment in violence. All such systems 'naturally' evolve under different circumstances, and all may be 'contractual' of course, but in the first extreme case the contract arises through mutual consent while in the second extreme it is established completely through duress. In between, the contract may have elements of both (e.g., the authority may exclusively extort, or combine some extortion with some true protection against outside threats, or actual assistance in the enforcement of internal consensual rules). Consider the two extremes as benchmarks against which to compare intermediate legal arrangements.

3.1 Institutions in a Consensual Legal System

Repeated games and reputation effects are likely to be sufficient to induce co-operation in a consensual legal system for many relationships. Indeed, there is often a simultaneous development of co-operation in law enforcement and other forms of voluntary interaction, since most interactions require some degree of certainty about legal obligations (Benson, 1989). Thus, when consensual groups form, institutions tend to evolve whereby group members are obligated to: (i) act as or provide access to third parties to clarify rules or change them if necessary, through arbitration or mediation of any dispute between members; (ii) assess new rules and dispute settlements to see that they are consistent with the group's goals and existing rules (e.g., customs, practices, contract clauses); and (iii) reinforce incentives to recognize rules, including participation in enforcement when necessary (Benson, 1990, 1994a).

Detailed discussion of all the institutions of a consensual legal system is not possible, given space considerations, but an example should suffice.[5] If a dispute arises, for instance, a mutually acceptable mediator or arbitrator might be chosen from among the respected members of the community, or from a pool of competitive dispute resolution specialists. Since the arbitrator/mediator must be acceptable to both parties, 'fairness' is embodied in the dispute-resolution process. As Buchanan emphasizes

(1975, p. 68), 'Players would not consciously accept the appointment of a referee who was known to be unfair in his enforcement of the rules of the game or at least they would not agree to the same referee in such cases'. Given that the chosen arbitrator/mediator convinces individuals in the group that a judgement should be accepted, the ruling can then be backed by a threat of ostracism by the entire membership. Indeed, refusal to behave accordingly to accepted rules of conduct, including acceptance of a fair settlement, can be 'punished' by exclusion from some or all future interaction with other group members (Benson, 1989, 1990, 1992b, 1994a, 1994b; Milgrom et al., 1990).[6] This sanction reinforces the self-interest motives to maintain reputation and repeated-dealing reciprocities, although in general, dispute resolutions are accepted in consensual groups because individuals recognize the benefits of behaving in accordance with members' expectations, not because they fear ostracism (or violence).

Demsetz (1967) explains that property rights will be defined when the benefits of doing so cover the costs of defining and enforcing such rights. Such benefits may become evident because a dispute arises, implying that existing rules do not adequately cover some new situation. Thus, the chosen arbitrator/mediator will often have to make more precise those rules about which differences of opinion exist, and at times even supply new rules because no generally recognized rules exist to cover a new situation (Hayek, 1973, p. 99). However, a dispute-resolution decision becomes a rule of law within the group only if it is seen as a desirable rule by all affected parties (Benson, 1989, 1990, 1992a, 1994a). It is not coercively imposed on a group by some authority. Thus, rules which best facilitate voluntary interaction tend to be selected over time, while decisions that do not facilitate interaction are not adopted as general rules of obligation.

Dispute resolution is not the only source of evolving rules. Individuals may simply observe that others are behaving in a particular way in light of a new situation, and adopt similar behaviour themselves, recognizing the benefit of avoiding a confrontation by trying to establish a different type of behaviour. As a consequence of adopting such behaviour, the individuals create an obligation to one another to continue the behavioural pattern. Alternatively, a new contract form may develop that improves on existing forms by reducing the potential for uncertainty. Others see the benefits of the new contract form and adopt it as well, so it becomes a standard practice in such situations. Fuller (1981, pp. 224–5) explains that 'the term *contract law*, therefore, refers primarily not to the law *of* or *about* contracts, but to the 'law' a contract itself brings into existence.' The expanding use of contract and development of contractual arrangements is, in fact, a natural event in the evolution of consensual law. As legal arrangements evolve and are improved upon, they tend to become more formal and, therefore, more explicitly contractual. In addition, as the group develops and expands, the trust relationships arising from frequent interaction and low cost information about reputations may be weakened, but conflicts can be avoided by explicitly stating the terms of the interaction *a priori*; that is, by contracting. A carefully constructed and enforceable contract can substitute for reciprocities and reputations.

In general, the institutions of consensual law are competitive (e.g., alternative sources of arbitration are likely to be available; see the discussion of inter-group interaction below for further examples), and voluntary (e.g. contracts) (Benson, 1994a). Contrast these institutions with those of authoritarian law.

3.2 Institutions of Authoritarian Command

Someone intent on establishing authoritarian law will attempt to *claim* exclusive 'sovereignty' (i.e., monopoly power) in the creation and execution of the law. A pure authoritarian system is a monopolized system.

After all, an individual cannot transfer wealth if the potential losers can either: (i) resist by turning to a consensual legal association to defend property against the authoritarian threat; or (ii) find another powerful individual with whom they might exchange relatively less wealth for protection against the claimant to legal authority. A legal system based on a monopoly in violence means that the commitment of the subjects to obey the authority arises exclusively out of fear, and that the authority will be the ultimate (final) source of all rules, all dispute resolution.

Individuals subjugated to authoritarian command have relatively strong incentives to break the law (e.g., steal, revolt) (Benson, 1994c). Therefore, an authority has incentives to insure against changes that might disrupt the stability of the wealth distribution established through force.[7] For instance, an authority may pay others who appear to have the potential to develop a similar comparative advantage in violence in order to reduce the likelihood of competition or resistance. Indeed, the extortionist also has incentives to reduce the cost of violence where it is profitable to do so. Thus, he is likely to buy acquiescence by transferring some wealth to potentially powerful individuals in exchange for an agreement not to oppose his extortion efforts directed at others who are less likely to be able to resist. Such payments may involve the use the authority's institutions of violence to grant to and protect property rights for those who are relatively strong, thereby focusing the tools of violence on relatively weak individuals. As a result, the authoritarian 'protection racket' involves a mix of extortion of the weak and protection of the relatively powerful.

The authority might attempt to insure against the consequences of changes in the distribution of power within his sphere of influence exclusively with pre-emptive large investments in violence, but this is very costly and there is another option. In order to maintain his hold on power, the authority can redistribute wealth as relative power changes. Thus, authoritarian systems tend to transfer to the wealthy and/or powerful. Of course, there is a potential danger of the poor organizing effectively and revolting too, so some transfers may flow in their direction as well, but in a relative sense, transfers to the wealthy and/or powerful will dominate. To facilitate this redistribution process, an authority will develop legal institutions whose primary functions are (i) taking wealth from some and transferring it to others, and (ii) discriminating among sub-groups on the basis of their relative power in order to determine who gains and who loses (Benson, 1990).

A detailed examination of the institutions of authoritarian law is not possible, but consider dispute resolution.[8] When a dispute arises under authoritarian law, wealth transfers are typically the goal of one litigant and avoidance of the transfer is the goal of the other. Under these circumstances, disputes are negative sum competitions: one party wins, another loses, and both incur dispute resolution costs. Such disputes are, therefore, much more adversarial than potential positive sum consensual law disputes.[9] As a result, adjudication, meaning that the judge is backed by threats of coercion to force the disputants into court and impose his decision, is generally necessary. The coercive threat against someone with little influence, who therefore expects to lose, often must involve severe physical or economic harm (imprisonment, confiscation of all property, mutilation, death) backed by institutions to make such threats credible (an army or strong police force).

The authority claims to be the source of all law, so disputes must be taken before his adjudication tribunal. The authority may actually take on a judicial role, as English kings did, for instance, and use military forces to back his rulings, although judicial and policing bureaucracies are certain to arise. As the scope of legal authority expands and property rights attenuations increase, the cost of judicial and policing activities rise.[10] The authority must maintain the claim of supreme law-maker, however, so the judicial system will be hierarchical, allowing appeal to the supreme court (e.g., the king).

A monopoly in legal authority is not likely to actually exist, of course. In reality, no single individual will be powerful enough to establish such an undisputed monopoly in law. A claimant to legal authority will have to compete with others who offer legal systems, some of which will also be potential claimants to sovereignty, and some of which will involve consensual arrangements whose members prefer independence. The authoritarian system alluded to above is what a claimant to authority strives to establish, whether it is ever fully achieved or not. The competition for authority also has implications for legal institutions, however.

3.3 Stability Considerations

As consensual legal arrangements evolve, the wealth-enhancing gains from voluntary interaction begin to materialize, repeated dealings and reputation effects develop, and incentives to maintain the arrangement and improve upon it become stronger. Thus, the *internal dynamics* of a consensual legal arrangement tend to support its maintenance. However, stability is less likely in an authoritarian legal system. A weak person might acquiesce to the demands of the strong but with the intention of breaking the agreement whenever possible and, given high transactions costs of policing, those possibilities will arise. Therefore, a weak individual's promises may not be credible, suggesting that the authority will have to be forever vigilant in policing his claims. Opportunistic breaches may involve theft, but organized revolt is also possible as numerous weak individuals form a co-operative group to take property from the powerful individual.[11]

Since power is a relative concept, the probability of winning in a conflict is a function of the strategies of both parties. Given diminishing marginal productivity in violence, it is easier to increase one side's power when it is lower than the other side's (Skaperdas, 1992, p. 724). The transactions costs of law enforcement under authoritarian command are likely to be high and rising then, relative to those of a consensual legal arrangement. Thus, the *internal dynamics* of authoritarian law are relatively unstable.[12] However, a significant threat to consensual legal arrangements arises from *external* sources.

4 INTERACTION BETWEEN LEGAL SYSTEMS: COMPETITION AND CO-OPERATION

No group is likely to develop its rules and institutions in complete isolation from other groups. Thus, inter-group interactions become probable, including both violent and non-violent competition, as well as legal emulation and co-operation.

4.1   Interactions Between Consensual Law Groups

Voluntary associations imply both the ability to voluntarily join a group, given acceptance by existing members, and to voluntarily withdraw, so inter-group movements are a distinct possibility (see, for example, Pospisil (1971), Umbeck (1981), Benson (1990, 1994a). Indeed, individuals have incentives to 'migrate' to the group which best facilitates voluntary interaction. Furthermore, individuals in groups that gain co-operative members enjoy more opportunities for mutually beneficial interaction so they have incentives to compete to attract or hold membership (the basis of consensual law groups may be geographical proximity, but it may also be kinship, functional proximity as in a trade association or the 'business community', religion, or any of a number of factors that create repeated dealings and/or reputation effects). As a result, members of consensual legal systems have incentives to improve rules faster than other groups, and to imitate desirable institutions and rules developed elsewhere. Competition and emulation lead to standardization of many rules and institutions across similarly functioning groups, although differences may remain, reflecting preferences of various groups' members.

A group does not necessarily have to expand to generate opportunities for beneficial interaction. Indeed, if individuals want to interact, but only on some dimensions, or if they want to maintain different sets of rules for different dimensions of interaction, then parallel 'localized' mutual support groups may be maintained while a 'second order of clustering' (Vanberg and Buchanan, 1990, p. 189) is established, facilitating a relatively limited scope for interaction.

A group whose members insist on strictly imposing their own morality and penalties on outsiders would probably be unable to initiate beneficial inter-group interaction. Thus, if people wish to simultaneously facilitate inter-group interaction and impose laws that differ substantially from the norms in other groups, they have strong incentives to inform outsiders of the differences in order to avoid conflict and minimize the difficulty of maintaining non-standard laws. Part of the reciprocal agreements with other groups may be the explicit recognition of differences in laws and procedures for treating conflicts. This in turn implies that, as inter-group interactions expand, a hierarchical jurisdictional arrangement may become necessary. For example, each localized group may have jurisdiction over disputes between its members, while disputes between members of a confederation of different groups are settled by some 'higher' confederation level court (see Pospisil (1971) and Benson (1990, 1992b, 1994a)). Note that these courts are not 'higher' courts as in authoritarian legal systems where disputes can be appealed and overturned by the supreme authority. Rather, this is a jurisdictional hierarchy defining the role of each court and allowing for increasingly more distant interactions (as in Pospisil (1971) and Benson (1992b, 1994a)). This allows for differences between the law applied within groups *and* between groups (Pospisil, 1971); a monopoly in law is not required.

A judgement involving an inter-group dispute will have to be considered to be a fair one by members of both groups, of course. Thus, an equal number of individuals from each group might serve as an arbitration board (see Benson (1990, 1992b, 1994a)), or a mutually acceptable third party (i.e., an arbitrator or mediator with a reputation for good judgement) might be chosen (as in Pospisil (1971), and Benson (1990, 1994a)). This provides another reason for the tendency toward standardization of rules across parallel groups with similar functions, at least for those functions carried out in the process of inter-group interactions.

Some individual members of each group must recognize the potential benefits of inter-group interaction and be willing to bear the cost of initiating institutional innovations. The resulting innovations must also involve more than just dispute resolution, because such interaction faces a particular transactions cost: the assurance problem. Each individual must feel confident that someone from the other group will not be able to renege on a promise and then escape to the protection of that other group. After all, at least initially, repeated game and reputation effects are localized within each group, and there is limited potential for a boycott sanction. Thus, for second order clustering to develop, some sort of inter-group insurance or bonding arrangement becomes desirable, as well as the establishment of an apparatus for inter-group dispute resolution. As inter-group interaction develops, the mutual support group becomes a surety group as well (Benson, 1990, 1992b, 1994a). Membership of a group then serves as a signal of reputable behaviour, and if a member of a group cannot or will not pay off a debt to someone from the other group, then the debtor's group will. The individual then owes his own group members, so the boycott threat comes into play once again.

The competition/co-operative relationship between consensual legal systems is driven by the desire to facilitate voluntary mutually-beneficial interactions rather than a desire for legal sovereignty. Thus, many different consensual systems can co-exist and interact. An understanding of consensual law requires that groups be the points of reference rather than 'society' as a whole:

'There may then be found utterly and radically different bodies of "law" prevailing among these small units, and generalization concerning what happens in "the" family or in "this type of association" made on the society's level will have its dangers. The total picture of law-stuff in any society includes along with the Great Law-stuff of the Whole, the sublaw-stuff or bylaw-stuff of the lesser working units' (Llewellyn and Hoebel, 1961, p. 28).

There are clearly limits to the extent of an inter-group network of co-operation determined by the relative costs and benefits of information about other groups and their legal systems. The costs of establishing inter-group legal arrangement depend in part on how 'distant' the groups are from one another, where distance can be in terms of geographic space, or in terms of the behavioural norms that are relevant to the groups. Thus, extensive interaction between starkly different groups may not arise. However, these limits are stretched as individuals become members of several groups. After all, as Mises (1985 p. 257) explains,

'Man is not the member of one group only and does not appear on the scene of human affairs solely in the role of a member of one definite group. ... The conflict of groups is not a conflict between neatly integrated herds of men. It is a conflict between various concerns in the minds of individuals.'

Indeed, in any complex society, there are many distinguishable systems of rules and institutions, and yet people from many of these different systems interact regularly without having to call upon any legal authority. Thus, inter-group co-operation appears to be the norm rather than the exception, and it appears to be quite widespread. And with good reason: as Gluckman (1955, p. 20) suggests, 'multiple membership of diverse groups and in diverse relationships is ... the basis of internal cohesion in any society'. An all-inclusive legal system would eliminate the benefits of competition and emulation and undermine the incentives for innovation.
Berman (1983, p. 10) explains that

'It is this plurality of jurisdictions and legal systems that makes the supremacy of law both necessary and possible. ... The very complexity of a common legal *order* containing diverse legal *systems* contributes to legal sophistication. Which court has jurisdiction? Which law is applicable? How are legal differences to be reconciled? ... The pluralism of ... law, ... has been, or once was, a source of development, or growth – legal growth as well as political and economic growth. It also has been, or once was, a source of freedom.'

Berman's 'or once was' phrase recognizes that diverse legal systems are increasingly being subjugated by authoritarian legal systems. Indeed, while consensual legal arrangements tend to be characterized by internal stability, they face a significant external threat to stability. The size of consensual groups and second order clusters are constrained by transactions costs, and in many cases such organizations have been unable to resist takeover by groups co-operating in the production of violence.

4.2 Competition for Authority: Between the Extremes of Pure Consent and Pure Command

As noted above, individuals who depend for their livelihood on a particular coercive institutional arrangement will always attempt to either eliminate or absorb any alternative legal arrangement. Effective authoritarian law requires a monopoly, so a legal authority must claim that it is the source of all law, including consensual law (e.g., custom, contract). In fact, in order to legitimize a claim to be the *one* source of law, an aspiring legal authority will often attempt to adapt many of the co-operatively produced legal institutions to its own purposes, while *selectively* enforcing some widely-held but voluntarily-produced rules and overturning others (Benson, 1990, 1992b, 1994a). Indeed, wealth must exist for a legal authority to have anything to transfer, and the creation of wealth depends on the existence of productive activity which in turn tends to be maximized under a system of private property rights. Thus, a legal authority faces a trade-off. As the transfer process attenuates property rights it reduces the production of wealth, so this long-run cost must be balanced against the short-run gains from transfers. The degree of property rights attenuation is a function of the authority's time horizon. If an authority's claim is relatively tenuous or if he is short-sighted for some other reason, incentives to transfer are relatively strong. A long time-horizon creates stronger incentives to maintain rules initially instituted through consensual legal systems. As a consequence, the break between consensual and authoritarian rules is not always clean.

Competition for legal sovereignty will require large investments in violence. Beyond that, authoritarian law requires much more force to maintain social order than is required under consensual law. It may well be that the scale of violence required to compete for and maintain authority is greater than a single individual can achieve. Therefore, in order to expand the scale of violence, an entrepreneur in extortion may attempt to establish a 'firm' for the co-operative production of violence: others who have a comparative advantage in violence but less entrepreneurial skills, sell their services to the authority as inputs (e.g., army or police personnel). The sale of inputs for the production of violence to an entrepreneurial leader is another reason for transfers of wealth to individuals who are relatively powerful themselves.

As noted above, authoritarian decision-makers discriminate between competing subgroups on the basis of what they can give to the decision-maker in order to insure against opposition. However, competition for authority similarly requires the taking of wealth from relatively weak subgroups in order to transfer it to relatively powerful subgroups in reflection of the self-interest motives of the legal authority (Benson, 1990).[13] Therefore, the discriminatory institutions will support an internal competition for wealth transfers resulting in an exchange between subgroups and the authority. The potential capacity for violence is the important discriminatory criterion in determining internal wealth transfers in a pure authoritarian system, because subgroups offer to support the authority indirectly by agreeing not to challenge his claim to sovereignty.

This capacity can also be extremely important when competition for authority exists. The control of military forces by earls and barons was one of the most important considerations in the early development of law under kingship in England (Benson, 1990, 1992b), for example, and threats of terrorism, strikes, riots and social unrest can be very effective in modern societies as well. But in addition, when competition for authority is important, a subgroup with a capacity for violence can support one competitor directly by selling their violence services.

When competition for authority exists on the higher or central level, a subgroup's ability to gain transfers may be a function of other factors as well. Competition for authority means that some economic wealth may be mobile and exit is possible, either by moving to the area currently controlled by another legal regime or by moving economic support to an internal competitor for authority. Thus, if some members have some property rights and therefore some economic power, the potential arises for making direct payments of tribute to or for withholding payments from particular competitors in exchange for favourable treatment such as protection of their property rights.

The number of members a subgroup has can also be important, perhaps because of the physical force they can bring to bear, but also perhaps because of the votes they can muster to support a particular claimant to authority against his internal competition, as in a representative democracy (clearly a legal arrangement that falls somewhere between the extremes of authoritarian and consensual). Some powerful

subgroups may simply give an authority their tacit support in exchange
for the authority's transfer of rights to them, protection of their property
rights, and/or various other privileges, some of which are suggested
below. Others may have to provide the authority with explicit support,
even yielding some tribute or taxes to the authority in exchange for an
agreement not to take the remainder of their property rights (e.g., there is
an extortion element to the exchange) as well as protection of those
rights from other threats (there is an element of true protection as well).
Still others pay only extortion and get very little protection because they
have virtually nothing to exchange with any of the competitors for
authority.

Individuals' incentives to establish exclusive claims to property, as
well as institutions that facilitate voluntary interaction, are not eliminated
with the advent of authoritarian law. Thus, the transactions costs of eliminating or absorbing consensual legal arrangements may be very high.
Individuals who are not involved in one-shot distribution disputes but,
rather, are attempting to clarify their agreed-upon rules of behaviour, will
often prefer to take disputes to arbitrators, for instance, rather than to the
authoritarian courts which specialize in adversarial disputes over the distribution of wealth. Legal authorities will attempt to eliminate these alternatives if they can, but if they cannot, they will raise the expected costs of
using them, perhaps by declaring them 'illegal' and driving them 'under-
ground', or perhaps by recognizing them but allowing appeal to authoritarian courts, mandating procedural changes, and so on (Benson, 1989,
1990, 1992b, 1994a, 1994b), and this effort will alter the consensual
process.

As the transactions costs associated with using alternative (competitive)
arrangements rise, they become relatively less attractive and their effectiveness is gradually undermined. Nonetheless, 'extrajudicial processes
will develop...; so will self-help procedures' (Nader and Todd, 1978,
p. 38). After all, if the physical and/or economic sanctions threatened by
the authority are less effective means of making promises credible than the
repeated-dealings and reputation effects (the threat of ostracism) in a consensual law group (a distinct possibility since the authority will back the
strongest interest groups even if they break promises) then violence can
increase as more individuals are incorporated into an authoritarian legal
system. Indeed, the role of unilateral violence in the protection of persons
and property re-emerges as the authority raises the costs of membership in
and undermines the cohesion of consensual groups. The authority will
declare 'vigilante' justice 'illegal' but the breakdown of consensual associations along with authoritarian institutions' focus on wealth distribution

rather than property rights leaves few alternatives for individuals with little 'political power'.

Whether intentional or not, deliberate efforts to create rules will tend to raise transactions costs:

> The spontaneous order arises from each element balancing all the various factors operating on it and by adjusting all its various actions to each other, a balance which will be destroyed if some of the actions are determined by another agency on the basis of different knowledge and in the services of different ends' (Hayek, 1973, p. 51)

Indeed, because legal authorities will not fully anticipate the consequences of their actions, an important implication of an authoritarian command is that there will be a train of readjustments through time. Under authoritarian law, property rights are never 'given': they are permanently 'in play' (Jasay, 1995). Furthermore, as Leoni (1961, p. 17) explains, 'the very possibility of nullifying agreements and conventions through supervening legislation tends in the long run to induce people to fail to rely on any existing conventions or to keep any accepted agreements'. Thus, when rights are significantly altered through authoritarian changes, or when they become sufficiently tenuous due to frequent changes, individuals' behaviour will change. Given the loss of right, for instance, individuals will quit performing previously worthwhile functions (e.g, providing goods or services). If the function is demanded by powerful groups, the legal authority will either try to force the previous behaviour, or directly produce the function (Benson, 1990, 1992b, 1994a, 1994b).

To the degree that a legal authority is successful in legitimizing its claims to sovereignty, the result is a perception of a single system of law.[14] Authoritarian legitimization has been so successful that, as Fuller (1981, pp. 156–7) suggests:

> '...instead of being perceived as distinctive interactional processes, [law is] seen as unidirectional exercises of ... power. Contract is perceived, not as a source of "law" or social ordering in itself, but of something that derives its whole significance from the fact that the courts of the [authority] stand ready to enforce it.'

Authoritarian law is far from completely dominant, however. Resistance to legal authority is most likely to arise where the benefits from voluntary interaction are very large and/or the group interacts across the jurisdictions of different authorities. The medieval 'Law Merchant' is one such example (Berman, 1993; Milgrom, et al., 1990; Benson, 1989, 1990, 1994a), and modern international commercial law is still largely voluntarily produced and enforced (Berman and Dasser, 1990; Benson, 1989, 1990, 1992a, 1994a). Many other consensual law systems have not survived however. At some point these evolutionary processes have been interrupted and/or redirected by internal or external forces. The interruption can be abrupt, through military conquest or a coup, or gradual, as the incentives to voluntarily interact for mutual gain breakdown because authoritarian institutions expand their scope and raise transactions cost for alternatives. Of course, a legal authority can also overstep his powers, leading to revolution and a movement back toward more consensual rules and institutions. Furthermore, revolutionaries may establish 'constitutional' constraints which separate powers, forcing competition between authoritarian institutions and slowing the evolution of authoritarian law. Thus, legal evolution is shaped by continuing conflict between voluntary arrangements and authority. In some cases voluntary arrangements dominate, while in others authority does; but in most cases, a combination exists in an unstable social order.

5 CONCLUSIONS

Consensual rules and institutions evolve through a process of natural selection. Presumably, this implies that rules and institutions which more effectively facilitate mutual interaction tend to replace those which are less effective.[15] Since authoritarian law often replaces or at least absorbs and builds upon rules and institutions established voluntarily, a 'consequentialist' (Jasay, 1995) could contend that the authoritarian system must be more effective. This is not the case, however, even if passing the test of survival implies that an institution is effective relative to its alternatives. It is certainly conceivable that the evolution of authoritarian law will be similar to the evolution of consensual law in the sense that the rules and institutions which best facilitate the purposes of the respective institutions might tend to survive while less effective rules and institutions are rejected.[16] Thus, the resulting institutions could be equally effective at fulfilling their purposes, but those purposes are different. Institutions which best facilitate involuntary transfers are quite different from those which best facilitate voluntary interactions.

Notes

1. The term 'institutions' is used in a variety of ways. As Vanberg and Kerber (1995, p. 1) note, it frequently means a 'configuration of interconnected rules', for instance, so the set of rules of conduct might be thought of as an institution. Here the term is used to describe the organizations or collections of institutions that support the rules of conduct (i.e., the configuration of organizational rules) as in Vanberg and Kerber, although it will be maintained that these institutions can evolve spontaneously, much as the configuration of general rules of conduct do.

2. Rider (1993) divides partial co-operation and conflict into two separate possibilities each, but a continuum of possibilities actually arises – see Benson (1994c) and note 3.

3. It may be that the person choosing to pay the tribute could effectively produce a sufficient counterforce to overthrow the subjugator, but if the tribute demanded is not too great, the opportunity costs of producing this counterforce is too high to make it worthwhile. Thus, the subjugator is constrained in how much he can extract. In this light, a continuum of 'tributes' is possible, ranging from 'slavery' (Rider, 1993) when one person has an absolute advantage in violence, to modest taxes for individuals who could also produce effective violence if pressed. See Benson (1994c) for discussion of this continuum of possible outcomes.

4. Umbeck's conclusion also appears to involve an assumption of no strategic kinds of behaviour on the part of the players; e.g., even with full knowledge of capacities for violence, if everyone believes that no one else is going to invest in violence, then everyone actually may have incentives to do so, given that the marginal product of violence is relatively high and/or a pre-emptive strike could win the conflict. This assumption might be very appropriate in Umbeck's case study of California gold camps, because the opportunity costs of violence was probably expected to be very high (sacrificing or mining activities). However, in a more generalizable setting, the likelihood of strategic interplay suggests that such a stable equilibrium is highly unlikely, reinforcing the arguments made below.

5. See Benson (1994a) for extensive discussion of consensual legal institutions for non-violent dispute resolution, participatory policing, ostracism sanctions, mutual insurance, surety or bonding, and legal change, and for references to literature examining many examples of such legal arrangements.

6. Ostracism evolves from individuals' responses to information about reputations, so consensual legal institutions evolve to facilitate the flow of such information (Benson, 1994a).

7. Consensual legal arrangements also may establish insurance systems to reduce the possibility of a property rights arrangement being disrupted (Benson, 1994a, 1994c).

8. See Benson (1990, 1992b, 1994a, 1994b) regarding the evolution of authoritarian institutions for policing, courts, prosecution, 'representation', punishment such as prisons, etc..

9. Disputes in a consensual system will also be adversarial, of course, as the immediate decision causes one party to gain and another to lose, but this short-term adversarial issue is only part of the outcome. Another part is that

solution of the dispute maintains or reestablishes long-term interactions of mutual gain.

10. As bureaux increase in number and/or size the ability of higher authorities to monitor their actions decreases, their power grows relative to the power of those they supervise (e.g, non-bureaucratic interest groups), and those they originally obtained authority from (e.g., kings and legislators). Furthermore, bureaucracies become interest groups which demand more rights modifications to enforce (Benson, 1990), thus resulting in wealth transfer to bureaucrats (i.e, larger budgets and/or more power).

11. Opportunistic breaches of consent contracts are also possible, of course. This incentives issue is a relative one rather than an absolute one. Under a consent contract, everyone is likely to be relatively better off than they would be if the contract breaks down and the group returned to the state of nature. A risk-averse individual will recognize this when considering an opportunistic breach, and consider the expected outcome given the probabilities of a successful and an unsuccessful breach, relative to the status quo. On the other hand, a slave could well be better off in a state of nature, given that the master is successfully overthrown, and the status quo is clearly relatively undesirable. Thus, the incentives to find a way to successfully breach are relatively strong. See Gauthier (1986, pp. 190–232) for related arguments.

12. As a consequence, of course, institutions will evolve to secure the authority's claim to power (i.e., to protect his source of wealth).

13. The theory of authoritarian law is not simply a restatement of the 'rent-seeking' theory of the state. For instance, powerful entities other than geographically-defined nation-states compete for authority and attempt to employ authoritarian legal institutions, such as the medieval Roman Church (Benson, 1990) and modern organized crime (Benson, 1994a).

14. See Benson (1994a) for additional examples of efforts to legitimize claims of legal sovereignty.

15. This discussion and others that have preceded it may imply that an 'efficient' system of property rights evolves under consensual law. Indeed, this may be a reasonable inference to draw, although it is not proven nor claimed here. At one level it is a trivial issue, of course. Given a consensual legal system, survival of a rule implies that is efficient because the transactions cost of changing it exceeds the benefits. However, in the context of a comparative institutions analysis, the issue is more complex. To make such a claim, factors like the potential outcome of alternative institutional arrangements, the extent of experimentation, competition and emulation, the ease of exit and entry, the size of consensual law groups and the extent of network externalities would all have to be addressed (Benson, 1994a) – a requirement that goes beyond the scope of the present discussion.

16. Whether this is in fact the case is certainly not proven here, nor is it claimed. There are 'consequentialists' who contend that if an institution passes the 'survival test' it must be efficient, however, and if they are correct, then the point made here is clearly relevant. The larger point is simply that the fact that institutions of authoritarian law are widely observed does not prove that they are necessary for facilitating voluntary interaction, or that they are even the most effective institutions for that purpose.

References

Benson, Bruce (1989) 'The Spontaneous Evolution of Commercial Law', *Southern Economic Journal*, 55: pp. 644–61.

_____ (1990) *The Enterprise of Law: Justice Without the State* (San Francisco: Pacific Research Institute for Public Policy).

_____ (1992a) 'Customary Law as a Social Contract: International Commercial Law', *Constitutional Political Economy*, 2: pp. 1–27.

_____ (1992b) 'The Development of Criminal Law and Its Enforcement: Public Interest or Political Transfers', *Journal des Economistes et des Etudes Humaines*, 3: pp. 79–108.

_____ (1994a) *An Economic Analysis of The Evolution of Law*. Florida State University: Mimeo.

_____ (1994b) 'Are Public Goods Really Common Pools: Considerations of the Evolution of Policing and Highways in England', *Economic Inquiry*, 32: pp. 249–71.

_____ (1994c) 'Emerging from the Hobbesian Jungle: Might Takes and Makes Rights', *Constitutional Political Economy*, 5: pp. 729–59.

Berman, Harold (1983) *Law and Revolution: The Formation of Western Legal Tradition* (Cambridge, Mass.: Harvard University Press).

_____ and Felix Dasser (1990) 'The "New" Law Merchant and the "Old": Sources, Content, and Legitimacy' in Thomas E. Carbonneau (ed.), *Lex Mercatoria and Arbitration: A Discussion of the New Law Merchant* (Dobbs Ferry, NY: Transnational Juris Publications).

Buchanan, James (1975) *The Limits of Liberty* (Chicago: University of Chicago Press).

Cheung, Steven (1974) 'A Theory of Price Control', *Journal of Law and Economics*, 17: pp. 53–72.

Demsetz, Harold (1967) 'Toward a Theory of Property Rights', *American Economic Review*, 57: pp. 347–59.

Fuller, Lon (1964) *The Morality of Law* (New Haven: Yale University Press).

_____ (1981) *The Principles of Social Order* (Durham, NC: Duke University Press).

Gauthier, David (1986) *Morals by Agreement* (Oxford: The Clarendon Press).

Gluckman, M. (1955) *The Judicial Process Among the Barotse of Northern Rhodesia* (Manchester University Press of the Rhodes–Livingston Institute).

Hayek, Friedrich (1973), *Law, Legislation, and Liberty*, Vol. 1 (Chicago: University of Chicago Press).

Jasay, Anthony (1995) 'Values and the Social Order', in Gerard Radnitzky (ed.), *Values and the Social Order* (Aldershot, England: Avebury).

Leoni, Bruno (1961) *Freedom and the Law* (Los Angeles: Nash).

Llewellyn, Karl and E. Adamson Hoebel (1961) *The Cheyenne Way* (Norman; University of Oklahoma Press).

Milgrom, Paul, Douglass North and Barry Weingast (1990) 'The Role of Institutions in the Revival of Trade: The Law Merchant, Private Judges, and the Champagne Fairs', *Economics and Politics*, 2: pp. 1–23.

Mises, Ludwig (1985) *Theory and History: An Interpretation of Social and Economic Evolution* (Auburn, Al.: Ludwig von Mises Institute).

Nader, Laura and Harry Todd, Jr. (1978) 'Introduction: The Dispute Process', in Laura Nader and Harry Todd, Jr. (eds), *The Disputing Process – Law in Ten Societies* (New York: Columbia University Press).

Pospisil, Leopold (1971) *Anthropology of Law: A Comparative Theory* (New York: Harper & Row).

Rider, Robert (1993) 'War Pillage, and Markets', *Public Choice,* 75: pp. 149–56.

Skaperdas, Stergios (1992) 'Cooperation, Conflict, and Power in the Absence of Property Rights', *American Economic Review,* 82: pp. 720–39.

Tullock, Gordon (1985) 'Adam Smith and the Prisoners' Dilemma', *Quarterly Journal of Economics,* 100: pp. 1073–81.

Umbeck, John (1981) 'Might Makes Right: A Theory of the Foundation and Initial Distribution of Property Rights', *Economic Inquiry,* 19: pp. 38–59.

Vanberg, Viktor and James Buchanan (1990) 'Rational Choice and Moral Order', in James Nichols, Jr. and Colin Wright (eds), *From Political Economy to Economics and Back?* (San Francisco: Institute for Contemporary Studies).

____ and Wolfgang Kerber (1995) 'Competition Among Institutions: Evolution Within Constraints'. In this volume.

7 Competitions of Socio-Economic Institutions: In Search of the Winners*

Pavel Pelikan

INTRODUCTION

This paper consists of three sections, each with a particular objective. The first section suggests a simple conceptual model of the role of institutions in social systems, to provide the present discussion with a clear conceptual framework, and perhaps also contribute to increasing the precision of the study of institutions in general. While the study of institutions is certainly more difficult to provide with a precise conceptual basis than quantitative studies of resource allocation, much improvement is still possible.

Section 2, assuming that in their competitions some institutions will win and other lose, inquires into the properties of potential winners. As I will argue that such winners can also be seen as potential institutional equilibria, to which social evolution, if not prematurely interrupted, might converge, properties of the winners will thus also be properties of such equilibria. But the paper aims only to inquire into such properties without aspiring to find them. Although some features of the winners will roughly be indicated, I wish above all to discuss the inquiry as such, to argue that it can be a fruitful one, and to point out the great social value of the knowledge that it can produce.

To avoid misunderstanding, two more points should be emphasized. First, institutional equilibria are of a substantially higher order than the resource allocation equilibria studied by standard economics. As will be explained more carefully below, to admit that the institutions of a society might stabilize is far from saying that such a society would petrify. Extensive social learning, restructuring and adapting may keep going on in a society with stable institutional rules – provided that they are what will be defined as 'adaptively efficient' – much as extensive learning, restructuring and adapting may keep going on in a brain with a stable set of

_____

*I thank Nicolai Foss, Lüder Gerken, Douglass North, and Viktor Vanberg for valuable comments on earlier drafts. The remaining errors and conclusions are mine.

177

genes. Second, to search for properties of institutional equilibria is not to try to predict the actual course of future social evolution. Such equilibria can only be used as orientation points in the space of alternative institutional forms, where the actual trajectories of social evolution can be mapped. Not even with the best knowledge of these equilibria could we predict how the trajectories will actually continue and where they will lead.

The concern for the actual outcomes of social evolution motivates the objective of section 3. While section 2 investigates effects of given institutions, and is thus about institutional statics, section 3 is about institutional dynamics. Its central questions are, what are the forces that drive institutional change?, and how can they be influenced by deliberate policies? The focus will be on policies that can help institutions to converge to a favourable equilibrium, or at least steer clear of deep crisis, and thus save societies from uninformed trials leading to costly errors. Theoretical knowledge, in particular of the kind that students of social evolution can produce, will be found to play a crucial role. Such knowledge will be predicted to grow in importance for the policies, and consequently also for the evolution studied.

In agreement with Hayek (1973, 1979), it is policies which modify or replace institutional rules, and not those intervening in specific outcomes, that will be found to have the greatest potential. But somewhat in opposition to his pessimistic view of limitations of human knowledge, the present argument will argue that much of relevant knowledge can be obtained, and that such knowledge will grow and become an increasingly important factor of future social evolution. It is with its help that costly policy errors can be avoided and institutional rules with intended consequences designed. To be sure, Hayek's criticism of the naive social engineering which caused so many disasters is fully shared. But considerable merit can be found in social engineering enlightened by relevant knowledge. Without such engineering, as the current problems with post-socialist transformation clearly show, the disasters caused by the naive engineers could hardly ever be repaired.

Strictly speaking, however, it is not entirely clear how much this view opposes Hayek. When he speaks of limitations of human knowledge, he usually means 'factual knowledge' of specific events in time and place (cf., e.g., Hayek, 1973, Chapter 1). But this is what in our computer age we would call 'data' rather than 'knowledge'. In the present argument, the relevant knowledge is about functional consequences of institutional rules. Thus, this is rather 'theoretical knowledge', concerned with functions and relationships, such as causal chains and natural laws, and not specific events. Hayek is less clear about human limitations in this type of knowledge, although some of his pessimism seems to persist even here. He often puts institutional rules in the class of phenomena that are the result of human actions, but not of human design (1973, p. 20), which can be interpreted to mean that humans cannot design rules with intended consequences. On the other hand, however, he engaged in designing such rules himself (Hayek, 1979).

The present argument is also somewhat more optimistic than that of North (1990), who seems to doubt that poor societies could ever break the dependence on their unfavourable initial paths. Without exaggerating the optimism, however, it only implies that production and dissemination of relevant knowledge can make such a break somewhat less unlikely, and thus increase the hope, be it only slightly, that even such societies will reach some favourable outcomes – or at least avoid the most disastrous ones.

This criticism of Hayek and North is not intended to negate the important contribution they both made to the production of relevant knowledge. It only intends to draw attention to their omission to endogenize the knowledge they produced into the social evolution they studied. It is an important part of the third objective to indicate how this omission could be corrected.

1 THE ROLE OF INSTITUTIONS IN SOCIAL SYSTEMS

1.1 Systems, Structures, and Institutions

In ordinary language, and sometimes also in theoretical discussions, the term 'institution' can mean two very different things: a lasting organization (e.g., a central bank, a ministry, an old firm), or a rule constraining choices (e.g., a law, a cultural norm). In agreement with most modern institutional economists, the term will be employed here only in its second meaning. In this meaning, 'institutions' correspond to what Hayek calls 'abstract rules of conduct' and can conveniently be visualized as the rules of a game.

Each organized social system (organization) – be it a nation-state, a national economy, a firm or an agency – can be seen to have a set of institutions of its own. They may be in part written and formally enforced, such as codified laws, and in part unwritten and informally sanctioned, as is the case with cultural norms.

A social system involves a collection of agents, who are organized, and/or organize themselves, into a certain (organizational) structure. Each agent assumes a certain role, characterized by a certain choice set and connected by certain channels – e.g., through a market or a hierarchy – to other roles, assumed by other agents. In this definition, 'structure' seems to roughly correspond to what Hayek calls 'order'. It contains not only abstract rules, but also agents that act and interact under the guidance (constraints) of the rules. It can be visualized as the operating and performing 'body' of the system.

To illustrate the difference between institutions and structures, let me consider a national economy. Examples of its institutions are property rights, corporate law, antitrust law and constitutional constraints on government economic activities. Examples of what constitutes its structure are established firms, existing markets and actual government agencies.

Within a structure, agents' choices may be about exchanges (transactions) along existing channels with agents in established roles – in other words, about actions which make an actual structure operate. But the choices may also concern modification of the channels and/or the roles and/or the assignment of agents to roles – in other words, the actions by which the structure is organized and reorganized.

In addition to other constraints – such as physical and economic ones – institutions constrain both kinds of choices. In other words, within the sets of physically and economically feasible actions which the agents might choose, given their inherent ('untamed') behavioural characteristics, institutions restrict their choices to certain permissible subsets. In this way, institutions influence (govern, regulate) both the operating and the organizing of the structure. If the structure is visualized as the system's 'body', institutions can be visualized as the system's 'genes' (Pelikan, 1988, 1992). To be sure, institutions are part of the structure, much as genes are part of the body. For institutions to be effective, they must indeed be internalized in each of the agents concerned. But from the point of view of system dynamics, this is a very special part: transcending individual agents, institutions may remain constant, while providing for and regulating changes of the structure – much as constant genes provide for and regulate the development of the body.

More precisely, system dynamics consists of three types of processes: (i) exchanges (transactions) of information and resources within an established structure; (ii) changes (evolution) of the structure under prevailing institutions; and (iii) changes (evolution) of the institutions.

For the study of institutions, it is the difference between (i) and (ii) on the one hand, and (iii) on the other hand, that is essential. While in (i) and (ii), institutions are seen to remain stable while regulating changes of other variables, in (iii) they are subject to changes themselves. In other words, (i) and (ii) belong to what may be termed institutional statics, whereas (iii) belongs to institutional dynamics.

In institutional statics, which will be the perspective of Section 2, the state of a system that changes over time thus consists of two main parts: (a) the state of the structure (the system's actual 'body'), which changes relatively slowly, and (b) the information and resources exchanged or stored within this structure, which change somewhat faster. Some of this information and/or resources may come from other systems; this is what constitutes the system's input. And some of the information and/or resources can go to other systems, which is what constitutes the system's output.

It is convenient, and for most of institutional economics fully sufficient, to think of discrete time consisting of a series of periods, in which the state of a system changes through a corresponding series of transformations. The system's state and input at the beginning of a period is transformed into the state (including output) at the end of the period. The system's institutions can then be seen as the transformation function that governs this process.

The fact that the transformations of stocks and flows of resources also strongly depend on the actual state of the structure, which is being transformed at a slower pace, makes the role of institutions somewhat more complex than this summary description implies. But it will be easier to discuss this complexity in the specific context of economic institutions (section 1.4) – the only context in which it will interest us here.

1.2 A Biological Lesson

The formal correspondence between the couple 'institutions-structure' and the couple 'genes-body' is instructive. It allows us to follow the old recommendation by Marshall and learn a lesson from biology, and more precisely from the relatively recent view that a body ('phenotype') is an *expression* of its genes ('genotype'). Emphatically, this does not mean that the genes alone determine the body. Much of the organizing of the body consists of spontaneous chemical reactions of atoms and molecules, possibly under a strong influence of environmental factors. But the genes are crucial in constraining the vast tree of all the chemically and physically possible reactions into a relatively narrow path that leads to the forming of a certain organism, and not others. The first lesson is that in a formally similar way, the structure of a social system can also be viewed as an expression of its institutions – provided that we replace the view of spontaneous chemical reactions of atoms and molecules by the view of spontaneous associating and (self-) organizing of human beings.

This reverses the usual perspective. An egg is no longer a chicken's way of making another chicken, but, as Samuel Butler put it more than a century ago, a chicken is an egg's way of making another egg. In biology, as exposed by Dawkins (1976, 1982), this reversed perspective can substantially improve our understanding of natural selection. The key is to see the units of selection as the genes, rather than the individual organisms or groups of organisms. The organisms that certain genes have helped to organize are only carriers of these genes and testing grounds of the genes' abilities. In fact, as Dawkins shows in his discussion of 'extended phenotypes', the testing grounds may include several more levels – such as artifacts and societies – where genes also express themselves, be it only at arm's length, and need to succeed.

The lesson can be summarized as follows. From the reversed perspective, it is the institutional rules that are basic, rather than the organizations as structures. It is these rules that are the units of selection in social evolution, whereas all the operating and interacting structures – be they tribes, firms, or nation-states – are only carriers and testing-grounds of the institutional rules which shape them and govern their functioning. The main outcome of social evolution, and the memory of the information produced, is thus a pool of institutional rules, rather than specific groups or societies – much as the main outcome of biological evolution are genetic pools, and not specific organisms or groups of organisms.

Biology, however, has its specific features, which set limits to what we can usefully learn from it. One of them is replication, in the sense of producing series of generations of offsprings. Replication is a clever trick by which nature increases the speed and the scope of its experimenting with genes, under the biochemical constraint that each organism is tied to a basically constant set of genes. Trying different sets of genes therefore requires new organisms, and usually also the death of old ones. Thus, contrary to what some evolutionary economists do, we should not try to find at any price an exact social analogue to biological replicating. Social and economic systems have other possibilities and constraints. New institutional rules can often be tried within an existing system, while some systems – such as national economies – can hardly die and can never start from zero again.

That new institutions can be tried within an existing organization qualifies the proposition that structures are expressions of institutions. This remains true only in the long run. In the short run, newly-tried institutions cannot help inheriting the structure from their predecessors. While within an inherited structure, choices of individual agents can be reoriented quite rapidly, it takes a much longer time before the structure itself becomes a reasonable expression of the new institutions – that is, before the inherited firms and markets are replaced by reasonably developed new ones.[1]

But this qualification does not change the basic view of institutions as the units of selection in social evolution. In this view, it is basically through competitions of institutions that this evolution proceeds. For students of social evolution, this Symposium could not indeed choose a more central topic.

1.3 A Simple Model of a Sovereign Social System

In general, social systems may form hierarchies. The member-agents of a social system are often systems of their own, made of smaller member-agents, while the entire system may be a member-agent of a larger system. A hierarchy of systems then implies hierarchies of structures and institutions. An example is a large firm that is a member-agent of a national economy. While both have institutions of their own, the firm's internal institutions must comply with the constraints of the national economic institutions (e.g., corporate law and labour law).

In most of the present discussion, however, it will be possible to avoid the problems of such hierarchies by focusing on social systems that can be classified as sovereign – in other words, that are not formally parts of larger social systems and thus subject to institutions of a higher level. Typical examples of such systems are modern nation-states and ancient tribes.

A fruitful way of depicting such a system is to divide it into three relatively separate systems: economic, political and cultural (in the broad anthropological meaning of this term). This division is of course highly stylized and corresponds more to the conventional division of labour in the social sciences than to hard empirical facts. The three systems have in common a population of individuals, who play the roles of economic agents, political agents, and cultural agents at the same time. It is through individual brains that the three systems are most importantly interrelated.

Let me briefly consider the systems one after the other, to note what in their states will be of importance for the present discussion. I see the economic system as meriting most attention. This is not because I happen to be an economist, but because the performance of this system turns out to play a privileged role in determining the fate of all types of institutions. We need to pay attention to both its structure and its output, and moreover to distinguish the supply structure, consisting of producers, from the demand structure, consisting of final consumers. We also need to note which of these agents have been implanted there by government. As will become clear below, much of the relevant knowledge about winning institutions is precisely about the economic role that they can allow, or must require, a politically selected government to assume.

The output of the economic system is important in two ways. It is, by definition, what provides all the private and public goods and services that the members of the society need for their physical survival and mental well-being, and also for their participation in the working of the political and the cultural systems. In addition, the experience with the economic system is an important source of information for both individual and social learning.

In the political and the cultural systems, we only need to consider a few aspects. In the political system, there are only two factors to assess: (i) codified law, which is the source of written and formally enforced institutional rules; and (ii) specific government, including government-selected economic agents – such as policy-making and/or planning agencies, agencies of procurement of public goods, and the principals of government-owned firms – to assume the economic roles that government is institutionally allowed or required to play.

In the cultural system we need to consider three aspects: (i) cultural norms (custom), that provide unwritten and informally-sanctioned institutional rules; (ii) preferences in the broadest meaning of this term, including tastes, interests, and values; and (iii) beliefs, including beliefs about the states and the behaviours of both nature and society. Preferences and beliefs are the main determinants of individual behaviour in all three systems. Preferences determine the objectives pursued and the types of incentives to which individuals effectively respond. Beliefs – based in different proportions on religions, ideologies, and scientific (refutable) knowledge – determine the mental models that individuals use to predict future states of nature and society, including consequences of their own actions.[2]

There is yet another important determinant of individual behaviour that social scientists should be particularly careful not to forget, as it lies outside all social systems. This is the genetic pool of homo sapiens that determines the cognitive and learning capacities of this species and their likely distribution in any human population. It is thanks to these capacities that cultural norms, preferences and beliefs can socially evolve and be individually learnt. But this also means that this evolution and learning can take place only to the extent for which these capacities allow. In other words, although the space within which social evolution can trace its trajectories is undoubtedly vast, it is nevertheless genetically limited.[3] The existence of such limits can now be deduced, and the old fuzzy view of human mind as a *tabula rasa* thus refuted, purely formally, from the basic logic of information processing systems: the more complex such a system is and the more learning capacities it is to have, the more information it must be given in the beginning (such as in the form of sophisticated learning programmes). Only the specific contents of such limits is a matter of empirical inquiry.

1.4 The Role of Institutions

The division of a society into the three systems implies division of its institutional rules into three corresponding subsets – economic institutions, political institutions and cultural institutions. Each system has institutions of its own which govern the transformations of its state over time. Property rights exemplify economic institutions, election procedures exemplify political institutions, and constraints on allowing new ideas and knowledge to modify preferences and beliefs exemplify cultural institutions. It is because each kind of institution is seen to take part in a competition of its own that the title of this paper mentions 'competitions' in the plural.

In the political and the cultural systems, where we do not pay attention to structures, the role of institutions is easy to describe. The political institutions govern the transformation of actual law and government into future law and government. The input that also influences the outcome includes actual preferences and beliefs, supplied by the cultural system. Analogously, the cultural institutions govern the transformation of actual norms, preferences and beliefs, into future norms, preferences and beliefs. The input that also influences the outcome includes the new knowledge learnt from experience with the economic and the political systems.

To illustrate, let me very roughly classify the forms of political and cultural institutions by choosing two broad families for each. For political institutions, let me choose 'democracy' and 'dictatorship'. As the usual meaning of these terms imply, democracy allows the preferences and beliefs of a majority to have more influence on future law and government than dictatorship, under which actual government also determines much of future law and government, while other inputs are largely ignored.

For cultural institutions, let me choose 'conservatism' and 'reformism'. Conservatism has the usual meaning of defending status quo norms, preferences, and beliefs, against both noise and new knowledge. As the term for what is in the present sense its opposite is not obvious, I choose 'reformism' to refer to such cultural institutions that ascribe a high weight to the input of new ideas and knowledge, and thus allow for an extensive learning process by which norms, preferences and beliefs may be modified.

In the context of political and cultural systems, it is particularly important to carefully distinguish between the state of a system and its institutions. What may cause confusion is that the two partly overlap. In both these systems, institutions not only govern the transformations of states, but are moreover part of the states. Codified law is produced as part of the state of the political system, but subsequently becomes an output that is divided among all three systems, including the political system itself, to form the written and formally enforced part of their respective institutions. Similarly, cultural norms are produced as part of the state of the cultural system, but subsequently are also divided among all three systems, including the cultural system itself, to form the unwritten and informally sanctioned part of the institutions.

But confusion is easy to avoid. The state of a system and the rules that govern its transformation can clearly be distinguished from each other, without excluding the possibility that a part of the state may become a part of the rules.[4] The point to keep in mind is that for any system, only those rules that participate in governing the transformation of its own state belong to its institutions. For example, property rights, although produced in part as cultural norms and in part as codified law, belong only to economic institutions. And among all the norms produced by the cultural system, it is only the ones which decide how the cultural system's own state is allowed to change that belong to cultural institutions.

In the state of the economic system, as noted, we need to distinguish between the relatively slowly changing structure and the more rapidly changing stocks and flows of resources, including the effective output. This complicates the role of economic institutions (cf. section 1.1). They govern the transformations of both, but there is a subtle point that it is important to understand. The actual state of the structure – e.g., the actually existing markets and the incumbent firms with their actual physical and human capital – is obviously a strong constraint on how the output can change over short periods of time. In the short run, the influence of the structure is indeed much stronger than the influence of the institutions. This also explains why non-evolutionary economics, limited to such a short run, has neglected institutions and spent all its efforts on analyzing resource allocation within constant structures. For the competition of institutions, however, it is the long run that decides. There, economic institutions have a strong and growing influence on how the structure itself evolves, to make it eventually become, in the sense of section 1.2, an expression of themselves. Economic institutions thus also have a strong influence on the output, but most of this influence is indirect and delayed, consisting of their cumulative past influence on the evolution of the structure.

It was Schumpeter who had the great merit of pointing out that the influence of institutions on the evolution of structures was more important than their influence on current resource allocation.[5] True, he omitted to mention institutions explicitly; he carefully examined this evolution only under the institutions of standard capitalism, and he entirely missed why industrial structures are bound to evolve toward inefficiency under socialism. But this does not diminish his great merit of pointing out the crucial problem. Once this is properly addressed by means of comparative institutional analysis, his omissions and errors become easy to correct.[6]

The closer attention to the economic system will often require to classify the forms of economic institutions into finer categories than just two broad families. The rough distinction between capitalism and socialism is now most often insufficient. For economic performance, institutional details often matter; today, as will be argued in a moment, the relevant question is no longer *whether* capitalism, but *which* capitalism?

2 WHICH INSTITUTIONS MAY WIN?

2.1 Conditions that Winning Institutions Must Meet

To discuss competitions of institutions, it is convenient to conceive of a space of institutional alternatives, where each alternative – a particular combination of economic, political and cultural institutions – corresponds to a certain point. This space can be subject to two inquiries: about properties of its points or regions (institutional statics), and about trajectories that social evolution can trace there by moving from one point to another (institutional dynamics).

An important task for institutional statics is to identify two kinds of regions: those that may contain potential winners and those that contain only definite losers.

The notion of 'potential winner' calls for clarification. A potential winner means a potential institutional equilibrium – a point which social evolution, if it arrived there, would not have to leave. But the real world keeps changing and social systems must keep adapting to it. This may give the impression that also institutions must keep changing. If this were the case, potential winners could not exist.

To be sure, as section 3 will consider in more detail, institutions may and do change. But it is important to understand that they need not always do so. To adapt to a changing world, a system needs above all to adapt its structure – this is, to recall, its functioning and performing 'body'. For example, new technologies and/or changes in relative prices may require new firms to enter and old firms to substantially reorganize or exit.

For institutions, two strategies are possible: (a) each time a new structure is necessary, find such new institutions that their expression will just be this structure; (b) find once for all such institutions that provide for the formation of a self-adapting structure – that is, structure that can keep adapting, under the same institutions, to a sufficiently wide range of possible states of the world.

In biological evolution, both strategies have been successful: the use of (a) is illustrated by insects, and the use of (b) by mammals, with humans exhibiting its most advanced form. This is worth emphasizing, for many social scientists seem to forget that all the wonderful flexibility and learning abilities of our brains, which make us more 'intelligent' than dogs and chimpanzees, are due to special information encoded in our genes, which themselves are not flexible at all, but rigidly stable and fortunately so.

In social evolution, in contrast, strategy (a) is at a clear disadvantage. If a structural change is necessary, many institutional alternatives must usually be tried before the one that provides just for that change can be found. Insects can cope with this disadvantage because of their enormous populations and high rates of replication. Perhaps strategy (a) may partly work in the competition of firms. An advanced economy typically contains many thousands of firms, of which some may indeed be of the insect type: they can be rigidly adapted to certain markets and technologies, and, if these change, be replaced by other firms, no less rigidly adapted to the new markets and technologies. But for nation-states, which on this planet are less than two hundred, which cannot simply disappear and be replaced by new ones, and which cannot keep changing their institutions without high risks and costs, strategy (a) is clearly unsuitable.

That is why in social evolution, strategy (b) is of prime importance, and therefore also, why some institutions may remain stable, even when the rest of the world keeps changing. The only question is, which institutions?

The first condition that such institutions must meet is to be 'adaptively efficient' – that is, to effectively provide for sufficient flexibility and adaptability of the structure over the range of the states that the world may happen to assume.[7]

Note that, in this definition, adaptive efficiency is a property of institutions, as opposed to the usual allocative efficiency, which is a property of structures. To be adaptively efficient, institutions must provide for such evolution of the structure that this remains reasonably efficient – or at least no more inefficient than its competitors – over the required range of states of the world.

But efficiency cannot suffice. The notion of efficiency, be it allocative or adaptive, must always be related to some objectives (values, preferences, objective functions). Standard economics allows them to be whatever consumers may wish ('consumer sovereignty'). But evolutionary analysis cannot be as liberal. It cannot help observing that the expected lifetime of social systems depends not only on their efficiency in the pursuit of given objectives, but also on what these objectives are – for instance, on their long-term ecological consequences and on their impact on the physical and mental health of the population. Hence institutions, to be potential winners, must also be able to induce the members of the society to choose objectives that do not destroy the basis on which continuing existence of the institutions depends. Let me call such objective 'wise' and denote this condition as the 'wisdom condition'.

If we again divide social institutions into economic, political and cultural ones, the efficiency condition can be identified as imposed on economic institutions, and the wisdom condition on the cultural ones. Moreover, additional necessary conditions appear, consisting of the requirements that the three kinds of institutions impose on each other.

Many social scientists (perhaps with the exception of economists) observed indeed that cultural, political and economic aspects of a society strongly condition each other. Cultural relativists even believed that the success of a society only depends on mutual adaptation of these aspects. It may therefore be useful to emphasize that the efficiency and wisdom conditions introduce severe absolute criteria, for which many mutually adapted institutions may nevertheless end up by being rejected.

2.2   The Efficiency Condition and Economic Institutions

The next question is, what do all these necessary conditions imply in terms of specific institutional properties? Without seeking to find a detailed answer, I wish to indicate some of its elements, and by doing so, to also indicate how a more thorough inquiry may be conducted and what social value the knowledge found may have.

The efficiency condition is a fruitful beginning. But, as non-economists, and in particular historians, may not be convinced about its importance, the following comment is in order. In the past, relatively primitive institutions causing much inefficiency could indeed allow both small tribes and large empires to maintain their existence for millennia. This may seem to imply that efficiency is not very important and that a return to similar institutions may also be an alternative for the future. The reason why this is not so is that institutional innovations and growing populations keep increasing the competitive pressures upon all societies. This, in turn, lowers the tolerance of inefficiency. Less and less inefficiency suffices to eliminate the institutions that caused it.

The properties necessary for efficient economic institutions were until recently an entirely open issue. To be sure, thanks to the work of Hayek, arguments claiming that it must provide above all for the spontaneous formation and functioning of competitive markets and must avoid all kinds of socialist planning have been known for a long time. But until the spectacular collapse of real socialism at the end of the 1980's, they were not given more weight among theoretical economists than the arguments claiming that socialist planning can be made efficient. While the weight of Hayek's pro-market arguments is now clearly increasing, they nevertheless do not seem able to settle the entire issue only by themselves. Their refutation of socialist planning is certainly powerful, but efficient market socialism of a new kind – using real markets, and not the refuted imitation of markets à la Oscar Lange – can still be claimed to have a future.[8]

In several of my papers (Pelikan, 1987, 1988, 1992, 1993), I elaborated a slightly different argument, which I believe brings the issue closer to a definitive conclusion. It is based on two theoretical novelties: (i) a comparative institutional analysis of the Schumpeterian dynamics of industrial structures ('creative destruction'), which Schumpeter carefully studied only for capitalism and Hayek mostly neglected; (ii) the recognition of economic competence as a scarce resource, whose allocation is intimately linked to this dynamics.

These novelties made it possible to produce a particularly strong argument in favour of a certain type of capitalist market institutions, which can be summarized as follows. To meet the requirements of the (adaptive) efficiency condition, economic institutions must provide not only for the formation and protection of reasonably competitive markets, including markets for capital and labour, but also require private and tradeable ownership of firms, and strongly limit the rights of government to intervene in the organization and management of supply. This argument thus refutes not only socialism with a central agency engaged in planning or market-imitating, but also all forms of socialism using real markets; it moreover exposes important constraints on government policies in mixed economies – that is, it shows the inefficiency of government ownership of firms and of selective industrial policies.

There is, however, one important difference from the usual pro-market arguments. The case for capitalist markets is strengthened only within the system of supply, whereas some mildly paternalistic and redistributive policies are shown necessary within the system of final demand (Pelikan, 1993). The case for such policies, which is based on the (adaptive) efficiency condition, with no reference to social (distributive) justice, becomes even stronger when the wisdom condition is also considered.

Although this difference may appear to weaken the case for capitalist markets, the true result is that it strengthens the case. This is because of the requirements that may be imposed on economic institutions by the cultural system. Hayek (1976) is certainly right that *if* people valued only the justice of rules, and not that of outcomes, *then* capitalist market institutions would be easy to implement and maintain. But what people value is part of the state of their cultural system, which is not easy to influence. There seem to be many cultures where what Hayek calls the 'atavism' of distributional justice is still going strong.[9] While it may be possible – as part of the transformation of the cultural system – to conduct educational campaigns aimed at convincing people to stop valuing distributional justice, the success of such an approach is uncertain and may take a long time to bear fruit. To show, as my argument does, that a certain type of capitalist market institutions provides for superior organization of production, regardless of the values concerning final consumption, makes such institutions more universally acceptable.

Although hierarchies of institutions are here left aside, a brief note about the competition of internal institutions of firms is instructive. The superiority of capitalist market institutions on the supply side is indeed largely due to their superiority in providing for this competition (Pelikan, 1989, 1993). Be the national economic institutions non-market or only non-capitalist, this competition will necessarily be distorted, and the quality of the winning firms will be worsened. To limit the entry to government-owned and/or employee-owned firms, or to allow policies to support unpromising firms (which policy-makers are unlikely to distinguish from promising ones) is bound to result in grossly inefficient production structures – as all the economies where some of this was allowed to take place amply illustrate. If organizationally or technologically inferior firms are allowed to dominate the supply structure, their dominance can only be temporary, for they must eventually cause the demise of the national economic institutions that made such arrangements possible.

To conclude this argument, let me emphasize an important qualification. Not all forms of capitalist market institutions are claimed able to win. It is fully admitted that some of them may lead to deep economic and/or social crises, and thus may end up among the losers. The argument claims that all potential winners must have economic institutions of this type – but not that all economic institutions of this type are potential winners. As I argued elsewhere (Pelikan, 1993), institutional details matter and to identify a winning form of such institutions may be difficult task for institutional design. And as will be discussed below, to make social evolution actually reach and stick to such a form may be a difficult task for public policy.

2.3   Implications for the Cultural and the Political Systems

From the economic system, there is a clear trail to the cultural and the political ones. Economic institutions, to be able to meet the efficiency conditions, impose specific requirements on both of them. Moreover, as noted, they must be adapted to each other and to themselves, and the cultural system must meet the wisdom condition.

What this implies for the cultural system can be summarized as follows. The wisdom condition directly concerns preferences. For example, to recall, they should not favour final consumption that undermines the physical or psychological health of the population, neglects education, or destroys the natural environment.

The economic system imposes three kinds of requirements. First, if its institutions are to be of a capitalist market type that can meet the efficiency condition, the cultural norms must provide all the necessary unwritten rules that such institutions may need. This includes, for example, a minimum respect for property rights, contracts, promises, and business ethics in general.[10] Second, the preferences must provide for sufficient propensities to save, take risks, invest, and take initiative ('entrepreneurship'), to make all the efficient markets and firms, for which such institutions provide potential space, actually form and develop. Third, the beliefs must be sufficiently rational, based to a large extent on scientific (refutable) knowledge, in order not to strangle the economy by shortages of economic or technological competence.

As we have not yet inquired into the form of political institutions, only two very general remarks can be made about what the political system requires. First, the cultural norms must again supply all the necessary unwritten rules for winning political institutions – whatever these may be. Second, the preferences and the beliefs must allow political agents to reach, under such institutions, all the political decisions required in the time required. If the winning institutions turn out to be of a democratic type (which they will indeed do in section 3.2 below), the two requirements will become quite severe. The first one will mean that the cultural norms must include acceptance of electoral results, including defeat. The second one will require the values to be sufficiently homogenous (or at least monotone), to avoid political crises caused by Arrow's Impossibility Theorem, and the beliefs to be sufficiently rational, to prevent democratic decisions from hindering socially valuable projects.

Finally, to be adapted to itself, the cultural system must supply all the unwritten rules for winning cultural institutions – again, whatever these may be. For example, if they belong to the conservative family, the norms would have to contain resistance to all changes of norms, preferences and beliefs. If they were of the reformist type, the norms would on the contrary have to contain openness to novelties and cultural learning.

Without any absolute condition to meet, the political system only needs to be adapted to the other systems and to itself. Much like the cultural system must supply all three kinds of institutions with suitable unwritten rules, the political system must supply all of them with suitable codified and formally enforced laws. In economic institutions, for example, the culturally-produced respect for property rights and contracts may have to be complemented by formal specification of details and by rules that the cultural system alone is unlikely to supply – such as suitable corporate law, antitrust law, and bankruptcy law. Cultural institutions, if conservative, may need a censorship law and, if reformist, laws on freedom of expression and perhaps also on critical thinking in education. Political institutions appear to be the greatest consumer of codified law: in modern nation-states, most of their rules appear necessary to codify.

Moreover, for the economic role that government is to play, the political system is required to choose government of sufficient integrity and competence to minimize efficiency losses due to unproductive rent-seeking and/or the incompetence of policy decisions. This requirement, however, is better seen as a problem of mutual adaptation between economic institutions and the political system. As the integrity and the competence of governments are always subject to binding constraints – which, although different in different cultures, are never negligible – economic institutions must compensate for these constraints by correspondingly restricting the economic role for government. Indeed, much of the earlier discussed case for capitalist market institutions follows from these constraints.

All this, of course, is only a very rough sketch of what the efficiency and the wisdom conditions imply for the cultural and political systems. But the main purpose, as noted, was to indicate how a fruitful inquiry into such implications can be conducted, rather than to reach specific results. The important point to note is that this line of inquiry, to however specific results it might lead us, is only about the states of these systems, but not about their institutions. To learn about these, we must examine how the required states can be obtained and maintained, and ask under what institutions this can happen.

But as long as we remain within institutional statics, limited to properties of supposedly given institutional alternatives, we cannot learn much. To see why, recall the space of institutional alternatives from section 2.1. Institutional statics can draw a map of this space, where points and regions can be marked by indications about their consequences on the working of social systems. What we have tried to learn is, which of these points are potential winners of the competitions of institutions (potential institutional equilibria)? Institutional statics leaves us with four broad regions where such points might be found. Although it can say much about specific properties of economic institutions, it cannot see why all four combinations of political and cultural institutions should not be possible: democracy and reformism, democracy and conservatism, dictatorship and reformism, and dictatorship and conservatism. To meet the wisdom condition and the requirements of efficient economic institution, the cultural and the political systems must only be maintained in certain required states. For institutional statics it is unimportant how this is achieved – whether the required laws are made by a parliament or a dictator, and whether all the required norms, preferences and beliefs are maintained by blind conservatism or by learning and reforming which no longer find rational reasons for change.

But in spite of this limitation of institutional statics, the map it produces can contain much of useful knowledge: although it cannot be very precise about potential winners, it can point out large regions as definite losers. The knowledge of this map, as will be argued below, is of great importance for institutional dynamics.

3 INSTITUTIONAL CHANGE, DELIBERATE POLICY AND THEORETICAL KNOWLEDGE

3.1 The Dynamics of Institutional Change

How institutions change and evolve can best be described as an experimental ('trial-and-error') evolutionary process, involving two phases: (i) designing and trying out of projects, and (ii) selecting or rejecting the projects tried according to their consequences.

An important question is, how much knowledge about the eventual consequences can inform phase (i). In biological (Darwinian) selection, it is none. At the other extreme, if all relevant knowledge were available, the process would not be evolution, but rather an exercise in perfectly rational design. According to the present argument, the evolution of institutions is an interesting intermediate case which is itself evolving from Darwinian beginnings to increasing use of relevant knowledge – although it is unlikely ever to reach the extreme of perfectly rational design.

Postponing the question of knowledge for a moment, let me briefly describe the two phases. In phase (i), the sources of design of institutional rules are seen here in the cultural and the political systems. The cultural system is the source of individualist trials modifying cultural norms, which spread from usually anonymous innovators through imitation by other individuals (cf. Hayek, 1967). The political system is the source of collectivist trials creating or changing codified law (cf. Vanberg, 1992). As attention is often paid to only one of these sources, it should be emphasized that both are important. No effective institutions can be made of legislated laws only; unless accompanied and complemented by suitable cultural norms, not even the best law can produce good results. But, at least in modern complex societies, the opposite is also true: unless complemented and supported by suitable law, not even the wisest cultural norms suffice to provide for efficiency.

It is phase (ii) that has the meaning of competitions of institutions. It is in this phase that winners are selected (maintained) and losers rejected.

To be maintained, the institutions of a system must effectively be respected by a quasi-totality of its agents. There are two main factors that can make an agent respect an institutional rule: (a) the fear of sanctions for non-respect; and (b) the belief that the rule is right, given the agent's preferences. To them the present argument adds a third factor, which can be seen as a derivative of (b): the knowledge that can – but perhaps only up to a certain point – replace the belief. Of course, to see knowledge as a derivative of beliefs raises the fine epistemological question of how to tell the difference between the two. But let me ignore this question for a moment, to return to it briefly in section 3.3.

For understanding phase (ii), it suffices to understand rejection, for selection is nothing but a long period without rejection. In general, an institutional rule is rejected when it is no longer supported (respected) by a sufficient number of agents. In detail, there are several ways in which this can happen. The most drastic one is the demise of the agents themselves. For example, some institutions may induce them to behave so inefficiently that they become unable to obtain the necessary quantities and qualities of food, shelter, medicine, and defence to physically survive. This is the principal way for rejecting genes in biological evolution, but is rarely used for rejecting institutional rules in social evolution. The reason is not that humans would be free of the danger of demise, but that thanks to their cognitive abilities they can often see the danger approaching and decide to reject such institutions before it is too late.

The human cognitive abilities are indeed the basis of all the other, less drastic ways of rejecting institutions. This has two important consequences. First, as these abilities are institutionally-conditioned, institutions become interdependent. For example, as pointed out in slightly different terms by North (1990), whether certain economic institutions are maintained or rejected strongly depends on the prevailing values and beliefs, which in turn strongly depend on the prevailing cultural institutions. As North points out, this makes social evolution path-dependent, for past values and beliefs may thus strongly influence the possibilities of future institutional changes. The present qualification is that this is true to the degree to which the cultural institutions are conservative; if they are reformist, the path-dependency is weaker. Moreover, as argued above, whether any institutions can be maintained depends in the last analysis on the economic output, including the production of new knowledge, which in turn strongly depends on the economic institutions.

Second, as the human cognitive abilities are imperfect, they may also be sources of important errors. In particular, false alarms may be given and potential winners may mistakenly be rejected. Hayek was among the first to warn that this was that happened in all the societies where Marx's alarm about the imminent collapse of capitalism was taken seriously enough to reject capitalist market institutions and start experimenting with its much poorer socialist alternatives. The opposite errors of maintaining eventual losers, in spite of growing signs of an approaching disaster, can also be committed. But such errors cannot last longer than the time it would take for the disaster actually to come and trigger the drastic way. The closer to this time they are allowed to last, of course, the higher the social costs incurred.

When this trial-and-error dynamics of institutional change is considered, it becomes clear why no knowledge of potential institutional equilibria that institutional statics might produce can predict the actual outcomes of future social evolution.

3.2 Political and Cultural Institutions: A Dynamic Point of View

In the previous section, cultural and political systems were exposed as sources of trials in institutional design. The question now is, what new can we learn about their institutions? As we can recall, institutional statics was not very informative. It admitted all of the considered combinations of political and cultural institutions as potential winners. Institutional dynamics might tell us more because it is also interested in the processes by which institutional alternatives can effectively be attained and/or maintained. In the case of institutional dynamics, this means to be interested not only in points, but also in the trajectories that can lead to and from the points. The question therefore is, whether we can discover some differences among alternatives of political and cultural institutions by investigating their chances of being effectively attained and maintained.

For cultural institutions, it is easy to find such differences. If the protection of status quo institutions is not absolutely errorless – which it never can be – institutional equilibria which rely on pure conservatism must clearly be unstable. Sooner or later they are bound to drift into disequilibria, which would then also be tried to be conserved – as no corrective feedback, based on observations, learning, and reforming, is in place. Of course, learning and reforming are not without problems. As noted, they risk being pursued erroneously. Then, instead of correcting a small disequilibrium, they can create a large one. But this does not cure the drawback of conservatism. What an institutional equilibrium needs, to be stable, is rational reforming based on relevant theoretical knowledge. Whether or not there can be stable institutional equilibria thus turns out to depend on whether or not humans are able to acquire relevant theories for correctly reforming their institutions – which includes keeping them stable, when they are in a favorable equilibrium, *and knowing it.*

The differences between alternative political institutions are somewhat harder to discover. When the importance of relevant knowledge is recognized, the crucial question is, who has it? To avoid misunderstanding, it should perhaps be emphasized once more that the relevant knowledge is not 'factual', which no single mind can possess, but theoretical. Its essential elements, if pedagogically explained, can be acquired by large numbers – for example, many people now understand why socialism cannot work.

Interesting differences between democracy and dictatorship then appear depending on how large a part of the population has the relevant knowledge – or at least have enough of it to know who has more of it. If a majority has this knowledge, democracy is clearly superior. The inferiority of dictatorship can then be exposed as follows. There is a non-zero probability that the decisive authority – be it as single dictator or a junta – is selected from the ignorant minority. The expected social losses under dictatorship must be higher than the expected losses under democracy, for there the relevant knowledge is used with certainty. But if only a minority has the relevant knowledge, an opposite ranking appears to be true. In this case, democracy will produce the wrong decisions, whereas dictatorship has a non-zero probability of being right.

This, however, does not mean that dictatorship will be part of a stable institutional equilibrium. There are two reasons why this is unlikely. First, knowledge spreads. If the relevant knowledge about favourable institutions is produced and if most people are reasonably able to learn it, the state in which it is limited to a minority is itself unstable. When this knowledge has spread to a majority, it is democracy that becomes superior. Of course, this does not exclude the possibility that a transitory use of dictatorship might have a positive expected value in a society with an actually ignorant majority. But, in the long run, dictatorship becomes inferior.

The second reason has to do with a particular kind of preferences (values) that seem to be present in all cultures. These are preferences over institutional rules as such, regardless of the outcomes to which these may lead. Often-discussed examples are preferences for democracy, regardless of what law and what government it may produce, and preferences for a market economy, regardless of what economic inequality it may cause. Dictatorship could be part of a stable institutional equilibrium only in a culture where preferences for dictatorship over democracy could lastingly be maintained. This appears unlikely, in particular when conservatism, which is the only type of cultural institutions under which such preferences could be maintained, is itself unstable. This reason would be strengthened, if Chomsky (1976) were right and human resistance to dictatorship moreover had a genetic basis (cf. section 1.3 and note 4).

Preferences over rules are of importance also from another point of view. According to Hayek (1976), it is upon them, and not upon preferences over actual outcomes, that modern large societies should be based. This is indeed how his argument in favor of 'abstract rules of just conduct' and his criticism of 'the atavism of distributional justice' can be put in present terms. The argument is right that a culture which values only institutional rules, and not outcomes, is less demanding, and therefore easier to endow with compatible and efficient economic institutions than a culture which also values actual outcomes. The obvious difficulty with the latter is that it risks overdetermining the economic problem: the preferred outcomes may not be obtainable under the preferred rules, or may not be obtainable at all. Cultures that insist on such outcomes destroy their economies and cannot last long.

But this is not the entire story. A culture which values only rules is also exposed to a serious risk, germane to that of conservatism. There is no guarantee that the rules that happen to be preferred are also those that result in meeting the efficiency and the wisdom conditions. If they are not, such a culture cannot last much longer than the one which overdetermines its economic problem. With no valuation of overall outcomes, there can be no corrective feedbacks, and therefore no hope for redress.

Institutional dynamics thus makes the result of institutional statics more precise: potentially winning institutional alternatives must provide not only for a capitalist market economy, but moreover for political democracy and cultural reformism.[11] It moreover shows that an important condition for a favourable equilibrium to be stable is widespread knowledge that this is a favourable equilibrium.

3.3 Deliberate Policies and Theoretical Knowledge

An important lesson of section 3.1 is that nature punishes societies that are far from any institutional equilibrium by economic and social crises, which force them to search for other institutions through costly and risky transformation processes. As these crises and processes usually cause much individual suffering and may threaten the very existence of organized society, it appears to be a natural objective for policy to try to attain and maintain a favourable institutional equilibrium.

Why the form of institutions should be a matter for deliberate policy, rather than left to spontaneous (cultural) evolution, may require a more thorough justification. Two cases are important to distinguish: (i) fortunate societies, which are in an institutional equilibrium – in other words, have institutions that allow them to meet both the (adaptive) efficiency condition and the wisdom condition; and (ii) unfortunate societies, whose institutions are far from any such state. Probably no real society strictly belongs to (i), but there are many real societies that definitely belong to (ii) – such as the 'Southern' nations with chronically underdeveloped economies, or the 'Eastern' nations, on the verge of economic and moral ruin after several decades of socialist experiments.

For case (ii) societies, the justification needs no advanced theoretical reasoning. Because of unfavourable cultural development and/or past policy errors, their institutions are in such a disastrous state that spontaneous recovery appears extremely unlikely. This is now also the prevailing belief (if not knowledge), for an intensive search for suitable transformation policies is being conducted in most of these societies. For case (i) societies, if they existed, the reason for deliberate policy is similar to the one which explains why conservatism is evolutionarily unstable. As follows from the previous section, without protection by deliberate policy, the favourable institutions would slowly dissolve by institutional drift – for example, through uninformed individualist experimenting.

When a deliberate policy of institutional change is justified, the crucial question is, how to prevent it from causing higher social losses than spontaneous social evolution. The answer is, of course, that this can never be guaranteed. The only promising avenue is to work on minimizing the expected losses of policy errors by producing and putting to use relevant theoretical knowledge, by which policy choices can be enlightened. Of course, both the production of such knowledge and its putting to practical use raise enormously difficult problems. But – and this is the final argument of this paper – modern societies have no other choice than do their best in struggling with them.

Before exposing the argument, brief comments on each of these problems are in order. Many students of institutions and institutional change are involved in producing relevant theoretical knowledge, yet they have not yet fully considered the impact of the knowledge which they produce on the evolution which they study. For example, much of the work of Friedrich Hayek and Douglass North contributed to this production and started to influence practical policy, although neither of them explicitly considered this influence.

But not all of what students of institutions produce can be considered relevant knowledge, so we have to define what such knowledge should consist of. A short way to describe it is to say that it should be about points and trajectories in the space of institutional alternatives (cf. section 2.1) – that is, about consequences of alternative institutions, as can be studied by institutional statics, and about the ways of attaining them and/or leaving them, as can be studied by institutional dynamics. The knowledge should be 'objective' in the sense that it is not subservient to our preferences (tastes, values, ideologies), but on the contrary allows us to study our preferences from a higher point of view and discover in them possible inconsistencies.[12] For example, much as medicine has found that the preference for longevity is incompatible with the preference for smoking, the social sciences should be able to find that the preference for civilization and welfare (in the broadest meaning of these terms) is incompatible with the preference for certain types of institutions.

Ideally, the knowledge should make it possible to identify both potential equilibria that policy should try to reach and preserve, and the unstable institutional alternatives, which lead to crises and disasters, that policy should avoid. In reality, however, it may never be possible to obtain all such knowledge. Although the knowledge is only about functional consequences ('general performance'), and not about specific ('factual') outcomes, its production is subject to at least two constraints. One is the openness to institutional alternatives. Institutional innovations, which are impossible to predict, keep appearing and enlarging the space. An alternative that today appears as an equlibrium may thus be displaced by a new alternative that will be discovered in the future. But this constraint is largely a matter of precision and should not be overestimated. Even if we can never know an institutional equilibrium in detail, we may learn to locate it within a certain region – for example, as was possible to do with regard to the identification of potential winning economic institutions in section 2.2. Moreover, much knowledge can definitely be obtained about institutions that lead to crises and disasters. To know which policies to avoid, even if we do not know which policies to recommend, has also positive social value.

The second constraint stems from the fundamental difficulty of distinguishing knowledge from mere conjectures and false theories. If Popper (1973) is right, we can never have true knowledge, only yet unrefuted theories. This means that we cannot exclude scientific errors, just as we cannot exclude policy errors. The theory of optimal socialist planning, which some of the best economists of their time helped to develop, and standard comparative economics, which failed to see the approaching collapse of real socialism, are spectacular examples of how serious errors can be produced by seemingly serious analysis. But this only confirms (or, to be Popperian, fails to refute) Popper's view of the evolution of sciences as an intellectual 'trial-and-error' process. Then, even if scientific inquiry can never yield true knowledge, to conduct it will still be of positive social value if its intellectual trials-and-errors can help to avoid some real policy errors.

In the social sciences, of course, intellectual errors should not be underestimated. False theories, if sufficiently believed, may have the effects of self-fulfilling prophecies. The Marxist theory of class struggle, which even predicted a specific trajectory from capitalist to socialist institutions, is a notorious example: where it was believed, destructive class struggle was organized and the theory thus appeared confirmed. But the influence of such theories can only be temporary (although perhaps not entirely reversible): sooner or later, differences between them and the real world are bound to appear and grow in importance – as happened, for example, with the Marxist theory, when it inspired real policies to try to follow the predicted trajectory. In the end, even this produced relevant knowledge, although at enormous social costs.

The difficulties with putting relevant knowledge to practical use are even difficult to survey, for there are many ways in which such knowledge can spread, and each has its specific obstacles. Efforts can be made to

In Search of the Winners

spread it directly to policy-makers or, in a democracy, to the electorate – neither of which may be easy. For example, in societies with conservative cultural institutions, an important obstacle is the above-mentioned path-dependency, which hinders new knowledge from modifying old beliefs, however harmful these might now be (cf. also North, 1990, and Denzau and North, 1994). To understand these difficulties in democracy, the usual theories, which see it only as a formal system for aggregating rational votes, are insufficient. Democracy must also be studied as a system of social learning and education, with the task of enlightening voters' choices by relevant knowledge.

A recent example of the importance of spreading relevant knowledge is the (relative) success of the Czech post-socialist transformation. Much of this success appears indeed due to such an enlightenment process. While the actually-taken policy measures were about the same as in many other post-socialist economies, the effort spent on explaining how markets work and why the measures were taken was unique. This appears indeed to be the only explanation why the Czech radical transformation policies could obtain and maintain broad political support, and why the Czech Republic is now the only post-socialist country where democracy did not bring back to power heirs of the old communist parties.

Of course, it can be objected that the Czechs just had good luck. They happened to begin the transformation process with a team of top policy-makers, chosen haphazardly in the turmoil of the 'velvet revolution', who happened to have the relevant knowledge (or beliefs reasonably close to it), together with the motivation and the pedagogical abilities to spread its most important elements rapidly to a critical mass of the electorate. Russia was less fortunate. Although many of its reformers had similar knowledge, they did not understand the importance of pedagogical explanations. Their electoral campaign was an offence to the reasoning abilities of an average voter and could not but bring their defeat. Ukraine was even more unlucky, for among her top policy-makers relevant knowledge appeared entirely missing.

Yet, in spite of all the difficulties with producing and spreading the relevant knowledge, modern societies have no alternative. They can no longer return to the paradise – if it ever existed – where life could go on under wise institutions, whose consequences no one had to understand. Once people started to try to understand and meddle with their institutions, however clumsily they may have done so, they chased themselves out of that paradise. They must now work in toil, if not necessarily in sweat, to learn to do it properly. However hopeless this task might be, not to work on it would leave for them even less hope.

Notes

1. The problem of speed differences between institutional and structural changes is of particular importance in the context of post-socialist transformation; see Pelikan (1992) for a more detailed discussion.
2. For an interesting account of the role of mental models in institutional economics, see Denzau and North (1994).
3. This view of genetic limits to social evolution can be seen as a loose extension of Chomsky's theory of 'universal grammar', which he defined as a genetically-given means and limit to the creation and learning of languages (for a popular presentation, see Chomsky, 1976). Chomsky also speculated about extending his theory to social evolution in general, and suggested an encouraging hypothesis that the genetic endowment of humans includes a need for freedom, which prevents them from permanently adapting to oppression.
4. A logically clear example of systems whose internal state includes the rules governing the transformation of this state is the modern computer. It was von Neumann who had the felicitous idea of storing computer programs, which govern operations with data, in the same memory as the data. This idea, which makes it possible to program modifications of programs, was perhaps the most important innovation in the architecture of automatically computing systems. In the 1950s, before such computers became common, they used to be distinguished as 'computers with internal control'.
5. Perhaps the best statement of this observation is the chapter on creative destruction in Schumpeter (1942/1976). Particularly telling is the following quotation: 'The problem usually studied is how capitalism administers existing structures, whereas the relevant problem is how it creates and destroys them' (p. 84).
6. This is at least what my study of this question allowed me to conclude (Pelikan, 1987, 1988, 1992).
7. While the term 'adaptive efficiency' was probably coined by Marris and Mueller (1980), its presently used definition is much of my own making. I was, however, greatly helped by personal discussions with Douglass North, who also showed how this term could productively be applied in his 1990 book.
8. For a recent blueprint for market socialism, see Bardham and Roemer (1992).
9. For a similar point see Choi (1993).
10. As follows from an interesting argument by Breton (1992), the lack of such cultural norms can be compensated by formally enforced law, which can thus make capitalist market institutions formally compatible with a wide variety of cultural norms. As he points out, however, such compensation is costly, in terms of enforcement and transaction costs. If paid, these costs may tax the resulting efficiency so heavily that the efficiency condition is no longer met. If not paid, the effective institutions would not be of the right type, and would therefore also fail to meet the condition.
11. As Lüder Gerken pointed out to me, this result is analogous with the result reached by Eucken in his study of interdependence of orders (1952/1990, pp. 180–5 and 332–4).
12. To be objective does not mean to be value-free. We cannot communicate in a value-free fashion, because all languages in which we may try to communi-

cate are inevitably value-loaded. All languages are based on categories that someone, in terms of some values, found important to distinguish. But there is a difference between referring to categories that can be valued, and actually valuing them. (In mathematics, this is the difference between listing the arguments of a class of objective functions, and assigning to these arguments particular weights, and thus determining a specific function within this class.) Thus, although all knowledge must be expressed in terms of valuable categories, it can be objective in the sense that it does not attach to these categories any specific values.

References

Bardham, P. and J.E. Roemer (1992) 'Market Socialism: a Case for Rejuvenation', *Journal of Economic Perspectives*, 6, pp. 101–16.

Breton, A. (1992) 'Markets, Cultures, and Asset Values'. Paper presented at the conference on Economics of Institutions: Government and Privatization, Charles University, Prague.

Choi, Y.B. (1993) 'Entrepreneurship and Envy', *Constitutional Political Economy*, 4, 331–48.

Chomsky, N. (1976) *Reflections on Languages* (New York: Fontana Books).

Dawkins, R. (1976) *The Selfish Gene* (Oxford: Oxford University Press).

_____ (1982) *The Extended Phenotype* (Oxford and San Francisco: W.H. Freeman and Co.).

Denzau, A.T. and D.C. North (1994) 'Shared Mental Models: Ideologies and Institutions', *Kyklos*, 47, pp. 3–30.

Eucken, W. (1952/1990) *Grundsätze der Wirtschaftspolitik* (Tübingen: J.C.B. Mohr (Paul Siebeck)).

Hayek, F.A. (1967) *Studies in Philosophy, Politics, and Economics* (London: Routledge and Kegan Paul).

_____ (1973) *Law, Legislation and Liberty: Rules and Orders* (London: Routledge and Kegan Paul).

_____ (1976) *Law, Legislation and Liberty: The Mirage of Social Justice* (London: Routledge and Kegan Paul).

_____ (1979) *Law, Legislation and Liberty: The Political Order of a Free People* (London: Routledge and Kegan Paul).

Marris, R. and D.C. Mueller (1980) 'The Corporation, Competition, and the Invisible Hand', *Journal of Economic Literature*, 18, pp. 32–63.

North, D.C. (1990) *Institutions, Institutional Change and Economic Performance* (Cambridge and New York: Cambridge University Press).

Pelikan, P. (1987) 'The Formation of Incentive Mechanisms in Different Economic Systems', in S. Hedlund (ed.), *Incentives and Economic Systems* (London and Sydney: Croom Helm).

_____ (1988) 'Can the Imperfect Innovation System of Capitalism be Outperformed?', in G. Dosi, C. Freeman, R. Nelson, G. Silverberg and L. Soete (eds), *Technical Change and Economic Theory* (London: Pinter Publishers).

_____ (1989) 'Evolution, Economic Competence, and the Market for Corporate Control', *Journal of Economic Behavior and Organization*, 12, pp. 279–303.

___ (1992) 'The Dynamics of Economic Systems, or How to Transform a Failed Socialist Economy', *Journal of Evolutionary Economics*, 2, pp. 39–63. Reprinted in H.J. Wagener (ed.), (1993) *On the Theory and Policy of Systemic Change* (Heidelberg: Physica-Verlag and New York: Springer-Verlag).

___ (1993) 'Ownership of Firms and Efficiency: the Competence Argument', *Constitutional Political Economy*, 4, pp. 349–92.

Popper, K. (1973) *Conjectures and Refutations: the Growth of Scientific Knowledge*, 4th revised edition (London: Routledge and Kegan Paul).

Schumpeter, J.A. (1942/1976) *Capitalism, Socialism, and Democracy* (New York: Harper & Row).

Vanberg, V. (1992) 'Innovation, Cultural Evolution, and Economic Growth', in U. Witt (ed.), *Explaining Process and Change: Approaches to Evolutionary Economics* (Ann Arbor: The University of Michigan Press).

Part II

Specific Aspects of Institutional Competition

8 Competition among Jurisdictions: The Idea of FOCJ*

Bruno S. Frey and Reiner Eichenberger

1 MONOPOLY VS COMPETITION OF GOVERNMENTS

The single European *economic* market has been a great success. The four freedoms relating to the movement of goods, services, labour and capital have without doubt significantly increased the welfare of the citizens within the European Union. With respect to *politics*, including economic policy, the picture is rather different. Essentially, one institution, the European Commission and its bureaucracy, has established itself as a *monopoly government* for European affairs, despite its so far limited powers. This paper argues that similar welfare improvements as in economic affairs could be reached in political affairs as well, provided the European Constitution allows for, and actively supports, *competition between governments at all levels*. The competition between already existing governments must be preserved but in addition a future European Constitution should foster the emergence of competitive new jurisdictions best serving individual preferences. These new governmental units are called FOCJ. The acronym relates to its four major characteristics:

F = *functional*, i.e. the new political units extend over areas defined by the tasks to be fulfilled;

O = *overlapping*, i.e. in line with the many different tasks (functions) there are many different governmental units extending over different geographical areas;

C = *competing*, i.e. individuals and/or communes may chose to what governmental unit they want to belong, and they have political

*We are grateful to Iris Bohnet, Isabelle Busenhart, Lüder Gerken, Felix Oberholzer, Dieter Schmidtchen, Jürg de Spindler and Christophe von Werdt for helpful remarks. Financial support by COST A7 is gratefully acknowledged.

rights to express their preferences directly via initiative and referenda;

J = *jurisdictions*, i.e. the units established are governmental, they have enforcement power and can, in particular, raise taxes.

While these FOCJ are in stark contrast to the concepts of federalism currently existing and proposed in the European Union, we intend to show that they are well-grounded in economic theory, and that successful precursors exist in European history. Indeed, we argue that Europe owes its rise as a dominant economic and intellectual centre to the competition among governmental units. A federalism imposed from above, on the other hand, cannot meet this requirement. We also intend to show that such functional competing units partially exist in present-day Europe and elsewhere, and that they perform well within the room accorded to them.

The second section of this paper specifies the concept of FOCJ more precisely and puts it into theoretical perspective. The third section outlines the major advantages of federalism based on FOCJ, and contrasts them to all-purpose jurisdictions confined to one particular, non-overlapping geographical area. The fourth section deals with partially existing FOCJ in Europe today, and discusses similar types of jurisdictions in the history of Europe. The relationship to US special districts and in particular to functional communes in Switzerland are also pointed out. Concluding remarks are offered in the fifth section.

2   THE CONCEPT OF FOCJ

The kind of federalism here suggested is based on theoretical propositions advanced in the economic theory of federalism but it nevertheless leads to a very different governmental system than is suggested in that literature. The economic theory of federalism (see Prud'homme, 1991, Bird, 1993, Breton, 1994, for surveys on its present state) starts from *existing* political units at the different levels of government (Weingast, 1993. p. 292), whereas we propose that jurisdictions should *emerge* in response to the *'geography of problems'*.[1] The four elements of FOCJ are now related to economic theory as well as to existing federal institutions, pointing out both similarities and differences to existing concepts.

2.1   Functional

In order for a political unit to optimally provide public services, the benefits and costs have to geographically match, i.e. spillovers have to be evaded. The different units are thus able to cater for differences in the population's preferences or, more precisely, to its demands. Moreover, the political units have to exploit economies of scale in production. As these may strongly differ between functions (e.g., between schools, police, hospitals, power plants and defence) there is an additional reason for unifunctional (or few-functional) governmental units. This is the central idea of 'fiscal equivalence' as proposed by Olson (1969) and Oates (1972). This endogenity of the size of governmental units constitutes an essential part of FOCJ. However, fiscal equivalence is little concerned with decision-making in those functional units. The supply process is either left unspecified or it is assumed that the mobility of persons (and of firms, a fact rarely mentioned) induces these units to cater for individual preferences. The same argument may be used against a concept closely-related to fiscal federalism, 'voting by foot' (Tiebout, 1956). In this process, political units grow in size if they are below optimum size, and if they are more efficient suppliers than the other units, and vice versa. According to this model of federalism, the political jurisdictions are exogenously given, are multi-purpose, do not overlap, and the political supply process is unspecified. In contrast, we emphasize the need to explicitly study the political supply process. In line with Epple and Zelenitz (1981), exit and entry is considered insufficient to eliminate rent extraction by governments. Individuals must also have the possibility to raise voice in the form of voting.

Buchanan's (1965) 'clubs' are similar to FOCJ because their size is determined endogenously by the benefits and costs of the club members (see Sandler and Tschirhart, 1980). Single-purpose districts as they exist in the United States (see Zax, 1988), or *Zweckverbände*, as they are aptly called in German-speaking countries, can be considered to be such clubs, except that the members do not consist of individuals but rather of communes, or even of cantons or provinces (in which case they are called *'Konkordate'*). However, in most countries such districts as clubs are not legally independent political entities (US and Swiss single-purpose communes are exceptions, see Mehay, 1984).[2] Club theory does not analyze the political process within the clubs, and the clubs as such do not have jurisdictional power as our FOCJ do. Moreover, FOCJ are not restricted to public goods but may also provide private goods as indeed many governments factually do.

Many privately arranged organizations performing a restricted 'public' function (and as such often receiving government subsidies) are flexible enough to adjust to the geography of problems. Examples are, in addition to social clubs and sports clubs, political parties and religious groups. In contrast, existing political jurisdictions perform many functions (they could be called APJ for All-Purpose Jurisdictions), and are therefore not designed to minimize functional spillovers and to maximally exploit economies of scale with respect to particular functions. An example are the regions as they exist in the European Union: their size is essentially historically determined. The politically much-propagated 'Europe of Regions' thus certainly does not meet federalism based on FOCJ.

Cross-national communes serving both allocative and distributional functions have been suggested for the European Union by Teutemann (1992). They differ in an important respect from FOCJ because they are determined and imposed from outside and from above whereas FOCJ emerge in response to the demand by individuals or, in a more aggregate way, by communes as the smallest existing political unit.

2.2 Overlapping

FOCJ may overlap in two respects. In the narrow sense two or more FOCJ catering to the same function may geographically intersect (e.g., a multitude of school FOCJ may exist in the same geographical area). In a wider sense FOCJ catering to different functions may overlap. As a result, an individual or a political commune normally belongs to various FOCJ at the same time. FOCJ need not be physically contiguous. They depart wholly from the identification of jurisdictions with a monopoly over a certain area of land. Thus they are an extreme counterproposition to archaic nationalism fighting about pieces of land – as we regrettably experience in former Yugoslavia and elsewhere. It also breaks with the notion of federalist theory that units at the same level may not overlap. On the other hand, in this respect FOCJ are similar to Buchanan-type clubs which may well intersect.

A good example for overlapping as a characteristic of FOCJ are religious groups of which several coexist in the same area, and between which individuals may freely chose. In many countries they are organized as legally public institutions. Swiss *Bürgergemeinden* ('citizens' communes') are another example for existing overlapping jurisdictions: in contrast to *Einwohnergemeinden* ('inhabitants' communes') they are composed of individuals with citizenship in a particular commune (there is no Swiss citizenship as such but it derives from citizenship in a commune), irrespective of where they live. *Bürgergemeinden* are thus separated from a particular geographical area but they entail a number of rights (e.g., in addition to voting, social welfare, housing support, scholarships for students and artists) and duties. They overlap in many respects with the

Einwohnergemeinden whose membership is defined by residency. Obviously single-purpose districts (for many examples from the United States see Tullock, 1993) or *Zweckverbände* are yet another case where governmental tasks are provided by overlapping public institutions.

2.3 Competing

Two mechanisms serve to induce the managers of FOCJ to conform closely to their members' preferences: the possibility to *exit* mimics market competition (Hirschman, 1970), and to *vote* establishes political competition (see Mueller, 1989). Migration is only one means of exit; membership in a particular FOCUS (which we take to be the singular of FOCJ) can be discontinued without changing one's location. Neither is exit restricted to individuals or firms; political communes as a whole, and even parts of them may also exercise this option.[3] Exit may moreover be total or only partial. In the latter case, an individual or commune only participates in a restricted set of FOCUS activities. For 'voting by foot' to function properly, it is necessary that exit is facilitated, and in particular that one can do so in part also. Otherwise the cost of exit may be so high that this competitive mechanism does not fulfil its task.

The importance of 'secession', that is the possibility for exit of jurisdictions (such as communes) to act as a restriction on the power of central states has been recognized in the literature (e.g., Zarkovic Bookman, 1992, Drèze, 1993), and has been suggested as an important ingredient for a future European constitution (Buchanan, 1991, European Constitutional Group, 1993). The right to secede stands in stark contrast to the prevailing concept of a state where this is strictly forbidden and often prevented by force. (Well-known examples are the American Civil War (1861–1865), the Swiss 'Sonderbundskrieg' (1847), or more recently Katanga (1960–63), Biafra (1967–70), Bangladesh (1970–71), and presently ex-Yugoslavia, all of which have been very bloody affairs.) Current European treaties do not provide for the secession of a nation from the European Union, and *a fortiori* for part of a nation. The possibility of lower-level jurisdictions to exit at low cost from the European Union as a whole as well as from particular subunits (nations, states, *Länder*, autonomous regions, etc.) thus depends strongly on the future European constitution.

For FOCJ to establish competition between governments, exit should be as free as possible; the conditions are to be regulated in a contract between the FOCJ's members. In contrast, entry need not necessarily be free. As for individuals in Buchanan-type clubs, jurisdictions may be asked a price if they want to join a particular FOCUS. The existing members of the

FOCUS have to collectively decide by democratic voting, whether a new member is welcome, i.e. whether their net benefits thereby increase.

Competition of this sort already exists today among public suppliers (e.g., between government hospitals) and, of course, private suppliers (e.g., between postal and other communication services). An individual as well as, say, a commune, may leave a particular supplier and become a customer of a competitor, therewith inducing some pressure for efficient supply. A similar competition exists between some sports organizations (for example, there exist three professional boxing organizations in the same market) and religious organizations. In the absence of monopoly powers these organizations have to make an effort to care for the demands of their actual and prospective members.

As has been pointed out, empirical evidence suggests that the exit option does not suffice to induce governments to act efficiently. Competition further needs to be secured by political institutions. The citizens should directly elect the persons managing the FOCJ, and should be given the right to initiate popular referenda on specific issues. These institutions are known to raise efficiency in the sense of caring well for individual preferences (for elections, see Downs, 1957, Mueller, 1989; for referenda Frey, 1994). Apart from American special districts and Swiss communes, existing overlapping jurisdictions such as the Swiss *Zweckverbände* or *Konkordate* have no such elements of *direct* democracy; they are only indirectly controlled by the fact that the managers of such units are delegated by democratically-elected bodies.

2.4 Jurisdictions

A FOCUS is a democratic governmental unit with authority over its citizens, including the power to raise taxes. Two cases can be distinguished: (a) Membership may be defined by the lowest political unit (normally the commune), and all corresponding citizens automatically become citizens of the FOCJ to which their unit (commune) belongs. In that case, an individual can only exit via mobility. (b) Individuals may freely choose whether they want to belong to a particular FOCUS but, while they are its citizens, they are subject to its authority. Some FOCJ may be non-voluntary in the sense that one must belong to at least one FOCUS, e.g., to one school district, and must pay the corresponding taxes (an analogy here is health insurance which in many countries is obligatory but where individuals are allowed to choose an insurance company). The citizens of a FOCUS devoted to education may, for example, decide that everyone must pay taxes in order to finance a particular school, irrespective of whether one (or one's children) attends the school. In this respect a minimal regulation by the central government may be in order so that citizens without children do not join 'school-FOCJ' which in effect do not offer any schooling but have correspondingly low (or zero) taxes.

The FOCJ as jurisdictions have the power to raise a price for entry. They provide particular services but do not necessarily produce it themselves if contracting-out to a public or private enterprise is advantageous. Existing overlapping institutions (special districts, *Zweckverbände*, etc.), on the other hand, normally do not have the legal status of governments; they are purely administrative units. Outsourcing or contracting-out by communes also differs from FOCJ as the former is restricted to production while FOCJ care for provision. As to theoretical concepts, Buchanan-type clubs differ from FOCJ because they are purely voluntary while FOCJ might not be.

FOCJ are far away from the jurisdictions of regions envisaged in the European treaties (see, e.g., Adonis and Jones, 1991). The major difference is that FOCJ emerge from below while the establishment of 'European regions' tend to be from above; they are a case of *'imposed subsidiarity'*, and their existence is strongly induced by the subsidies flowing from the European Union. In contrast, the concept of FOCJ corresponds to Hayek's (and Buchanan's) non-constructivist process view; it cannot *a priori* be determined from outside and from above which FOCJ will be efficient in the future. This must be left entirely to the competitive democratic process taking place at the level of individuals and communes; the central European constitution must only make sure that no other government units, in particular the nations, may obstruct the emergence of FOCJ. In contrast to Hayek, however, our scheme allows for a (closely-restricted) set of central regulations, as mentioned above. Moreover, Hayek measures efficiency by survival in the evolutionary process while we define efficiency more directly in terms of the fulfilment of citizens' demands.

The discussion of the characteristics of FOCJ should reveal that this concept of federalism and competition among governments differs basically from *existing European institutions*. 'Subsidiarity' as proclaimed in the Maastricht Treaty is generally recognized to be more a vague goal than a concept with content (see, for instance, Centre for Economic Policy Research, 1993, p. 19–23). Even if subsidiarity were taken seriously, it would not lead to a real federal structure because many (actual or prospective) members of the European Union are essentially unitary states without federal subunits of significant competence (examples are the Netherlands, France or Sweden). The 'regions' existing in the European Union (examples are Galicia and Cataluña in Spain, or South Tyrol and

Sicily in Italy) are far from being units with significant autonomous functional competencies; they heavily depend on the central state and the European Union from which they receive subsidies as their major source of income.

The Council of Ministers is a European decision-making institution based on federal principles (but nations only are represented) and organized according to functional principles (or at least according to the corresponding administrative units). However, this Council is only indirectly democratic (the ministers are members of governments which are democratically legitimized by the representative system) and the deliberations are not public. Exit from the European Union is not formally regulated, and exceptions to specific aspects of agreements reached (as in the Maastricht Treaty concerning the European Monetary Union and the Protocol on Social Policy, or the Schengen Treaty concerning the free movement of persons) are granted reluctantly, and are indeed seen as damaging to the 'spirit of Europe'. In a system of FOCJ, in contrast, such functional units not covering everyone are taken as the welcome expression of heterogeneous demands among Europeans.

FOCJ also differ in many crucial respects from the *proposals* advanced for a future European constitution. Among scholars, one of the most prominent was Buchanan's (1991) concept which stresses individual nation's right to secede but, somewhat surprisingly, does not build on Buchanan-type clubs. The European Constitutional Group (1993) focuses on the example of the American constitution, and presents a constructivist proposal concerning the houses of parliament and the respective voting weights of the various countries. Overlapping jurisdictions and referenda are not allowed for, and the exit option is strongly restricted. Another group of researchers (see Blöchliger and R.L. Frey, 1992; Schneider, 1992) suggest a strengthening of federalism in the traditional sense (i.e. with multi-purpose federal units) but do not envisage overlapping jurisdictions. The report by the Centre for Economic Policy Research (1993) criticizing 'subsidiarity' (as used in the Maastricht Treaty) as an empty concept argues that good theoretical reasons must be provided for central government intervention. But the report does not deal with the institutions necessary to guarantee that policy follows such theoretical advice. The idea of overlapping, not geographically-based, jurisdictions is briefly raised (pp. 54–5) but is not institutionally or practically worked out; nor is the need for a democratic organization and the power to tax acknowledged.

The recent proposal from politicians (Herman Report of the European Parliament, 1994) mainly deals with the organization of the parliamentary systems (the houses of parliament and the national vote weights) and to a substantial extent accepts the existing treatises as the founding blocks of the European constitution. The idea of competition between governments (which is basic for FOCJ) is neglected or even rejected in favour of 'co-operation' between governments.

It might be argued that the idea of FOCJ is exotic and has no chance of ever being put into practice. A careful consideration of policy-making in Europe reveals, however, that there is a wide range of functional issues to which FOCJ could profitably be applied. A practical example is the policing of the Lake of Constance (which borders on two German *Länder*, two Swiss Cantons, and one Austrian *Land*) which involves the regulation of traffic, environmental protection, the suppression of criminal activities and the prevention of accidents. Formally, the various local police departments are not allowed to directly collaborate with each other, not even to exchange information. Rather, they must advise the police ministries of the *Länder* and cantons, which then have to notify the respective central governments which then interact with each other. Obviously, such a formal procedure is in most cases vastly inefficient and unnecessarily time-consuming. In actual fact, the problems are dealt with by direct contact among the local police commissioners and officers, but this is outside the law and depends to a substantial extent on purely personal relationships (which may be good or bad). A FOCUS committed to policing the lake would allow a pragmatic, problem-oriented approach within the law – and would, moreover, be in the best 'spirit' of Europe.

The possibility for FOCJ to emerge is not restricted to such small-scale functional issues but are relevant for all levels of government and major issues. An example would be Alsace which, while remaining a part of France in other respects, might partially exit by joining, say, the German social security or school system (with German as the main language), or might join a university-FOCUS involving also the Swiss university of Basle and the German university of Freiburg. Another example refers to Corsica which, according to Drèze's (1993) suggestion, should form an independent region of Europe because of its dissatisfaction with France. However, most likely the Corsicans are only *partially* dissatisfied with France which suggests that one or several FOCJ, e.g., according to ethnic or language boundaries, or especially focused on its economic problems as an island, provide a better solution (partial instead of total exit). A further example would be a FOCUS on tourism policy of the eastern Mediterranean including Asia Minor's coastline of Turkey, the Ionic islands of Greece and the divided island of Cyprus. An important area for FOCJ are with respect to transport issues, in particular railroads. Despite the membership of various countries in the (then) European Community, railroad policy was not co-ordinated to exploit possible economies of scale, but a FOCUS may constitute a well-suited organization to overcome such shortcomings.

3   THE CASE FOR FOCJ

3.1   Advantages

Various strong points of FOCJ have already been mentioned while describing the concept. On the *demand* side, the possibility and incentives to satisfy heterogeneous preferences of individuals are crucial. Due to the concentration on one functional area, the citizens of a particular FOCUS have better information on its activity, and are in a better position to compare its performance to other governments. As many benefits and costs extend over a limited geographic area, FOCJ are usually small which is also helpful for voters' evaluations. The exit option opened by the existence of overlapping jurisdictions is an important means to make one's preferences known to governmental suppliers.

On the *supply* side, FOCJ are able to provide public services at low cost because they are formed in order to minimize interjurisdictional spillovers and to exploit economies of scale. The specialization on one function further contributes to cost efficiency due to the advantages of specialization. As FOCJ raise their own taxes to finance their activity, it pays to be economical. In contrast, in APJ (All-Purpose Jurisdictions) financed from outside lacking such fiscal equivalence, politicians have an incentive to lobby for ever-increasing funds, and thereby push up government expenditures, because taxation is a public good (or bad) and therefore need not be considered as a cost to any particular jurisdiction. The incentive to economize in a FOCUS induces its managers to contract-out whenever production costs can thereby be reduced which leads to a stronger market orientation of FOCJ than of APJ. The threat of dissatisfied citizens or communes leaving, and the benefit of new citizens and communes joining, gives an incentive to take individual preferences into account, i.e. FOCJ are not only cost-minimizers but have an incentive to provide the public services efficiently. Quite another advantage of FOCJ is that they open up the politicians' cartel ('classe politique') to functionally competent outsiders. While in All-Purpose Jurisdictions persons with broad and non-specialized knowledge are attracted to become politicians, in FOCJ it is rather persons with a well-grounded knowledge in a particular functional area (such as education or refuse collection).

The possibility to form FOCJ helps to deal with issues raised by fundamentalist sentiments. In contrast to a system of all-purpose governments, political movements focused on a single issue (such as ethnicity, religion and environment) are not forced to take over governments *in toto* but can concentrate on those functions they are really interested in. The 'Greens', for example, do not have to take a stand on foreign policy (for which they are dogmatically ill-equipped) but can devote their energy to FOCJ dealing with environmental issues. Similarly, an ethnic group need not disassociate itself from the state they live in as a whole, but may found FOCJ which care for their preferences, especially with respect to schooling. South Tyroleans, for example, unhappy with the language domination imposed by the Italian state, need not leave Italy in order to fulfil their demands for cultural autonomy buy may establish corresponding FOCJ.

The possibility to exit partially (e.g., only with respect to ethnic issues) does not lead to trade barriers often going with the establishment of newly-formed all-purpose political jurisdictions. FOCJ thus meet the criterion of market-preserving federalism (see Weingast, 1993).

With respect to a future Europe, a federal system of FOCJ certainly affects the role of the nation-states. They will certainly lose functions they presently do not fulfil according to the population's preferences. On the other hand, the scheme does not purport to do away with nations (this would anyway seem to be a hopeless endeavour at present) but seeks for multinational alternatives where they are desired by the citizens. In those areas where native states perform according to the voters' preferences, they will remain.

3.2　Alleged Problems

In a federal system of FOCJ, each individual is a citizen of various jurisdictions, according to the number of functions differentiated. It might be argued that the individuals are overburdened by voting in elections and referenda taking place in each FOCUS and consequently would respond by political abstinence.

There are three reasons why this view is unwarranted. First of all, low political participation does not constitute a problem as such as rational citizens do not vote if they are satisfied with the public services provided by a FOCUS. What matters is that vote participation is variable, and in particular that it increases when individuals are dissatisfied. The costs of organizing the vote can be reduced by bundling elections and referenda of various FOCJ. Secondly, the break-up of government activity in several functional dimensions helps citizens to identify issues more clearly than when they have to evaluate complex, multi-functional public supply. Formal voting theory assumes that the voters evaluate separately each part of government activity which affects their preferences (e.g., Downs, 1957 or, for a survey, Mueller, 1989). This breakdown according to various dimensions is to a substantial extent performed by FOCJ. Finally, the burden of having to vote at many different elections and referenda is alleviated by institutions which arise to deal with the problem. At elections, citizens may vote for one delegate who sits in various FOCJ, or may simply follow parties' recommendations.

A second alleged problem of the federal system here suggested concerns *co-ordination* between the large number of FOCJ. It should be made clear that co-ordination between governments is not good as such (as assumed by many political scientists) but often serves as a cartel among the members of the 'classe politique' to evade, or even exploit, the population's wishes (see Vaubel, 1986, 1992, CEPR, 1993, Frey, 1994). As far as welfare-increasing co-ordination is concerned, its need is reduced compared to APJ because the FOCJ emerge so that externalities are minimized, i.e. a Coasian process of endogenous adaption works. If major spillovers between FOCJ exist, new FOCJ will emerge taking care of these externalities. As the number of FOCJ is restricted due to the transactions costs involved, less important externalities between FOCJ will remain. However, spillovers also exist in a system of APJ, and the crucial question therefore is in what system they can be better dealt with. Some spillovers explicitly existing between FOCJ take a different form in APJ where they are implicit between administrative units, e.g., between the department for environment and the department of transport. The respective civil servants have a muted incentive to take these spillovers into account. Interministerial commissions need to be established, but then the decision situation is similar to co-operation efforts between FOCJ.

A third alleged problem with FOCJ is that the separation along functions prohibits vote trading and therefore restricts the expression of different preference intensities. In a system of APJ in contrast, minorities with strong preferences in one dimension (function) can exchange votes with groups who have strong interests in other functions, leading to a Pareto-superior outcome. First of all it should be noted that vote trading does not always induce a Pareto-superior outcome. 'Log-rolling' is only beneficial to those groups involved – it may well damage others. According to the vote trading paradox (see Riker and Brams, 1973), log-rolling may even be costly for all the groups involved, when government activity is not effectively limited to allocative functions. Furthermore, preference intensities can generally be expressed by higher vote participation and/or by a higher probability to vote for a desired alternative (see on probabilistic voting, Lafay, 1993). Finally, a federal system based on FOCJ is flexible enough to allow minorities with intensive preferences to establish new FOCJ which care for their preferences.

A final major objection against FOCJ is that redistribution based on solidarity is claimed to break down and that FOCJ emerge on the basis of income. (Of course, this criticism also holds against Tiebout's model of voting by foot.) One solution would be that the constitution gives the European central government the power to impose income redistribution. Alternatively, a FOCUS specialized on interregional redistribution may emerge but this presupposes barriers to entry (in analogy to insurance systems with cross-subsidization). Recent empirical research (Gold, 1991, Kirchgässner and Pommerehne, 1993) suggests that 'local' redistribution is feasible, as mobility by persons (and to a lesser extent also by firms) is sufficiently costly to allow a significant amount of redistributive action by governments.

3.3 Why has the System of FOCJ not Emerged?

In view of the major advantages outlined, and the futility of much of the criticism of FOCJ the economist's standard question arises: if this type of federalism is so good, why does it not exist?

There are two major reasons why the organization of states does not follow the model of FOCJ. An obvious, but crucial, one is that individuals and communes are prohibited to establish such jurisdictions, and in many countries of the European Union communes are not even allowed to formally collaborate with each other without the consent of the central government. When spillovers exist, the normal procedure in all member countries is to shift the task to a higher level which leads to increasing centralization (an example is environmental protection which to a considerable extent is local but where the existence of partial externalities have led to a centralized administration).

The second reason why the system of FOCJ is not observed is that it violates the interests of politicians and public officials at the higher levels of government. The emergence of FOCJ reduces their power because they control public supply to a lesser extent. As politicians' discretionary room and therefore the rents appropriable are the larger, the higher the federal level, they favour a shift of competencies in this direction, and oppose local decision-making, especially by FOCJ.[4]

It follows that under existing constitutional conditions in the countries of the European Union (and elsewhere) a federal system of FOCJ is unlikely to arise.

3.4   Creating a Favourable Environment

A system of government where the federal jurisdiction emerges from below as a response to citizens' preferences, and is not dictated from above, requires a *constitutional decision* (see Buchanan and Tullock, 1962 and more recently Frey, 1983, Mueller, 1994). A minimum provision – one would name it 'the fifth freedom' – must ensure that the emergence of FOCJ may not be blocked by existing jurisdictions, be it by competitors or governments on a higher level. Every citizen and commune must have the right to directly appeal to the European Court if barriers to the competition between governments are established.[5] Positively, the European constitution must give the lowest political units (communes) a measure of independence so that they can engage in forming FOCJ. The citizens must be given the right to establish FOCJ by popular referenda, and political entrepreneurs must be supported by the institution of popular initiatives. The FOCJ themselves must be granted the right to raise taxes to finance the public services provided.

4   HISTORICAL PRECURSORS AND PARTIAL EXISTENCE OF FOCJ

Decentralized, overlapping political units have been an important feature of European history. The competition between governments in the Holy Roman Empire of German Nations, especially in today's Italy and Germany, was intensive. Many of these governments were of small size. Several scholars have attributed the rise of Europe to this diversity and competition of governmental units which fostered technical, economic and artistic innovation (see, e.g., Hayek, 1960, Jones, 1981, Schwarz, 1993, Weede, 1993 and Baumol and Baumol, 1992, who also give a lively account of how the musical genius of Wolfgang Amadeus Mozart benefited from this system of government). While the Chinese were more advanced in very many respects, their superiority ended with the establishment of a centralized Chinese Empire (Pak, 1993, Rosenberg and Birdzell, 1986). The unification of Italy and Germany in the nineteenth century, which has often been praised as a major advance, partially ended this stimulating competition between governments and lead to deadly struggles between nation-states. Some smaller states escaped unification; Liechtenstein, Luxembourg, Monaco, San Marino and Switzerland stayed politically independent, and at the same time grew rich. Today, there is a tendency to disintegrate again, as the division of Czechoslovakia, and the strong centrifugal movements in Belgium, Spain and Italy show. These governmental units were not FOCJ in the sense outlined above but they shared the characteristic of competing for labour and capital (including artistic capital) among each other. However, history also reveals examples of jurisdictions close to FOCJ. The problems connected with Poland's strong ethnic and religious diversity (Catholics, Protestants and Jews) were at least partly overcome by jurisdictions organized along these features, and not along geography (see Rhode, 1960 and Haumann, 1991). The highly successful *Hanse* prospered from the twelfth to the sixteenth century, and comprised *inter alia* Lübeck, Bremen, Köln (today German), Stettin and Danzig (today Polish), Kaliningrad (today Russian), Riga, Reval and Dorpat (today parts of the Baltic republics) and Groningen and Deventer (today Dutch); furthermore, London (today British), Bruges and Antwerp (today Belgian) and Novgorod (today Russian) were *Handelskontore* or associated members. It clearly was a functional governmental unit serving trade and was not geographically contiguous.

The European Community started out as a FOCUS designed to establish free trade in Europe, and was from the very beginning in competition with other trade areas, in particular North America and Japan. In many other respects there emerge FOCJ-like units within Europe such as with respect to police, education, environment, transport, culture or sports though they have been prevented to become autonomous jurisdictions with taxing power. Most of these functional units are not congruent with the area of the European Union. Some are smaller (e.g., those organized along ethnic or language functions), and some are larger. Several East European countries and Switzerland which are not EU members are certainly fully involved in areas like European culture, education and crime-prevention. FOCJ of the nature understood in this paper may therefore build upon already existing structures, and are in the best of European traditions.

There are two countries in which functional, overlapping and competing jurisdictions exist (though they do not in all cases meet the requirements of FOCJ specified above).

US special districts. Single-purpose governments play a significant role in the American federalist system. Their number has rapidly increased; 1967–72 by 30.4 per cent, 1972–84 by 19.7 per cent, in both cases more quickly than other types of jurisdictions (Zax, 1988). There are both autonomous and democratically-organized as well as dependent special districts (e.g., for fire prevention, recreation and parks). Empirical research suggests that the former type is significantly more efficient (Mehay, 1984). Our theoretical hypothesis of the opposition of existing jurisdictions against the formation of special districts is well borne out. In order not to threaten the monopoly power of existing municipalities statutes in eighteen states prohibit new municipalities within a specified distance from existing municipalities (ACIR, 1982, Zax, 1988, p. 81); in various states there is a minimum population size required and various other administrative restrictions have been introduced (see, e.g., Nelson, 1990). Empirical studies reveal that these barriers imposed by Local Agency Formation Commissions (LAFCO) tend to reduce the relative efficiency of the local administration (Di Lorenzo, 1981, Deno and Mehay, 1985), and tend to push upwards the local government expenditures in those municipalities which have introduced LAFCOs (Martin and Wagner, 1978).

Swiss Communes. Many Swiss cantons have a structure of overlapping and competing functional jurisdictions which share many features of FOCJ. In the canton Zurich (with a population of 1.2 million, an area of 1700 km² and tax revenue of SFr. 2800 million) there are 171 political communes (with a tax revenue of SFr. 3900 million) which in themselves are composed of three to six independently-managed, democratically-organized communes devoted to specific functions and raising their own taxes. A typical example will illustrate this. The political commune of Niederhasli (population 5900, size 11 km²) finances its expenditures of SFr. 11 million (in 1991) by raising a tax equivalent to 38 per cent of the cantonal tax rate (in addition it raises various charges and receives a limited amount of subsidies from the canton). A commune devoted to the education from years 1 to 6 of schooling has expenditures of SFr. 5.8 million and raises a tax of 55 per cent of the cantonal tax. A corresponding commune concerned with education from years 7 to 9 spends SFr. 4.9 million and raises 22 per cent of the cantonal tax rate. There are two church communes having tax rates of 10 per cent and 11 per cent of the cantonal tax rate, respectively. The two school communes and the two religious communes are essentially self-financing. The sixth commune (*Zivilgemeinde*) is devoted to providing water, electricity and a TV antenna, and finances itself solely by user charges. These communes often overlap with neighbouring political communes. In the case of Niederhasli, the advanced school commune also comprises the political commune of Niederglatt (pop. 3300) and parts of Oberglatt (pop. 4300) (where the other part of pupils attends school in yet another school commune). The

Zurich canton is no exception concerning the multitude of types of functional communes. A similar structure exists, e.g., in the Glarus or
Thurgau cantons (for the latter, see Casella and Frey, 1992). Various
efforts have been made to suppress this diversity of functional communes, usually initiated by the cantonal bureaucracy and politicians.
However, most of these attempts were thwarted because the population is
most satisfied with the public supply provided. The example from
Switzerland – which is generally considered to be a well-organized and
administered country – shows that a multiplicity of functional jurisdictions under democratic control is not merely a theorist's wishful thinking
but has also worked well in reality.

5 CONCLUDING REMARKS

Europe owes its position as an economically rich and intellectually and
artistically powerful continent in large measure to the great variety of governmental jurisdictions in competition with each other. This basic insight
was overshadowed by the unification movements especially in Italy and
Germany. The European movement follows the historic lesson by opening
up trade barriers and supporting economic competition, and this with great
success. However, the historic lesson has not been followed with respect
to establishing competition between existing and new governments.

This paper proposes that the future European constitution should allow,
and actively promote, the evolution of functional, overlapping and competing governmental jurisdictions (FOCJ). They fulfil many of the
welfare-enhancing qualities of theoretical concepts such as Tiebout's
voting by foot, Olson's and Oates' fiscal equivalence, or Buchanan's
clubs. It is shown that FOCJ are feasible, that there are successful historical examples, and that they partially exist in the form of US special districts and Swiss functional, democratic and overlapping communes.

Notes

1. There are precursors to FOCJ in the economics literature though the concept
    has, to our knowledge, not been applied to the European Union. As in several
    other areas of economics, Tullock (1985, 1994) has been one of the inventors;
    he somewhat misleadingly calls it 'sociological federalism'. See also Casella
    and Frey (1992) and the literature cited therein. A recent Centre for Economic
    Policy Research Publication (CEPR, 1993) shortly refers to the possibility of
    establishing overlapping jurisdictions in Europe (pp. 54–5) but does not work
    out the concept nor is there reference to previous research (except to Drèze
    1993 on secession).

2. In the Swiss canton Zurich which has 171 political communes (and in addition many hundreds of functional communes, see below Section 4) there are (in 1991) 174 *Zweckverbände* of which 30 care for waste water and purification plants, 21 for water provision, 15 for cemeteries, 14 for hospitals, 10 for regional planning, 10 for refuse collection etc.

3. Again there are many examples in Switzerland: Communes decided by referendum, whether they wanted to join the new canton Jura established in 1978, and in 1993 communes in the Laufental could opt between staying in canton Basel-Land or Solothurn. Communes also frequently change districts (the federal level below cantons) by referendum.

4. A formal reason is that vote cycling is more prevalent, the more alternatives (functions) there are (see, e.g., Kramer, 1973). Normally, lower level jurisdictions have more institutions for citizen participation, and they are used more widely, so that the politicians' discretionary room and rents are lower (see, e.g., Oakerson and Parks, 1988, Cronin, 1989).

5. As mentioned above, the central government should be able to impose some restrictions on FOCJ to guarantee minimum standards. The European constitution must explicitly limit such intervention because they may well serve the purpose of undermining competition.

References

Adonis, Andrew and Stuart Jones (1991) 'Subsidiarity and the European Community's Constitutional Future', *Staatswissenschaft und Staatspraxis*, 2, pp. 179–96.

Advisory Commission on Intergovernmental Relations (ACIR) (1982) *State and Local Roles in the Federal System*, Report A-88 (Washington DC: US Government Printing Office).

Baumol, William J. and Hilda Baumol (1992) 'On the Economics of Musical Composition in Mozart's Vienna'. *Economic Research Reports* RR 92–45 (New York: C.V. Starr Centre for Applied Economics, New York University).

Bird, Richard M. (1993) 'Threading the Fiscal Labyrinth: Some Issues in Fiscal Decentralization', *National Tax Journal*, 46, pp. 201–21.

Blöchliger, Hansjörg and René L. Frey (1992) 'Der schweizerische Föderalismus: Ein Model für den institutionellen Aufbau der Europäischen Union?', *Aussenwirtschaft*, 47, pp. 515–48.

Breton, Albert (1994) *Competitive Governments. Toward a Positive Wicksellian Theory of the Public Finances* (New York: Cambridge University Press).

Buchanan, James M. (1965) 'An Economic Theory of Clubs', *Economica*, 32, pp. 1–14.

_____ (1991) 'An American Perspective on Europe's Constitutional Opportunity', *Cato Journal*, 10, pp. 619–29.

_____ and Gordon Tullock (1962) *The Calculus of Consent. Logical Foundations of Constitutional Democracy* (Ann Arbor: University of Michigan Press).

Casella, Alessandra and Bruno S. Frey (1992) 'Federalism and Clubs: Towards an Economic Theory of Overlapping Political Jurisdictions', *European Economic Review*, 36, pp. 639–46.

Centre for Economic Policy Research (CEPR) (1993) *Making Sense of Subsidiarity: How Much Centralization for Europe?* (London: CEPR).

Cronin, Thomas E. (1989) *Direct Democracy. The Politics of Initiative, Referendum and Recall* (Cambridge, Mass.: Harvard University Press).

Deno, Kevin T. and Stephen L. Mehay (1985) 'Institutional Constraints on Local Jurisdiction Formation', *Public Finance Quarterly*, 13, pp. 450–63.

Di Lorenzo, Thomas J. (1981) 'Special Districts and Local Public Services', *Public Finance Quarterly*, 9, pp. 353–67.

Downs, Anthony (1957) *An Economic Theory of Democracy* (New York: Harper and Row).

Drèze, Jacques (1993) 'Regions of Europe: a feasible status, to be discussed', *Economic Policy*, 17, pp. 266–307

Epple, Dennis and Allan Zelenitz (1981) 'The Implications of Competition Among Jurisdictions: Does Tiebout Need Politics?', *Journal of Political Economy*, 98, pp. 1197–1217.

European Constitutional Group (1993) *A European Constitutional Settlement.* (Draft document) (London: European Constitutional Group).

Frey, Bruno S. (1983) *Democratic Economic Policy* (Oxford: Blackwell).

_____ (1994) 'Direct Democracy: Politico-Economic Lessons from Swiss Experience', *American Economic Review*, 84, pp. 338–42.

Gold, Steven D. (1991) 'Interstate Competition and State Personal Income-Tax Policy in the 1980s', in Daphne A. Kenyon and John Kincaid (eds), *Competition among States and Local Governments* (Washington DC: Urban Institute Press), pp. 205–17.

Haumann, Heiko (1991) *Geschichte der Ostjuden* (München: dtv).

Hayek, Friedrich August von (1960) *The Constitution of Liberty* (Chicago: Chicago University Press).

Herman, Fernand (reporter) (1994) *Zweiter Bericht des Institutionellen Ausschusses über die Verfassung der Europäischen Union.* Europäisches Parlament, Sitzungsdokumente (A3-0064/94).

Hirschman, Albert O. (1970) *Exit, Voice and Loyalty* (Cambridge, Mass.: Harvard University Press).

Jones, Eric L. (1981) *The European Miracle* (Cambridge: Cambridge University Press).

Kirchgässner, Gebhard and Werner W. Pommerehne (1993) 'Tax Harmonization and Tax competition in the European Community: Lessons from Switzerland'. Paper presented at the ISPE Meeting, Linz, Austria, August 19–21.

Kramer, Gerald H. (1973) 'On a Class of Equilibrium Conditions for Majority Rule', *Econometrica*, 41, pp. 285–97.

Lafay, Jean-Dominique (1993) 'The Silent Revolution of Public Choice', in Albert Breton, Gianluigi Galeotti, Pierre Salmon and Ronald Wintrobe, *Preferences and Democracy*, Villa Colombella Papers (Dordrecht: Kluwer), pp. 159–91.

Martin, Dolores and Richard Wagner (1978) 'The Institutional Framework for Municipal Incorporation', *Journal of Law and Economics*, 21, pp. 409–25.

Mehay, Stephen L. (1984) 'The Effect of Governmental Structure on Special District Expenditures', *Public Choice*, 44, pp. 339–48.

Mueller, Dennis C. (1989) *Public Choice II* (Cambridge: Cambridge University Press).

228 The Idea of FOCJ

____ (1994) *Constitutional Economics*. Book manuscript, University of Maryland.

Nelson, Michael A. (1990) 'Decentralization of the Subnational Public Sector: An Empirical Analysis of the Determinants of Local Government Structure in Metropolitan Areas in the US', *Southern Economic Journal*, 57, pp. 443–57.

Oakerson, Ronald J. and Roger B. Parks (1988) 'Citizen Voice and Public Entrepreneurship: The Organizational Dynamic of a Complex Metropolitan County', *Publius: The Journal of Federalism*, 18, pp. 91–112.

Oates, Wallace E. (1972) *Fiscal Federalism* (New York: Harcourt Brace Jovanovich).

Olson, Mancur (1969) 'The Principle of "Fiscal Equivalence": The Division of Responsibilities among Different Levels of Government', *American Economic Review*, 59, pp. 479–87.

Pak, Hung Mo (1993) 'Effective Competition, Institutional Choice and Economic Development: A Factor that Makes China China'. Mimeo, Department of Economics, School of Business, Hongkong Baptist College.

Prud'homme, Remy (ed.) (1991) *Public Finance with Several Levels of Government* (The Hague/Koenigstein: Foundation Journal Public Finance).

Rhode, Gotthold (1960) 'Staaten-Union und Adelsstaat: Zur Entwicklung von Staatsdenken und Staatsgestaltung in Osteuropa, vor allem in Polen/Litauen, im 16. Jahrhundert', *Zeitschrift für Ostforschung*, 9, pp. 185–215.

Riker, William H. and Steven J. Brams (1973) 'The Paradox of Vote Trading', *American Political Science Review*, 67, pp. 1235–47.

Rosenberg, Nathan and L.E. Birdzell (1986) *How the West Grew Rich. The Economic Transformation of the Industrial World* (London: I.B. Tauris).

Sandler, Todd and John T. Tschirhart (1980) 'The Economic Theory of Clubs: An Evaluative Survey', *Journal of Economic Literature*, 18, pp. 1488–1521.

Schneider, Friedrich (1992) 'The Federal and Fiscal Structures of Representative and Direct Democracies as Models for a European Federal Union: Some Ideas using the Public Choice Approach', *Journal des Economistes et des Etudes Humaines*, 3, pp. 403–37.

Schwarz, Gerhard (1993) 'Wettbewerb der Systeme – eine ordnungspolitische Sicht'. Paper presented at the Institut für Auslandsforschung, Zürich, November 23, 1993.

Teutemann, Manfred (1992) *Rationale Kompetenzverteilung im Rahmen der europäischen Integration* (Berlin: Duncker & Humblot).

Tiebout, Charles M. (1956) 'A Pure Theory of Local Expenditure', *Journal of Political Economy*, 64, pp. 416–24.

Tullock, Gordon (1985) 'A new Proposal for Decentralizing Government Activity', in Helmuth Milde and Hans G. Monissen (eds), *Rationale Wirtschaftspolitik in komplexen Gesellschaften* (Stuttgart: Kohlhammer), pp. 139–48.

____ (1994) *The New Federalist* (Vancouver: Fraser Institute).

Vaubel, Roland (1986) 'A Public Choice Approach to International Organization', *Public Choice*, 51, pp. 39–57.

____ (1992) 'The Political Economy of Centralization and the European Community', *Journal des Economistes et des Etudes Humaines*, 3, pp. 11–48.

Weede, Erich (1993) 'The Impact of Interstate Conflict on Revolutionary Change and Individual Freedom', *Kyklos*, 46, pp. 473–95.

Weingast, Barry R. (1993) 'Constitutions as Governance Structures: The Political Foundations of Secure Market', *Journal of Institutional and Theoretical Economics*, 149, pp. 286–311.

Zarkovic Bookman, Milica (1992) *The Economics of Secession* (New York: St. Martin's Press).

Zax, Jeffrey S. (1988) 'The Effects of Jurisdiction Types and Numbers on Local Public Finance', in Harvey S. Rosen (ed.), *Fiscal Federalism: Quantitative Studies* (Chicago: The University of Chicago Press), pp. 79–106.

9 The European Market for Protectionism: New Competitors and New Products[*]

Andreas Freytag

1 THE PROBLEM

The 1990s show the danger of emerging protectionism all around the world. The most important trading nations are imposing new trade barriers or at least threatening to do so. The US Government has already reimposed Super 301 of the 1988 Omnibus Trade Act. Even the completion of the Uruguay Round on December 15, 1993 was not judged unequivocally. Whereas some observers talk about the most successful round ever completed, others are unsatisfied because the results are not stated very precisely and several goals have been missed.

Although some relatively new theoretical thinking (Dixit, 1984, Krugman, 1984) suggests that under certain circumstances a protectionist trade policy may lead to welfare improvements, there is no doubt that in general free trade and open markets lead to the highest welfare level. Protectionism is a serious threat to growth and employment, both in those countries imposing protectionist measures and in those countries submitted to protectionism. Despite this well-known phenomenon no serious efforts for liberalization are taken. A very important player in this negative-sum game is the European Union. Up to the 1980s the crucial points of European Protectionism were the Common Agricultural Policy and some 'Heckscher–Ohlin-Industries' like steel and textiles. Recently there has been an interesting tendency in the trade policy of the European Union: tariffs are more and more substituted by non-tariff barriers, especially some new forms of them, for example anti-dumping policy, technology policy and strategic trade policy. The aim of tariff reduction which is laid down in the GATT Treaty may be one reason for substituting tariffs

*I gratefully acknowledge helpful comments by Louis De Alessi, Lüder Gerken, Mónica G. Mastroberardino and Carsten-Patrick Meier.

231

for non-tariff barriers. Another probably more important reason is given by the new structure of trade policy in Europe.

The political economy explains the formation and existence of protectionism by using a market model. In this context, we use a very comprehensive definition of protectionism: every measure taken in order to support an industry or an enterprise. Hence, not only trade policy, but also subsidies, tax reliefs, regulations and so on are included. The new forms of protectionism – what we call 'new products on the political market' – can either be new instruments of trade and industry policy or new conceptions of promoting industries.

Demanders of protection in this model are industries under import competition and industries under pressure of structural change. The suppliers are politicians who worry about their (re-)election and bureaucrats who are interested in increasing their influence and importance by covering certain industries. This model is theoretically and empirically confirmed. The level and the structure of protectionism in developed countries is explained very well by political economy models. In a stable economy a long-term equilibrium in the political market can be achieved.

The situation changes when regional integration takes place. In the European Union the political markets seem to be subject to considerable changes. We use an extended market model to point out and explain these changes. Our central hypothesis is that the Commission as a relatively new institution is trying to establish itself on the European political market.

However, there is one problem concerning the political market in comparison with other markets. The behaviour of the participants has to be derived from the results; they probably would never admit to behave in the assumed mode. In addition, the contracts made on the political markets are implicit. No accounting is done. Hence, the economic analyst has only a few means to confirm his theoretical hypotheses. One of these means is an econometric analysis where the endogenous variable is the structure of protection and the exogenous variables are proxies for the ability of pressure groups to satisfy their demands (Anderson and Baldwin, 1981). This approach is not appropriate to our hypothesis because the number of observations is far too small. Only a few industries are subject to new forms of protection. Therefore, it is impossible to use a cross-section model. Instead, we concentrate on the analysis of two case studies. We analyze one instrument of strategic trade and industrial policy of the Union and the promotion of one special sector. The problem with case studies is that the results of one or two studies are not necessarily valid in general. This will be kept in mind when drawing conclusions.

The paper is organized as follows. In the next section the theoretical background is developed. Starting from the positive theory of trade policy, the market for protection in the European Union is presented. The market structure is shown and a process of creative destruction on this market is described. The market participants are national and supranational institutions as suppliers and interest groups as demanders. The third and the fourth section are dedicated to two fields of EU trade and industry policy where the persuasiveness of the theoretical results is evident. The first study deals with the Common Technology Policy as a relatively new instrument of common policies. In the second case study we concentrate on the promotion of a special industry which hitherto has been supported only by national institutions: the aircraft industry, especially Airbus Industries. The EU Commission now also wants to promote it. The fifth chapter is dedicated to the conclusions.

2 THE POLITICAL MARKET IN THE EUROPEAN UNION

2.1 The Structure of the Political Market before and after Integration

To understand the existence of protectionism and the suboptimal outcome of economic policy in the EU the concept of the social welfare function is inappropriate since it cannot explain why a government chooses a policy that reduces overall welfare. In order to explain such a policy, one has to focus on the gainers and losers of protection. Hence, we use the classical market model where the interaction between the supply and demand curves determines the quantity and the price of the product, which in our case is protection.[1] The suppliers are politicians and bureaucrats, and the demanders are interest groups, consumers and taxpayers. Of course, consumers and taxpayers are frequently the same people. Since strategic trade and industrial policy is particularly expensive, it is worthwhile distinguishing between these groups. Suppliers and demanders exchange measures of trade and industrial policy. Thus, the political outcome in this model is endogenous as opposed to the 'benevolent dictator model'. For instance, a political party offers a policy mix which favours particular interests. The supported lobby pays for the protection by providing enough votes for the party to be (re-)elected.

The suppliers of protection are policy-makers and bureaucrats. Like all other participants in markets they are seen as utility-maximizers. The utility functions of politicians and bureaucrats contain several arguments.

These are, among others, personal influence, higher income, ideology, higher budgets and – last but no least – social wealth (Willgerodt, 1979, p. 200ff). The suppliers carry out their policies in order to reach the highest possible personal utility level under political budget constraints. In the case of politicians the budget constraint is the probability of the (re-) election (Magee, Brock and Young, 1989, pp. 43ff). They are only able to maximize their utility if they succeed in general elections. Political parties offer a policy mix in order to maximize their probability of being elected. Once in office, they try to maximize their utility. Bureaucrats face a different constraint since they are usually controlled by politicians and their range of influence is limited. Both factors lead to a restriction of their position compared with politicians. But, usually, they do not have to fear competition, and they normally cannot be put out of office. In this respect, they are better off than politicians. Thus, bureaucrats can be seen as 'partial dictators' (Messerlin, 1981, p. 472). These different limitations lead to the conclusions that bureaucrats try to offer more differentiated and therefore more distorting measures of protection on a higher level than politicians (Messerlin, 1981, pp. 480ff).

The demanders of protection are the producers of commodities and services. They are represented by lobbies. Producers, especially import-competing industries, demand tariffs and non-tariff barriers which improve their welfare. The worse their economic performance is, the less are their opportunity costs of demanding protection, and the higher are the import barriers they call for. Exporters, consumers and taxpayers of course prefer and demand open markets and free trade. Which group is more successful in the political market? Following Olson (1965) it is obvious that producers' interests are easier to organize than the interests of consumers and taxpayers for three reasons: first, the group of producers is smaller in number than the group of consumers. Therefore, 'free-rider' problems are small. The gainers from the public good that the group produces are easily identified. Second, the individual gains from protection are higher for producers than the individual losses for consumers and taxpayers. Thus, the opportunity costs of lobbying are lower to producers than to consumers. Following from these reasons the producers, third, have much more incentives to be informed about the incidence of a special policy measure than consumers who have to judge the whole political programme of parties in which protection is not necessarily the most important field.

Looking at national political markets in developed countries one recognizes a stable equilibrium. The most protected industries are those which face fierce competition from developing countries and which are not willing and able to cope with the structural change which

Heckscher–Ohlin industries in developed countries find themselves confronted with. The determinants of this structure of protectionism are very similar across industrial countries: a sector is the more likely to be protected, the lower its international competitiveness is, the more concentrated its output is, the less skilled its labour force is, the less value added per capita it produces, and the higher its labour adjustment costs are (Anderson and Baldwin, 1981). Without an exogenous shock one can imagine this structure being valid over a long time. It could not last indefinitely because of the rising costs of a repressed structural change; the losers from protection will feel growing concern and will try to organize their interests better than before. But that scenario is a long-term one.

The equilibrium may be thrown off balance at short notice by economic integration (Olson, 1982). This shock has several possible changes regarding the level and structure of protectionism in the participating countries. The integration inside Europe started when the European Union was founded. The EU as a whole cannot be classified unambiguously in one of the known forms of integration. In its treatment of agricultural policies, for instance, it can be viewed as a common market. Yet in the range of trade and industrial policy, the EU should be treated analytically as a customs union. In a customs union, internal protection is to be dismantled and common trade barriers towards other countries are to be made uniform. Still, free trade is far from being realized inside the Union. Many internal trade-barriers – even in agricultural trade – prevent the allocation from being optimal. The following theoretical exposition tries to give an explanation for this and other phenomena.

By agreeing upon a customs union the member countries had to create a new bureaucracy which is responsible for the common external trade policy and for internal free trade. The Commission of the EU plays this role. As regards trade and industrial policy it works in two ways: first, it makes suggestions for the common trade policies which the Council has to decide on (Article 113, EC Treaty). It acts as a monopolist concerning propositions because no other institution or person is allowed to suggest common policies. Second, it has to watch if the member countries perform the treaties, particularly that they do not pursue trade policy of any kind on their own (Article 92–94, EC Treaty). National institutions should in general withdraw from trade policy and concentrate on regional fields of activities. Only in some exceptional cases can the member countries carry out some trade or industrial policy measures (Article 115, EC Treaty). As a result, internal free trade policy should be adopted, with the well-known positive welfare effects. But does this newly installed division of labour work correctly?

Before European integration, national politicians and members of the
bureaucracy worked as suppliers of trade and industrial policies. They
alone were responsible for the political outcome, given their political
budget constraints. In the course of the integration process institutional
competition emerged. One can identify at least two new competitors, the
EU Commission and the European Court of Justice. We shall focus on the
more important institution in terms of external trade and industrial policy.
This is the EU Commission in its role as the Union's bureaucracy. It is
vested with all nominal power concerning external trade policies. It aims
to establish itself as the real powerful institution whereas the national suppliers have withdrawn from these areas slowly and reluctantly. Which are
the appropriate strategies the three competitors, that is the EU-
Commission, national governments and national bureaucracies, choose?

2.2   The Strategies of the Players after the Integration

The EU Commission

As the new supplier the Commission is in a special position because it is
the only competent authority in common trade and industrial policy.
Therefore, it is suitable to call the Commission a 'general dictator'. But it
faces some political budget constraints we have not mentioned yet. First,
there is the GATT. The GATT aims at liberalization, with a reduction of
tariffs, a uniform tariff structure and the outlawing of non-tariff trade barriers. The last restriction is not a very tight one since all contracting parties
are searching for new forms of protectionism which do not violate the
GATT. In order to establish oneself on the political market in Europe, non-
tariff barrier seem to be appropriate, especially for a bureaucracy. Second,
the EU Commission has no tax sovereignty. It depends on funds which the
national governments spend on common policies. Other fund-raising
sources are fractions of the VAT revenues, customs revenues and price
adjustment levies in agricultural trade. Therefore, the Commission is low in
funds. Since the importance of tariffs and customs revenues is diminishing,
and since many non-tariff barriers put the Commission to great expense, it
is not able to offer all the political products it otherwise would. Moreover,
the national suppliers of protection are not willing to leave the field to the
Commission and are therefore reluctant to provide more money for the promotion of a common policy. To overcome these problems the Commission
can use four strategies: the use of Article 93, EC Treaty, the formation of
coalition with some member countries, the exploitation of its monopoly to
suggest common policies, and the creation of new political products.

One way to repress national protectionism is the use of Article 93, EC Treaty. The Commission is authorized to control the subsidies that member countries pay to their national firms. If the subsidies disturb the Common Market the Commission requests the member country to stop or change it within a deadline. In order to put through such a request the Commission can appeal to the European Court of Justice. A closer look at the facts shows that the Commission has usually won such cases. But this strategy alone is not appropriate in order to be successful as supplier in the political market.

With a view to establishing itself as competitor on the market for protection more is needed. A strategy which may be very successful would be to combine two or more different policy measures in order to form a coalition. If the governments of some member countries do not want the commission to carry out a special policy because it has been their own field of action hitherto, whereas other member countries are indifferent because they have not been involved in this policy yet, the Commission may try to combine the first policy with another policy which is important to the second group of member countries. In a 'log-rolling' process the second group supports the Commission's efforts, whereas the Commission in return either carries out a policy in favour of these countries or allows them to carry out own trade or industrial policy without calling for Article 93, EC Treaty. As will be shown in the third section of the paper, the Commission has used this strategy successfully in order to set up a common technology policy.

But the Commission is also able to establish itself on the political market without taking into account national suppliers. It has the monopoly on the suggestion of common trade policy measures in the Union. It seems advantageous for it to adopt distorting measures whose consequences cannot easily be assessed, therefore non-tariff barriers are much more suitable than tariffs. Distorting measures help the Commission to become the 'general dictator'. The Council and national governments are dependent on proposals and advices made by the Commission, which has now become irreplaceable. The Common Agricultural Policy provides an example of such a strategy. The set of rules is so intricate that national institutions, the Council and third persons have many difficulties in assessing the economic consequences of certain measures.

Another strategy to reduce the Commission's political budget constraints would focus on the demanders of protection. The Commission can attract demand for protection by placing new products in the political market, for example the so-called strategic trade and industrial policy which, in the last decade, has won an enormous academic reputation. Many studies have theoretically shown the positive welfare effects of trade and industrial policy when the market structure is oligopolistic[2] or when spillovers of research and development activities are at hand (Grossman and Helpman, 1990). Although it is convincingly argued that it is impossible to pursue such a policy (Donges, 1994), it is fashionable to plead for it. Rent-seeking lobbies can argue with logically consistent arguments, and the public opinion is more easily convinced that strategically-oriented protection helps countries out of structural crises. Since the EU Commission has adopted this positive attitude its political budget constraints have been reduced. Its chances of fund-raising are growing because the national governments may be forced to help it. If they do not do so, they are likely to lose electoral support because the Commission's advocacy of strategic trade and industrial policies is something which the voters are in favour of. The Commission's behaviour can therefore be compared with the behaviour of entrepreneurs who seek new opportunities by selling new products (Schumpeter, 1942/1976, pp. 81ff).

The national institutions

The national politicians and governments have at least four ways to react to the new situation. The least likely is that they will withdraw and leave the field to the commission. They do not often choose this first strategy. Second, they try to offer some new political products to their demanders. This may work for some time. But once the Commission has recognized national trade and industrial policies it insists on compliance with Article 93 or 115, EC Treaty. Thus, this strategy only seems to be a short-term reaction, intended to gain time. There is a similar strategy, however. The national suppliers are able to react on the product innovation of the EU Commission in just the way that Schumpeterian theory would suggest: The Commission places its strategic-oriented protection as political product innovations and behaves as a Schumpeterian entrepreneur. The national institutions would then behave as imitators by offering a similar political product. They would also impose strategic trade and industrial policies. Although national technology policies had already existed no member country had emphasized the strategic aspect before. This is a new element but it is also open to criticism because the Commission will probably react by calling for Article 93, EC Treaty.

The fourth and most appropriate option in the eyes of national governments is to become an intermediary on the political market. They could demand protection from Brussels which they would offer to their national demanders. These demanders continue to be dependent on national institutions. The price the governments pay is the loss of competence in trade and industrial policy but they do not have to withdraw from the market completely. They can provide the Commission with high enough funds to offer an expensive strategic trade and industrial policy. The Commission itself can accept national protectionism. At least it can reduce its efforts to control these national activities. This can be seen as a log-rolling process at the expense of consumers and taxpayers. Furthermore, the Commission and national institutions can divide labour in the following way: the Commission plans and monitors all programmes and measures while the national and local institutions carry out the programmes in detail. Both national and supranational level are still at work as suppliers of protection. The use of this strategy has another valuable advantage for national governments. Not being responsible for common policies gives the opportunity of diminishing the political budget constraints in the case of unpopular decisions made by the Commission: the Commission does the dirty work for the governments (Vaubel, 1991, p. 36). Their chances of being (re-)elected are not restricted by the political decision even if they participated in the decision process.

The national bureaucracies do not feel that comfortable with the new competitor since trade and industrial policy is now to be centralized. Presuming that the Commission succeeds in using Article 93, EC Treaty, they have less chances to keep their position as partial dictators. As autonomous suppliers, they lose importance. Because their areas of competences are too small from the beginning, they cannot become intermediaries. Thus, the only option they have is to withdraw from the market for protection, at least in the long run. Naturally, they will try to delay this process. If the qualified staff members try to leave their national bureaucracy and join the Commission the imbalance gets worse (Vaubel, 1993, pp. 10ff). Taking into account that the salaries in Brussels are much higher than in the national bureaus, this is a very probable outcome.

The demanders of protection

Which participant on the demand side can cope better with the new structure on the supply side of the integrated political market? Generally, more competition on the supply side means better or cheaper products. A priori it does not seem clear, whether demanders for protection (producers of commodities) or demanders for open markets (consumers, taxpayers and some exporters) can face the situation more adequately. Before the integration took place, the lobbies of the producers only concentrated their activities on national suppliers. It seems plausible that they would need time to reorganize after the integration. It takes time to establish a lobby in

Brussels. An industry with national interest groups located in the national capitals is unable to found a supranational organization at once for two reasons. First, the structure of the supply side is not clear to them a priori. So they have to establish contact with national suppliers and the EU Commission. Secondly, there are principal–agent problems between the lobby as agent and the firms as principal. Even if it was necessary to concentrate only on rent-seeking activities in Brussels the lobbies in the national capitals would not be willing to withdraw because the jobs and income of people working at the lobbies depend on staying in the capitals. Hence, during the process of reorganization some rents may be invalidated (Tiedemann, 1994). But after a while, the producers will have reorganized and formed a top organization in Brussels since they still are relatively small groups which can be organized (Olson, 1965). This is by no means the case with consumers and taxpayers. It has already been nearly impossible to express their interest in national markets. In an integrated political market, with some ten different languages and more than 300 million people, this is even more difficult. Hence, one can easily imagine that the producers' advantages will grow when the political market is enlarged because of the integration.

2.3   Short Summary of the Theoretical Results

This short exposition shows that in general the European market for protection works in a similar way to markets for commodities and services. The integration has led to the installation of a new bureaucracy, particularly the EU Commission, which has tried to establish itself as a supplier on the political market. Its strategies are the following: first, it tries to control the efforts of the national institutions to offer their own trade policy. Secondly, it forms coalitions by combining different fields of policy. This log-rolling process can be used to place its own products on the political market and to crowd out national suppliers. Thirdly, its policy is made mostly selective and intricate in order to become the general dictator. Fourthly, it places product innovations, namely some means of strategic-oriented protection. These innovations are placed in order to attract the demand to the new supplier. The national suppliers have only a few possible ways to react. They can imitate the new products, or they can become intermediary for the protection the Commission offers to the European lobbyists. The second strategy seems to be the more successful one because the EC Treaty does not allow national institutions to carry out trade and industrial policies.

In this respect, the political market does not differ widely from normal markets: A process of creative destruction takes place such that the new competitor tries to crowd out the old one by placing new products. The established suppliers refuse to withdraw from the political market. So they become intermediaries or behave as imitators. But if we take another view the analogy to commodities markets is not evident: normally, this process of innovation and imitation leads to welfare improvement for the consumers of goods and services. As pointed out, the integration only improves the position of producers of commodities on the political market. Generally, they demand protection whereas the consumers are better off with free trade. The above-mentioned product innovations do not lead to more free trade; rather they mean more selective and thus more costly interventions. Regional – not worldwide – integration creating new bureaucracies probably raises the level of protectionism. (Frey and Buhofer, 1986). Thus, the changes in the political market leave the consumers worse off.

3 TECHNOLOGY POLICY IN THE UNION

This section focuses on the process of creative destruction on the political market. It shows how the Commission tries to place its new political product 'Common Technology Policy', how the national suppliers react and behave as intermediaries, particularly in Germany, and how the vote trading in the log-rolling process takes place. The first subsection discusses the arguments in favour of technology policy. Some facts of the Common Technology Policy are shown in the second subsection. In the third subsection, we explain the behaviour of the participants on the market for R&D support. From this behaviour we derive the results, the process of log-rolling and the crowding out of national suppliers.

3.1 Pros and Cons of Technology Policy

The first case study deals with an instrument of EU industrial policy which is not normally quoted in the context of protection. Technology policy is usually justified by positive externalities caused by research and development, an argument of market failure. In addition, the very high risk of R&D-spendings is a second argument in favour of technology policy. Both arguments are correct as far as basic research is concerned, which indeed is characterized by high positive externalities. The revenues of the expenditure on R&D are not only collected by the firms that invested in the project, but other firms can also benefit; in other words, the revenues are partly social. Thus, basic research will not be provided sufficiently by the market. State interventions are needed to guarantee sufficient efforts in R&D. But it is different with applied research. The revenues derived from applied research are wholly private. Hence, it is by no means necessary and economically justified to support it, and the governmental attempt to stimulate applied R&D is of course an instrument of protection. The range of arguments against this kind of technology policy is wide:

The first argument against selective R&D promotion is that it means 'pretence of knowledge' (Hayek, 1974/1992). Second, enterprises which are applying for funds in order to carry out a research project will not suggest projects which are very likely to be successful. Instead, they will probably suggest very risky projects, and an adverse selection will take place (Klodt, 1987, p. 83). Third, promoted enterprises do not have too high an incentive to achieve very fast progress. A step-by-step strategy is more often adopted in order for them to obtain more and more funds. Fourth, the higher the funds of technology support are, the more scientists are busy applying for these resources instead of searching for new technologies. The amount of technology allowances determines the allocation of talent (Murphy, Shleifer and Vishny, 1990).

3.2   Some Facts of the Common Technology Policy

Technology policy is a traditional policy field of the more developed member countries, especially France, Germany, Great Britain and the Netherlands. Most of the funds are dedicated to applied research of large-scale enterprises although the promotion of smaller firms is emphasized in official statements (Klodt et al., 1988, pp. 3ff). The efforts of the Commission to support R&D started in the early 1960s, but it was not until 1984 that a regular Common Technology Policy was established.

One can distinguish two different kinds of support; the direct and the indirect. The direct approach is intended to support basic research. In order to allow the promotion of R&D the Commission organizes Framework Programmes in four- or five-year-terms. The first lasted from 1984 to 1987 and provided ECU 3.7 billion, the second program (1987–1991) was endowed with 5.1 billion ECU, and in the third one (1990–1994) ECU 5.4 billion were available, which of course was more since 1990 and 1991 were counted twice so that real endowment was ECU 8.8 billion (Harrop, 1992, p. 128). The financial endowment of the Fourth Framework Programme (1994–1998) is set to be even higher. It will provide about ECU 13 billion.

Table 1   The Second and the Third Framework Programme (ECU millions)

Industry	Second Programme (1987–91) Funding Absolute	Percentage	Third Programme (1990–94) Funding Absolute	Percentage
Information and Communication	2,275	42.3	2,221	38.9
Energy	1,173	21.7	814	14.3
New Materials	845	15.6	888	15.7
Biotechnology (a)	280	5.2	714	13.0
Environmental Research	375	6.9	518	9.1
Resources and Mobility	–	–	518	9.1
Others	448	8.3	–	–
Total (b)	4,396	100	5,910	100

Source: OECD, 1992, pp. 330ff.
Notes:
(a) Biotechnology includes Agrotechnology, Medicine and related areas.
(b) Some measures are counted twice, so that in total the sum is higher than ECU 3.7 billion (1987–91) and ECU 5.4 billion (1990–94).

Table 1 shows the crucial points of the Common Technology Policy during the Second and Third Framework Programmes. It becomes clear that it concentrates only on a few industries; in other words it is rather selective. Three quarters of the funds of the Third Programme are dedicated to five major industries: information, communication, energy, new materials and biotechnologies. The support of biotechnologies has been raised from 5.2 per cent to 13.0 per cent. Environmental research has also gained in importance, whereas the promotion of energy has been cut. The distribution of funds suggests that this form of support favours applied research more than basic research. The selection is made by the EU which consults enterprises and scientists. Therefore, the direct approach is often called 'top-down' approach.

In addition, an indirect, or 'bottom-up', approach exists. Any interested enterprises are invited to take the initiative if they need support. There are no common funds available but it is possible to acquire national financial endowments (Starbatty and Vetterlein, 1990, p. 88). The Union, together with the EFTA countries and Turkey, has established EUREKA as a reaction to the SDI Program of the United States. The objective of this approach is to promote the co-operation of enterprises in R&D. It is intended to strengthen the international competitiveness of European enterprises.

3.3   The Political Economy of Technology Policy in EU

The EU Commission

The participants in the political market of course have different interests. The Commission of the EU wants to broaden its range of competence. In other words, it tries to place new products on the political market. Technology policy is a very useful product in attracting demand to the Commission because it seems to be economically rational. The Commission faces the problem that the established suppliers of technology policy do not want to give up their positions. Hence, they are going to counteract efforts of the Commission that, without its own budget, depends on the approval of the member countries. In the Council, some 70 percent of the votes are necessary to get a Framework Programme through. To overcome these difficulties, the Commission uses three strategies.

First, it combines technology policy with regional policy to gain the votes of the relatively less developed member countries. These countries a priori have only small interest in supporting R&D. The expenditure on R&D in these countries is still much lower than in the northern member countries (OECD, 1992). The Commission has to convince them. By promising them growing funds for regional projects, it buys their votes in the Council. That is how the majority for a Common Technology Policy can be obtained in the Council. The Commission forms a coalition which even worsens the situation of consumers and taxpayers. Not only do they pay the bill for the promotion of applied R&D but, beyond that, new expenses occur in order to provide new means of regional policy.

Second, the Commission can force more developed countries to agree to a common technology policy. The case of Germany may demonstrate the possibilities. The German Government refused its consent to the common promotion of R&D throughout the 1980s by quoting the principle of *Ordnungspolitik* and the subsidiarity principle. The first means that technology policy should concentrate on basic research, that is selective interventions should be avoided. The subsidiarity principle claims that a policy measure should be carried out on that political level that can do it in the most efficient way. If spillovers of R&D exist overall in the Union a common promotion is appropriate. If spillovers are not EU-wide, national or regional institutions are better qualified to perform the task. Although the argument makes sense it is possible that this is not the only motivation for preventing the Commission from offering its own technology promotion. The model of political economy suggests that the second intention of the government was to stay in the political market. The Commission reacted by ignoring those German enterprises which were among the applicants when it allocated the funds of the First Framework Programme. Only when the German Government abandoned its position were the German enterprises taken into consideration (Starbatty and Vetterlein, 1990, p. 117).

Third, the Commission, in trying to expand its competence uses the application of Article 93, EC Treaty, in order to crowd out its national competitors. Throughout the 1970s and 1980s, it examined many national promotion projects in the field of R&D. In most cases, it made no objections (Klodt et al., 1988, pp. 126ff). Although at the first glance Article 93 seems not to be the most relevant strategy, the examination alone may be suitable to repress national efforts because of the danger of a formal proceeding. If the national governments lose a formal proceeding their political budget constraints at home are likely to raise.

The national institutions

The other potential suppliers of technology policy are the member countries. They can be divided into two groups; one group that offers technology policy, the other that does not. Thus, they have different interests and react in a different way when a new competitor appears. In the northern countries, national institutions are by no means willing to retire from the political market. However, as shown above, it is far from easy to stay in the market. The first possible reaction is the attempt to prevent the Commission from promoting R&D by referring to the subsidiarity principle, but seeking just to oppose the new supplier proved vain, especially since Article 130iff, Maastricht Treaty, vests the Commission with power. The commission was able to repress opposition to Common Technology Policy from Germany by neglecting German firms when it allocated the R&D funds. This strategy helped to compel the German Government to give up its position (see above). German firms now benefit from the Common Technology Policy in the same way as other firms.

Instead of being opposed to the Commission's offer, the second possible reaction for the national institutions is to neglect it and the Article 93, EC Treaty. In spite of this restriction, they would still place their political products in the market. Up to now it has been possible to do this because it proved quite difficult for the Commission to show that national R&D support seriously disturbs the allocation on the Common Market. Nevertheless, sooner or later the national supplier could be forced to withdraw.

Faced with this problem, the national institutions have chosen a third option. As pointed out above, the strategic-oriented and selective technology policy is a successful product innovation. Before the 1990s, the national suppliers did not call their R&D support strategic oriented, but they subsequently noticed the positive public image of such a policy. So they found it appropriate to postulate a strategic-oriented technology policy. Again, the German example will serve as an illustration. The Federal Government and some State Governments (Bavaria, Baden-Württemberg) have installed technology councils where politicians, managers of important enterprises and scientists (no economists!) discuss probable developments and possible strategies to face them. A second step has not been taken yet. Moreover, all relevant political parties in Germany call for the promotion of key industries in their election platforms. The national institutions behave as imitators. The Commission's successful product innovation in the political market inspired the national institutions to react with a similar product. In addition, by installing technology councils, the national institutions are subject to a change. Hitherto they have only been suppliers; now they are also intermediaries. It is probable that proposals and demands for projects within the Common Technology Policy are made in the technology councils. While being in close contact to the demanders of R&D support the national governments and bureaucracies can bring these in contact with the EU Commission. National institutions are able to stay in the market in this manner.

The southern member countries are much more at ease with the efforts made by the Commission to establish itself as a competitor in the market for technology policy. They had had no competence in this policy field before the Commission started its own technology policy. Since the Commission and the northern countries have diverging interests concerning this topic they can offer their votes in the European Council to either side. The price for this deal depends on their performance in the bargaining. In the case of technology policy, the Commission bought their votes by raising the regional allowances given to them. Thus, the institutions in the southern countries have also become intermediaries. The politicians and bureaucracies there have to allocate the allowances and to watch over the usage of the funds. That means new fields of activity for them. Both the demanders for and the suppliers of Common Technology Policy depend on them. Moreover, the Commission may not control them too much as it depends on their votes.

The demanders

The last groups to be mentioned in this context are the interest groups as demanders of technology policy. For them more competition on the supply side is an advantage. Since both suppliers advertise for their product, the demanders can ask for more R&D support in Brussels and at home. As long as the Commission has not fully established itself and the national suppliers have not completely withdrawn they will do so. Moreover, they have another advantage. They are better informed about technological trends and new products (on the commodity markets) than the suppliers. Thus, they are involved in the decision-making process on R&D support from the beginning: many programmes are inspired and planned by the concerned industries which even drafted the contracts (Ullrich, 1990, pp. 173ff). In particular, the Commission, as a newcomer on the political market, needs their help, so that even the 'top-down' approach is characterized by the interests of the demanders, particularly the large ones. They are better equipped for lobbying than the smaller firms so that the imbalance in favour of large-scale enterprises on a national level is not likely to disappear in Europe.

4   THE AIRCRAFT INDUSTRY

After looking at a generally-used instrument of strategically-oriented trade and industrial policy, we shall now examine a specific industry, the aircraft industry. It is necessary to consider whether the strategy of the Commission, in aiming to gain an attractive position on the political market, is changed when it is concerned with a specific industrial sector rather than in introducing general protectionist measures. The proceeding is similar to that chosen in section 3. First, an economic assessment of the promotion of the European aircraft industry is given. Second, the political market for this special segment is explained. The explanation focuses on the role of the Commission: Does it behave in the way which the theoretical analysis would suggest?

4.1   Promotion of Aircraft Industry in Europe: No Economic Success

On the world market for large aircrafts American firms are traditionally in a leading position. It was not before the early 1980s that their European competitors could stabilize their market shares at some 20 per cent (Bletschacher and Klodt, 1992, p. 79). Other competitors do not exist. This oligopolistic market structure is caused above all by barriers to entry, namely sunk costs which make the entry into the market impossible, at least without state interventions. Moreover, another special property of the market, dynamic economies of scale, is also likely to prevent newcomers from entering the market. In addition, economies of scope and network externalities are often cited as making the entry for a newcomer very difficult.[3]

Why should the state support the entry into the market for aircrafts? Two reasons which can make economic sense are to be considered. The first refers to high return in oligopolistic markets as the theory of strategic trade policy suggests (see above). If these high returns exist, the European Union should support the European aircraft industry in order to make profit-shifting from the United States to Europe possible. The whole economy can improve in welfare. The second reason is often seen in spillovers for other industries, generated by R&D efforts in the aircraft industry. However, up to now neither any profit-shifting (Bletschacher and Klodt, 1992, pp. 90ff) nor the empirical relevance of positive externalities (Schrader, 1990, pp. 225ff) could be shown.

Nevertheless, the Commission of the EC (1992) puts forward these arguments. Moreover, the Commission quotes some other arguments in favour of supporting the aircraft industry: the enormous expenditure on R&D which the industry has to make in order to be internationally competitive; and the high level of investment necessary to start production.[4] Private enterprises are considered unable to afford such high amounts. Hence, they have to be supported by the state until the investments pay off. These two arguments do not make much sense: if an investment is likely to be success it should be possible to collect enough capital on the international market for venture capital which normally works well. The third reason the Commission quotes for the state to intervene is the endeavour to be technologically independent which is considered to be very important. Because this objective is a political one it cannot be judged economically. But economists can say something about the efficacy of the methods which are applied to pursue this goal. From this standpoint, assuming that there is access to all technology, then autarchy is to be rejected because it is too expensive. Instead, the best way to achieve independence is through international trade; most individuals and countries are going to become independent because they depend on each other. To draw a conclusion, all these arguments cannot bear close examination (Donges, 1994).

Table 2 shows that the economic performance of the aircraft industry in Europe seems to be strong by normal standards. The growth of production

Table 2   Economic indicators of the aircraft industry
(partly including aerospace)

Indicator	1982	1984	1986	1987	1988	1989	1990
Production (a)	18.4	21.5	27.5	29.4	32.8	36.1	38.7
EC Exports (a)	4.2	6.3	6.2	6.0	10.8	14.5	17.4
EC Imports (a)	3.6	5.0	6.2	6.1	10.2	14.2	18.8
RCA (b)	0.31	0.23	–0.02	–0.01	0.11	0.1	0.04
World Market Shares (%) (c)	(1981–85): 19.5				(1986–90): 20.1		
Investments over Production	4.1	3.0	3.5	3.9	4.2	n.a.	n.a.
Productivity (d)	92.4	100	107.3	106.1	111.6	128	127.4
Real Growth (e) Divided by the Growth of GNP	(1982–85): 2.35				(1986–90): 1.58		

Source: EUROSTAT, 1992 and 1993; Bletschacher and Klodt, 1992, p. 79.
Notes:
(a) Billion ECU; current prices.
(b) Revealed Comparative Advantage:
Ln $(X/M/x/m)$ where X = all exports of the EC;
M = all imports of the EC;
x = aircraft and aerospace exports of the EC;
m = aircraft and aerospace imports of the EC.
(c) Large civil aircraft
(d) 1984 = 100 (EUROSTAT, 1992).
(e) Per annum.

exceeds the growth of GNP in the Union. Exports exceeded imports almost throughout the 1980s. Thus, the RCA is positive most of the time. This indicator is often quoted as important, although it is just the expression of comparative advantages a country or region has. Besides, the indicator in this case is a function of all the protectionist measures in favour of the aircraft industry.

Moreover, all indicators should be treated carefully. The growth rate, the development of production, exports and imports, and the world market shares are surely determined by the huge allowances that the national governments gave to the European aircraft and aerospace industry. They should be interpreted under this reservation. The enormous rise of productivity can be interpreted as an indicator of the industry's high research-intensity. But it is not clear whether these gains are due to private efforts or to state interventions. In addition, the productivity index is not explained any further by the Commission. One has to be very careful about the index. The volume of annual investments is unsatisfactory. The investment in the aircraft and aerospace industry is by no means higher than in other industries. In order to figure out if sunk costs exist, one ought to have data of the capital stock which are not available. Last but not least, no information about the profits exists, or if it does, it is not given to the public. As this is the most relevant indicator by which to judge an industry's performance, our conclusion must remain incomplete.

4.2   Concorde and Airbus: Two Big Shots of Industrial Policy?

The first considerable attempt of European countries to pursue industrial policy in favour of the aircraft industry was the Concorde, which was a common project of Great Britain and France. It failed because of lacking economic rationality. The participating firms did not pay attention to the costs. Instead, the main motivation was a technical enthusiasm. Moreover, the division of labour between the enterprises did not work well since none of them was willing to specialize exclusively in one working area, but wanted to participate in most of the new knowledge (Berg and Mammen, 1981, p. 352). The project was cancelled in 1978 since only 14 aircrafts had been sold.

Some of these mistakes were avoided when in 1967 the Airbus, a common project of firms from Belgium, France, Germany, Great Britain, the Netherlands and Spain, was brought into being. The partners founded an enterprise called Airbus Industries, which better took the costs into account and which practiced a higher internal specialisation. Nevertheless, Airbus Industries is far from being organized efficiently. The production is allocated by quotas referring to the financial engagement of the partner firms, not to real comparative advantages. The national partners take most of the decisions; Airbus Industries itself has only a few competences (Yoffie, 1990, pp. 339ff) which keeps allocation from being optimal and the planning process from being as fast as possible (Feldmann, 1993, p. 157).

The promotion of Airbus comprises allowances of R&D, production and sales. A fourth element, the guaranty of exchange rates was dropped in 1992 because it violated the GATT rules (FAZ, 1992). Although this project works much better than the Concorde, it is far from being an economic success. The subsidies had risen to US $ 20 billions at the end of the 1980s (Bletschacher and Klodt, 1992, p. 92). Not profit-shifting, but loss-shifting, has taken place.

4.3   The Commission as a New Competitor

From the beginning the support for Airbus Industries has been granted by the member governments, not by the Union (Hayward, 1988, p. 15). The only suppliers of protection have been national institutions. Because of the technological fascination of aircraft one can imagine the opportunity costs of protecting this industry for politicians and bureaucrats being low. The political budget constraints which the national suppliers face are not high. Thus, the national institutions surely want to continue in offering this product notwithstanding that the costs for the economy as a whole are high.

Since 1988 the Commission has tried to change this situation. It created so-called Action Programmes for special industries, of which one was dedicated to the aircraft industry (Commission of the EC, 1992). In this programme, some proposals are made to strengthen this industry's international competitiveness. The crucial points are the following: (1) bundling of R&D efforts in order to raise efficiency; (2) harmonization of technical standards, scientific education, training of personnel and registration requirements of aircraft; (3) a guarantee fund to minimize the exchange rate risk; and (4) the pressure on the United States and on the member countries to comply with the rules of fair competition.

The hypothesis of this section is that the Commission tries to establish itself further on the political market for protection by presenting such an action programme. The crucial points of the programme can especially support this hypothesis. In order to test the hypothesis we now take a closer look at the economic rationality of the four elements. The hypothesis cannot be rejected if the action programme lacks economic rationality.

The Commission proposes to bundle national R&D efforts in order to minimize costs which are high due to research taking place at seven places in Europe up to now. On the one hand, this measure may raise economic efficiency if it helps to avoid two or more scientists doing the same job. On the other hand, such duplication of research can create competition between scientists and lead to better and earlier results. Another advantage of parallel and decentralized research is that the fields of research can be chosen by the scientist alone. Centralized efforts involve the danger of being selective even more than national efforts. This can have even worse effects for economic growth and employment. The Commission could be tempted to lay down the scientific topics a priori which can have the disadvantage that national pretence of knowledge is only substituted by a common one.

The same ambivalent criticism applies to the second proposal, the harmonization of standards and regulations. Harmonization can save costs.

However, Airbus Industries probably would have reduced costs if this had been possible. As pointed out above, the structure and the decision-making process of Airbus Industries did not allow an efficient use of the resources dedicated to R&D. So harmonization must be accompanied by the reorganization of the firm's structure which is better made by Airbus Industries itself, not by the Commission. In addition, harmonization can cause even higher costs if the technical or educational standard that has a priori been chosen by the Commission later proves to be an inferior one.

The third proposal deals with the industry's problem to cope with the volatility of the exchange rate of the US Dollar with regard to the currencies of the European Monetary System (EMS). The sales of the aircraft are invoiced in US Dollars; the costs, however, are to be paid in European currencies. In three cases the Commission identifies a problem for Airbus Industries: the US Dollar is soft at the time when (1) starting the production process; (2) when the aircraft are paid by the buyer; or (3) when Airbus Industries wants to invest the revenues. If the US Dollar is strong, the Commission sees the problem for the European airlines that their capital is too expensive. It seems that there is no exchange rate appropriate for the European seller or buyers of aircraft. Therefore, the Commission pleads for the installation of a guaranty fund which should be financed by the aircraft industry itself, but it does not say how this fund should work.

At first glance, the proposal seems to be in accordance with market rules. But if a fund which is financed by the industry is really necessary no efforts of the Commission are required. The aircraft industry is by no means the only industry facing long-term exchange rate risks. Since no other sector facing this difficulty is protected that way such a fund seems to be rather unnecessary. Moreover, nowadays a huge range of possibilities to hedge against exchange rate risks exist. One also has to look at the incidence of the payments dedicated to the fund. Even if the industry provides the funds it does not necessarily really bear all the costs as well. Subsidies for production, sale and export could be used for it. In this case the behaviour of the Commission would not be in accordance with the GATT.

The fourth element of the action programme is also a serious one although it looks as if it was in compliance with the GATT and with market rules. The Commission urges the United States to keep to the rules of the bilateral agreement, signed in 1992. The agreement aims at fair competition rules in the market for large aircraft, by limiting the direct subsidies to 30 per cent of total costs and by limiting R&D support, that is indirect subsidies, to 5 per cent of total sales. In the past, the US Government mainly supported the American aircraft enterprises by defence spending. This was often criticized by the Commission. Furthermore, following the agreement the market is to be organized more transparently than before. The Commission claims that the origin of the permanent disagreement between the EU and the US lies in a different logic concerning aircraft in both regions. However, it is by no means clear why there should be a different logic. The statement is very imprecise. Concerning the Common Market, the Commission refers to Article 85f and Article 92–94, EC Treaty. In a very careful way, it points out the problems of mergers of the enterprises in the aircraft industry and the limits of national promotion.

One can interpret this part of the programme in two ways: first, it could be meant as a reminder to all participants in this market to stick to the rules of fair competition. Second, it could be seen as a first, careful trial to gain a foothold in this segment of the market for protection. We prefer the second interpretation for two reasons: If it had really been meant as a reminder to free (or at least freer) trade, the Commission would not have spent so much energy on the other three elements which mainly counteract any plea for fair trade. In addition, the Commission's efforts to restrict the national promotion of the aircraft industry are quite insufficient; nothing is said about the high subsidies, the distortions caused by the burden which is borne by the taxpayers, and the misallocations which are due to these distortions.

The established national suppliers did not react directly on the action programme. They probably did not see the necessity although it should be obvious to them that this was only the beginning of the Commission's efforts to offer protection in this market segment. As long as the Commission proposes complementary rather than substitutive policy measures, for example technology policy instead of production allowance, the national suppliers may face even lower political budget constraints than before. They are still able to protect Airbus Industries while saving own funds which the Commission provides instead. Therefore, they can still offer their political product in order to be successful on their national political market (Freytag, 1993, pp. 304ff).

The demanders of protection in this market segment differ from those in other segments. Whereas the normal demander of protection is an enterprise which was founded in order to produce commodities and/or services, Airbus Industries can be treated as if it was created by the suppliers of protection, in other words it is a case of Say's Law. The behaviour of Airbus Industries differs from that of other demanders, too. Normally, the demanders try to create and exploit asymmetric information, so that consumers and taxpayers do not see their losses. Instead, Airbus Industries seems to be very self-assured; they take the view that they are working in compliance with GATT rules (FAZ, 1993) although not firms, but countries, should argue in such a manner.

As shown above, Airbus Industries is not homogenous. Therefore, one can imagine that its attitude towards the new competitor is conflicting. On the one hand, the new competitor is welcome for more suppliers can bring an even higher protection. On the other hand, there exists a danger that the Commission in the future is going to combine the promotion with regional policy. In this case, Airbus Industries probably will be divided: its subsidiary companies have their own interests. They still need their national suppliers in order to protect them and do not want to see them disappear from the political market.

After analyzing the market for protection in favour of the aircraft industry we draw a first conclusion. Although the strategy of the Commission is more subtle than in the case of technology policy one can hardly reject the hypothesis that the Commission is trying to establish itself also in this market segment. This purpose proves very difficult compared with the efforts concerning technology promotion. National efforts to support the aircraft industry obviously do not generally fall under Article 92–94, EC Treaty, because several member countries are involved. Besides, the Commission cannot claim a domination of the market by one or few enterprises (Article 85f, EC Treaty) since Airbus Industries was created solely to break the dominance of American firms. The relevant market in the case of large aircrafts is the world market, not the European market. The Commission only has the chance to use its monopolistic situation concerning proposals on common policies. By mixing technology policies with the promotion of a special industry it can make a first successful attempt to compete with the established suppliers of protection within the Union. Another problem of the Commission is with the financial endowments of the action programme. Hitherto no funds were necessary because of the programme. The Commission will only give a more precise estimate of costs when it has to make detailed proposals in order to specify the programme (Commission of the EC, 1992, p. 32). We can make the forecast that in this case the resistance of the national suppliers will grow. Nevertheless, the Commission has taken a successful first step to establish in the market for protecting European aircraft industries. Others will probably follow.

5 CONCLUSIONS

This paper intended to explain how the political markets in Europe are subject to changes due to their increasing integration. Generally, political economy is able to help in understanding policy-making. There is no doubt that economic policies in developed countries have certain patterns which are related to the ability of interest groups to safeguard their interests. Under normal circumstances, trade and industrial policy is likely to leave producers better off and to worsen the situation of consumers and taxpayers. In addition, not all producers are protected, but mainly the import-competing industries.

Economic integration disturbs this equilibrium if it is followed by new rules and new institutions, which is the case inside the European Union. Trade policy towards third countries has been subject to harmonization, and internal free trade has been agreed upon. A new institution, the EU Commission, is responsible for imposing external trade policy measures and for keeping internal free trade. However, the national institutions do not withdraw as suppliers of protection without offering some resistance. Hence, the EU Commission acts as their competitor in the political market in Europe. It wants to attract the demand for protection to itself. The proceedings are similar to the proceedings in markets for commodities and services: a process of creative destruction with innovation and imitation takes place.

The market for technology policy can be explained especially well by this model. The Commission is trying to establish itself on the market for technology policy by offering political product innovations, that is strategically-oriented technology policy, by repressing the national suppliers and by forming a coalition with previously uninterested member countries. The national suppliers react by providing similar products to their pressure groups, that is imitation, and by changing their position: instead of being suppliers, they are now intermediaries.

The second example was the market for promoting the European aircraft industry. The result here is not as convincing as the examination of the Common Technology Policy. The Commission has not yet had the same possibilities to establish itself in this market. The preconditions for this purpose are not that good. Neither Article 85f nor Article 93, EC Treaty, provide the chance to intervene easily. The Action Programme which the Commission presented can be seen as a first attempt in order to claim competence to support this industry. It is by no means an effort to stimulate economic growth and employment within the Union. This holds true all the more since the protection of Airbus Industries has proved to be an economic fiasco. The two examples show that both existing and potential suppliers of protection do not only take economic performance into account when they impose policy measures; political considerations are also important.

The results of the theoretical analysis cannot be rejected. Nevertheless, one has to treat the findings carefully. Two case studies, one of them convincing, the other one a little less persuasive, do not allow the drawing of any definite conclusion that all EU policies are just imposed in order to maximize the individual utility of the bureaucrats working in the Commission. Instead, many staff members are surely of the firm conviction that they can do something useful by promoting special industries. The logical stringency of the political market model is not as high as in markets for commodities and services. Our analysis need not be at any rate appropriate to explain political outcome. Not every political activity is of such individual rationality as the model would suggest. However, one should keep in mind that the motivation for any decision-maker to pursue a certain policy is by no means as important as the economic outcome. A benevolent dictator will change a policy if it proves inefficient; an option the Commission has not chosen.

After all, the results provide useful hypotheses of how the policy-making may take place. These hypotheses can be used to predict policies in the future. We suggest that the EU Commission will try to place more new products on the political market in Europe and that the national institutions react in a way similar to that we noticed in our case studies. Perhaps it will be possible in the future to use econometric analysis in order to test the market model we developed in this paper.

Notes

1. A comprehensive introduction into the international political economy can be found in Frey (1984).
2. See for instance Krugman (1984), Spencer and Brander (1983), and Dixit (1984).
3. See for example Baldwin and Flam (1989), Klepper (1990), and Bletschacher and Klodt (1992, pp. 69ff).
4. These arguments should not be confused with the argument of dynamic economies of scale and the argument of sunk costs.

References

Anderson, Kym and Robert E. Baldwin (1981) 'The Political Market for Protection in Industrial Countries: Empirical Evidence', *World Bank Staff Working Papers* No. 492 (Washington, DC: The World Bank).
Baldwin, Richard and Harry Flam (1989) 'Strategic Trade Policies in the Market for 30–40 Seat Commuter Aircraft', *Weltwirtschaftliches Archiv*, 125, pp. 484–500.

Berg, Hartmut and Gerhard Mammen (1981) 'Alternative Strategien staatlicher Technologieförderung: Eine Analyse der Projekte "Concorde" und "Airbus"', in Harald Jürgensen *et al.* (eds), *Jahrbuch für Sozialwissenschaft*, 32, (Göttingen: Vandenhoeck und Ruprecht), pp. 346–79.

Bletschacher, Georg and Henning Klodt (1992) *Strategische Handels- und Industriepolitik* (Tübingen: J.C.B. Mohr (Paul Siebeck)).

Commission of the EC (1992) *Die europäische Luftfahrtindustrie: Bestandsaufnahme und mögliche Gemeinschaftsaktionen* (Brussels: EC Commission).

Dixit, Avinash (1984) 'International Trade Policy for Oligopolistic Industries', *The Economic Journal*, 94, pp. 1–16.

Donges, Juergen B. (1994) 'Kritisches zu den Forderungen nach einer strategischen Industriepolitik', in Rolf H. Hasse, Josef Molsberger and Christian Watrin (eds), *Ordnung in Freiheit*. Publication in Honour of Hans Willgerodt (Stuttgart, Jena, New York: Gustav Fischer), pp. 182–99.

EC Treaty (1993) (München: Beck), pp. 4–126.

EUROSTAT (1992) *Panorama der EG-Industrie, Statistischer Ergänzungsband 1992* (Luxemburg: Amt für amtliche Veröffentlichungen der Europäischen Gemeinschaft).

EUROSTAT (1993) *Panaroma der EG-Industrie* (Luxemburg: Amt für amtliche Veröffentlichungen der Europäischen Gemeinschaft).

Feldmann, Horst (1993) 'Konzeption und Praxis der EG-Industriepolitik', *ORDO-Jahrbuch*, 44, pp. 139–68.

'Airbus-Kurssicherung ein GATT-Verstoß', *Frankfurter Allgemeine Zeitung (FAZ)*, 17 January 1992, p. 13.

'Bonn will die Luftfahrtindustrie weiter fördern', *Frankfurter Allgemeine Zeitung (FAZ)*, 29 April 1993, p. 15.

Frey, Bruno S. (1984) *International Political Economics* (Oxford and New York: Basil Blackwell).

Frey, Bruno S. and Heinz Buhofer (1986) 'Integration and Protectionism: A Comparative Institutional Analysis', *Aussenwirtschaft*, 41, pp. 167–88.

Freytag, Andreas (1993) 'Zur Rolle der EG-Kommission in der Europäischen Industriepolitik', *Zeitschrift für Wirtschaftspolitik*, 42, pp. 295–307.

Grossman, Gene M. and Elhanan Helpman (1990) 'Comparative Advantage and Long-Run Growth', *American Economic Review*, 80, pp. 796–815.

Harrop, Jeffrey (1992) *The Political Economy of Integration in the European Community* (Aldershot: Edward Elgar).

Hayek, Friedrich August von (1974/1992) 'The Pretence of Knowledge', in *Nobel Lectures (Nobel Memorial Lecture) in Economic Science (1969–1980)*. (Singapore: World Science), pp. 179–188.

Hayward, Keith (1988) 'Airbus: Twenty Years of European Collaboration', *International Affairs*, 64, pp. 11–26.

Klepper, Gernot (1990) 'Entry into Market for Large Transport Aircraft', *European Economic Review*, 34, pp. 775–803.

Klodt, Henning (1987) *Wettlauf um die Zukunft*, (Tübingen: J.C.B. Mohr (Paul Siebeck)).

Klodt, Henning *et. al.* (1988) *Forschungspolitik unter EG-Kontrolle*, (Tübingen: J.C.B. Mohr (Paul Siebeck)).

258 The European Market for Protectionism

Krugman, Paul R. (1984) 'Import Protection as Export Promotion: International Competition in the Presence of Oligopoly and Economies of Scale', in Hendryk Kierzkowski (ed.), *Monopolistic Competition and International Trade* (Oxford: Oxford University Press), pp. 180–93.

Magee, Stephen P., William A. Brock and Leslie Young (1989) *Black Hole Tariffs and Endonenous Policy Theory* (Cambridge, New York, Port Chester, Melbourne, Sydney: Cambridge University Press).

Messerlin, Patrick A. (1981) 'The Political Economy of Protectionism: The Bureaucratic Case', *Weltwirtschaftliches Archiv*, 117, pp. 469–96.

Murphy, Kevin M., Andrei Shleifer and Robert W. Vishny (1990) *The Allocation of Talent: Implications for Growth*, NBER Working Paper 3530, (Cambridge Mass.: NBER).

OECD, (1992) *Wissenschafts- und Technologiepolitik*, (Paris: OECD).

Olson, Mancur (1965) *The Logic of Collective Action* (Cambridge Mass. and London: Harvard University Press).

—— (1982). *The Rise and Decline of Nations* (New Haven and London: Yale University Press).

Schrader, Klaus (1990) 'Einzelwirtschaftliche Wirkungen von Rüstungs- und Raumfahrtausgaben in den Vereinigten Staaten - eine Literaturanalyse', *Zeitschrift für Wirtschaftspolitik*, 39, pp. 211–62.

Schumpeter, Joseph A. (1942/1976) *Capitalism, Socialism and Democracy* (New York: Harper & Row).

Spencer, Barbara J. and James A. Brander (1983) 'International R&D Rivalry and Industrial Strategy', *Review of Economic Studies*, 50, pp. 707–22.

Starbatty, Joachim and Uwe Vetterlein (1990) *Die Technologiepolitik der Europäischen Gemeinschaft* (Baden-Baden: Nomos).

Tiedemann, Rüdiger (1994). *Aufstieg oder Niedergang von Interessenverbänden? Rent-Seeking und europäische Integration* (Baden-Baden: Nomos).

Treaty on the European Union (Maastricht Treaty), in Presse- und Informationsamt der Bundesregierung (ed.), Bulletin No. 16 of 13 February 1992, Bonn, pp. 113–84.

Ullrich, Hans (1990) 'Europäische Forschungs-und Technologiepolitik und die Ordnung des Wettbewerbs im Gemeinsamen Markt', in Erik Boettcher, Philipp Herder-Dorneich, Karl-Ernst Schenk and Dieter Schmidtchen (eds), *Jahrbuch für Neue Politische Ökonomie*, 9 (Tübingen: J.C.B. Mohr (Paul Siebeck)), pp. 169–95.

Vaubel, Roland (1991) 'A Public Choice View of International Organization', in Roland Vaubel and Thomas D. Willett (eds), *The Political Economy of International Organizations*, (Boulder, San Francisco and Oxford: Westview Press), pp. 27–45.

—— (1993) 'Perspektiven der europäischen Integration: Die Politische Ökonomie der Vertiefung und Erweiterung', in Horst Siebert (ed.), *Die zweifache Integration: Deutschland und Europa, Workshop zur Strukturberichterstattung* (Tübingen: J.C.B. Mohr (Paul Siebeck)), pp. 4–31.

Willgerodt, Hans (1979) 'Wirtschaftsordnung und Staatsverwaltung', *ORDO-Jahrbuch*, 30, pp. 199–217.

Yoffie, David B. (1990) *International Trade and Competition* (New York St. Louis, San Francisco: McGraw-Hill).

10 Liberty, Competition, and the Rise of Coercion in American Federalism
John Kincaid

Changing conceptions of liberty and equality in the United States have given rise in recent decades to a new, coercive phase of American federalism in which the federal government engages in unprecedented regulation of state and local governments and displacement of their sovereign powers. This coercive federalism reflects a shift in federal policy-making from places (i.e., state and local jurisdictions) to persons (i.e., individual citizens). In order to protect individual rights and provide benefits to persons, the federal government has increasingly pre-empted state and local powers and required state and local governments to implement federal policies and comply with federal rules. As a result, the federal government is occupying a more monopolistic position in the federal system. Acting more like a monopolist, the federal government has sought to suppress intergovernmental competition in the federal system and has fewer incentives to behave as a co-operative partner with state and local governments.

I BALANCING ANARCHY AND MONOPOLY IN FEDERALISM

Federalism is a form of constitutional governance dedicated to liberty and predicated partly on the assumption that both political anarchy and political monopoly are antithetical to law and liberty. Federalism, however, has been difficult to define precisely because, unlike the one-sided sovereignty in classic confederal and unitary regimes, a federal polity divides and shares sovereign powers. As such, federalism can be construed, as a relationship, a covenantal relationship (Elazar, 1987) in which power is naturally in flux and assertions of power often require co-ordinate consent and action (Hayek, 1960). In contrast to issues of structure prominent in confederal and unitary schemes, issues of relationship – conflict, co-operation, competition, collusion and coercion – pervade federal arrangements.

In effect, federalism is a balance between anarchy and monopoly requiring sufficient powers for the general (i.e., nationwide) government to prevent relations between the constituent governments from plunging into anarchy (such as has occurred with the disintegration of Yugoslavia), while reserving to the constituent units sufficient powers to prevent the general government from becoming a monopoly (as with the military regimes in Nigeria). Such a balance seems to require, among other things, a degree of competition between governments sufficient to constrain both anarchy among the constituent governments and monopoly in the general government. Such competition also undergirds classic notions of dual and co-operative federalism because neither anarchy nor monopoly is conducive to dualism or co-operation. Anarchy represents a breakdown of co-operation and a fragmentation of power, while a monopolistic government has no incentive to co-operate or to legitimize countervailing governments. In these respects, competition is essential to the operation of dual and co-operative federalism.

A federal polity also faces a second balancing challenge: one between individual liberty and communitarian liberty or, in shorthand, the rights of persons (personal freedoms) versus the rights of places (states' rights). Federalism's protections of the rights of places do not necessarily protect the rights of persons, while protections of the rights of persons do not necessarily protect the rights of places. In principle, each constituent polity could exclusively define the rights of persons, and one can even conceive of competition among these jurisdictions to offer variable packages of liberty (e.g., the right to die) tailored to the diverse preferences in a federation, but this principle is muted by the requisites of interjurisdictional mobility in a common federal market as well as by the modern Western principle of individual equality, which treats rights as universal. This expansive principle creates a widening circle of 'equal' rights for persons in polities dedicated to such protection. The principle of equality produces ever less tolerance for perceived peaks and valleys of individual liberty found in a union of sovereign polities. To realize equality, it is necessary to smooth out the peaks and valleys, usually by elevating valley jurisdictions to the level of peak jurisdictions. Such egalitarian landscaping, however, displaces powers exercised by the constituent governments, and the only government available to displace them is the national government.

A third balancing challenge for a federal system is between the claims of citizenship and the desires of consumership (Kincaid, 1993b). A classic feature of federalism is dual citizenship, whether *de jure* or *de facto*. Citizens frequently experience tension between these citizenships, and politics in a federation often entails clashes between cosmopolitans who value national citizenship and locals who value citizenship in their constituent polity. Establishment of a common market under a federal regime, however, also creates tension between local citizenship and national consumership. This tension has become especially evident in the United States where the consumer society has transformed nearly all local citizens into cosmopolitan consumers able to access goods and services, not only nationally but also globally.

This tension arises from the dynamics of consumerism, which increase incentives for citizens to demolish jurisdictional barriers that inhibit the movement of goods and services across the boundaries of the constituent governments within the federation's common market. Free trade requires diminution of the powers of self-government exercised by the constituent governments because variable exercises of such powers by fifty states and 86, 692 local governments would fragment the marketplace and frustrate consumers. Yet these powers of regional and local self-government are prized by locals who seek to maintain communal values and public policies that suit their preferences as local rather than national citizens. The more that citizens pursue consumership interests in the national marketplace by levelling jurisdictional barriers, however, the more they reduce the effective scope of their local citizenship rights. Thus, while local citizenship has centrifugal effects on power in a federal system, national consumership has centripetal effects.

Distinctions between private and public goods also lose force under consumerism because federal regulation of the national market for private goods requires regulation of public goods (e.g., transportation) relevant to interjurisdictional commerce, many of which are provided in state and local markets. Federal regulation of state and local public goods constrains the exercise of other constituent government powers and creates incentives for monopoly behaviour by the federal government, thus bringing more state and local public goods under federal regulation.

The manner and extent to which egalitarian and consumerist conceptions of liberty affect a federal system, however, are shaped by culture as well. Where concentrations of ethnic, religious, and/or linguistic groups cognizant of their communal identities largely coincide with constituent jurisdictional boundaries, there is likely to be resistance to federal intrusions upon constituent government powers (e.g., Taylor, 1993). Although, historically, the United States has had cultural regions defensive of states' rights (e.g., the South and the Utah-based Mormon area), the appeals of egalitarianism and consumerism for most Americans have eroded such concerns.

As a result, power in the United States has shifted toward monopoly as the federal government has sought to promote equal rights and liberties for persons and greater national prosperity for consumers. The federal system, therefore, is less dualistic, less co-operative and more coercive (Kincaid, 1990) than ever, because the federal government can achieve egalitarian and consumerist objectives only by pre-empting and conscripting state and local government powers. Given that these governments historically exercised the 'lion's share' of domestic powers, especially those of coercion, the federal government has assumed the advantageous position of legitimizing its movement toward monopoly by appearing to liberate persons from the tyranny of state and local governments. This national liberation of persons from the grip of small places, epitomized by the federal assault on states' rights segregationists in the 1950s and 1960s, has produced a considerable centralization of power since the 1960s, even though there is still considerable decentralization of administration, and even though the 'New Federalisms' of Presidents Richard M. Nixon (1969–1974) and Ronald Reagan (1981–1989) appeared, on first viewing, to be anti-centralist.

Alexis de Tocqueville, of course, argued that centralization would be a logical outcome of the democratic passion for equality. Centralization may not be inevitable, but its seeds were planted during the founding era when the Federalists sought to stem competition and conflict between the states, liberate persons from the tyranny of state legislatures, extend the authority of the Union directly to citizens, and build a great commercial republic. The Federalists were only modestly successful in the 1780s but, over time, the federal system became more nationalized and coercive, especially as the federal government responded to the direct interests of persons rather than those of state and local governments (i.e., places). Federal relations with persons are coercive for constituent places because, given the historically broad state–local responsibility for citizen well-being, the federal government can benefit persons only by circumventing state and local governments (e.g., direct payments to individuals, such as Social Security), displacing traditional state and local authority (e.g., pre-emption), or requiring state and local governments to implement federal policies (e.g., mandates and conditions of aid). The federal government now employs all three mechanisms to unprecedented extents.

2   FROM PLACES TO PERSONS IN AMERICAN FEDERALISM

During debate over the union in the 1780s, leading Federalists, such as Alexander Hamilton, argued that 'we must extend the authority of the Union to the persons of the citizen, the only proper objects of government'(*Federalist* 15). Under the Articles of Confederation (1781), the

Union could not penetrate state sovereignty to touch the persons of citizens for purposes of taxation, economic regulation, law enforcement or conscription. The confederal government could legislate only for persons in the western territories. According to Hamilton, therefore, the great innovation of the new Constitution of the United States was its authorization for the federal government to enact laws, within a limited sphere of delegated powers, applicable to persons (*Federalist* 15 and 16). This limited authority over persons, more than any other feature of the US, Constitution, transformed confederalism into federalism.

This new 'federalism' was to have a strong general government able to enhance national defence, in part by suppressing rivalry among the states; promote commercial prosperity, in part by imposing common-market rules against state trade barriers; and secure liberty, in part by counterbalancing state legislative power. The latter aspect of this new federalism would provide, according to James Madison, 'a double security' for 'the rights of the people' (*Federalist* 51). Madison, who became the fourth president of the United States (1809–1817), is often called the father of the US Constitution.

Given that the new government could legislate for persons within the states, the Constitution, unlike the Articles of Confederation, established federal courts with jurisdiction separate from state courts. This innovation, among others, violated many Americans' understanding of federalism as purely confederation, and evoked fears of a tyrannical central government. Many Anti-Federalists, who opposed the proposed Constitution, saw the US Supreme Court as an engine of centralization. Essentially, then, while the Federalists were alarmed by anarchy, which they saw as the effectual condition of the Confederation, the Anti-Federalists were alarmed about monopoly, which they saw lurking behind the proposed Constitution.

As the price of ratification, Anti-Federalists who were open to compromise insisted on a Bill of Rights, which became the first ten amendments to the Constitution in 1791. The first nine amendments protect citizens directly against federal tyranny (by promoting rights such as the freedom of speech, press and religion); the Tenth Amendment provides further protection by reserving to the states 'or to the people' all powers not delegated to the United States or prohibited the states by the Constitution.

2.1 Dual Federalism

The Tenth Amendment and the separate federal and state courts fostered a vision of dual federalism articulated most fully by the courts, which tried to maintain a strict separation of the powers and activities of the state and federal governments. Although political practices were often more co-operative than dualistic (Elazar, 1962), the reigning principle was minimal federal interference with state sovereignty. The weight of this principle was demonstrated after the Civil War (1861–1865) when, despite the war's nationalizing effects, the federal government withdrew from the South in 1873 to 1876 and allowed the southern states to assert the fiction of 'separate but equal' 'Jim Crow' laws (*Plessy*, 1896), which required race segregation. This encouraged the South to maintain 'states' rights' as a fundamental tenet of federalism, despite the Fourteenth Amendment's (1868) federal guarantees of due process and equal protection of the laws for all persons in all states.

Under dual federalism, the federal government provided benefits to persons by working around the states, in parallel with the states, and occasionally through the states. After the Civil War, for example, the federal government awarded bonus and pension payments to veterans and widows of veterans of the Union army and navy. By 1890, such payments made up more than a third of federal expenditures. This first federal welfare system lasted for more than a century, and the federal government still operates veterans' hospitals outside of state and local health-care systems. Generally, though, the federal government exercised most of its authority over persons outside the states, namely, in the western territories where it dispossessed the Indians of much of their land and delivered it to Euro-American settlers through homestead grants after 1862 and to states and railroad corporations through land grants.

The federal government worked in parallel fashion as well, for example by establishing its own bank, although its authority to create a national bank was controversial. In a resurgence of states' rights, President Andrew Jackson destroyed the Bank of the United States in 1832, in part because he supported public demands for deposits of US funds into state banks. A dual banking system was established during the Civil War, however, and, unlike Canada, which has a single banking system, the United States still maintains dual (federal and state) banking.

The federal government also worked through the states, even in some areas of its exclusive constitutional authority, such as the postal service where jobs were federal patronage 'plums' awarded to state and local political supporters. The federal government also assisted the states through 'pork-barrel' appropriations, public-works projects executed by the US Army Corps of Engineers, land grants for colleges and universities, and the first cash grants-in-aid in 1879.

Thus, dual federalism was quite intergovernmental and often co-operative. The federal government was expected to serve state and local government interests, but the idea of dual federalism sustained the principle that while the federal and state governments could interact, they could not invade each other's sovereign spheres. Few conditions, therefore, were attached to federal aid to states and localities. The federal government, moreover, exercised little direct authority over persons within the states. The benefits it delivered to persons had to be provided either to settlers in the territories or to persons connected to federal service.

Nevertheless, dual federalism was often described as competitive, which, in the view of some observers, was the intent of the US Constitution. As the governor of Utah recently put it:

> The Constitution established a balanced competition among levels and branches of government. The people are protected only when those levels and branches are willing and able to compete. If a level or branch is unwilling or unable to compete, power will be concentrated improperly and the rights of the people will be endangered. (Leavitt, 1994)

James Madison, who supported a stronger national government in the 1780s, had anticipated intergovernmental competition, in part out of realization that the new federal government would have to win the public's trust. This would be, he argued, a largely positive development:

> If . . . the people should in future become more partial to the federal than to the State governments, the change can only result from such manifest and irresistible proofs of a better administration, as will overcome all their antecedent propensities. And in that case, the people ought not surely to be precluded from giving most of their confidence where they may discover it to be most due. (*Federalist* 46)

By the end of the nineteenth century, many reformers came to regard competition under dual federalism as detrimental to liberty and equality, partly on the ground that concentrations of power in the private sector (e.g., robber-baron monopolists) required countervailing concentrations of power in the public sector. Progressive historians, such as Charles Beard, argued that economic elites designed the US Constitution to advance their class interests by fragmenting power through such devices as the separation of powers within governments and the dualistic distribution of powers between governments. As a leading legal scholar and advocate of national supremacy later wrote, the competition embedded in dual federalism blocked government action. The 'relationship which . . . prevailed with the [US Supreme] Court was a competitive conception.' Given that 'the

National Government and the states [were seen] as rival governments bent on mutual frustration', it was 'the supreme duty of the Court to maintain the two centers of government in theoretical possession of their accustomed powers, however incapable either might be in fact of executing them' (Corwin, 1941, p. 98).

The case against intergovernmental (i.e., federal – state – local) competition and interjurisdictional (i.e., interstate, interlocal) competition (Kenyon and Kincaid, 1991) rested mainly on two grounds. First, intergovernmental competition allowed economic elites to divide and conquer the public sector so as to defeat policies beneficial to the general public good. Second, interjurisdictional competition drove social policies (e.g., welfare benefits and environmental protection) and business regulation to their lowest common denominators. A leading advocate of co-operative federalism used as her major example of baneful competition the 'helplessness of individual states to protect themselves against . . . competition in convict-made goods' (Clark, 1938, p. 124). Similarly, Paul A. Freund argued that 'states are gravely handicapped if they are subjected to the competition of other states having much lower standards of wages and working conditions' (Freund, 1968, p. 47). Although empirical evidence for these effects of competition was, and remains, scant, these views of competition became major justifications for expanding the power of the federal government. Such views remain prominent, as reflected, for example, in a report of the National Commission on the State and Local Public Service:

> States could . . . seek to shift the burden [of health-care reform] to the private sector; the preferred approach would be to mandate employer coverage. When considering this approach, states must naturally contend with the threat from both large and small businesses that the new burdens will persuade them to move elsewhere, for such is the nature of interstate competition for business. (1993, p. 27)

No evidence is given to support this proposition.

2.2   Co-operative Federalism

The initial response to these arguments was not a massive increase in federal power, but articulation of the concept of co-operative federalism, which began to take shape under President Theodore Roosevelt's 'New Nationalism'. In his last State of the Union message in 1908, for example, Roosevelt assured the nation that enhancement of federal power to accomplish new national purposes 'does not represent centralization'. In turn, President Woodrow Wilson (1913–1921) expressed as a basic tenet of his New Freedom: 'Co-operation amidst variety is what we seek'.

Reformers promoted 'co-operation' in two basic ways. One was to increase the competitive power of citizens against both corporate and party bosses by, for example, allowing them to organize unions and vote in primary elections. This approach also produced a major constitutional change in federalism: direct election of US senators in 1913. The second approach was to enhance the competitive position of government against business by increasing the power of the federal government – mainly through a strong presidency, a professional bureaucracy, and an activist judiciary – and by giving the federal government new revenue-raising authority to extend its reach and redistribute income. This approach produced another major constitutional change in federalism: the federal income tax amendment of 1913.

Thus, co-operative federalism emerged as an effort to accommodate Progressive desires for a more powerful national government to the political realities of a society that still had one foot in the dual federalism of places and the other foot in an emerging social pluralism of persons. Indeed, co-operative federalism presupposes dualism because co-operation, by definition, implies the existence of independent entities capable of forging a partnership. The Progressives, who constituted a social reform movement at the turn of the century and who tried briefly to become a political party, dismantled pieces of the constitutional foundation of dual federalism, but could do little damage to the political foundation of dual federalism. The federal government was too weak and distant to compete effectively against state and local governments, and Americans remained fearful of centralization.

Co-operative federalism was marked by expanding federal power accompanied by sensitivity to state and local government concerns in policy-making. Although the New Deal (1933–1945) is often regarded as a great centralizing period, New Deal policies did little to disturb state and local powers, primarily because President Franklin D. Roosevelt refused to attack the powerful state and local political bosses (Kincaid, 1987). The New Deal's major legislative legacy, the Social Security Act of 1935, was a paradigm of co-operative federalism, with a touch of dual federalism in its provision of direct federal payments to senior citizens. Despite expanded federal economic regulation, the Congress maintained dual federal-state regulation and taxation of the banking, telecommunications and securities industries; countermanded the US Supreme Court by preserving exclusive state regulation of insurance; and interfered little with state-local regulation of small businesses and licensing of occupations. The federal government also poured money into state and local governments with few conditions attached to the funds and no apparatus to audit expenditures. Finally, and importantly for the preservation of state and local powers, the New Deal did not champion nationalization of the US Bill of Rights under the Fourteenth Amendment, nor did it disturb race segregation in the South. Thus, despite expanded federal activity, the federal government still had little direct contact with the persons of most citizens.

The New Deal's great federalism case – *United States* v. *Darby Lumber Co.* in 1941 – did sound the death knell for the Tenth Amendment by declaring it merely 'a truism', but it had little practical effect on federalism. The Fair Labor Standards Act (FLSA) upheld in *Darby* applied to employees of private industry, not to state and local government employees. State and local political bosses, therefore, had little reason to oppose the FLSA, and they never suspected that the Congress would extend the FLSA to state and local employees three decades later (Kincaid, 1993a).

The New Deal did, however, lay the groundwork for the demise of co-operative federalism in several respects.

First, local governments, especially big cities (most controlled by Democrats), were awarded a seat at the federal bargaining table as full 'third partner' in the federal system, thus undercutting the legitimacy of the states as the constitutionally authorized partner in co-operative federalism. Among other things, cities sought direct federal aid that bypassed their state governments.

Second, the federal government became the dominant fiscal partner. In 1927, federal spending accounted for only 31 per cent of all own-source government expenditures, compared to 52 per cent for local governments and 17 per cent for state governments. The federal share increased to 50 per cent by 1940 and to 72 per cent by 1952, before dropping to 65 per cent in 1957 – about where it stands today. In turn, state and local governments became more dependent on federal funds, often willingly so.

Third, the New Deal fostered the belief that state and local governments could not respond to the problems of an urban–industrial society or cope with a national crisis, such as the Great Depression. Americans also began to view the federal government as the most progressive partner in the federal system – an engine for social change and personal benefits.

2.3   Collapse of Co-operative Federalism

Co-operative federalism can be said to have collapsed in August 1968 during the tumultuous, national, presidential nominating convention of the

Democratic party in Chicago. Reformers drove the traditional state and local political bosses out of the nominating system and reoriented the representative base of the Democratic party from places to persons by establishing rules to ensure proportional representation of blacks, women, young adults and other minorities and by emphasizing primary elections for presidential aspirants. In short, descriptive representation of persons took precedence over the political representation of places in the party.

The Republican party was more resistant to these reforms. Consequently, while federalism virtually disappeared as an issue for the Democrats, the Republicans continued to defend federalism, a position that fitted nicely with Richard M. Nixon's southern-state election strategy.

The 1968 Democratic convention dramatically reflected the confluence of political, social and cultural forces that had been unleashed during the 1960s. This was a decade of personal liberation, and the pre-eminent struggle for the liberation of persons from the coercion of places was the African American civil rights movement. Hence, federalism became associated with states' rights, and states' rights became associated with racism (Riker, 1964). In order to liberate persons from the coercion of places, the federal government invaded historic realms of state and local authority.

Several major factors induced the collapse of co-operative federalism.

For one, the US Supreme Court nationalized much of the US Bill of Rights by incorporating it into the Fourteenth Amendment so as to protect rights against state as well as federal action. Beginning with *Brown* v. *Board of Education* in 1954–1955, which struck down race segregation in public schools, the Court initiated a massive expansion of federal power not only to protect individual rights but also to reform state and local governments. Although this activism largely ended after the Court struck down state anti-abortion laws in 1973 (*Roe* v. *Wade*), the federal courts had achieved unprecedented levels of rights protection and intervention into state and local affairs, from which there has been little retreat, except in criminal rights.

Second, the US Supreme Court's 'one person, one vote' rulings in 1964 (*Wesberry* and *Reynolds*) shifted representation in both the US House of Representatives and the state legislatures from places to persons. Before 1964, most election districts conformed to substate juridictions, usually county boundaries, thereby emphasizing the representation of local government jurisdictions rather than individuals or social groups in legislative bodies. The full impact of reapportionment was felt in the early 1970s, at which time the Congress became more 'atomistic' (Hertzke and Peters, 1992) as the members became more attentive to interest groups representing persons and less attentive to state and local government officials.

Third, many of the interest groups that emerged on the national scene under the spotlight of the new media were not simply indifferent to federalism, but hostile to it. Virtually all groups defined as 'minorities' despised federalism as a mask for oppression and advocated centralization for purposes of liberty and equality. State and local governments, therefore, became objects of hostility because they exercised most of the powers of government over persons in the federal system. In the drive to rescue 'minorities' from the coercive powers of state and local governments, the federal government was urged to exercise coercive power over those governments.

Fourth, the social movements of the 1960s and the interest groups formed around them generated broad awareness of public problems, such as environmental degradation, which were seen as cutting across state and local boundaries. More and more public issues were said to have negative spillovers requiring direct action by the federal government. This was reflected, for example, in the Omnibus Crime Control and Safe Streets Act of 1968, which opened the door to a growing federalization of criminal law.

Fifth, the equality revolution of the 1960s undermined the legitimacy of the place diversity sustained by federalism. Reformers asked why, for example, a woman should have a right to an abortion in one state but not in another. Equality, therefore, was seen to require a displacement of the peaks and valleys of variable state and local laws by uniform federal law.

Sixth, the last of the powerful state and local political party machines and bosses had collapsed by the mid-1970s. Southern white political machines were decimated by the civil rights movement, federal legislation, and migration to the Sunbelt. Northern big-city political machines collapsed as white voters moved to the suburbs, the federal government imposed restrictive rules on urban aid, and the courts cleaned up municipal government.

Seventh, the demise of political machines facilitated the rise of professional state and local bureaucracies and public employee unions, which experienced considerable growth despite the decline of private-sector unions in post-industrial America. When state and local bosses controlled patronage employees, they faced no opposition to their prerogatives. Civil service employees and their unions, however, frequently welcome federal intervention, as in the 1968, 1974 and 1985 extensions of the Fair Labor Standards Act (FLSA) to state and local governments. Civil service employees seek federal intervention to compel their state and local government employers to provide better job benefits, more funds for their agencies, and more support for agency programmes. State chapters of the National Education Association (NEA), for example, which were 'tea-and-cookie' clubs in the 1950s, developed by the 1980s into the most influential lobbies in most state capitals. NEA, which represents public school teachers, has sought to shift power from elected local school boards to the state capitals and to the federal government. In addition, state and local bureaucrats often develop close ties with their federal counterparts with whom they share policy interests that may not correspond to the interests of their elected state and local superiors.

In some cases, state and local administrators have used the federal courts to extract funds or policy concessions from elected state and local officials.

Finally, the lifeblood of co-operative federalism began to hæmorrhage as the federal government experienced shortfalls of hard money. The federal government has incurred budget deficits every year since 1968, thus making it more difficult and less appealing to fund state and local governments. Funding problems also became more acute after 1972 when the US economy entered a long period of slow growth. Hence, rather than funding state and local governments to implement federal policies co-operatively, the federal government turned more to requiring implementation without financial aid.

In the final analysis, the collapse of co-operative federalism represented a victory of persons over places, of an insurgent national pluralism constituted by autonomy-seeking persons conscious of their First and Ninth Amendment rights over an embattled federalism constituted by sovereignty-protecting places conscious of their Tenth and Eleventh Amendment rights. As a result, the federal government became the centre of political attention and embarked on unprecedented concentrations of powers.

3 CHARACTERISTICS OF COERCIVE FEDERALISM

Contemporary US federalism can be regarded as coercive insofar as it entails unprecedented federal interventions into state and local affairs, placing the federal government in a virtual monopoly position (Kincaid, 1993c). This coercive federalism exhibits nine major characteristics, which reflect both decreased co-operation and increased coercion.

3.1 Diminished Federal Aid to States and Localities

Although federal aid to state and local governments increased from $7.1 billion in 1971 to about $204 billion in 1993, aid peaked in 1978 at 27 per cent of state and local expenditures and 17 per cent of federal outlays. In 1992, federal aid accounted for 22 per cent of state-local outlays and 13 per cent of federal outlays (US Advisory Commission on Intergovernmental Relations [US ACIR], 1993b).

Of greater significance is a steep drop in direct federal aid to local governments. The federal contribution to fifty big-city budgets, for instance, fell from 18 per cent in 1981 to about 5 per cent in 1992 (although states increased aid to localities from $81 billion in 1980 to $183 billion in 1991). One reason for the decline is that President Reagan opposed federal aid to local governments. Viewing federalism as a federal-state relationship, Reagan refused to accept local governments as the third partner. Hence, two major local programmes were terminated: General Revenue Sharing (GRS) in 1986 and Urban Development Action Grants (UDAGs) in 1988. The termination of UDAGs, which had especially benefited big cities, also reflected a new demographic reality important to Republicans: by 1990 more than 50 per cent of Americans lived in suburbs.

3.2 Aid to Persons Over Places

Aid to local governments would have declined anyway, however, because federal aid for persons (e.g., Medicaid and Aid to Families with Dependent Children [AFDC]) now outstrips aid for places (e.g., highways and urban renewal). In 1993, 62 per cent of all federal aid to states and localities was dedicated for payments to persons, compared to 32 per cent in 1978. Most of the 88 per cent increase in federal aid of the last six Reagan-Bush years was for payments to persons. Aid for persons is mostly entitlement money for which states have primary administrative responsibility; hence, 89 per cent of all federal aid now goes to states. Medicaid, for example, is the nation's principal health-care programme for the poor. The federal government provides states with between 50 and 79 per cent of the funds for benefits (depending on a state's per capita personal income). Medicaid amounts to about 38 per cent of all federal aid to state and local governments.

Federal spending on Medicaid and AFDC is expected to increase by 66 per cent by 1999, while federal domestic discretionary spending is expected to decrease by 0.3 per cent. Most federal aid to localities comes from this discretionary pot. In turn, states will spend about $68 billion more on Medicaid and AFDC in 1999 than they do now; hence, they may also have less money for their local governments. Thus, federal entitlement programmes for persons have not only captured the largest share of the federal budget but also commandeered state and local budgets, leading some big-city officials to make desperate pleas for money, such as a proposal by the mayor of Philadelphia that US foreign aid be distributed abroad as vouchers redeemable only in 'distressed' US cities.

This shift in federal aid from places to persons also elevates current consumption over future investment, and is driving state and local budgets in the same direction. Consequently, public funds for capital investment in infrastructure and economic development and for higher education are declining, and governments are being driven into borrowing and imposing user fees to raise revenue.

3.3   Conditions of Aid to States and Localities

Under his New Federalism, Reagan sought to reduce conditions (e.g., regulations) of aid by convincing the Congress to consolidate 77 categorical grants into nine block grants in 1981 so as to give state and local officials more discretion to spend federal aid in broad policy areas. Most block grants are for states (e.g., the Job Training Partnership Act and Social Services Block Grant). The major city programme is the Community Development Block Grant. Total federal grant programmes, therefore, fell from 539 in 1981 to 404 by 1984, with 12 block grants included among these.

The Congress's preference for conditions, however, is reflected in its funding of 578 categorical grants and only 15 block grants in 1993. About 90 per cent of all aid money was placed in the categoricals. The Congress has also reattached many conditions to block grants. In 1993, President Clinton agreed to a proposal from governors and state legislators, which had been requested by President Bush, to ask the Congress to consolidate 55 categoricals into block grants. This consolidation, however, would include only about 6 per cent of all federal-aid money.

States view Medicaid as the most fiscally onerous categorical programme. In 1989, the fifty governors urged a two-year moratorium on enactments of conditions, but the Congress added more rules. Because of aid conditions, as well as inflation and voluntary state expansions of Medicaid during more affluent years, Medicaid increased from 7 per cent of state general spending in 1970 to about 17 per cent in 1993. The three largest state spending categories are now elementary and secondary education followed by Medicaid and then higher education.

Another facet of conditions attached to federal aid has been an increased use of crossover sanctions (US ACIR, 1984), especially in the major intergovernmental place programme: federal-aid highways. At least 17 crossover conditions are attached to federal highway aid. A significant example was a 1985 condition requiring states to raise to 21 the legal age for purchasing alcoholic beverages as a condition for receiving full federal highway funding. This device allowed the federal government to circumvent its lack of constitutional authority to regulate the drinking age. The US Supreme Court upheld this condition of aid in one of the most significant federalism cases of the 1980s (*South Dakota*, 1987). Although the Court has noted that conditions of aid 'might be so coercive as to be unconstitutional' (*South Carolina*, 1988), it has been reluctant to invalidate conditions because any state is legally free to refuse federal funds, even though, as a matter of fiscal and political reality, state and local governments cannot withdraw from the major and most conditioned aid programs, such as Medicaid and highways. Hence, federal aid is no longer a co-operative federal-state-local partnership. The extent to which the Congress can carry conditions of aid was demonstrated in 1993 when legislation was enacted to reduce highway funding to states that do not eliminate within two years their economic sanctions against South Africa.

3.4   Federal Mandates on States and Localities

Federal mandates are legal requirements that state or local officials perform functions under pain of civil or criminal penalties. Little or no federal money is ordinarily provided for compliance. In late 1993, the National Conference of State Legislatures identified 132 bills in the Congress containing new mandates. The US Conference of Mayors estimated that, on average, ten major federal mandates consumed 11.7 per cent of big-city tax revenues in 1993. The National Association of Counties estimated that 12 major federal mandates consumed 12.3 per cent of county tax revenues.

Mandating reflects another significant change in federal behaviour. Before the mid-1960s, the Congress limited its infrequent interventions mostly to conditions of aid and to prohibitions of certain state or local actions. The first major mandate was enacted by the Congress in 1931 (the Davis–Bacon Act). Another was enacted in 1940; none were enacted from 1941 to 1963; nine were enacted from 1964 to 1969; 25 were enacted during the 1970s; and 27 were enacted during the 1980s (US ACIR, 1993a).

Mandating has transformed state and local elected officials into pleading interest groups. For example, state and local officials mounted the first nationwide protest, called National Unfunded Mandates Day, on 27 October 1993. President Clinton issued an executive order on 26 October to restrain administrative mandating. Reagan and Bush had also pledged to reduce mandates. Given the federal government's budget problems, however, unfunded mandates rather than grants-in-aid have become a major mechanism for initiating new federal policies for persons.

3.5   Federal Pre-emption of State and Local Authority

Pre-emption of state and local powers has also reached unprecedented levels since the 1960s. Of 439 explicit pre-emption laws enacted by the Congress from 1789 to 1991, 233 (53 per cent) were enacted after 1969 (US ACIR, 1992). There is a larger, though unknown, number of implied pre-emptions, namely, non-explicit statutes interpreted by federal agencies and courts as pre-empting state-local powers. Although states won more pre-emption cases (51 per cent) before the US Supreme Court in 1970–1991 than in 1930–1969 (41 per cent), pre-emption cases increased from 95 in 1930–1969 (2.4 per year) to 232 in 1970–1991 (10.5 per year) (O'Brien, 1993).

The rise of pre-emption is due partly to the paradox of coercive federalism and the widely noted 'resurgence of the states' (Bowman and Kearney, 1986). For example, as states improved their regulatory capacities while the federal government pursued deregulation under Presidents Carter, Reagan, and Bush, many businesses advocated federal pre-emption of state regulation. As business lobbyists put it, they prefer to be regulated by one 500-pound gorilla in Washington than by 50 monkeys on steroids. Governors have also urged pre-emption in the belief that uniform national economic and environmental regulation will make the United States more globally competitive. Consequently, despite his New Federalism rhetoric, Reagan signed more pre-emption laws than any president in US history.

3.6   Intergovernment Tax Immunities

In the past, the federal government permitted many state and local tax immunities, but as federal expenditures and deficits have grown, it has intruded on state and local revenue bases. In 1986, for example, the Congress eliminated deductions of state and local sales taxes from federal personal income tax liabilities and placed restrictions on state and local tax-exempt bond financing. In 1990, the Congress outlawed health-provider taxes being levied by states to help raise Medicaid matching funds. The Congress also required certain state and local government employees to pay federal Social Security taxes. This will entail significant costs, especially for big cities and counties.

3.7   Decline of Co-operative Programmes

The co-operative features of major intergovernmental programmes, such as Medicaid, have eroded in recent years. To mask deficits, for example, federal officials have delayed and reduced disbursements to the states from the highway, mass transit, and aviation trust funds and from the Employment Security Administrative Account for state unemployment insurance. Also, in 1990, the Congress raised the federal motor-fuel tax by five cents but, for the first time, did not dedicate the entire increase to highway aid. State legislators argued that while this increase would raise $25 billion for the federal treasury, it would reduce state gas-tax revenues by about $2.8 billion because of reduced gasoline consumption and voter opposition to state motor-fuel tax increases.

3.8   Federal Court Orders

Despite establishing a State and Local Legal Center in 1983 to help defend state and local interests before the US Supreme Court, state and local governments won only 39 per cent of the federalism cases decided by the Court in 1981–1989 (Kearney and Sheehan, 1992). The most significant federalism case in recent decades was *Garcia* v. *San Antonio Metropolitan Transit Authority* (1985), in which the Court applied the Fair Labor Standards Act (FLSA) to state and local government employees, thereby overturning a 1976 ruling (*National League of Cities*) that blocked application of this law on Tenth Amendment grounds. The Court opined in *Garcia* that states cannot expect the judiciary to protect their powers from federal encroachment by invoking the Tenth Amendment; instead, they must lobby in the national political process like other interest groups. This case epitomizes the shift from places to persons under coercive federalism because, for the first time, the Court legitimized federal regulation of all persons employed by state and local governments. The authority of a government to control its own personnel is a basic attribute of sovereignty (Kincaid, 1993a).

Federal court orders and litigation are now salient for state and local officials, especially in mental health, education, welfare, public housing, environmental protection and corrections (e.g., prisons). While facing a budget crisis in 1991, for example, Massachusetts was ordered by a federal court to comply with a consent decree entered into with mental retardation interest groups sixteen years earlier. A federal district court's desegregation order affecting the Kansas City, Missouri, School District may cost the state and city $1 billion (*Missouri*, 1990). With respect to democratic state and local self-government, the court order overrode five voter rejections of property-tax increases as well as state constitutional and statutory tax limits, including a voter-initiated 1980 amendment to the Missouri Constitution.

Dissents have been sounded by Justice Sandra Day O'Connor, who has attempted to defend state powers under the republican guarantee clause of the US Constitution (Art. IV, Sec. 4) rather than the Tenth Amendment. In *Gregory* v. *Ashcroft* (1991), for example, the Court held that the US Age Discrimination in Employment Amendments of 1986 did not pre-empt the Missouri Constitution's mandatory retirement age for state judges. O'Connor opined that the right of state citizens to determine the qualifications of their chief public officials is fundamental to a republican form of government, which cannot be abrogated by the federal government. However, this reasoning has been developed in only a few cases, and it has not attracted majority support on the Court.

3.9 Dismantling Federal Intergovernmental Institutions

As federal policy-making shifted decisively from places to persons in the 1980s, the federal government also dismantled or weakened intergovernmental institutions that were established to promote co-operative federalism. The intergovernmental division of the president's Office of Management and Budget was abolished in 1983, as were the federal regional councils created by President Nixon. Intergovernmental relations offices in most of the Cabinet departments were downsized and placed under firm presidential political control. After Democrats recaptured the US Senate in the 1986 elections, the Senate's activist Subcommittee on Intergovernmental Relations was reorganized into a low-prestige Subcommittee on Government Efficiency, Federalism, and the District of Columbia. The House retained its subcommittee, which had been reorganized as Intergovernmental Relations and Human Resources in 1977, but renamed it in 1987 as Human Resources and Intergovernmental Relations. The intergovernmental division of the Congress' General Accounting Office was eliminated in 1992. In addition, efforts were made to abolish the US Advisory Commission on Intergovernmental Relations in 1985, 1989, 1993 and 1994; instead, the Commission's appropriations were cut by 53 per cent in 1985 and by 44 per cent in 1993.

Thus, the decisive decade in the rise of coercive federalism was the 1980s, during which the US Supreme Court redefined the states as little more than interest groups, and Americans essentially redefined themselves as a pluralistic nation or rights-bearing consumers rather than as a union of 'sovereign' places. In contrast to Reagan's contention in his first inaugural address (1981) that 'the Federal government did not create the States; the States created the Federal government', Justice Harry A. Blackmun pointedly asserted that: 'Ours . . . is a federal republic, conceived on the principle of a supreme federal power and constituted first and foremost of citizens, not sovereign states' (*Coleman*, 1991). State and local governments were severely disadvantaged by this redefinition because they had historically exercised most of the coercive powers of government over persons. The federal government, whose authority barely touched the persons of citizens for nearly 180 years, gained the political advantage of being able to liberate persons from this state and local coercion, thus making itself the source of protection and largesse for citizens and legitimizing its movement toward a monopoly position in the federal system.

4   CONCLUSION

Among the results of coercive federalism is a deterioration of what Friedrich von Hayek saw as one of the 'excellencies' of the federal Constitution, namely, 'the fact that certain kinds of coercion require the joint and co-ordinated use of different powers or the employment of several means, and, if these means are in separate hands, nobody can exercise those kinds of coercion . . . . Federal government is thus in a very definite sense limited government' (1960, p. 185). Today, there is virtually no field in which federal officials feel unauthorized to exercise power unilaterally.

Another result is that the federal Bill of Rights, including the Ninth Amendment for which Hayek had much enthusiasm, has, through the Fourteenth Amendment, become a vehicle for expanding federal power. The extent to which the role of the federal government in American society has changed was evident in recent US Senate debate over a bill to establish an Office of Gender Equity in the US Department of Education. Commenting on the bill, Senator Edward Kennedy of Massachusetts said, 'You have first-, second-, and third-grade harassers. You have kindergarten harassers. We're reaching out and identifying them at the earliest grades, disciplining these individuals.'

Hayek also emphasized the importance of US Supreme Court limits on the power of the Congress and, to some extent, the state legislatures. However, with respect to the constitutional foundation of federalism, especially the Tenth Amendment, the Court has abandoned its defence of the Constitution against congressional legislation. Under dual and co-operative federalism, the Court was viewed as the 'umpire' of the federal system, but in *Garcia*, the Court left the players to fend for themselves. In that decision, the Court accepted the argument that it is obligated to police the Bill of Rights for persons but not the Tenth Amendment for places (Choper, 1980). As such, the Court vitiated Hayek's argument that:

> the small can preserve their independence in the international as in the national sphere only within a true system of law which guarantees both that certain rules are invariably enforced and that the authority which has the power to enforce these cannot use it for any other purpose. While for its task of enforcing the common law the supranational authority must be very powerful, its constitution must at the same time be so designed that it prevents the international as well as the national authorities from becoming tyrannical. (1944, p. 236)

This lack of judicial restraint on congressional power over the states has diminished citizen control over their state and local legislative bodies, which must often raise taxes, alter spending priorities, and promulgate policies in response to federal rules rather than constituent preferences. This may be one factor behind citizen movements to impose state constitutional tax and expenditure limits on their state and local governments as well as term limits on state and federal legislators.

As a result, coercive federalism has constricted local self-government. Again, as Hayek wrote, echoing Tocqueville, 'Nowhere has democracy ever worked well without a great measure of local self-government' (1944, p. 235).

Whether this American escape from federalism is 'the road to serfdom' remains to be seen, but a reversal of coercive federalism is likely to be difficult because the federalism of the past has come to be associated with the 'liberty of places' (i.e., states' rights and local self-government) while coercive federalism is associated with the 'liberty of persons' regardless of place. A graphic illustration occurred on 28 April 1994 when leading state and local officials testified before the US Senate on behalf of a bill to prohibit unfunded federal mandates. The room was filled by persons with disabilities intent on defeating the bill and defending the unfunded mandates contained in the Americans with Disabilities Act of 1990.

Although recent scholarship has revived the notion of competitive federalism (e.g., Dye, 1990, US ACIR, 1991, Kenyon and Kincaid, 1991), such competition is viewed with alarm by many conservatives as well as liberals, both of whom see in a more monopolistic federal government opportunities to institutionalize their policy preferences. Thus, while modern Democratic presidents, such as Franklin D. Roosevelt and Lyndon B. Johnson, are rightly associated with swings toward federal monopoly, Ronald Reagan signed more legislation pre-empting state powers and mandating federal policies than any previous president.

References

Bowman, Ann O'M. and Richard C. Kearney, (1986) *The Resurgence of the States* (Englewood Cliffs, NJ: Prentice-Hall).
Brown v. *Board of Education of Topeka* (1954) 347 US 483 and 349 US 294, 1955.
Choper, Jesse H. (1980) *Judicial Review and the National Political Process: A Functional Reconsideration of the Role of the Supreme Court* (Berkeley: University of California Press).
Clark, Jane Perry (1938) *The Rise of a New Federalism: Federal-State Cooperation in the United States* (New York: Columbia University Press).
Coleman v. *Thompson* (1991) 111 S. Ct. 2546.
Corwin, Edward S. (1941) *Constitutional Revolution Ltd.* (Claremont, CA: Claremont Colleges).
Dye, Thomas R. (1990) *American Federalism: Competition Among Governments* (Lexington, MA: D.C. Health).
Elazar, Daniel J. (1962) *The American Partnership: Intergovernmental Co-operation in the Nineteenth-Century United States* (Chicago: University of Chicago Press).
____ (1987) *Exploring Federalism* (Tuscaloosa: University of Alabama Press).
Federalist Papers, The (1961) (Edited by Clinton Rossiter.) (New York: New American Library).
Freund, Paul A. (1968) 'The Supreme Court and the Future of Federalism', in Samuel I. Shuman (ed.), *The Future of Federalism* (Detroit, MI: Wayne State University Press).
Garcia v. *San Antonio Metropolitan Transit Authority* (1985) 469 US 528.
Gregory v. *Ashcroft* (1991) 111 S. Ct. 2395.
Hayek, Friedrich A. (1944) *The Road to Serfdom* (Chicago: University of Chicago Press).
____ (1960) *The Constitution of Liberty* (Chicago: University of Chicago Press).
Hertzke, Allen D. and Ronald M. Peters (eds) (1992) *The Atomistic Congress: An Interpretation of Congressional Change* (Armonk, NY: M.E. Sharpe).
Kearney, Richard C. and Reginald S. Sheehan (1992) 'Supreme Court Decision-Making: The Impact of Court Composition on State and Local Government Litigation', *The Journal of Politics*, 54 (November), pp. 1008–25.
Kenyon, Daphne A. and John Kincaid (eds) (1991) *Competition among States and Local Governments: Efficiency and Equity in American Federalism* (Washington, DC: Urban Institute Press).
Kincaid, John (1987) 'Frank Hague and Franklin Roosevelt: The Hudson Dictator and the Country Democrat', in Herbert D. Rosenbaum and Elizabeth Bartelme (eds), *Franklin D. Roosevelt: The Man, The Myth, The Era* (Westport, CT: Greenwood Press).

___ (1990) 'From Co-operative to Coercive Federalism', *The Annals of the American Academy of Political and Social Science*, 509 (May), pp. 139–52.

___ (1993a) 'Constitutional Federalism: Labor's Role in Displacing Places to Benefit Persons', *PS: Political Science & Politics*, 26 (June), pp. 172–7.

___ (1993b) 'Consumership versus Citizenship: Is There Wiggle Room for Local Regulation in the Global Economy?', in Brian Hocking (ed.), *Foreign Relations and Federal States* (London: Leicester University Press), pp. 27–47.

___ (1993c) 'From Cooperation to Coercion in American Federalism: Housing, Fragmentation and Preemption, 1780–1992', *The Journal of Law and Politics*, 9 (Winter), pp. 333–40.

Leavitt, Michael O. (1994) *Conference of the States* (Salt Lake City, UT: Governor's Office) (20 March).

McConnell, Grant (1966) *Private Power and American Democracy* (New York: Alfred A. Knopf).

Missouri v. *Jenkins* (1990) 495 US 33.

National Commission on the State and Local Public Service (1993) *Frustrated Federalism: Rx for State and Local Health Care Reform* (Albany, NY: Nelson A. Rockefeller Institute of Government, State University of New York).

National League of Cities v. *Usery* (1976) 426 US 833.

O'Brien, David M. (1993) 'The Rehnquist Court and Federal Preemption: In Search of a Theory', *Publius: The Journal of Federalism*, 23 (Fall), pp. 15–31.

Plessy v. *Ferguson* (1896) 163 US 537.

Reynolds v. *Sims* (1964) 377 US 533.

Riker, William H. (1964) *Federalism: Origin, Operation, Significance* (Boston: Little Brown).

Roe v. *Wade* (1973) 410 US 113.

South Carolina v. *Baker* (1988) 485 US 505.

South Dakota v. *Dole* (1987) 483 US 203.

Taylor, Charles (1993) *Reconciling the Solitudes: Essays on Canadian Federalism and Nationalism* (Montreal and Kingston: McGill-Queen's University Press).

US Advisory Commission on Intergovernmental Relations [US ACIR] (1984) *Regulatory Federalism. Policy, Process, Impact and Reform* Washington, DC: ACIR.

___ (1991) *Interjurisdictional Tax and Policy Competition: Good or Bad for the Federal System?* (Washington, DC: ACIR).

___ (1992) *Federal Statutory Preemption of State and Local Authority* (Washington, DC: ACIR).

___ (1993a) *Federal Regulation of State and Local Governments: The Mixed Record of the 1980s* (Washington, DC: ACIR).

___ (1993b) *Significant Features of Fiscal Federalism* (Washington, DC: ACIR).

United States v. *Darby Lumber Co.* (1941) 312 US 100.

Wesberry v. *Sanders* (1964) 376 US 1.

11 Standardization: The Evolution of Institutions versus Government Intervention*

Günter Knieps

1 INTRODUCTION

Standards of compatibility have gained considerable attention in recent economic modelling in industrial economics (for example, Gilbert (ed.), 1992) as well as in public policy (see Commission of the European Communities, 1991).[1] Within large technical systems (e.g. railway systems, telecommunications systems) the complicated procedure of standard-setting has gained particular attention (e.g. Weinkopf, 1993, Genschel and Werle, 1992). Hierarchical control of standard-setting within network monopolies is considered no longer appropriate due to the recent trend towards vertical disintegration, deregulation and internationalization (for further discussion, see Knieps, 1993). As a consequence of the growing number of interfaces between decentralized subsystems, alternative external institutions, in particular committees, markets and regulatory commissions, play an increasing role within the standardization processes.

The aim of this paper is to analyze the role of competition among standard institutions as an alternative to the design of an 'ideal' standard institution. For this purpose it seems to be of particular importance that the chosen case studies (telecommunications and railway systems) point out the importance of variety and search for new solutions which can most successfully be found by a variety of competing institutions. Moreover, the question arises whether common rules with respect to standard-setting should be designed and enforced by regulatory authorities in order to harmonize the competition process between standard institutions.

---

*Critical comments by Charles B. Blankart and Lüder Gerken on an earlier version of this paper are gratefully acknowledged.

In section 2 the increasing trend towards committee-based standardization procedures in telecommunications and railway systems is demonstrated. Actual competition among committees, entry of new committees, division of labour and co-operation between committees, mergers of committees may arise to solve pure co-ordination problems as well as possible conflicts of interest, inherent in standardization processes. As one corner-solution the independent actions of market participants may occur.

The next section assesses whether committee-based standardization procedures should be left unregulated or be sustained by regulatory authorities. Government interference can encompass different modes, among others the application of common rules to all standardization bodies and the requirement of transparent and nondiscriminatory standards (as proposed by Commission of the European Communities, 1991: C 20/15, C 20/10).

In section 3.1 the question is analyzed whether the design and enforcement of common rules for committees by government regulation can be recommended. It will be argued that the enforcement of common rules to all standardization bodies might distort incentives to collective action by a committee. This may lead to an inferior non-co-operative production of standards.[2] Co-ordination of different standardization bodies including the support of co-operation, seems also superfluous. If the cost duplication effect is larger than the heterogeneity advantages of different committees, then it is likely that mergers of committees will follow.

In spite of the recent trend towards vertical disintegration, deregulation and internationalization large technical systems may entail parts, where the incumbent carriers are able to disturb the process of competition among standard committees, for example by their ownership of railroad tracks. It is argued in section 3.2 that, nevertheless, government agencies should refrain from interference into the standard-setting process. Neither active standard-setting nor the design and enforcement of rules to market power biased committee procedures can be recommended. Instead, remaining market power in large technical systems should be directly disciplined. Examples could be the abolishment of legal entry barriers to telecommunication networks or access-regulation of owners of railroad tracks.

2 FROM HIERARCHICAL CONTROL OF STANDARD-SETTING TOWARDS COMMITTEE-BASED STANDARDIZATION PROCEDURES

2.1 Standardization Within Integrated Large Technical Systems

It is well known that large technical systems depend heavily on standardization: railroad gauges, buffer heights and car brakes have to be standardized in order to allow trains to run. In the past bureaucracies preferred fully standardized train systems such as the French TGV and the German ICE and typically allowed only one of these systems on their networks. Therefore, the most important parts of standardization were carried out under the hierarchical design of national railway companies.

The International Union of Railways (UIC) was put in charge of inter-country standardization, representing the interests of the national railway companies (see Union Internationale des Chemins de fer (UIC) (1990/1991)). The resulting international standardization has either been rather weak or totally missing. Indeed, we can find only minimal requirements on loading, brakes and schedules at the international level (e.g., Blankart and Knieps, 1993, p. 50). Incompatibility can be observed on such important components as electricity power and train control systems and signal technologies.[3]

A similar situation of hierarchical control of standard-setting also prevailed in the telecommunications sector. In the United States vertical integration between the network carrier AT&T and the equipment manufacturer Western Electrics based standard-setting on direct organizational integration. In European countries the so-called 'unitary concept of technology' (*Einheitstechnik*) predominated on the national level. This concept has been applied for all parts of telecommunication systems including switching systems and terminal equipment. All the technical requirements and physical dimensions including the quality aspects have been rigidly specified by the national telecommunications administrations (PTTs).[4] Technically new and innovative concepts could only be implemented when the national carriers, in discretionary consultation with its main suppliers, incorporated these new standards.

Within the international telecommunications regime the International Telecommunication Union (ITU) was founded as the central international organization, mainly representing the interests of the national telecommunication administrations. The branch of the ITU which is especially concerned with the process of standard-setting is known as the International Telegraph and Telephone Consultative Committee (CCITT).

As long as telecommunications remained chiefly a domestic issue – with minimal interconnection between countries and almost no international trade of telecommunication equipment – co-ordination remained at a low level.

2.2   Vertical Disintegration, Deregulation and Internationalization and the Increasing Dominance of Standard-Committees

Large technical systems are presently characterized by an increasing trend towards vertical disintegration, deregulation and internationalization. This has led to a growing number of interfaces between decentralized subsystems. Consequently, the nature of the standardization processes is changing from hierarchical control of standard-setting by national carriers towards committee-based international standardization procedures. The following section will demonstrate these developments as they affect railway systems and telecommunication networks.

The current development of European railway systems is mainly based on two different approaches. Firstly, free entry of service companies to the tracks is being introduced; thus a policy towards vertical disintegration becomes inevitable (Commission of the European Communities, 1992). Free access to the different national rail networks demands the co-ordination of national railway infrastructures towards a European Railway infrastructure on which customized transport services can be supplied. Therefore, technical harmonization of traffic and train control systems on a European scale has now gained increasing importance (Ploeger, 1991). Secondly, in 1986 the national railways of Community member countries, together with those of Austria and Switzerland, (now known as the Community of European Railways) decided to formulate proposals for a European, broadly integrated, high-speed rail network. The high-speed notion has now developed its own momentum in Europe (Community of European Railways, 1989).

The internationalization of railway networks together with free market entry on the railway networks creates an increasing potential for committees. New train companies will occur (possibly a large number) which may either try to build their own committees (for example a service companies' committee) or to enter the traditional railroad associations (in particular the International Union of Railways (UIC) and the Community of European Railways). Newly-founded committees could be of particular importance in order to exploit the potential for new, innovative train services which are not included in the service spectrum of the traditional railroad companies.

Nevertheless, the evolution of competing standardization committees cannot be observed until now. In contrast, the traditional railroad association UIC and the Community of European Railways benefit from the increasing trend towards internationalization by increasing their co-ordination and harmonization activities.

In the course of the actual reform of European railway policy the increasing international co-ordination requirements enlarged the task of the International Union of Railways (UIC), whereas the national railroad companies suceeded in keeping the management of train traffic control and safety processes (e.g. Ploeger, 1991). From the perspective of the national railroad carriers and their associations this seems a rational policy. Railroad owners would lose discretionary power with respect to the access of service companies, whereas the incumbent railroad associations would lose an important co-ordinating task. Moreover, since new service companies completely depend on the access and co-ordination policies of the railroad owners and their associations, they cannot separate and create their own associations. Instead they will have to join the traditional railroad associations, although one can expect that power shall be asymmetrically distributed in favour of the national railroad carriers which also own the tracks. In the following section we shall discuss the resulting regulatory problems from any attempt to discipline market power. The current development of telecommunication systems is mainly based on three different lines.

Firstly, the shift from electromechanical systems to digital systems shortens life cycles of equipment and greatly increases the importance of fixed R&D costs associated with the programming of adequate software. Therefore, the importance of economies of scale in equipment production gained considerable importance. Consequently, the national-bound (quasi) vertical integration between equipment producers and network carriers is broken up. National barriers to entry for foreign suppliers are decreasing and international trade in equipment is growing (e.g., Knieps, 1994, Neu et al., 1987, Müller, 1992).

Secondly, free entry of telecommunication service companies and customer premise equipment manufacturers has become possible due to deregulations on the European as well as on national levels.[5] Although the national carriers' policy has been to keep the network monopoly (as well as the voice telephone monopoly), even here changes towards liberalization can currently be observed. From 1998 onwards free entry into European voice telephone markets will be allowed (e.g., Ungerer, 1994).

Thirdly, an increasing challenge of traditional network monopolies shall take place due to the increasing importance of alternative networks based on different technologies. At the moment mobile communication carriers and satellite carriers have already entered the network market parallel to the traditional cable-based network carriers. Furthermore, the national railroad companies are currently planning to build a Europeanwide fibre-optics network along their rails.

These developments strongly change the nature of standardization processes in telecommunications, in particular the role of committees.

Firstly, due to the convergence of information and communications technologies, computer manufacturers as well as their associations gained increasing importance within telecommunication standardization processes. Organizations whose standardization needs were not fully considered by the traditional incumbent organizations could congregate to form their own standardization bodies. For example, the twelve leading European information technology manufacturers established in 1983 the Standards Promotion and Application Group (SPAG) in order to develop common European standards for data communication. Traditional international standardization organizations like the International Standardization Organization (ISO) and the International Electrical Commission (IEC) gained influence in the standardization of telecommunications (Genschel and Werle, 1992, pp. 27, 29).[6] Moreover, new continental standard committees were founded in order to promote cross-border-oriented standardization processes. In the United States, T1, the Accredited Standards Committee for Telecommunications was formed after the break of AT&T in 1984 (e.g., David and Greenstein, 1990). In Japan, TTC, (the Telecommunications Technology Council) was formed in 1985, and in Europe, ETSI (the European Telecommunications Standard Institute) started its work in 1988.

The International Telecommunication Union (ITU) in principle admits only the national telecommunication administrations (PTTs) to membership (from more than 160 member countries) which are allowed to vote. Non-PTT organizations (private operating agencies and firms from the telecommunications industry) may participate in the work process[7] provided they are authorized by the respective PTT (e.g., Genschel and Werle, 1992, pp. 14, 28, Monopolkommission, 1992, p. 351). In contrast members of ETSI are much more heterogeneous, including network carriers, equipment producers, PTTs, user organizations, service providers and research institutes, provided they are located within the geographical area of EEC and

EFTA members. More than 50 per cent of the members of ETSI are from the industry (Monopolkommission, 1992, p. 349). Co-ordination and division of labour with the other European standardization organizations are motivated to avoid inefficient cost-duplication of standardization (see Monopolkommission, 1992, p. 350). The major task of the European Committee of National Standard Bodies (CEN – Comité Européen de Normalisation) and the European Association of National Electronical Committees (CENELEC – Comité Européen de Normalisation Electronique) includes harmonization between European countries of a broad range of standards, of which telecommunications plays only a part (e.g. Commission of the European Communities, 1991).

In spite of this entry of committees, the traditional incumbent organization ITU/CCITT still seems to play an important role in the international standardization process.

The question arises as to whether ITU/CCITT will lose pre-eminence in setting international telecommunication standards in the future. Instead of competition, until now signals of willingness to co-operate – with the aim of developing a division of labour – between CCITT and the newly-founded continental committees ETSI, T1 and TTC have been observed (e.g. Genschel and Werle, 1992, p. 30). Nevertheless, increasing conflicts between CCITT and the other standard committees can be expected, which may finally lead to a decreased importance of ITU/CCITT in the arena of international standard-setting. Within ITU/CCITT, the interests of service companies, equipment producers and user organizations are traditionally much lower represented than within the newly-founded continental organizations ETSI, T1 and TTC. An important strength of ITU/CCITT has been its large number of 'powerful' members, the telecommunications administrations of more than 160 countries which are still defending their monopoly rents (e.g. Genschel and Werle, 1992, p. 30). Therefore, a rapid change in the interests and behaviour of such a large bureaucratic organization as ITU/CCITT cannot be expected. As a consequence, incentives for co-operation should be much stronger between the continental committees rather than between the committees and CCITT. Moreover, as soon as network competition increases, new carriers will prefer the option to attain the support of continental committees. This may finally lead to a reduction of ITU/CCITT members, if some national carriers completely disappear. One may even speculate that the International Standardization Organization (ISO) may prefer to collaborate with the new continental committees rather than with ITU/CCITT, because the committees represent a larger spectrum of interests.

3 REGULATION OF COMMITTEE-BASED STANDARDIZATION PROCEDURES?

3.1 Enforcement of Common Rules for Committees?

Committees or associations of committees may have rules of self-regulation. In the United States, the American National Standards Institute (ANSI), itself not a standards-developing organization, designs the voluntary, consensus-based process to which all accredited standards-writing organizations must conform to generate so-called American National Standards.

Within the EU it is currently proposed to found a European Standardization Council, a new institution responsible for the overall policy of European standardization. A European Standardization Board would act as the executive body of the Council, responsible for the management and co-ordination of European standardization. Although the role and organizational shape of such a European Standardization Council is still rather vague, a basic objective of the European Council seems to be to develop and maintain common rules to all standardization bodies within Europe (Commission of the European Communities, 1991, C 20/15–16).

However, such a development of common rules by regulation and its global enforcement seems inadequate, given the complex nature of standard-setting processes. Since it is impossible that a social planner can optimize the trade-off between standardization and variety in a dynamic world (e.g., Blankart and Knieps, 1992), it is also impossible to design 'ideal' rules for standard committees. In contrast, a variety of committees with possibly different rules seems to be the adequate procedure to initiate the search for new standards (technologies) and to find viable standard 'clubs', whose members are satisfied with the intrinsic solution of the trade-off between the advantages of network externalities and variety. Therefore, the set-up of new committees (e.g., representing the interests of new service providers) should not be hindered for the reason that they are specializing on the interests of particular groups with no overall balancing potential.

If there exist strong preferences for a simultaneous use of different technologies and if network externalities only play a negligible role there seems to be no potential for standard committees at all. Instead, unco-ordinated market solutions with resulting incompatibility can be expected to evolve.

Since standard-setting is a costly procedure there exists an intrinsic incentive for mergers of committees if the cost-duplication effect dominates the advantages of variety (specialization) and search. For the case that the standard problem has the nature of a pure public good, where only the externality problem has to be solved (no preferences for variety and no search) then probably only one standard committee will evolve.

Summing up, in a dynamic world where the search for network islands of common standards is a central problem, the enforcement of common rules for committees seems to be detrimental. In large technical systems, such as railroads and telecommunications, a large spectrum of services is unexplored until now. Specialized applied networks may emerge in response to supply and demand of participants with relatively homogeneous interests (e.g., banks, consumer goods industries, etc.). Special standard committees may evolve to solve their standardization problems according to their own rules. Even within such subsystems where traditionally network externalities – and subsequently a large user base – have played a dominant role (e.g., basic telecommunication networks), nowadays the search for variety and the introduction of new technologies becomes increasingly important. The evolution of new committees to solve the standardization problems of new transmission technologies (e.g., mobile communication) should not be hampered by the enforcement of common rules of standardization.

3.2 Direct Co-ordination of Different Standardization Committees?

Not only the enforcement of common rules but also the direct co-ordination of different standardization bodies by government regulation seems detrimental. One extreme case which tries to make co-ordination superfluous is the requirement by the Commission of the EU that standard committees are only recognized officially, if they agree to give up parallel standardization activities on the national level (Gabler, 1989, p. 574). It seems obvious that such requirements hinder the decentralized search process for new technological solutions, focussing only on the role of network externalities and possible cost-duplication of standard-setting.

Nevertheless, standard committees should have the freedom and competency to solve the trade-off between network externalities and cost-duplication of standard-setting on the one hand, and the advantages of variety and search for new solutions on different regional levels on the other hand. Although incentives for voluntary co-ordination of different standardization bodies already have a long tradition, increasing co-ordination activities (for example between ETSI, T1 and TTC) can be expected as a consequence of the increasing internationalization. Although until now only national standardization organizations are represented in international standard committees, European organizations are increasingly involved in co-ordination activities – e.g. between CEN/CENELEC and ISO/IEC (see Monopolkommission 1992, p. 352). Regulatory activities in order to stimulate the co-ordination of continental and international organizations, however, seem superfluous or detrimental, because the sophisticated search procedure on which geographical level the standard-setting process should best be located would be disturbed.

3.3   Regulation of Market Power?

In spite of the recent trend towards vertical disintegration, deregulation and internationalization, large technical systems may entail subparts, where market power of the incumbent carriers plays a dominant role. This is the case if at least one market side is characterized by a non-contestable natural monopoly (e.g. Baumol, Panzar and Willig, 1982). For example, railway tracks must be regarded as sunk costs, which cannot be shifted to another market. Therefore, if a potential competitor plans an entry with a parallel track, the incumbent railway owner could reasonably claim to reduce his tariffs to the level of short-run variable costs. Once a railway network is completed, one cannot thus expect further entries with additional tracks. The decision-relevant costs of entry include the costs of tracks, which could not be covered by tariffs based on short-run variable costs. In contrast to the supplier of rail-services[8] the track owner in question has therefore obtained market power (Fremdling and Knieps, 1993, pp. 149–50).

In the past telecommunication systems have also been considered as a case of a natural monopoly where due to cable-based transmission technology sunk costs play an important role. In recent times the role of natural monopoly in telecommunication networks has been diminishing. The construction of competitive network infrastructures in the high-volume long-distance traffic of the industrialized countries cannot be expected to create a significant waste of costs (e.g., Knieps, 1990, p. 76). Nevertheless, until now most telecommunication operators in Europe have some market power due to legal network monopoly (e.g., Blankart and Knieps, 1994, p. 6). However, some elements of network competition are possible due to entry by new technologies (mobile communication, satellites).

It can be expected that market power within individual sectors of large technical systems will also have a direct impact on the process of competition among standard committees. As has already been indicated the traditional railway companies, as owners of the tracks, still play a dominant role in the standard-setting process. The increasing internationalization is only reflected in an increasing importance of the International Union of Railways (UIC). The process of entry by new train service companies has not yet gained its own momentum. Nevertheless, the potential role of standard committees based on new service companies and the role of new service companies within the UIC must be viewed rather sceptically as long as the traditional railroad companies determine access conditions to their tracks.

Within the telecommunication sector the legal monopoly of cable-based network carriers creates at first glance a comparable situation. Since at least a partial bypass of traditional network monopolies (e.g., by mobile and satellite technologies) is possible, new service providers, however, are less dependent on the access conditions of the legal cable-based network owners. In addition, there is increasing pressure from data network suppliers. The increasing spectrum of standard committees within the telecommunication sector already indicates these differences of market power of traditional network owners between railroads and telecommunication carriers.

Since in the non-contestable cases power is still involved negotiations within committees are likely either not to take place upon the same footing or else to involve strategic behaviour. As a consequence, variety and the search for new solutions may be hampered. Therefore, government inter-ference seems to be required. Government may need its legal power to neutralize market power (e.g., Blankart and Knieps, 1994, p. 79).

Several alternatives may be available. Firstly, governments may try to develop and prescribe standards where competition among committees fails. A 'public interest'-oriented government agency may choose the concept of open regulation as proposed in Blankart and Knieps (1992, p. 59). For those components of a large technical system which exhibit a large degree of externalities, but little variety and search, government may (if at all) contribute to the definition of a common standard in order to reach the critical mass of users so that the system becomes economically viable.

However, the incentives of government agencies have to be taken into account when alternative standard-setting procedures are considered. Unfortunately, the tendency of committees to neglect the search for new solutions due to market power does not necessarily disappear when gov-ernment standard-setting activities are introduced. On the contrary, a large spectrum of recent activities by the European Commission indicates a ten-dency towards highly structured standards which leave very little room for variety and innovation. Governments will presumably maximize the depths of standardization because this approximates to influence (or power) maximization. Therefore, it most probably enforces common tech-nologies on those who prefer to specialize and it precludes market search and, hence, innovation. Once governments have the legitimacy to design standards, they may even become active if the committee process is not biased by market power at all (e.g., Blankart and Knieps, 1993, pp. 46, 50, Blankart and Knieps, 1994, pp. 7–10). We can conclude that the first alternative, that of active standard-setting by government agencies, is most probably inadequate to solve the market power problem of standard committees.

A second alternative may be that governments should design and enforce rules to which the standard-setting of market power-biased committee processes must obey. This alternative also seems rather problematic. Either such rules are too general (e.g. transparency and non-discriminatory behaviour within standard committees) such that market power is not effectively disciplined or the danger increases that the dominating partners will leave the committee (which may result into an inferior non-co-operative standard-setting).

From our point of view, the third alternative is most likely to be successful. Government agencies should refrain from interference into the standard-setting processes and leave these to the committees. Instead, regulatory tools should be applied to discipline market power of the network carriers by focussing on the issue of access conditions. Quality and price regulations (e.g., Braeutigam, 1981, Spulber, 1989) would reduce monopoly power to an extent to which the incentives to prevent the evolution of competing standardization committees would be eliminated. In addition, legal network monopolies should be abolished and vertical disintegration (e.g. between tracks and train traffic control systems) supported. As a result, an adequate functioning process of competition among standard committees in the area of large technical systems can be expected, providing an adequate solution of the difficult balance between network externalities, variety and search.

Notes

1. Quality, safety and environmental standards are not considered here (e.g., Leland, 1979).
2. Farrell and Saloner (1988) have shown that committees solving pure co-ordination problems – everyone would prefer any proposed co-ordinated standardized outcome to the result of each going his own way, but in which the participants disagree on which of the co-ordinated outcomes is better – do better than the market, when there is no value attached to speed. The role of committees versus markets is also discussed in Berg (1989, pp. 367 ff).
3. See also the illustrative examples in Weise (1992, p. 54).
4. Since in European countries telecommunications administrations are traditionally under the same roof as postal service administrations, the organization is called PTT (Postal, Telegraph and Telephone administration).

5. See for example the 'Green Paper on the Development of the Common Market for Telecommunication Services and Equipment' – issued by the Commission in June 1987 (Commission of the European Communities, 1987).
6. An important example is the OSI (Open Systems Interconnection) – a seven-layer frame of references for systems of standards – which was developed at the International Standardization Organization (ISO) with multiple contributions from national standards bodies, user groups, manufacturers' associations etc. (see e.g. Collins, 1986, p. 2). After approval of the OSI frame by the most relevant standardization organizations of information technology *and* telecommunications it was established in the early 1980s (Genschel and Werle, 1992, p. 35).
7. However, they are not allowed to vote.
8. In fact trains, like planes, do not need to be considered as sunk costs. They can be used to serve other networks in different locations once demand in the former network has dropped too far to keep up a profitable train service. Therefore, inefficient allocation of inputs, inefficient production technologies etc. automatically lead to market exit (e.g., Knieps, 1993, p. 203).

References

Baumol, W.J., J.C. Panzar and R.D. Willig (1982) *Contestable Markets and the Theory of Industry Structure* (San Diego: Harcourt Brace Jovanovich).

Berg, S.V. (1989) 'The Production of Compatibility: Technical Standards as Collective Goods', *Kyklos*, 42, pp. 361–83.

Blankart, Ch. B. and G. Knieps (1992) 'The Critical Mass Problem in a Dynamic World: Theory and Applications to Telecommunications', in F. Klaver and P. Slaa (eds), *Telecommunication – New Signposts to Old Roads* (Amsterdam, Oxford, Washington, Tokyo: IOS Press), pp. 55–63.

____ (1993) 'State and standards', *Public Choice*, 77, pp. 39–52.

____ (1994) 'Market-Oriented Open Network Provision', Discussion Paper No. 9, Institut für Verkehrswissenschaft und Regionalpolitik, Freiburg.

Braeutigam, R.R. (1981) 'Regulation of Multiproduct Enterprises by Rate of Return, Mark Up and Operating Ratio', *Research in Law and Economics*, 3, pp. 15–38.

Collins, H. (1986) 'Data Communications Standards: A Report from the War-Zone'. Paper presented at the Conference on Product Standardization and Competitive Strategy, Paris.

Commission of the European Communities, (1987) 'Green Paper on the Development of the Common Market for Telecommunications Services', KOM (87) 290 endg., Brussels.

____ 1991. 'Commission communication on the development of European standardization – Action for faster technological integration in Europe', *Official Journal of the European Communities*, 34, C 20, 28 January 1991.

____ (1992) 'Draft Proposal for a Council Directive amending Council Directive 91/440/EEC on the development of the Community's railways'. Brussels.

Community of European Railways (1989) 'Proposals for a European High-Speed Network'. Paris, January.

David, P.A. and S. Greenstein (1990) 'The Economics of Compatibility Standards: An Introduction to Recent Research', *Economic Innovation and New Technologies*, 1, pp. 3–41.

Farrell, J. and G. Saloner (1988) 'Co-ordination through committees and markets', Rand Journal of Economics, 19, pp. 235–52.

Fremdling, R. and G. Knieps (1993) 'Competition, Regulation and Nationalization: The Prussian Railway System in the Nineteenth Century', Scandinavian Economic History Review, 41, pp. 129–54.

Gabler, H. (1989) 'ETSI-European Telecommunications Standards Institute'. Nachrichtentechnische Zeitung (ntz), 42, pp. 574–9.

Genschel, P. and R. Werle (1992) 'From National Hierarchies to International Standardization: Historical and Modal Changes in the Coordination of Telecommunications'. Max-Planck Institut für Gesellschaftsforschung, MPIFG Discussion Paper 92/1, February.

Gilbert, R.J. (ed.) (1992) 'Symposium on Compatibility', The Journal of Industrial Economics, 40, pp. 1–123.

Knieps, G. (1990) 'Deregulation in Europe: Telecommunication and Transportation', in G. Majone (ed.), Deregulation or Re-regulation? Regulatory Reform in Europe and the United States (London: Pinter Publishers), pp. 72–100.

——— (1992) 'The Challenge of the European Railways'. Research Memorandum No. 481, Faculty of Economics, University of Groningen.

——— (1993) 'Competition, coordination and cooperation. A disaggregated approach to transportation regulation', Utilities Policy, 3, pp. 201–7.

——— (1994) 'Die Telekommunikation als Gegenstand der Industriepolitik in Europa, den USA und Japan aus wirtschaftswissenschaftlicher Sicht'. Forthcoming in E.J. Mestmäcker (ed.), Ordnungsprinzipien im Wirtschaftsrecht der Telekommunikation (Baden-Baden: Nomos).

Leland, H.E. (1979) 'Quacks, lemons and licensing: A theory of minimum quality standards', Journal of Political Economy, 86, pp. 1328–46.

Monopolkommission (1992) Wettbewerbspolitik oder Industriepolitik. Hauptgutachten 1990/1991 (Baden-Baden: Nomos).

Müller, J. (1992) 'Scenarios of 1992 and Consequences for Euro-Japanese Relationship', in F. Meyer, Kramer, J. Müller and B. Preißl (eds), Information Technologies: Impacts, Policies and Future Perspectives (Berlin, Heidelberg, New York: Springer).

Neu, W., K. -H. Neumann and T. Schnöring (1987) 'Trade patterns, industry structure and industrial policy in telecommunications', Telecommunications Policy, 11, pp. 31–44.

Ploeger, L.F. (1991) 'Revolution on rails'. European rail, Communities of European Railways, Newsletter, No. 10, Sept.–Oct.

Spulber, D.F. (1989) Regulation and Markets (Cambridge: MIT Press).

UIC (1990) 'Geschäftsbericht 1990-1991'.

——— (1994) 'UIC-Reform', Pressemitteilung No. 67, 25 January 1994.

Ungerer, H. (1994) 'Maßnahmen der EG zur Öffnung der Telekommunikations-Dienstleistungsmärkte für neue Wettbewerber'. Euroforum Konferenz, Bad Homburg.

Weinkopf, M. (1993) 'Ökonomie des ONP-Konzeptes'. Diskussionsbeitrag No. 118, WIK, Bad Honnef, November.

Weise, H. (1992) 'Nichts paßt bei der Bahn, Europas Eisenbahnen: Jeder macht, was er will, keiner macht was er soll, aber alle machen mit', Die Zeit, No. 48, November 20, p. 52.

12 Transformation of the Economic System in the Russian Federation: What Role for Competition among Regional Governments?*

Matthias Lücke

1 INTRODUCTION

Even more than in other former planned economies, the successful transformation of the economic system in the Russian Federation will involve a 'sea change' in the running of its political and economic institutions. A short, and far from exhaustive, list includes the following measures: restructuring of government budgets at the national, regional and municipal levels; introduction of financial discipline in enterprises; reforming the financial system; privatizing the means of production. The required changes are particularly far-reaching and difficult to implement because Russia has practically no experience of market-type relations between economic agents.

This raises the question of whether such changes can be imposed from above, that is, by the central government (with the possible support of foreign economic advisors). At least three objections can be raised. First, the diversity of economic conditions in the country suggests that the time path of institutional change may vary across regions. Second, it would be a hazardous task to define, *a priori*, the model to be followed. Institutions in market economies are far from uniform, having evolved over long periods

*This paper is part of a research project on the prerequisites for integrating the former Soviet Union into the world economy. The project has received financial support from the Alfried Krupp von Bohlen und Halbach Stiftung. Vitali Naishul has provided some of the data and made very helpful comments. Constructive criticisms and suggestions have also been received from Rolf J. Langhammer, Martin Raiser and the editor of this volume. The usual disclaimer applies.

of time in response to specific national conditions. Third, while Western attention so far has focussed on the federal (central) institutions in Moscow, their ability to ensure that decisions taken at the national level are implemented locally is now severely limited. Arguably, therefore, the activities of regional (*oblast*-level) governments are at least of equal importance for the ultimate success, or otherwise, of economic transformation in Russia.

An alternative view of institutional change proceeds from the Hayekian notion of institutions as spontaneous social inventions. This view suggests that, with appropriate incentives, individual institutions will adjust to changes in their environments, and new institutions will be created spontaneously when old ones turn out to be unreformable. The implied process of trial-and-error can only be sustained in the presence of competition among existing and newly-created institutions. This view is particularly attractive in relation to the present situation in Russia because it allows specific national circumstances to influence institutional change and, additionally, permits regional diversity.

The purpose of this paper is to discuss whether greater regional autonomy, and the ensuing opportunities for competition among regional governments, can promote economic reform in Russia. The theoretical background is provided by the fiscal federalism debate: First, economic transformation in Russia will lead to substantial shifts in relative income positions, and thus to demands for protection and compensation. Second, certain inevitable government expenditures have to be financed at the national level (such as the conversion of the defence sector), requiring a substantial fiscal burden to be distributed among the regions. Therefore a strong constitutional framework may well be needed to keep 'free-rider' problems in check and ensure that competition among regional governments does not lead to the progressive impoverishment of disadvantaged regions.

This paper starts by reviewing the theoretical and empirical literature on the benefits and limitations of government decentralization and interjurisdictional competition (section 2). Then the role is described that the regions have played so far in the economic transformation of the Russian Federation (section 3). In the following two sections the conclusions drawn from the survey of the literature in section 2 are applied to the current situation in the Russian Federation. First, an attempt is made to assess empirically the extent to which interregional differences in popular support for reform stem from genuine differences in political preferences, rather than from distributional concerns (section 4). Second, the opportunities for, as well as limits to, interregional competition in Russia are discussed with a view to throwing some light on the appropriate constitutional framework. Guiding principles for the assignment of functions to the various tiers of government are also devised (section 5). Several lessons are finally drawn from this discussion for the future re-ordering of intergovernmental relations in Russia (section 6).

2 DECENTRALIZATION OF GOVERNMENT AND INTERREGIONAL COMPETITION: BENEFITS AND LIMITATIONS

The economic arguments in favour of decentralization derive mainly from two sources.[1] The first is the theory of fiscal federalism, for which the Musgravian distinction between the allocation, stabilization, and distribution functions of government still provides a suitable starting point. The conclusion of this literature is, briefly, that the macroeconomic stabilization function should rest with the central government. Likewise, central government has a leading role to play in the distribution function, partly because of the potential mobility of the poor. There may, however, be an efficiency argument for some local poor relief (Oates, 1991, p. 4). By contrast, preferences regarding the provision of public goods are likely to differ across regions, particularly in countries as diverse as Russia. Allocation decisions should therefore be taken by those regional units whose citizens will benefit from a particular decision (Boss, 1993).

Hence benefits from decentralization are seen to stem mainly from the optimal allocation of resources in the production of public goods when regional preferences differ. On the other hand a large number of contributions to the literature on fiscal federalism point to potentially large distortionary effects of interjurisdictional competition on the provision of public goods (for example, Oates and Schwab, 1988, Taylor, 1992, Wildasin and Wilson, 1991). Such findings (including whether there is over- or underprovision of public goods) are highly sensitive to the underlying assumptions, especially regarding the tax system. Nevertheless it may be concluded that unless there is pure benefit taxation, competition among jurisdictions will be distortionary more often than not in welfare analytic terms. Pure benefit taxation (such as a head tax), however, is a very restrictive and even implausible assumption if regional authorities are to have any substantial responsibilities and, therefore, financing needs (Musgrave, 1991).

The resulting bias of traditional welfare analysis against decentralization is challenged by a more recent literature that emphasizes the disciplinary role of interjurisdictional competition with respect to government activities.

The central assumption is that government bureaucrats tend to pursue their own agenda rather than the common good. Empirical studies have shown that, under specific circumstances, budget-maximizing behaviour (or perhaps, plain inefficiency) on the part of bureaucrats may be contained through tight electoral control (Pommerehne, 1989). Frequently, however, direct democracy such as through obligatory referenda may be infeasible or ineffective, especially at levels of government above the municipality. Then the ability of mobile factors of production to emigrate from a high-tax area may exert a similar disciplinary effect. Bureaucrats would find their power to increase taxes and expenditures constrained as the exit of mobile resources leads to a shrinking tax base. In representative democracies, they might also run the risk of not being re-elected by voters whose incomes are diminished by the exit of mobile resources (Sinn, 1990).

A related point has been made in the Hayekian tradition by Vihanto (1992). He argues that competition among regional governments may be viewed as a discovery procedure that is likely to unearth information that would otherwise not be available. Hence the possible distortionary effects of competition among jurisdictions (which are known, in principle at least, or may be estimated) have to be weighed against the (*a priori* unknown) benefits from making discoveries that would otherwise not be made.

The empirical evidence on the *Leviathan* hypothesis, that is, the effectiveness of interjurisdictional competition in containing the size of government expenditures, is mixed. The studies reviewed in Pommerehne (1989) point to a clearly discernible relationship between the institutional arrangements governing decision-making on taxes and expenditures on the one hand, and the size of government and the cost of specific government services on the other. The contrast here is between direct and representative democracy, however, rather than between decentralized and centralized government. Only if decentralized government implies more stringent control over bureaucrats by the electorate may Pommerehne's findings be interpreted as supporting the *Leviathan* hypothesis. Similarly, Oates (1991) concludes a survey of empirical studies by suggesting that the degree of centralization has only a weak impact, at best, on the size of government. Measures other than decentralization should be sought if one's objective is to contain the size of government. Jansen (1991) undertakes an extensive econometric analysis of the determinants of local government spending in the USA and finds that, after accounting for a variety of conceptual and statistical problems, the evidence in favour of the *Leviathan* hypothesis is rather weak.

This brief survey is sufficient to demonstrate that the costs and benefits of decentralization depend on the circumstances of each country. Judging the desirability, or otherwise, of interregional competition therefore presupposes empirical study. Because of the great importance of distributional issues, the conclusions may also depend crucially on value judgements.

3   THE POSITION OF REGIONS IN THE ECONOMIC TRANSFORMATION OF RUSSIA

The transformation of former planned economies requires policy measures in the areas of macroeconomic stabilization, economic restructuring and institutional change (Siebert, 1991). The optimal timing and sequencing of reforms in these three areas has been extensively discussed under the heading of gradualism versus shock therapy. By now a majority view appears to have emerged that, on the one hand, the interdependence of the issues requires the simultaneous adoption of policy measures in all three areas. On the other hand, the weakness of existing institutions and the lack of administrative capacity, especially in the former Soviet Union, make it imperative to concentrate on a limited number of reform projects at any given time. The upshot of these arguments is the 'minimum bang' strategy (Williamson, 1992). It implies that right from the start of reform, a 'critical' mass of changes should be introduced that is large enough to be consistent and credible, and still sufficiently small to be feasible in the face of limited administrative capacity (Lücke, 1993).

The policy of the Russian political leadership since the beginning of 1992 has differed substantially from this prescription (DIW et al., various issues). At the national level, attempts at macroeconomic stabilization have been thwarted by the failure of government and parliament to agree on a strategy for consolidating the federal budget. Structural adjustments have been hampered by the unwillingness of the political leadership to. allow domestic relative prices to adjust fully to the world market relationships. Energy prices in particular are still controlled and remain far below the world market level, in spite of the January 1992 'general' price liberalization and the nominal liberalization of coal and oil prices in the first half of 1993.

In the area of institutional reform some progress has been made with privatization in services and industry. Nominal change in ownership alone, however, will not transform socialist enterprises into capitalist firms. It is also of crucial importance to eliminate the lack of financial discipline, sometimes termed the 'soft budget constraint', which characterized enterprise behaviour under the old system (Kornai, 1993).[2] The required

changes in the financial and legal systems, however, have not been introduced. In sum, while the traditional system of intermediation is clearly
gone for good, attempts at economic reform have been constrained by the
inability of the government and parliament to agree on, and implement a
consistent programme for market-oriented reform.

The continuing conflict between the government and parliament over
economic policy has led to widespread uncertainty about which legal rules
are in force in many crucial areas. The relationship between the central
and regional (*oblast*-level) governments has been a particularly prominent
victim of the ensuing institutional anarchy. During Soviet times, the
regions within the Russian Federation were *de facto* little more than
administrative units, independent of their legal status as autonomous
republics, *krais*, or *oblasts*. Throughout the former Soviet Union, a complicated system of direct and indirect interregional transfers was used by
the 'centre' to channel savings into centrally directed investment, and to
ensure that regional standards of living did not diverge excessively
(Orlowski, 1992; 1993). Details of the transfer system remained secret
(and are still difficult to ascertain today), and there was not even an open
debate permitted about the system in general terms.

The dissolution of the Soviet Union has entailed the disintegration of
the transfer system among its former constituent republics. Direct (bud-
getary) transfers were terminated immediately. Now the gradual adjustment of relative prices in inter-state trade to world market relationships is
doing the same to indirect transfers, which occurred mainly through
underpriced energy exports from Russia.

Within Russia, the traditional transfer system through the central government has been undermined by several separate developments. For a
number of years now, increased freedom of debate has enabled the populations of resource-rich areas, particularly in Siberia, to demand (and go on
strike for) restrictions on the implicit outflow of funds from their areas,
given their own miserable living conditions. Recently many regions have
obtained the right to an enlarged share of the revenue from the sale of
local natural resources. This is equivalent to giving regions a greater share
of the resource rent. In a related development, many regions also enforced
restrictions on extra-regional exports by local enterprises when the interregional payments system broke down in early 1992 and both foodstuffs
and critical industrial inputs could often be obtained only through barter
deals.

Since early 1992, the national government has been pushing down
responsibility for several types of expenditure to *oblast*-level governments
without providing compensation in the form of increased transfers. Such

expenditures include not only consumer price subsidies for some basic foodstuffs and cash payments to certain vulnerable groups, but also capital investment projects of national importance such as airports, utilities, and housing for military personnel (Wallich, 1992, p. 42). Local governments (which are in turn funded largely by *oblast*-level budgets) have also had to take over many social services previously provided by enterprises.

Saddled with new tasks but without the proper means to fulfil them, *oblast*-level governments have increasingly defaulted on the transfer of locally collected taxes to the central government. At present, these regions have only limited control over their tax revenue. They have recently been allowed (within certain limits) to set the rate of the regional portion of the corporate profit tax, which is of dubious value when enterprises are frequently lossmaking or otherwise default on payments. They also receive fixed shares of the revenue from the personal income tax, some excises, resource taxes, and other, less important taxes over whose bases or rates they have no control. The federal government continues to hold exclusive control, however, over several important taxes such as the value added and export taxes (Wallich, 1992, p. 31, DIW et al., 1994, pp. 18ff).

The relatively small size of many *oblast*-level units has entailed a need for co-operation among regions, both in terms of co-ordinating policies (such as on inter-regional trade) and jointly representing regional interests *vis-à-vis* the central government. Regional governments responded to this need quickly by setting up 'regional associations' almost throughout the territory of the Russian Federation (Radvanyi, 1992, Jarygina and Martschenko, 1993, pp. 217ff, Hughes, 1993). While the scope of the activities and the political clout of these regional associations differ considerably, their spontaneous formation suggests that regional governments are both aware of and willing to realize the benefits of co-operation. In a certain sense, the regional associations in Russia may be compared to new types of specialized, supra-regional institutions set up in many Western countries to perform tasks not adequately dealt with either at the national or the local level. These include public transport authorities in metropolitan areas, boards of education, and bodies running specialized hospitals (Oates, 1991).

This brief review of the role of regions in the economic development of Russia since early 1992 supports the view articulated by Schlögel (1994) that during a time of severe economic, social and political upheaval, regional governments have played a crucial role in stabilizing the evolution of events. They have provided a buffer between the majority of the population caught in the economic relationships and the habits of thinking of the old system, and the often unpredictable developments in Moscow. In providing stability, however, many regional governments relied on defensive strategies to protect their interests, and used command methods familiar from the old system. Without clearly defined rights and obligations, they were by and large unable to actively promote economic transformation at the regional level.[3]

This raises the question of whether, in a reformed policy environment, regions can make a more constructive contribution to economic transformation. Since many regional administrations are dominated by unreformed cadres of the old regime, fundamental reform may also be required at the level of the regional units themselves. This may involve organizational reform to shake up established relationships among individual bureaucrats, or even the redrawing of borders to form larger regions with clearer regional identities. The following two sections enquire to what extent certain preconditions for successful decentralization and inter-regional competition are satisfied, and establish some general guidelines for the constitutional framework and assignment of functions to the central versus regional government.

4   DETERMINANTS OF POPULAR ATTITUDES TOWARDS ECONOMIC AND POLITICAL REFORM

It has been pointed out in section 2 that the concept of competition among jurisdictions relies on the assumption that preferences for the provision of public goods vary across jurisdictions. The results of several nationwide elections and referenda in Russia since 1991 do indeed point to pronounced inter-regional differences in popular support for market-oriented economic and political reforms. Several studies conclude, however, that such support is mainly a function of regional economic structures that determine how voters' incomes will be affected by reforms (Yasin et al., 1994). These studies suggest that distributional concerns, rather than diverging preferences regarding public goods such as the *Wirtschaftsordnung* (economic system) *per se*, dominate popular attitudes towards reform. If this hypothesis is true, the case for decentralization in Russia would be weakened to the extent to which economic reform is sought as a vehicle for income redistribution, rather than as a means for satisfying diverging preferences for the provision of particular public goods. The purpose of this section is to undertake an empirical test of the relative importance of genuine diverging political preferences versus distributional concerns in determining attitudes towards reform.

To this end it is necessary, first, to measure popular support for reform in individual regions. Of the seven indicators employed in this analysis, four relate to the results of the Spring 1993 referendum on whether people supported ('reformist') President Yeltsin personally (*YEL93*), or the ('reformist') economic and social policies of the government at the time (*ECSO93*), or whether they supported early elections to replace the ('reformist') president (*ELPR93*), or to replace the ('conservative') parliament (*ELPA93*). Information is available on actual regional percentage shares of 'yes' votes on each of these question (Yasin et al., 1994: Annex 1). By contrast the results of the December 1993 parliamentary election and of the referendum on the new constitution are not available in full (*RFE/RL News Briefs*, 21–25 February 1994). The only available source of information is newspaper reports with maps of Russia containing the information represented by the (dichotomous) *DEMOCRD* and *CONSTID* variables (*Segodnya*, 21 December 1993). *DEMOCRD* takes the value of '1' if pro-reform, or 'democratic' parties (VR, RDDR, Yabloko, PRES) obtained more votes than conservative groups (LDPR, KPRF, Agrarian Party RF). *CONSTID* is set to '1' if more than half of the votes cast were in favour of the new constitution. *LLYEL* represents analysts' judgements on where support for Yeltsin has been weakest from 1991 through 1993, and is equal to '1' for all other areas.[4]

These indicators of regional support for reform are employed as dependent variables in regression and probit analyses, depending on whether each dependent variable is dichotomous or not. The explanatory variables in these analyses have been chosen to reflect both possible distributional concerns, and regional characteristics that may be related to diverging preferences for public goods.

It is assumed, in line with the studies previously cited, that distributional concerns are related to the structure of regional output: Regional electorates are suspected to be more or less supportive of economic and political reform depending on how their predominant sources of income are likely to be affected. For example, regions which depend on heavy industry for a large share of their employment are suspected to be less favourably inclined towards reform, *ceteris paribus*, because many enterprises may no longer be viable once economic reform has lead to the adjustment of relative input prices to world market levels.

While it would have been desirable to use sectoral shares in regional value added, this was impossible because, due to still widespread price distortions, no meaningful data are available. The number of variables that was subsequently chosen to describe regional production structures would have been too large to allow meaningful regressions to be run. Therefore

Table 1 Economic Determinants of the Popular Attitude towards Economic Reform – OLS Regression and Probit Estimation Results

Equation No. Dependent Variable	(1) YEL93	(2) ECS093	(3) ELPR93	(4) ELPA93	(5)[a] DEMOCRD	(6)[a] DEMOCRD	(7) CONSTID	(8) LLYEL	(9) PCAPY
C	22.17*	19.63*	63.00***	37.09***	-0.42	-1.39§	-0.49	-1.45	2.11*
DNAT	-3.07	-2.87	0.14	-3.07		0.27§	-0.16	0.04	
URBPOP	2.81	2.55	-13.65**	-4.90		0.85§	-0.54	-0.23	4.07***
PCAPY	0.54-02***	0.46***	-0.25E-02***	0.15E-02***		0.10E-03§	0.26E-03§	0.40E-03§	
ANIMAL	-4.01***	-3.40***	1.93***	-0.20	-0.26§		-0.15	-0.10	0.12
CEREAL	-1.59	-0.91	0.72	0.24	-0.29§		-0.11	-0.06	-0.13
VEGEGG	-2.38	-2.36	0.55	-1.32*	-0.10§		0.04	0.19	-0.22E-01
PREMET	-2.50**	-2.10*	1.46**	-0.51	0.05		-0.17	0.07	0.48***
OILGAS	-0.20	0.14	0.54	0.02	1.21§		0.08	2.04	0.37***
IRONTIN	-0.16	-0.22	0.31	-0.29	0.01		-0.40§	0.85	-0.39E-01
LEADCOAL	-0.26	-0.25	-0.29	-0.59	0.04		0.22	1.47	-0.13
SILVTIT	-3.09***	-2.80***	1.48***	-0.53	-0.03		-0.23	-0.86	0.41***
MERCOP	0.67	0.56	-0.51	0.18	0.22		0.03	3.62	0.37E-01
BAUXITE	-2.09*	-1.95*	0.72	-1.25*	-0.13		-0.03	-4.39	0.15E-01
FERROALL	1.44	1.30	-0.56	0.63	0.08		-0.12E-02	9.51	0.40E-01
HEAVY	1.61	2.20	-0.35	0.49	0.07		0.05	-0.05	-0.56***
LIGHT	-1.11	-0.73	1.27**	0.76	0.32E-2		0.79E-02	0.14	-0.13

Table 1—continued

Equation No. Dependent Variable	(1) YEL93	(2) ECS093	(3) ELPR93	(4) ELPA93	(5)[a] DEMOCRD	(6)[a] DEMOCRD	(7) CONSTID	(8) LLYEL	(9) PCAPY
FOOD	-2.46**	-2.19	1.04*	-0.04	0.02		-0.25§	-0.52§	0.38***
MILIND	0.02	0.64E-02**	0.12E-02	0.02	-0.12E-2		0.43E-02	-0.74E-02	-0.18E-02
TERTIAR	0.08	0.17	-0.23	0.04	0.01		-0.93E-02	-0.69E-02	0.36E-01
N	85	85	85	85	86	86	65	87	85
R^2	0.56	0.56	0.63	0.16	0.77	0.31	0.39	0.85	0.57
F	6.59***	6.55***	8.56***	1.83**	–	–	–	–	7.67***
per cent pos. obs.	–	–	–	–	33.7	33.7	63.1	63.2	–

Notes:

Equations 1, 2, 3, 4, 9: OLS regressions; equations 5, 6, 7, 8: probit analysis $(dP(DEPVAR = 1)/dx)$.

Definitions of variables – dependent variables see text; C: constant; DNAT: autonomous areas dummy, URBPOP: share of urban in total population; PCAPY: per capita income; ANIMAL, CEREAL, VEGEGG (vegetables and eggs): factors representing agricultural output; PREMET (precious metals, diamonds), OILGAS, IRONTIN, LEADCOAL, SILVTIT (silver, titanium), MERCOP (mercury, copper), BAUXITE, FERROALL (ferroalloys): factors representing output of mineral raw materials; HEAVY, LIGHT, FOOD: factors representing industrial output; MILIND, TERTIAR: employment share of military industrial complex and tertiary sector.

[a] Estimate did not converge for the full set of explanatory variables $(R^2 = 1.00)$. – ***, ** (*): Significantly different from 0 at the $\alpha = .01$ (.05; .10) confidence level (two-tailed t test). – § t-statistic (parameter estimate divided by standard error) greater than or equal to 2.

Source: Data see text; own calculations with TSP Version 4.2B software.

factor analysis has been applied to each of three sets of variables representing the output of agriculture, raw materials and industry. In this way it has been possible to condense the information contained in each subset of data into a manageable number of explanatory variables (factors), each with an economic interpretation (see Table 1).[5]

The three remaining explanatory variables are supposed to represent political preferences not directly linked to distributional concerns. *DNAT* takes the value of '1' if a region enjoys autonomous status (republic, oblast, or okrug) because of the presence of a significant non-Russian population. Autonomous regions are generally thought to have benefited from greater independence due to political reform.

URBPOP represents the degree of urbanization measured as the percentage of the population residing in urban-type settlements according to the traditional Soviet definition. Almost universally, urban people tend to be less conservative than rural populations. *PCAPY* is per capita 'money' (that is, household) income of the population in 1991. It is plausible to assume that economic restructuring, which had not started in earnest in 1991, will entail a substantial redistribution of incomes. If this is true, 1991 income per head may not be a reliable predictor of future, post-reform income. Instead, it may be thought of as proxying factors such as educational attainment, political awareness, and so on.

The results of the OLS regression and probit analyses are reported in Table 1. Without going into the fine points of particular regression results, three important determinants of support for reform may be identified. First, regions with high per capita household incomes in 1991 tended to support reforms, *ceteris paribus*. Second, regions with substantial agricultural output (particularly animal products and cereals) or large employment in the food industry tended to be more conservative. Third, regions with substantial deposits of precious metals and similar natural resources (*PREMET*: gold and diamonds; *ARGTIT*: silver and titanium) were also more conservative, *ceteris paribus*.

Remarkably, the remaining independent variables do not have a clearly identifiable impact on regional support for economic reform. This applies not only to the legal status of regions (autonomous area or not), but also to their dependence on employment in the main branches of civilian and military industry, and to the local availability of mineral raw materials except precious metals. Hence our empirical findings provide no support for the hypothesis (popularized, *inter alia*, by the *Economist*, 25 December 1993–7 January 1994) that there exists a North–South divide in political preferences in Russia along the lines of resource-rich versus industrial rust-belt regions. If there is a divide with well-defined regional groupings on either side, it is more likely to be along the lines of more versus less agriculture and high versus low income.[6]

These findings now need to be interpreted in terms of our distinction between distributional concerns and diverging political preferences. It is doubtful whether the negative coefficient of the agricultural variables indicates distributional concerns, because it is far from obvious that agricultural areas would lose form market-oriented reforms. It seems more plausible to interpret this finding in terms of diverging political preferences as indicating that rural people are more conservative. Similarly, people in resource-rich areas may no longer feel a need for change now that their relative income situation has improved considerably.

The interpretation of the positive coefficient of per capital household income is more complicated. On the one hand, as suggested above, people in high-income areas may be more fully aware of the inevitability and long-term benefits of reform, independent of how it affects the population in the short-to medium-term. On the other hand, they might view transition to a market economy as an opportunity to improve their incomes and living conditions generally. They might believe, in particular, that existing interregional income differences will widen if redistribution through the centre is weakened by economic and political reform. In fact, equation (9) in Table 1 demonstrates that per capita income in 1991 was positively correlated with the presence of sectors whose prospects are generally considered relatively good, such as precious metals, oil and gas, silver and titanium, and food processing. By contrast, there is a negative correlation with heavy industry where there is usually thought to be a great need for restructuring. Hence, while our findings point to the presence of substantial differences in 'genuine' political preferences, the possibility cannot be discarded that *PCAPY* also reflects distributional concerns.

5 GUIDELINES FOR A CONSTITUTIONAL FRAMEWORK AND ASSIGNMENT OF GOVERNMENT FUNCTIONS

We now draw on these empirical findings and the discussion in section 2 to discuss the future contribution of decentralization to economic transformation in the Russian Federation. We first look at the potential benefits, and then address some of the possible pitfalls. On the basis of this discussion, we shall formulate some guiding principles for a constitutional framework for interregional competition, and for the assignment of functions to the central versus regional governments.

The empirical analysis in section 4 has emphasized the wide interregional diversity of preferences for political and economic reform. The inability of national political institutions to implement a coherent economic policy may also be interpreted as a reflection of irreconcilable differences between the sectoral and regional interests that each institution represents. Decentralization would give individual regions considerable leeway in choosing their own paths for structural adjustment and institutional reform, such as privatization. Hence it would permit the provision of public goods in the form of rules for adjustment to conform more closely to the wishes of regional electorates. This argument is in line with the traditional theory of fiscal federalism.

Because of the wide differences in local conditions it would probably be difficult, if not impossible, to devise optimal transformation strategies from the centre. Hence the formulation of policies for transformation may benefit from the availability of local information that can only be obtained through the process of search and discovery initiated by interregional competition. This is the Hayekian argument as applied by Vihanto (1992).

A new political culture in Russia is still evolving, and it is certainly too early to state that (even representative) democracy has taken firm roots at the central as well as the regional level. Hence it would be desirable if there existed some check on the behaviour of regional governments in the absence of effective electoral control. Such a check could be provided by interjurisdictional competition if the cost of migration of factors of production were sufficiently low. This is a variant of the *Leviathan* argument.

The review of theoretical approaches to interjurisdictional competition in section 2 also suggests a number of qualifications on any overly optimistic view of the net benefits of decentralization in Russia. These qualifications centre around the questions of first, how large are the distortions produced by interregional competition?, and second, are the necessary conditions for effective interregional competition satisfied? After discussing each qualification, we suggest its possible implications for the future relationship between central and regional governments in Russia.

The first qualification stems from the importance of distributional issues. Much of the increase in regional power that has occurred so far has been driven by discontent with the traditional system of explicit and implicit interregional transfers. However, starting conditions differ substantially across regions. The legacy of the old economic and political system frequently includes not only distorted structures of regional output, but also serious ecological damage, or concentrations of military units in particular areas. On the positive side, resource-rich regions still benefit from centrally-directed investment in the past.

Without substantial redistribution conditions of life would therefore vary substantially across regions while it would be beyond the power of many regional governments to improve local conditions significantly. Such income differences would be unjustified economically as they would be the result of 'free-riding' by particular regions on a common financial burden. Hence they would probably be politically unacceptable if there were a large number of relatively poor regions, or if powerful groups (such as the military) ended up with incomes below the subsistence level. While theoretically the financial legacy of the past could be distributed among the regions once and for all (compare Drèze, 1993, pp. 179ff), this is not a practical option because many of the relevant costs are not yet known. The implication of these arguments is that the Russian regions' common past will necessitate a significant degree of income redistribution for the foreseeable future.[7] Should individual high-income regions wish to leave the Russian Federation, an economic case may be made for requiring them to compensate the remaining areas to the extent of their probable future contributions.

The second qualification relates to the legal status of the constituent regions of the Russian Federation. The essence of intergovernmental relations in a federation is that the allocation of responsibilities to the centre versus the regions is decided upon by a central body, such as a constituent assembly. The upshot of this assumption is that citizens are expected to identify, in the first place, with the country as a whole, and only then with a particular region. If this is the case, interregional redistribution of incomes may be organized on the presumption that people are prepared to pay for the creation of similar living conditions throughout the country.

Although the present redistribution of incomes among regions in Russia proceeds along these lines, it is not clear that such a consensus still exists. The persistent conflicts between the Russian central government and a number of regions, particularly certain autonomous republics, raise the question of whether Russia should not rather be thought of as a confederation. As such, it would consist of sovereign subjects that have freely decided to delegate certain functions to the confederation, and would be free to decide to leave the confederation should they find this to be in their best interest. Some observers look upon that possibility as the beginning of the disintegration of Russia (for example, Yasin et al., 1994). Certainly it would not facilitate the definition of rules for the sharing of the common financial burden from the past. On the other hand, it is difficult to see how the central government can hold on to responsibilities that a substantial number of regional governments claim for themselves.

Independent of whether the status of Russia is formally changed to a confederation, it may therefore be useful to allocate responsibilities to the centre only if the vast majority of regions find this in their best interest. This is in line with the subsidiarity principle. At the same time, a framework for supra-regional co-operation should be created that can be used by groups of regional units according to their individual needs. The advantage of such a scheme would be that allocating only limited responsibilities to the centre would allow even regions with limited common interests to participate in the confederation. At the same time, regions with a need for closer co-operation would be free to set up medium-level governmental organizations that would cater to their greater needs for co-operation. Such a reform should also provide for a uniform status of the regions because the distinction between autonomous areas (with a significant non-Russian ethnic group) on the one hand and *oblasts* and *krais* on the other is becoming obsolete. The cultural identity of ethnic minorities may be protected more effectively by other means.

The third qualification relates to the preconditions for well-functioning competition among jurisdictions. It is far from obvious that these are in place throughout Russia. The fear has even been expressed that decentralization would ultimately lead to the disintegration of Russia into fiefdoms (Yasin et al., 1994), where local warlords might not be inclined to submit to democratic elections, and the cost of emigration for individuals might be prohibitive. The history of inter-war China provides a graphic example of the type of 'low-level equilibrium' that might result. In some parts of the North Caucasus such a situation may already be arising. Given the large amounts of weaponry (conventional and other) left over from the Cold War, this prospect seems rather undesirable.

It is difficult to see how any institution other than national legislative and jurisdictional bodies can guarantee the preconditions for effective competition. These include, *inter alia*, an encompassing legal system, guarantees for human rights and, especially, the right to free interregional movement for people, goods, and money. Given such guarantees, it seems likely that a substantial number of people would be willing to migrate in search of better living conditions. Past experience shows that people have been attracted to live and work in adverse conditions (for example in Siberia or in the northern territories) by high pay and a generous supply of consumer goods. With the possible exception of certain autonomous areas, there is also a fair degree of cultural homogeneity across Russia, including, importantly, the common language. What would be required in recipient regions, however, is sufficiently flexible labour and housing markets to accommodate immigrants.

Similar considerations apply to capital movements across Russia. At present the overall investment climate is rather difficult, and formal financial institutions are on the whole underdeveloped. Nevertheless extensive flight of capital out of Russia and the existence of networks of private traders all over the country suggest strongly that even now capital must in fact be highly mobile. Over time improvements in the formal banking system, especially the emergence of sound private investment banks, should reduce transaction costs and lead to the partial substitution of formal for informal channels of capital movements. In sum, therefore, the potential migration of factors of production could be large enough to lead to effective competition among regional governments.

Finally, it may be noted that the human capital required for rational economic policy-making seems to be in short supply in Russia. In such cases it is generally advisable to centralize decision-making in order to make the best possible use of the available administrative capacity, rather than to spread it out thinly across regions.[8] This observation strengthens the case for centralizing those tasks where there would otherwise be duplication of effort. These include the provision of national public goods such as defence, diplomatic relations and macroeconomic management.

6 CONCLUSIONS

In sum, will far-reaching decentralization and competition among regional jurisdictions promote economic transformation in Russia? The answer suggested by the above arguments is cautiously affirmative. A return to a unitary state, or to a federation with only very restricted powers for the regions, presently seems out of the question. It is hardly conceivable that regional elites will give up the powers they have wrought from the centre (and the rents that come with them). This should be true even if there were a conservative backlash in national politics. After all, regional elites have long wielded effective power, even under the former 'bureaucratic market' system of intermediation (Naishul, 1993), although this was not obvious in terms of formal institutions. Further decentralization would give the more reform-minded regions a chance to go ahead, and their example might well transpire to the presently conservative regions.

It is beyond the scope of this paper to discuss in detail possible strategies for decentralization in areas such as expenditure and tax assignment, privatization policy, financial system reform, and so on. This applies particularly because it is not clear whether *oblast*-level regions will survive in their present form. In devising such strategies, however, three lessons from the above discussion may be drawn upon.

First, the effectiveness of interregional competition will depend on a constitutional framework that can only be provided by the central political institutions. This should include not only basic human rights, but also economic rights such as the free movement of people, goods, and money throughout Russia. In addition, there are also areas such as the legal system and macroeconomic policy where interregional differences in preferences are probably small, and which may therefore be delegated to the centre to avoid duplication of effort.

Second, an economic case may be made for requiring all regions to share in the financial burdens resulting from Russia's communist past. Apart from economic considerations, there is also the possibility of political upheaval if powerful groups stand to suffer excessive income losses. In all likelihood, burden-sharing will require a substantial interregional redistribution of income that may well have to be organized through the centre.

Third, an institutional framework should be created that takes into account the existing interregional differences in political preferences and in the need for interregional co-operation. It seems advisable, conceptually, to reconstruct the federal system from bottom to top, and to allocate responsibilities to the centre only if this is in the interest of a large majority of regions. More limited interregional co-operation that involves only subgroups of regions may occur through specialized supra-regional, medium-level government institutions that are controlled by the participating regions.

On a cautionary note, we emphasize that the complexity of the current situation does not lend itself to sweeping generalizations. Competition among regions in the framework of a confederation might well leave many Russian citizens worse off than they would be if there were a central government with bureaucrats whose objective function contained only the common good. Such a point of reference, however, is clearly irrelevant. Under present circumstances, formally acknowledging the decentralization that has already taken place, and giving regions well-defined responsibilities and sources of income offers the best hope of regaining the momentum of economic reform. Relieving the centre of responsibilities that are best borne by the regions should also free administrative capacity for those tasks that only central institutions can take care of adequately.

Notes

1.   In a brief summary such as the present one it is obviously impossible to do full justice to the very diversified literature that has sprung up particularly in

recent years. The purpose of this section is to identify lessons which are independent of the precise formulation of the underlying assumptions, and which may therefore be drawn upon in the present policy-oriented discussion.

2. The traditional system of interactions among economic agents is often referred to as central planning. Naishul (1993) has pointed out that, during the last two decades at least, the term 'bureaucratic market' is more appropriate to characterize the system of intermediation in the former Soviet Union.

3. One obvious exception is Nizhnii Novgorod oblast where a number of factors combined to make the oblast an experimenting ground for the potential for local economic reform (Cline, 1994). The attempts made by the central government to formalize relationships with the regions through the Federation Treaties signed in early 1992 are reviewed by DIW et al. (1993) and Shaw (1992).

4. The large number of possible indicators raises the question to what extent they are correlated with one another; that is whether they tend to identify similar sets of regions as supportive of, or opposed to reform. In order to analyse the degree of interdependence, correlation or contingency coefficients have been calculated for each pair of indicators, depending on whether at least one in a given pair is categorical. Generally speaking, correlation among these variables is found to be high but less than perfect. By using a variety of indicators, this empirical analysis seeks to put into perspective the difficulties that may be involved in the interpretation of the results for any one variable.

5. The raw data and details of the calculations are available from the author upon request.

6. One might think of a cluster analysis as a way of identifying groups of regions with similar characteristics. It was found in an earlier analysis of regional economic structures in the Russian Federation, however, that the results of a cluster analysis were quite sensitive to the essentially arbitrary choice of the independent variables (Lücke, 1994). The purpose of that study was to identify regions sufficiently different from the majority of areas to possibly benefit from separatism. While the choice of independent variables or of the clustering method did not significantly affect the identification of such outliers, it did have a marked impact on the grouping of the remaining regions.

7. The recent literature shows that redistribution does not depend on the existence of a central institution (Thomas, 1993). It may also be organized through agreement among rationally acting regional governments. The mechanism is essentially migration, coupled with the cost of overcrowding in particularly attractive regions. The effectiveness of migration in the Russian context is discussed below.

8. A similar point has been made by Levy (1988) who seeks to explain the relatively large size of exporting footwear producers in South Korea compared with Taiwan. Levy argues that business, and particularly international marketing–skills were in relatively short supply in post-war Korea. Hence it was desirable to have relatively large firms. The shortage of such specialized skills was arguably less stringent in Taiwan, where firm size is found to have been significantly lower.

References

Boss, Alfred (1993) 'Wettbewerb der Regionen und Finanzverfassung: Prinzipien einer Reform des Finanzausgleichs in der Bundesrepublik Deutschland', in

Probleme des Finanzausgleichs in nationaler und internationaler Sicht, Beihefte der Konjunkturpolitik, (Berlin: Duncker and Humblot), 41, pp. 79–98.

Cline, Mary (1994) 'Nizhnii Novgorod: A Regional View of the Russian Elections', *RFE/RL Research Report*, 3, No. 4, pp. 48–54.

Deutsches Institut für Wirtschaftsforschung (DIW), Institut für Weltwirtschaft an der Universität Kiel (IfW) and Institut für Wirtschaftsforschung Halle (IWH) (1993) *Die wirtschaftliche Lage Rußlands. Systemtransformation auf dem Rückzug?* Zweiter Bericht. Kiel Discussion Papers, 208/209 (Kiel: Institut für Weltwirtschaft).

_____. (1994) *Die wirtschaftliche Lage Rußlands. Durch Konzeptlosigkeit zum Kollaps* Vierter Bericht. Kiel Discussion Papers, 232 (Kiel: Institut für Weltwirtschaft).

Drèze, Jachques (1993) 'Regions of Europe: A Feasible Status, To Be Discussed', *Economic Policy*, 17, pp. 265–307.

Hughes, James (1993) 'Yeltsin's Siberian Opposition', *RFE/RL Research Report*, 2, No. 50, pp. 29–34.

Jansen, Annica Carol (1991) 'Does Decentralization Control Local Government Spending? A Test of the Leviathan Hypothesis'. Diss. Cornell University.

Jarygina, T. and G. Martschenko (1993) 'Regionale Prozesse in der ehemaligen UdSSR und im neuen Rußland', *Osteuropa*, 3, pp. 211–28.

Kornai, Janos (1993) 'The Evolution of Financial Discipline Under the Postsocialist System'. Collegium Budapest: Mimeo.

Levy, Brian (1988) 'Transaction Costs, the Size of Firms and Industrial Policy: Lessons from a Comparative Case Study of the Footwear Industry in Korea and Taiwan'. Research memorandum, 112 (Williamstown, Mass.: Williams College, Center for Development Economics).

Lücke, Matthias (1993) 'Policy Options for Economic Transformation in the Republic of Belarus'. MOCT-MOST 3, pp. 53–71.

_____ (1994) 'Wirtschaftliche Grundlagen des Regionalismus in der Russischen Föderation', *Zeitschrift für Wirtschafts- und Sozialwissenschaften*, 114 (forthcoming).

Musgrave, Peggy (1991) 'Merits and Demerits of Fiscal Competition', in Remy Prud'homme (ed.), *Public Finance with Several Levels of Government*. Proceedings of the 46th Congress of the International Institute of Public Finance, Brussels, (The Hague), pp. 281–97.

Naishul, Vitali (1993) 'Liberalism, Customary Rights and Economic Reforms', *Communist Economies and Economic Transformation*, 5, 1, pp. 29–43.

Oates, Wallace E. (1991) 'Fiscal Federalism: An Overview', in Remy Prud'homme (ed.), *Public Finance with Several Levels of Government*. Proceedings of the 46th Congress of the International Institute of Public Finance, Brussels (The Hague) pp. 1–18.

_____ and Robert M. Schwab (1988) 'Economic Competition Among Jurisdictions: Efficiency Enhancing or Distortion Inducing?', *Journal of Public Economics*, 45, pp. 333–54.

Orlowski, Lucjan T. (1992) 'Direct Transfers between the Former Soviet Union Central Budget and the Republics: Past Evidence and Current Implications'. Kiel Working Papers, 543 (Kiel: Institut für Weltwirtschaft).

—— (1993) 'Indirect Transfers in Trade Among Former Soviet Union Republics: Sources, Patterns and Policy Responses in the Post-Soviet Period'. Kiel Working Papers, 556 (Kiel: Institut für Weltwirtschaft).

Pommerehne, Werner W. (1989) 'The empirical relevance of comparative institutional analysis'. Discussion Papers, October 1989, (Saarbrücken: University of Saarland).

Radvanyi, Jean (1992) 'And What If Russia Breaks Up? Towards New Regional Divisions'. Post-Soviet Geography, 32, pp. 69–77.

Schlögel, Karl (1994) 'In der Provinz entscheidet sich, was aus Rußland werden wird', Frankfurter Rundschau, 11 March 1994, p. 12.

Shaw, Denis J.B. (1992) 'News Note: Russian Federation Treaty Signed', Post-Soviet Geography, 33, pp. 414–17.

Siebert, Horst (1991) 'The Transformation of Eastern Europe', Kiel Discussion Papers, 163 (Kiel: Insitut für Weltwirtschaft).

Sinn, Stefan (1990) 'The Taming of Leviathan: Competition among Governments'. Kiel Working Papers, 433 (Kiel: Institut für Weltwirtschaft).

Taylor, Leon (1992) 'Infrastructural Competition Among Jurisdictions ', Journal of Public Economics, 49, pp. 241–9.

Thomas, Ingo (1993) 'Allokationseffizienz, Interregionaler Finanzausgleich und Föderalismus bei hoher Arbeitsmobilität: Eine theoretische Analyse'. Working Papers, 598 (Kiel: Institut für Weltwirtschaft).

Vihanto, Martti (1992) 'Competition Between Local Governments as a Discovery Procedure', Journal of Institutional and Theoretical Economics, 148, pp. 411–36.

Wallich, Christine I. (1992) 'Fiscal Decentralization. Intergovernmental Relations in Russia'. Studies of Economies in Transformation Papers, 6 (Washington, DC: The World Bank).

Wildasin, David E. and John Douglas Wilson (1991) 'Theoretical Issues in Local Public Economics. An Overview', Regional Science and Urban Economics, 21, pp. 317–31.

Williamson, John (1992) 'The Eastern Transition to a Market Economy: A Global Perspective' Occasional Paper, 2, Centre for Economic Performance (London: London School of Economics).

Yasin, Y., S. Alexashenko, A. Neshchadin, O. Grigoryev and M. Malyutin (1994) Russian Regions in Transition (Moscow: The Expert Institute, Russian Union of Industrialists and Entrepreneurs).

Author Index

322 *Author Index*

Subject Index

323

324

Subject Index

citizens *continued*
supranational economic associations 21
citizenship, and federalism 260–1
class struggle theory 201
claw-back clauses 110
Clinton, Bill 274
clubs
and FOCJ 211
perspective of institutional competition 25
protectionism policies 17–18
theory of 17, 129, 143n.16, 145n.39, 211
clustering, second order 164, 165, 167
codes, legal 90
codified law 184, 186, 193, 195
coercive federalism 259, 271–8
cognitive abilities 196
collective competition 7
collective property 82
command, law by 154–9, 161–3, 167–71
committee-based standardization procedures 283, 290–4
common markets 21, 261
Common Technology Policy 241–7
communes 43, 47, 212, 213, 221, 224–5
Communism 81, 82
Community Development Block Grant 273
competence, economic and technological 192
competing FOCJ 209–10, 213–14
Competition
as a discovery procedure *see* discovery procedure, competition as
by obstruction 16
by performance and efficiency 16, 51, 54–5
competitive advantage 23, 41, 45, 48, 60n.21
competitive order 51, 52, 53–7
see also Wettbewerbsordnung
competitive pressure, jurisdictions 45
computers 203n.4
Concorde 250
conditional evolutionary conjectures 50–1
conduct, rules of 3, 7, 37
abstract 198
design 4
evolution 160, 172n.1
non-constitutional 7
spontaneous formation 4
confederations 311–12
conflict 154–5, 156–7, 161, 166
Congress, US 269

connecting factors 93–6
consent, law by 154–61, 164, 164–71, 172n.7
conservatism 185, 193, 194, 196, 197, 198
Constance, Lake of 217
Constitution of Totalitarianism 82
Constitutional Economics 54
constitutional rules 7, 25, 171
constitutionally-constrained competition 48–53, 57
constitutions 19
Russia 298, 305, 309–13
USA 263–5
constrained competition 21, 90
construction products 113
consumer preferences 46, 51
consumer sovereignty 50, 52, 54–5, 189
consumership, and federalism 260–1
Contestable Markets, theory of 5
contracts
consent 173n.11
incentives 156–7, 160–1
law 160
co-operation
evolution of law 155–6, 157–9, 163–71
federalism 259–60, 266–71
rents 129–31, 135–7, 140
corporations 92
corridoring 113–15
corruption 68, 83
Corsica 217
Council of Ministers 216
court orders, federal 276–7
creative destruction 910, 203n.5, 241, 255
process of 5
credibility, sources of 156–8, 162, 163, 169
credible threat 99
crises 73–4, 80–2, 199
crossover sanctions 273–4
Cuba 82
cultural institutions 185–6, 193, 196–9
cultural norms 186, 195
cultural relativists 189
cultural system 183, 184, 192–4
customs unions 21, 235
Czech transformation policies 202

Darwinian selection 194
Darwinism 59n.17
deadlocks, political 102–4
decentralization
cycles 83
and federalism 262
and jurisdictions 47–8, 56

ignorance, rational 70, 73
imitation 40, 46–7, 190
immigration 18
  policies 143n.21
  taxes 125, 132–5, 137
import restrictions 15, 17, 18
Impossibility Theorem 193
impure public goods 18
incentive mechanisms 46–8, 56
income distribution 68, 154, 157, 161–2
incompetent policy decisions 193
inconsistencies between designed and
  spontaneous rules 8
individual competition 6–7
Industrial Organization Approach 5
inflation 83
  see also hyperinflation
informal constraints 3
information 66–7
infrastructure, public 13
innovations
  and constitutional constraints 48
  cyclical processes 40
  effects of institutional competition 101
  incentives 165
  institutional 165
  literature 58n.8
  need for 42
  reasons for divergences in 66
  and state activity 73, 80
  trial-and-error nature 40
institutional alternatives, space of 187,
  194, 200–1
institutional drift 199
institutions 172n.1
  at choice 92
  coercive 154
  income distribution 154
  as rules 2, 37–9
insurance law 111–13
interest groups
  organization 72
  public choice theory 11, 16–17, 19
interests 184
intergovernmental competition 20, 259, 266
  see also vertical competition
inter-group interactions 164–5
interjurisdictional competition 20, 266
  see also horizontal competition
intermediaries, national institutions as
  238–9
international competition 13–14, 60n.21
international migration 119–21, 137–40
  inefficiencies 121–8
  policies 131–7

international standardization 285
International Standardization Organization
  (ISO) 288, 289
International Telecommunication Union
  (ITU) 285, 288–9
International Telegraph and Telephone
  Consultative Committee (CCIT) 285,
  289
international trade 17, 68, 77
International Union of Railways (UIC)
  285, 286–7, 293
internationalization 284
intervention
  levels 80
  rights 190
Ionia 76

Jackson, Andrew 264
Japan 79
Job Training Partnership Act 273
Johnson, Lyndon B. 280
jurisdictional FOCJ 210, 214–18
jurisdictional mobility 56
jurisdictions
  competition among: case for FOCJ
  218–22; constitutional constraints
  51–3; historical precursors and
  partial existence of FOCJ 222–5;
  as knowledge-creating process
  42–8; monopoly versus competition
  209–10
  competitive order 55–6, 58
  concentration 56
  limited 95–6
  population approach 39

Kansas City, Missouri 276–7
Kennedy, Edward 278
knowledge
  pretence of 242
  problem 40, 44–5, 127
  socio-economic institutions 178–9, 184,
  192, 195, 197, 200
knowledge-creating process, competition as
  5–6
  constitutional constraints 48
  evolutionary perspective 39
  among jurisdictions 42–8
Kuomintang 81

labour
  division of 77
  mobility 22
  transmission mechanisms of institutional
  competition 13